Crystal Ster

ID Guide vol. 1 a

from

REPLACEMENTS, LTD.
China, Crystal & Silver • Old & New

Bob Page & Dale Frederiksen

Acknowledgments

We would like to thank the following individuals from within the Replacements, Ltd. community for their work in creating this book, the most extensive identification book of its kind. Only through the commitment, enthusiasm, and dedication of this caring and skilled team could this book have been possible.

JoNell Bakanec
Sherry Blankenship
Amy Fisher
Todd Hall
Randy Harris
Chris Kirkman
Roberta Newman
Karen Pirello
Jaime Robinson
Dean Six
Kristi Stratton
Pat West

Special thanks is given to the staffs of the Research and Imaging Services departments at Replacements, Ltd. Their countless hours identifying, verifying, photographing and drawing stemware patterns have been invaluable in the completion of this book.

Published by
Replacements, Ltd.
Greensboro, North Carolina

ISBN# 978-1-889977-17-1
Copyright © 2013 by Replacements, Ltd.

Additional copies of this book may be ordered from:

REPLACEMENTS, LTD.
China, Crystal, Silver & Collectibles • Old & New
1089 Knox Road, PO Box 26029 Greensboro, NC 27420
1-800-REPLACE (1-800-737-5223) *www.replacements.com*

Table of Contents

—— On the Cover ——

Massena
by
Baccarat

Nudes–Royal Blue
Stem 3011
by
Cambridge

Mayfair–Pink
by
Anchor
Hocking

Introduction

This is the first volume in our Crystal Stemware ID Guide series. With more than 5,900 patterns illustrated in volume 1, this guide is by far the most extensive ever published. We are confident that it will be a primary source for identifying the crystal patterns that come your way. While not trying to be a comprehensive pattern guide on any one manufacturer, it represents the vast majority of the most collectible and sought after stemware patterns of yesterday and today.

This guide is a compilation of a great deal of resource material covering many glass manufacturers and importers that are requested today. A line drawing representation of each pattern based on inventory, manufacturer literature, photographs, etc., has been created to make viewing the details of each pattern easier at a glance, making identification faster.

How to Use This Guide

In our new Crystal Stemware ID Guide series, we have also included many Early American Pattern Glass, Pressed Glass, Carnival Glass, and Depression Glass patterns.

Volume 1 includes patterns from 211 companies with names that begin with numerals or the letters A–F, such as 111 State Crystal, Anchor Hocking, and Atlantis, through those such as Fostoria, Franciscan, and Furstenberg. We have tried to make researching patterns easy for you. The layout of the book is alphabetical by manufacturer. Since most of the companies represented have only a small number of patterns, your research should be both efficient and successful.

Within each manufacturer, the patterns are arranged in a visually intuitive fashion by the stem or bowl shape. By organizing patterns in this way, you can compare the stem and bowl shape of your pattern to those similar from each manufacturer. Once the shape is located, if your pattern has a design it can be compared to the other patterns shown on that shape to find a match. In most cases, if the same pattern was made in different color variations, with varying optics, and/or different trim colors, a single drawing may have been used and the variations noted beneath that pattern.

Four of the larger manufacturers, Bryce, Cambridge, Duncan, and Fostoria, have information at the beginning of their sections showing examples of each stem or line shape and the page on which it begins. With these particular companies, comparing your pattern to the stem or line shapes first will make it faster to locate your pattern.

You will notice that some patterns shown throughout the guide are labeled without a name, but instead have numbers or a combination of letters and numbers. For example, "Melrose" by Fostoria is the name of that pattern. Another example would be "896-3" by Bryce. This shows the factory assigned stem number or line, "896", with an unknown design. The unknown design or decoration is the third we have documented on that stem. "AIG 1" by Abigails, as shown on page 1, is an example of our Replacements, Ltd. manufacturer code followed by our assigned number, since we do not currently know the stem or line number given by the manufacturer. AIG 1 represents the company Abigails, and "1" is the first pattern we have documented.

We have also included a list of the manufacturers that commonly mark their products on pages 408-409. Most commonly, the maker would acid etch their name or maker's mark on the foot of the stemware. In some cases the name or mark would be engraved in the foot. When the glassware is marked, the name of the company is often spelled out. Examples of maker's marks have also been added to help you identify the maker when the company name is not spelled out. A "•" indicates those companies whose merchandise is almost always marked. Care should be taken in purchasing patterns from these companies when the pieces are not marked. Second quality pieces often are unmarked. In the case of Lenox, there are second marks which have broken circles through the name or around the "L."

Some patterns appearing in the Crystal Stemware ID Guide series will be identical from one company to another. Manufacturers such as Spiegelau, Nachtmann, and Schott, major European glassmakers, create many of the wares that are sold by other companies such as Gorham, Mikasa, and Oneida. Sometimes the only difference between patterns will be maker marks or paper labels that appear on the items.

Sphere
Frosted Stem
111 State Crystal

2ST 1
Wine Shown
Gold & Jewel
Encrusted Stem
2 Saints

2ST 2
Red & Green Floral Stem
2 Saints

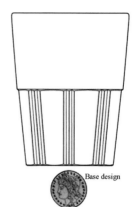

Base design

U. S. Coin
Tumbler Shown
Newer, Clear/Frosted,
Coin Motif
AA Importing Company

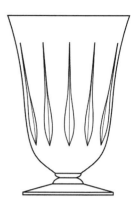

Chiara Vertical
Vertical Cuts
Abbiamo Tutto

AIG 3
Optic Bowl, Oversized,
Plain
Abigails

AIG 3
Optic Bowl, Oversized,
Gold Band on Stem,
Gold Bowl & Foot Trim
Abigails

AIG 6
Optic Bowl,
Gray Cut Grapes,
Leaves & Vines
Abigails

AIG 1
Optic Bowl,
22K Gold Speck Stem
Abigails

Fortunata
Gray Cut Floral
Abigails

Savannah
Wine Shown
Gray Cut Grass
Abigails

Romanza
Spiral Optic Bowl
Abigails

Pariz
Wine Shown
Horizontal, Diagonal &
Fan Cuts
Abigails

Belle Epoque
Wine Shown
Red Bowl,
Fan, Dot & Panel Cuts
Abigails

AIG 2
Blue Optic Bowl,
Twisted Stem
Abigails

Adriana
Wine Shown
Various Color Bowls,
Twisted Stem
Abigails

Arlington
Ruffled Bowl,
Twisted Stem
Abigails

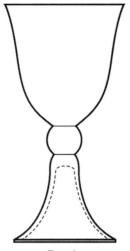

Royale
Hollow Stem
Abigails

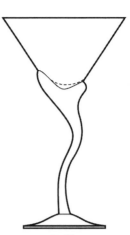

Buffy
Martini Shown
Wavy Stem
Abigails

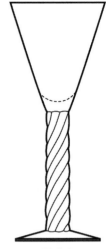

Twist
Twisted Stem
Abigails

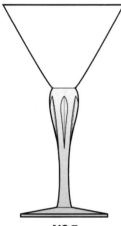

AIG 7
Martini Shown
Various Color Stems
Abigails

Hortense
Champagne/Tall Sherbet Shown
Amber Bowl,
Clear or Blue Stem
Abigails

AIG 5
Wine Shown
Blue Bowl, Square Foot
Abigails

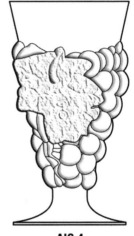

AIG 4
Footed Tumbler Shown
Molded Grapes
Abigails

Amber Fins
Blue Bowl,
Amber Fins & Foot
Abigails

Sapphire
Blue Bowl & Foot,
Gold Wafer Stem
Abigails

Danube
Champagne Flute Shown
Clear or Blue Bowl,
Oval Cuts
Abigails

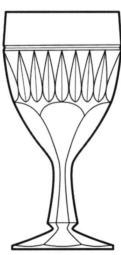

AI 1
Horizontal, Vertical &
Panel Cuts
Pressed Glass
Action Ind. Crystal

AI 2
Crisscross Cuts,
Pressed Glass
Action Ind. Crystal

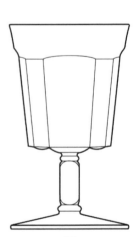

75
Plain, Pressed Glass
Adams & Company

75S
Cut Floral
75
Adams & Company

Daisy & Button
Daisies & Buttons,
Thumbprint Panels
Adams & Company

Baltimore Pear/Gipsy
Pears, Circa 1874,
Pressed Glass
Adams & Company

Wildflower
Clear or Various Colors,
Diamonds & Floral,
Pressed Glass
Adams & Company

Good Luck
Horseshoe & Floral,
Pattern Glass
Adams & Company

Apollo
Acid Etched Floral,
Pressed Glass
Adams & Company

Plume
Plumes,
Pressed Glass
Adams & Company

Garfield Drape
Floral/Bead Drape,
Pressed Glass
Adams & Company

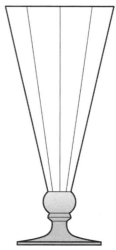

A1G 1
Iced Tea Shown
Multisided Bowl,
Frosted Ball Stem
Aderia Glass

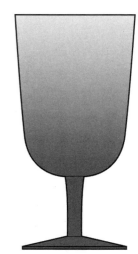

AFO 2
Smoke, Plain
Afors

Drake
Vertical & Panel Cuts
Afors

Chateau
White Wine Shown
Plain
Aida Crystal

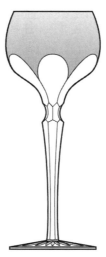

Malene
Wine Shown
Various Color Bowls,
Panel Cuts
Ajka Crystal

Edina
Champagne Flute Shown
Various Color Bowls,
Panel Cuts
Ajka Crystal

Taormina
Wine Hock Shown
Various Color Bowls,
Laurel & Panel Cuts
Ajka Crystal

Marsala
Various Color Bowls,
Grape & Star Cuts
Ajka Crystal

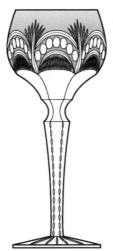

Cleantha
Wine Shown
Various Color Bowls,
Arch & Fan Cuts
Ajka Crystal

Carolyne
Wine Shown
Various Color Bowls,
7-Point Fan & Crisscross Cuts
Ajka Crystal

Caroline
Various Color Bowls
9-Point Fan & Crisscross Cuts
Ajka Crystal

Earlene
Wine Shown
Ruby Bowl,
Vertical & Star Cuts
Ajka Crystal

Rilette
Wine Shown
Various Color Bowls,
Crisscross & Wide Fan Cuts
Ajka Crystal

Carilla
Wine Shown
Various Color Bowls,
Crisscross & Thin Fan Cuts
Ajka Crystal

Florderis
Wine Shown
Various Color Bowls,
Dot & Fan Cuts
Ajka Crystal

AJC 16
Various Color Bowls,
Crisscross & Fan Cuts
Ajka Crystal

Sandrina
Wine Shown
Various Color Bowls,
Pinwheel & Fan Cuts
Ajka Crystal

Adorlee
Wine Hock Shown
Various Color Bowls,
Pinwheel & Fan Cuts
Ajka Crystal

Albracca
Wine Hock Shown
Various Color Bowls,
Pinwheel & Crosshatch Cuts
Ajka Crystal

Maralah
Cobalt Bowl,
Grape, Star & Fan Cuts
Ajka Crystal

Arabella
Wine Hock Shown
Various Color Bowls,
Crisscross & Vertical Cuts
Ajka Crystal

Cadessia
Wine Shown
Various Color Bowls,
Crisscross & Vertical Cuts
Ajka Crystal

Estella
Wine Shown
Various Color Bowls,
Vertical & Fan Cuts
Ajka Crystal

Ariadne
Wine Shown
Various Color Bowls,
Vertical Cuts
Ajka Crystal

AJC 14
Wine Hock Shown
Various Color Bowls,
Vertical Cuts
Ajka Crystal

Alberga
Various Color Bowls,
Vertical Cuts
Ajka Crystal

Saarburg
Green Bowl,
Arch & Fan Cuts
Ajka Crystal

Alva
Iced Tea Shown
Cobalt Bowl, Vertical Cuts
Ajka Crystal

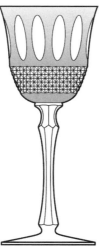

Willamette
Roemer Wine Shown
Various Color Bowls,
Crisscross & Thumbprint Cuts
Ajka Crystal

Valara
Wine Shown
Various Color Bowls, Dots,
Crisscross & Vertical Cuts
Ajka Crystal

Ardella
Various Color Bowls,
Dots, Crisscross &
Vertical Cuts
Ajka Crystal

Melitta
Wine Shown
Various Color Bowls,
Panel Cuts
Ajka Crystal

Egbertina (Ruby Bowl)
Hadria (Black Bowl)
AJC 17 (Cobalt Bowl)
Wine Shown; Crisscross Cuts
Ajka Crystal

Edmanda
Wine Shown
Various Color Bowls,
Crisscross & Fan Cuts
Ajka Crystal

Voletta
Wine Shown
Various Color Bowls,
Panel Cuts
Ajka Crystal

Saxonia
Various Color Bowls,
Crosshatch & Vertical Cuts
Ajka Crystal

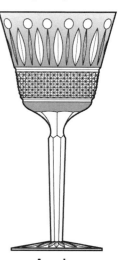

Amorica
Various Color Bowls,
Crosshatch, Vertical &
Dot Cuts
Ajka Crystal

Lynn/Linne
Wine Shown
Various Color Bowls,
Panel Cuts
Ajka Crystal

AJC 5
Cobalt Bowl
Crisscross & Vertical Cuts
Ajka Crystal

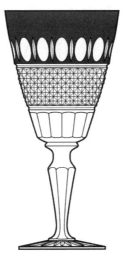

Guendolen
Wine Shown
Cobalt Bowl, Crosshatch
& Thumbprint Cuts
Ajka Crystal

Regan
Wine Shown
Various Color Bowls,
Honeycomb Cuts
Ajka Crystal

Patrizia
Various Color Bowls,
Vertical Cuts
Ajka Crystal

Morrigan
Wine Shown
Amber Bowl, Panel Cuts
Ajka Crystal

Arietta
Various Color Bowls,
Honeycomb Cuts
Ajka Crystal

Angilde
Dark Ruby Bowl,
Thumbprint Cuts
Ajka Crystal

Tilda
Wine Shown
Various Color Bowls,
Arch Cuts
Ajka Crystal

Idelle
Wine Shown
Various Color Bowls,
Vertical Cuts
Ajka Crystal

Domella (Red Wine 8¾")
Docilla (White Wine 8⅜")
Black Bowl, Vertical Cuts
Ajka Crystal

AJC 18
Cordial Shown
Cobalt Bowl, Vertical Cuts
Ajka Crystal

Albinka
Martini Shown
Various Color Bowls,
Vertical Cuts
Ajka Crystal

AJC 13
Martini Shown
Horizontal, Diagonal,
Dot & Fan Cuts
Ajka Crystal

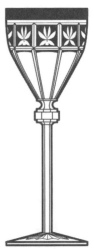

Radella
Black Bowl,
Fan, Square & Panel Cuts
Ajka Crystal

Amarante
Green Bowl,
Thumbprint Cuts
Ajka Crystal

Olinda
Wine Shown
Various Color Bowls,
Crosshatch & Vertical Cuts
Ajka Crystal

Mercia
Wine Shown
Amethyst Bowl,
Grape & Star Cuts
Ajka Crystal

Monferrato
Clear or Various Color
Bowls, Clear Stem,
Geometric Cut Band
Ajka Crystal

Cadyna/Cadena
Wine Shown
Cobalt Bowl, Vertical Cuts
Ajka Crystal

Alacoque
Wine Shown
Ruby Bowl,
Crisscross & Fan Cuts
Ajka Crystal

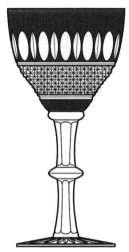

AJC 15
Red Wine Shown
Ruby Bowl, Crosshatch
& Vertical Cuts
Ajka Crystal

Proinnseas
Iced Tea Shown
Various Color Bowls,
Floral & Vertical Cuts
Ajka Crystal

Hilaeria
Wine Shown
Various Color Bowls,
Laurel & Panel Cuts
Ajka Crystal

Csopak
Pinwheel & Crisscross Cuts
Ajka Crystal

AJC 10
Wine Shown
Panel Cuts
Ajka Crystal

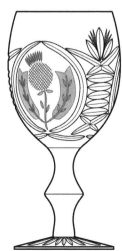

Jammertal
Wine Shown
Thistle & Fan Cuts
Ajka Crystal

AJC 1
Various Color Bowls,
Dragonfly & Floral Cuts
Ajka Crystal

Spadafora
Ruby Bowl,
Floral & Panel Cuts
Ajka Crystal

AJC 11
Champagne Flute Shown
Red Bowl, Cut Hearts
Ajka Crystal

Ajka Crystal

Donnafugata
Wine Shown
Ruby Bowl,
Grape & Star Cuts
Ajka Crystal

Elida
Leaf & Berry Cuts
Ajka Crystal

Anita
Ruby Bowl,
Thumbprint Cuts
Ajka Crystal

Roncada
Amethyst Bowl,
Vertical, Horizontal &
Dot Cuts
Ajka Crystal

Ancelin
Wine Shown
Various Color Bowls,
Dot Cuts
Ajka Crystal

Alcamo
Wine Shown
Azure Bowl,
Geometric Cuts
Ajka Crystal

Esmeralda
Wine Shown
Ruby Bowl,
Vertical & Horizontal Cuts
Ajka Crystal

Devonna
Cobalt Bowl,
Single Vertical Cut
Ajka Crystal

Reinheld
Wine Shown
Black Bowl & Stem,
Square Cuts
Ajka Crystal

Renella
Wine Shown
Black Bowl & Stem,
Horizontal Cut Rings
Ajka Crystal

Skyla
Wine Shown
Cobalt Bowl
Ajka Crystal

Volterra
Ruby Bowl & Stem,
Crosshatch & Fan Cuts
Ajka Crystal

Edlin
Wine Shown
Various Color Bowls,
Panel Cuts, Multisided Foot
Ajka Crystal

Avarona
Wine Shown
Ruby Bowl, Panel Cuts
Ajka Crystal

Wigburg
Wine Shown
Ruby Bowl,
Vertical & Dot Cuts
Ajka Crystal

Mertise
Various Color Bowls,
Grape & Leaf Cuts
Ajka Crystal

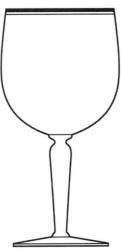

AAN 1
Gold or Platinum Trim
Aladdin Crystal

Petite Rose
Cut Rose
Aladdin Crystal

Princess
Goblet/Wine Shown
Gold Jeweled Ball Stem
Alan Lee Collection

Variegated
Goblet/Wine Shown
Gold Bands,
Gilded Gold/Copper Foot
Alan Lee Collection

Tuscany
Goblet/Wine Shown
Amethyst, Copper, Green, Blue
or Ruby Bowl, Gold Bands
Alan Lee Collection

Sienna
Goblet/Wine Shown
Gold Bowl & Bands, Black Foot;
Green Bowl, Gold Bands & Copper Foot
Alan Lee Collection

Polka Dot
Goblet/Wine Shown
Seafoam Green Bowl, Clear
Dots, Gold Bands & Foot
Alan Lee Collection

Decadent
Goblet/Wine Shown
Crimson & Gold Lower Bowl
& Foot, Gold Bands
Alan Lee Collection

Mosaic
Goblet/Wine Shown
Copper, Gold & Silver
Gilded Bowl, Gold Bands
Alan Lee Collection

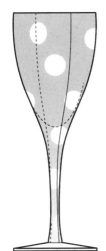

Polka Dot Square
Goblet/Wine Shown
Square; Seafoam Green,
Clear Dots
Alan Lee Collection

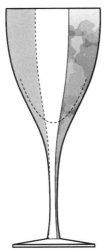

Variegated Square
Goblet/Wine Shown
Square; Clear, Frosted &
Gold/Copper Sides
Alan Lee Collection

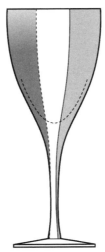

Tuscany Square
Goblet/Wine Shown; Square;
Clear, Various Color, Gilded
Gold/Silver or Frosted Sides
Alan Lee Collection

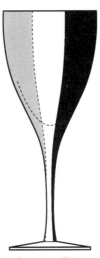

Cosmopolitan
Goblet/Wine Shown
Square; Clear, Black &
Frosted Sides
Alan Lee Collection

Princess Conical
Goblet/Wine Shown
Gold Jeweled Stem
Alan Lee Collection

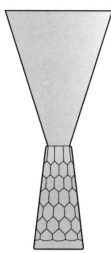

Tuscany Conical
Goblet/Wine Shown
Amethyst, Copper, Blue, Green or
Ruby Gilded Bowl, Cut Frosted Stem
Alan Lee Collection

Orseggi
Red Wine Shown
Plain
Alessi

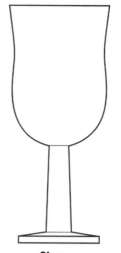

Ginerva
Wine Shown
Plain
Alessi

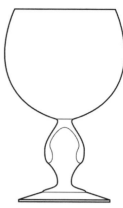

Porthos
Wine Shown
Plain
Alessi

Din-Don
Blue Stem
Alessi

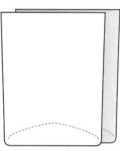

Colombina Collection
Tumbler Shown
Clear or Frosted
Alessi

Lappland
Plain,
Bubble in Stem
Alsterfors

Jostan
Vertical Cuts,
Bubble in Stem
Alsterfors

ATR 1
Thumbprint & Plant Cuts,
Bubble in Stem
Alsterfors

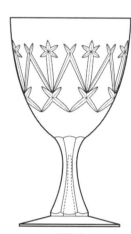

ATR 2
Diamond & Star Cuts,
Bubble in Stem
Alsterfors

ATR 3
Crisscross Cuts,
Bubble in Stem
Alsterfors

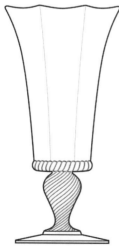

Angelica
Champagne Flute Shown
Multisided Bowl,
Twisted Stem
Amalfi Crystal

Perlina
Wine Shown
Clear, Amber or Green,
Molded Swirl
Amalfi Crystal

Serafina
Wine Shown
Green, Molded Bands
Amalfi Crystal

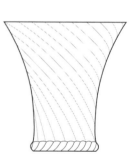

Rivolo
Clear, Amber or Green,
Swirl Optic Bowl, Rope Foot
Amalfi Crystal

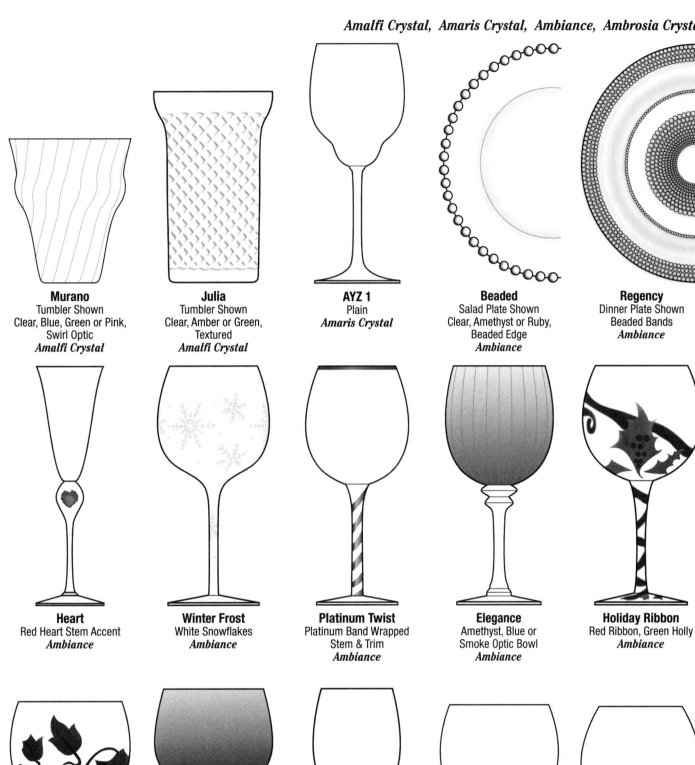

Murano
Tumbler Shown
Clear, Blue, Green or Pink,
Swirl Optic
Amalfi Crystal

Julia
Tumbler Shown
Clear, Amber or Green,
Textured
Amalfi Crystal

AYZ 1
Plain
Amaris Crystal

Beaded
Salad Plate Shown
Clear, Amethyst or Ruby,
Beaded Edge
Ambiance

Regency
Dinner Plate Shown
Beaded Bands
Ambiance

Heart
Red Heart Stem Accent
Ambiance

Winter Frost
White Snowflakes
Ambiance

Platinum Twist
Platinum Band Wrapped
Stem & Trim
Ambiance

Elegance
Amethyst, Blue or
Smoke Optic Bowl
Ambiance

Holiday Ribbon
Red Ribbon, Green Holly
Ambiance

Naturals
Green Painted Ivy
Ambiance

Trumpet
Cobalt or Chocolate Bowl,
Hollow Stem
Ambiance

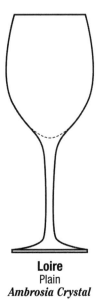

Loire
Plain
Ambrosia Crystal

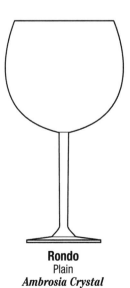

Rondo
Plain
Ambrosia Crystal

Trio
Plain
Ambrosia Crystal

Ambrosia Crystal, Amcaro, American Atelier, American Cookware

Aria
Gold Trim
Ambrosia Crystal

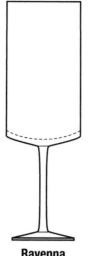

Ravenna
Plain
Ambrosia Crystal

Estate
Plain
Ambrosia Crystal

Gold Net
Gold Lines & Trim
Amcaro

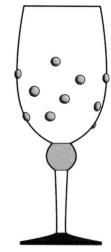

Ena
Blue Dots & Ball with
Green Foot; or Yellow Dots &
Ball with Red Foot
Amcaro

Flora
Various Color Bowls,
Green Stem & Foot
Amcaro

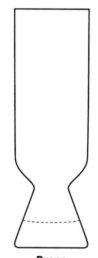

Drops
Champagne Flute Shown
Plain
Amcaro

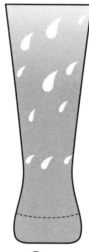

Drops
Champagne Flute Shown
Frosted, Clear Drops
Amcaro

Centro
Pilsner Shown
Green, Purple, Red or
Yellow Band
Amcaro

AA 1
Green, Orange, White or
Yellow Disk
American Atelier

Carnival Splash
Blue/Aqua Color in Bowl
American Atelier

Mardi Gras
Old Fashioned Shown
Multicolored Confetti,
Barware
American Atelier

AA 2
Highball Shown
Cobalt or Amethyst Base
with Bubbles, Barware
American Atelier

AY 1
Wine Shown
Smoke Bowl & Stem
American Cookware

AY 2
Taupe Brown, Plain
American Cookware

12

Barbara
Pinwheel & Fan Cuts,
See Eleanor for Barware
326
American Cut

Princess Irene
Crisscross & Fan Cuts
American Cut

Joy
Vertical Cuts
American Cut

Jewel
Crisscross, Vertical &
Horizontal Cuts
American Cut

Nancy
Vertical & Horizontal Cuts,
Multisided Foot
American Cut

President
Panel Cuts,
Multisided Foot
American Cut

Eleanor
Pinwheel & Fan Cuts
326
American Cut

Brilliant
Crisscross & Fan Cuts
American Cut

Vega
Gray Cut Floral,
Clear Crisscross & Arch Cuts
American Cut

Juliette
Pinwheel, Crisscross &
Vertical Cuts
American Cut

Lace
Vertical & Star Cuts
American Cut

Laura
Crisscross & Laurel Cuts
American Cut

Golden Lorelei
Platinum Lorelei
Gold or Platinum Encrusted
Bands & Leaves
American Cut

Montreal
Pinwheel & Crisscross Cuts
American Cut

Pinwheel
Wine Shown
Pinwheel & Vertical Cuts
American Cut

Savoy
Diagonal Cuts
American Cut

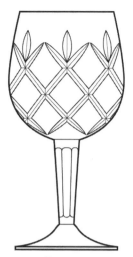

Regency
Crisscross & Vertical Cuts
American Cut

Monte Carlo
Panel Cuts
American Cut

Yale
Panel Cuts
American Cut

Marcia
Wine Shown
Vertical Cuts
American Cut

Leanore
Pinwheel, Arch & Fan Cuts
American Cut

Statesmen
Crisscross & Vertical Cuts
American Cut

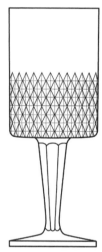

Americana
Crosshatch Cuts
American Cut

Aristocrat
Crosshatch & Vertical Cuts
American Cut

Stella
Pinwheel, Arch & Fan Cuts
American Cut

Tamara
Vertical Cuts
American Cut

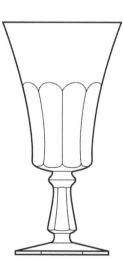

Diplomat
Panel Cuts,
Multisided Foot
American Cut

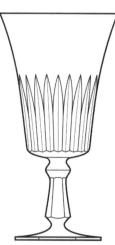

Imperial
Vertical Cuts,
Multisided Foot
American Cut

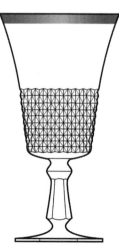

Gold Diamond
Crisscross Cuts,
Multisided Foot, Gold Trim
American Cut

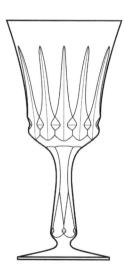

Eliza
Wine Shown
Vertical Cuts
American Cut

English
Crisscross & Arch Cuts
American Cut

Iris
Wine Shown
Plain
American Cut

AMC 9
Wine Shown
Vertical Cuts
American Cut

AMC 7
Wine Shown
Platinum Trim
American Cut

AMC 12
Wine Shown
Vertical & Oval Cuts
American Cut

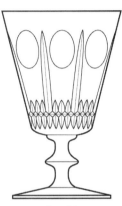

Ingrid
Thumbprint & Vertical Cuts
American Cut

AMC 11
Wine Shown
Gold Encrusted Bands
& Leaves
American Cut

Corinne
Plain
American Cut

Georgian
Crisscross Cuts
American Cut

Ruby Amber
Red Bowl
American Cut

Lima
Plain
American Cut

Mexico
Platinum Trim
American Cut

Optic
Optic Bowl
American Cut

Satellite
Plain
American Cut

Fany
Hollow Stem
American Cut

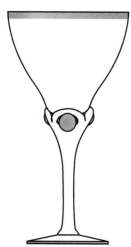

Golden Suszy
Platinum Suszy
Gold or Platinum
Stem Accents & Trim
American Cut

Tulip
Tulip Shaped Stem
American Cut

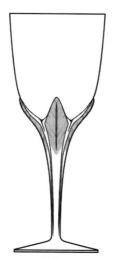

Erica
Frosted Leaves on Stem
American Cut

Roberto
Twisted Stem
American Cut

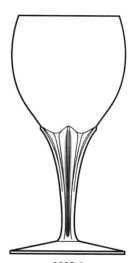

AMC 2
Cordial Shown
Red Stripe in Stem
American Cut

Satin Rose
Oversized Goblet Shown
Frosted Rose Stem
American Cut

Rain
Vertical Cuts,
Square Foot
American Cut

Gold Rose
Gold Encrusted Floral,
Gold Trim
American Cut

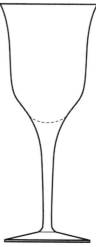

Astrid
Plain
American Cut

Leaves
Etched Leaves
American Cut

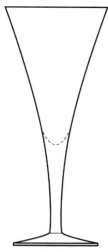

Janice
Plain
American Cut

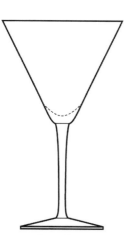

Occasions
Plain
American Cut

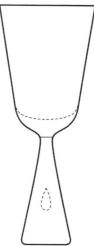

Princess
Bubble in Stem
American Cut

Simplicity
Plain
American Cut

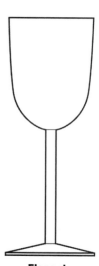

Elegante
Plain
American Cut

Optique
Optic Bowl
American Cut

Twist
Twisted Stem
American Cut

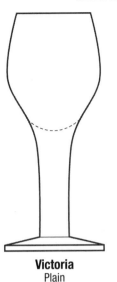

Victoria
Plain
American Cut

Helena
Plain
American Cut

Starlight
Star Cuts
American Cut

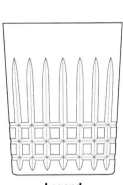

Legend
Double Old Fashioned Shown
Polished Vertical &
Horizontal Cuts
American Cut

AMC 6
Highball Shown
Bubble in Base, Barware
American Cut

AMC 4
Double Old Fashioned Shown
Raised Gold Dots,
Bubble in Base, Barware
American Cut

AMC 5
Double Old Fashioned Shown
Cobalt & Gold Accents,
Barware
American Cut

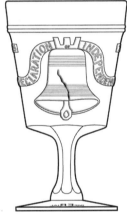

Liberty Bell
Bicentennial,
Liberty Bell Motif
American Historical

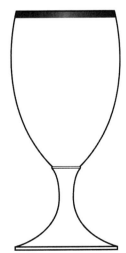

AMH 1
Platinum Trim
American Hostess

Wedding Band
Smooth Stem,
Platinum Trim
American Hostess

Wedding Band
Disc/Ball Stem,
Gold or Platinum Trim
American Hostess

Blue Lace
Cut Floral
American Hostess

Manor Rose
Single Cut Rose
American Hostess

Ancestral Wheat
Cut Wheat
American Hostess

Spring Glory
Clear or Pink,
Cut Floral
American Hostess

Evangeline
Cut Floral
American Hostess

Whitney
White Wine Shown
Swirl Optic Bowl
American Living

Le Bleu
Smokey Blue, Plain
American Manor

Chantilly
Etched, Platinum Trim
17702
American Manor

Ebony
Black, Plain
17703
American Manor

Wedding Day
Bubble in Stem,
Platinum Trim
17625
American Manor

Riviera
Cut Plants,
Platinum Trim
17676
American Manor

Finale
Gold or Platinum Encrusted
Trim, Bubble in Stem
17614
American Manor

Melody Platinum
Platinum Trim
American Royalty

Carmel
Clear or Various Colors,
Plain
American Stemware

Carmel Frost
Frosted Stem & Foot
American Stemware

Wild Rose Frost
Pink Bowl,
Pink Frosted Stem & Foot
American Stemware

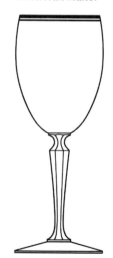

Carmel
Gold or Platinum Trim
American Stemware

Biltmore
Gray Cut Floral
American Stemware

Lakeshore
Vertical Cuts
American Stemware

AMS 1
Vertical Cuts
American Stemware

Elite
Plain
American Stemware

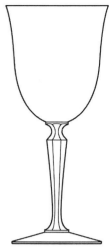

Westport
Clear or Various Colors,
Plain
American Stemware

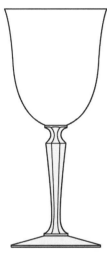

Westport
Frosted Stem & Foot
American Stemware

Westport
Clear or Various Colors,
Optic Bowl
American Stemware

AMS 2
Pale Pink, Cut Floral
American Stemware

AMS 3
Cut Floral
American Stemware

AMS 5
Crisscross & Fan Cuts
American Stemware

Princeton
Clear or Various Colors,
Plain
American Stemware

Princeton
Frosted Stem & Foot
American Stemware

Princeton
Optic Bowl
American Stemware

Princeton
Gold or Platinum Trim
American Stemware

AMS 4
Gray Cut Laurel
American Stemware

Sanibel
Plain
American Stemware

Sanibel
Swirl Optic Bowl
American Stemware

Penthouse
Clear or Various
Color Stems
American Stemware

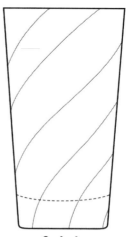

Carivele
Highball Shown
Optic
American Stemware

Kenilworth
Beverage Shown
Plain
American Stemware

Kenilworth
Beverage Shown
Gold or Platinum Trim,
Barware
American Stemware

Ligonier
Beverage Shown
Plain
American Stemware

Ligonier
Beverage Shown
Gold or Platinum Trim,
Barware
American Stemware

AAG 1
Multicolored Frosted Bowl,
Frosted Stem
Amisco Art Glass

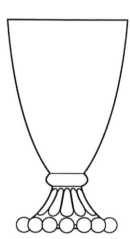

Boopie
Clear or Various Color
Bowls, Plain,
Ball Design on Foot
Anchor Hocking

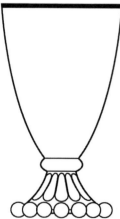

Boopie
Gold Trim,
Ball Design on Foot
Anchor Hocking

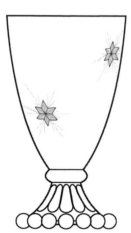

Sparkling Star
Gray Cut Stars,
Boopie Stem
Anchor Hocking

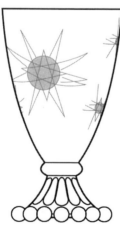

AHC 8
Gray Cut Starbursts,
Boopie Stem
Anchor Hocking

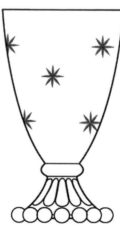

AHC 23
Gray Cut Stars,
Boopie Stem
Anchor Hocking

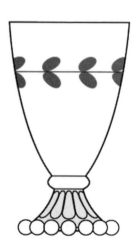

AHC 29
Gray Cut Laurel,
Yellow Foot,
Boopie Stem
Anchor Hocking

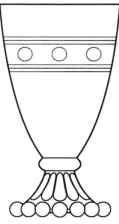

AHC 3
Gray Cut Circles & Bands,
Boopie Stem
Anchor Hocking

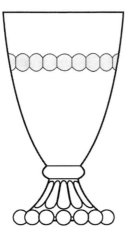

AHC 2
Gray Cut Circles,
Boopie Stem
Anchor Hocking

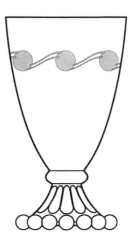

AHC 28
Gray Cut Dots & Swirls,
Boopie Stem
Anchor Hocking

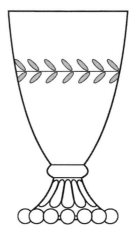

Laurel
Goblet/Iced Tea Shown
Gray Cut Laurel,
Boopie Stem
Anchor Hocking

AHC 7
Gray Cut Floral,
Boopie Stem
Anchor Hocking

AHC 10
Gray Cut Floral,
Boopie Stem
Anchor Hocking

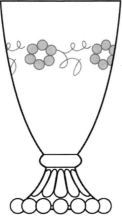

AHC 48
Gray Cut Floral &
Squiggly Lines,
Boopie Stem
Anchor Hocking

AHC 32
Gray Cut Floral,
Boopie Stem
Anchor Hocking

AHC 16
Gray Cut Leaves,
Boopie Stem
Anchor Hocking

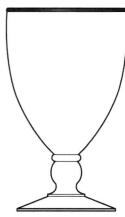

AHC 56
Platinum Trim
Anchor Hocking

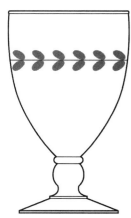

AHC 62
Gray Cut Laurel
Anchor Hocking

Bubble Foot
All Clear or All Avocado;
Green or Ruby Bowl with
Clear Bubble Foot Stem
Anchor Hocking

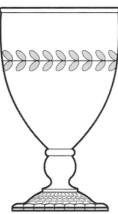

AHC 4
Gray Cut Laurel,
Bubble Foot Stem
Anchor Hocking

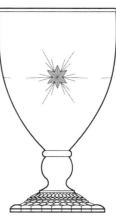

AHC 61
Gray Cut Stars,
Bubble Foot Stem
Anchor Hocking

AHC 43
Gray Cut Rose,
Bubble Foot Stem
Anchor Hocking

AHC 11
Gray Cut Rose,
Bubble Foot Stem
Anchor Hocking

Burple
All Clear or with
Ruby or Green Bowl,
Plain or Gold Trim
Anchor Hocking

Legacy
Crisscross Vertical Cuts,
24% Lead, Plain
Anchor Hocking

Legacy
Crisscross Vertical Cuts,
Gold or Platinum Trim
Anchor Hocking

Canfield
Diamond & Vertical Cuts,
Pressed Glass
Anchor Hocking

Courtney
Clear or Various Colors,
Panel Cuts
Anchor Hocking

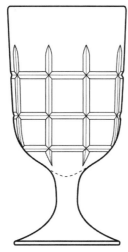

Tartan
Clear or Various Colors,
Vertical & Horizontal Cuts
Anchor Hocking

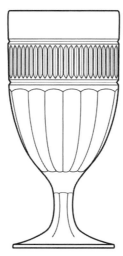

Annapolis
Clear or Various Colors,
Vertical & Panel Cuts
Anchor Hocking

Savannah
Clear or Blue,
Embossed Floral, Giftware,
Pressed Glass
Anchor Hocking

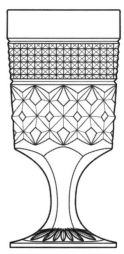

Wexford
Clear or Various Colors,
Crisscross Cuts,
Pressed Glass
Anchor Hocking

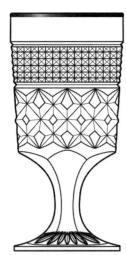

Wexford
Crisscross Cuts,
Platinum Trim,
Pressed Glass
Anchor Hocking

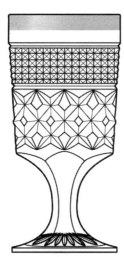

Wexford
Crisscross Cuts,
Gold Band,
Pressed Glass
Anchor Hocking

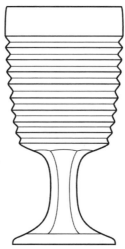

Park Avenue
Clear, Blue or Green,
Horizontal Ribs
Anchor Hocking

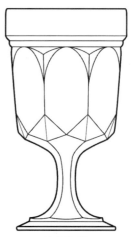

Fairfield
Clear or Various Colors,
Pressed Glass
1200
Anchor Hocking

Georgian
Clear or Various Colors,
Honeycomb Cuts,
Pressed Glass
Anchor Hocking

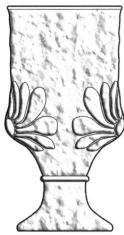

Rainflower
Clear or Various Colors,
Textured Body,
Embossed Floral
Anchor Hocking

Miss America
Clear or Various Colors
Anchor Hocking

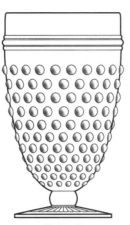

Hobnail
Clear or Various Colors
Anchor Hocking

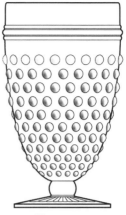

Moonstone
Clear or Green Opalescent,
Hobnail Design
Anchor Hocking

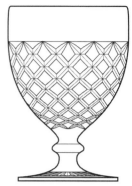

Waterford
Clear or Various Colors,
Waffle Design
Anchor Hocking

Monarch
Royal Ruby, Plain
Anchor Hocking

Fairfield
Plain
Anchor Hocking

Mayfair
Goblet Shown 5¾"
Clear, Various Colors or
Frosted, Open Rose Design
Anchor Hocking

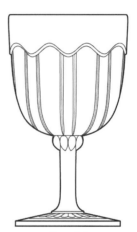

Colonial
Clear or Various Colors,
Ribs & Panels
Anchor Hocking

Cameo
Clear or Various Colors,
Optic Bowl
Anchor Hocking

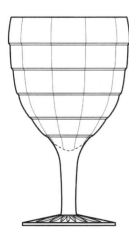

Block Optic
Clear or Various Colors,
Optic Bowl,
Smooth Straight Stem
Anchor Hocking

AHC 55
Gray Cut Laurel &
Horizontal Bands
Anchor Hocking

Mayfair
Goblet Tall Shown 7¼"
Various Colors,
Open Rose Design
Anchor Hocking

Panelled Ring-Ding
Black, Red, Yellow,
Orange & Green Stripes
Anchor Hocking

Block Optic
Various Colors,
Optic Bowl, Bulbous Stem
Anchor Hocking

23

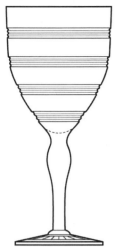

Banded Rings
Clear or Various Colors,
Plain
Anchor Hocking

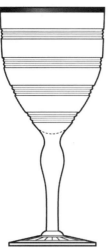

Banded Rings
Platinum Trim
Anchor Hocking

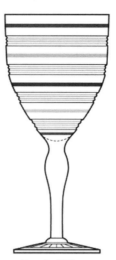

Banded Rings
Multicolored Rings
Anchor Hocking

AHC 18
Clear or Various Colors,
Rippled Optic Bowl
Anchor Hocking

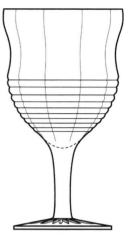

Circle
Clear or Various Colors,
Optic Bowl
Anchor Hocking

Royal Ruby
Wine Shown
Dark Red
Anchor Hocking

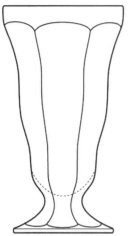

Fountainware
Soda Tumbler Shown
Clear or Various Colors,
Panel Design
Anchor Hocking

Princess
Footed Tumbler Shown
Various Colors
Anchor Hocking

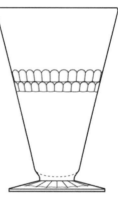

Roulette
Footed Tumbler Shown
Clear or Various Colors
Anchor Hocking

Manhattan
Footed Tumbler Shown
Clear or Various Colors,
Horizontal Ribs
Anchor Hocking

Sandwich
Footed Tumbler Shown
Clear or Various Colors,
1940s–1960s Glassware
Anchor Hocking

Stars & Stripes
Champagne/Tall Sherbet Shown
Eagle Center, Ribbed
Anchor Hocking

Excellency
Wine Shown
Plain
Anchor Hocking

Everton
Water/Wine Goblet Shown
Plain
Anchor Hocking

Celebrate
Wine Shown
Clear & Black Stems,
Ribbed & Smooth Bowls
Anchor Hocking

Gabriella
Wine Shown
Plain
Anchor Hocking

Flair
Gray Cut Buds & Leaves
Anchor Hocking

Bravo
Gray Cut Cones
Anchor Hocking

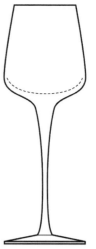

Aries
White Wine Shown
Plain
Anchor Hocking

Classico
Iced Tea Shown
Plain
Anchor Hocking

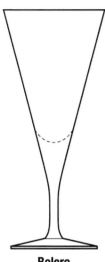

Bolero
Plain
Anchor Hocking

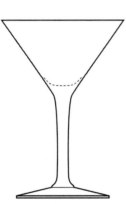

Ashbury
Martini Shown
Plain
Anchor Hocking

Hollywood
Martini Shown
Various Color Stem Accents
Anchor Hocking

Berkeley
Iced Tea Shown; Clear or
Various Colors, Vertical Cut
Corners, Square Base
Anchor Hocking

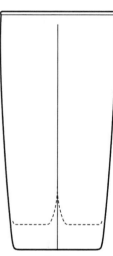

Alexis
Highball Shown
Plain, Square Shape
Anchor Hocking

Central Park
Iced Tea Shown
Clear or Various Colors,
Vertical Wave Cuts
Anchor Hocking

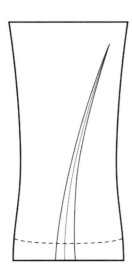

Flair
Tumbler Shown
Curved Vertical Lines
Anchor Hocking

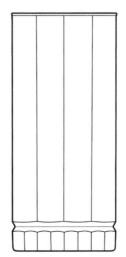

Essex
Iced Tea Shown
Clear or Various Colors,
Multisided
Anchor Hocking

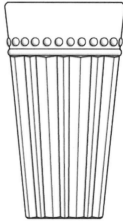

Olivia
Tumbler Shown
Vertical Lines & Dots
Anchor Hocking

Prescut
Tumbler & Flat Iced Tea Shown
Clear or Various Colors,
Stars & Fans, Pressed Glass
Anchor Hocking

Prescut Pineapple
Ruby Flash,
Pressed Glass
Anchor Hocking

AHC 15
Flat Iced Tea Shown
Clear or Various Colors,
Star & Cameo Design
Anchor Hocking

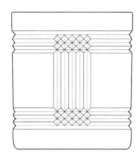

Aberdeen
Tumbler Shown
Vertical & Horizontal Cuts
Anchor Hocking

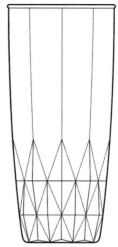

Crown Point
Flat Iced Tea Shown
Diamond & Vertical Design,
Pressed Glass
Anchor Hocking

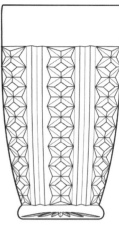

Diamond
Tumbler Shown
Clear or Various Colors,
Crisscross & Panel Design
Anchor Hocking

Swirl
Tumbler Shown
Ruby Red, Swirl Design
Anchor Hocking

Windsor
Tumbler Shown
Clear or Various Colors,
Geometric Cube Base
Anchor Hocking

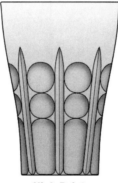

High Point
Flat Juice Shown
Ruby Red,
Circles & Ridges
Anchor Hocking

Coronation
Footed Tumbler Shown
Clear or Various Colors,
Vertical Ribs & Panels
Anchor Hocking

Fortune
Flat Juice Shown
Clear or Various Colors,
Vertical Ribs
Anchor Hocking

Pillar Optic
Tumbler Shown
Various Colors,
Panel Design
Anchor Hocking

Old Cafe
Tumbler Shown
Clear or Various Colors,
Vertical Ridges
Anchor Hocking

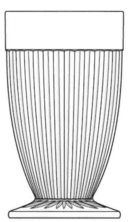

Queen Mary
Footed Tumbler Shown
Clear or Various Colors,
Vertical Ribs
Anchor Hocking

Colonial Tulip
Tumbler Shown
Various Colors,
Tulip & Swag Design
Anchor Hocking

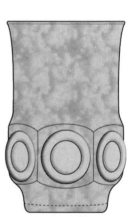

Heritage Hall
Tumbler Shown
Various Colors, Textured,
Embossed Circles
Anchor Hocking

Milano
Flat Juice Shown
Clear or Various Colors,
Textured Bark Design
Anchor Hocking

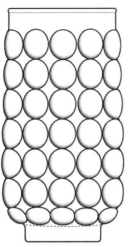

Bubble
Lemonade Tumbler Shown
Clear or Various Colors,
1940s-1960s Glassware
Anchor Hocking

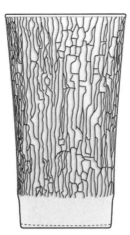

Pagoda
Tumbler Shown
Various Colors, Textured,
Square Bark Design
Anchor Hocking

Tahiti
Tumbler Shown
Various Colors,
Bamboo Design
Anchor Hocking

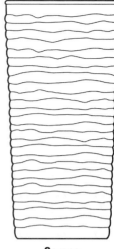

Soreno
Flat Iced Tea Shown
Clear or Various Colors,
Pressed Bark Design
Anchor Hocking

AHC 64
Tumbler Shown
Plain
Anchor Hocking

Finlandia
Tumbler Shown
Clear, Avocado or Mocha
Anchor Hocking

Newport
Tumbler Shown
Royal Ruby
Anchor Hocking

Roly Poly
Flat Iced Tea Shown
Royal Ruby or Forest Green
Anchor Hocking

Beverly
Tumbler Shown
Royal Ruby or Forest Green
Anchor Hocking

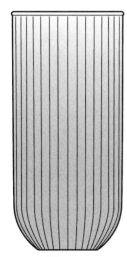

Monaco
Flat Iced Tea Shown
Pink, Vertical Ribs
Anchor Hocking

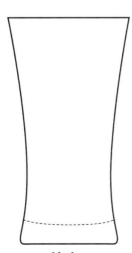

Linden
Tumbler Shown
Clear or Mocha
Anchor Hocking

Chateau
Tumbler Shown
Royal Ruby
Anchor Hocking

Belmont
Tumbler Shown
Forest Green
Anchor Hocking

Forest Green
Tumbler Shown
1940s-1960s Glassware
Anchor Hocking

Baltic
Footed Tumbler Shown
Royal Ruby or Forest Green
Anchor Hocking

AHC 22
Tumbler Shown
Green, Swirl Design
Anchor Hocking

Whirly Twirly
Tumbler Shown
Royal Ruby or Forest Green,
Wavy Rings
Anchor Hocking

AHC 31
Tumbler Shown
Clear or Green,
Ring Design, Barware
Anchor Hocking

Martinique
Tumbler Shown
Plain
Anchor Hocking

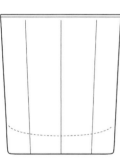

AHC 12
Old Fashioned Shown
Panel Design
Anchor Hocking

Heavy Base
Highball Shown
Plain, Barware
Anchor Hocking

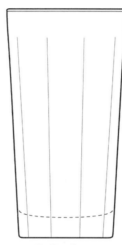

Reflections
Flat Iced Tea Shown
Clear or Light Blue,
Heavy Optic
Anchor Hocking

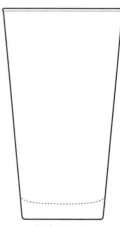

Refreshers
Tumbler Shown
Clear or Cobalt,
Plain
Anchor Hocking

AHC 59
Tumbler Shown
Blue, Swirl Optic
Anchor Hocking

Grecian Classic
Tumbler Shown
Clear Cut Laurel Band
Anchor Hocking

Laurel
Tumbler Shown
Polished Cut Laurel Band
Anchor Hocking

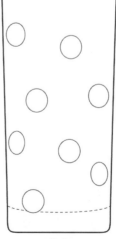

Dot
Tumbler Shown
Cut Dots
Anchor Hocking

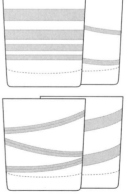

Cut Glass
Double Old Fashioned Shown
Frosted Cut Rings,
Multi-Motif
Anchor Hocking

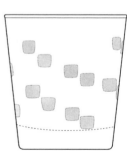

Cubist
Tumbler Shown
Gray Cut Abstract Squares,
Barware
Anchor Hocking

AHC 46
Flat Juice Shown
Red Cherries
Anchor Hocking

Oranges
Flat Juice Shown
Oranges, Green Leaves
Anchor Hocking

3519B
Tumbler Shown
Tri-Colored Cherries
Hanging From Branch
Anchor Hocking

Fiesta Bands
Tumbler Shown
Various Color Bands
Anchor Hocking

Green Corduroy
Flat Ice Tea Shown
Green & Peach
Bands & Stripes
Anchor Hocking

Horse and Buggy
Tumbler Shown
Gold & White, Horses,
Colonial/Dutch Design
Anchor Hocking

AHC 27
Highball Shown
Forest Green, White Decal,
People & Trees
Anchor Hocking

Golden Peaks
Tumbler Shown
Black & Gold
Geometric Decoration
Anchor Hocking

Gazelle
Tumbler Shown
White Gazelle on Green
Anchor Hocking

Dogwood
Tumbler Shown
White Enameled Dogwoods
on Forest Green
Anchor Hocking

Gay Nineties
Tumbler Shown
Straight Shell, Forest Green,
White Decals, Multi-Motif
Anchor Hocking

AHC 63
Flat Iced Tea Shown
Gold & White Decal, Eagles,
Colonial Motifs
Anchor Hocking

3526
Cooler Shown
Various Color Dots
on White Background
Anchor Hocking

Polka Dots
Tumbler Shown
Forest Green, White Dots
Anchor Hocking

English Country
Tumbler Shown
Hearts, Homes & Trees
Anchor Hocking

AHC 54
Tumbler Shown
Blue Band, Squares,
Hearts & Flowers
Anchor Hocking

Twelve Days of Christmas
Tumbler Shown
12 Days of Christmas Decals
Anchor Hocking

AHC 30
Tumbler Shown
Red/Yellow Apples on
Frosted Background
Anchor Hocking

Gay Nineties
Tumbler Shown
Roly Poly, Forest Green,
White Decals, Multi-Motif
Anchor Hocking

AHC 40
Tumbler Shown
Holly & Berries,
Red Stripes
Anchor Hocking

Cardinal
Tumbler Shown
Cardinal Bird Design,
Pressed Glass
Anchor Hocking

76 Grape
Tumbler Shown
Forest Green, White Grape
& Leaf Decal
Anchor Hocking

Modern Blocks
Tumbler Shown
Black, Coral & Blue
Blocks & Rectangles
Anchor Hocking

AHC 52
Tapered Tumbler Shown
Gold Leaves on
Royal Ruby
Anchor Hocking

AHC 49
Old Fashioned Shown
Gold Eagles/Stars,
Arrows & Branches
Anchor Hocking

Let It Snow
Tumbler Shown
Let it Snow &
Snowmen Decals
Anchor Hocking

ANN 1
Pinwheel & Fan Cuts
Anna Hutte

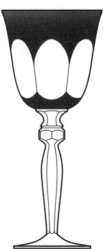

ANN 4
Various Color Bowls,
Panel Cuts
Anna Hutte

Optical
Optic Bowl
Anna Hutte

Medici
Vertical & Dot Cuts
Anna Hutte

Dunja
Thumbprint & Fan Cuts
Anna Hutte

Geraldine
Crisscross Cuts
Anna Hutte

Nepel
Vertical Cuts
Anna Hutte

Nostalgia
Laurel & Thumbprint Cuts
Anna Hutte

Madame
Panel Cuts
Anna Hutte

Rosentraum
Floral & Panel Cuts
Anna Hutte

ANN 5
Various Color Bowls,
Panel Cuts
Anna Hutte

ANN 3
Wine Hock Shown
Various Color Bowls
Anna Hutte

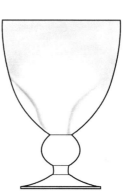

Antwerp
Green, Yellow or Blue Bowl
Anthropologie

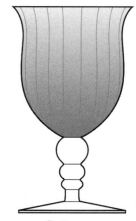

Buttercup
Wine Shown
Amber or Green Optic Bowl
Anthropologie

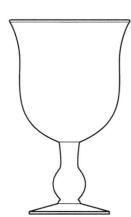

AOG 2
Plain
Anthropologie

Backyard (Green Bowl)
Stafford (Amber Bowl)
Wine Shown
Optic Bowl
Anthropologie

Encased Amber
Optic Bowl,
Amber Flower Stem Accent
Anthropologie

Spiral Bud
Wine Shown
Purple Swirl Optic Bowl
Anthropologie

Horta
Etched Floral Vines
Anthropologie

Captured Silverware
White Wine Shown
Utensil Encased Stem
Anthropologie

Air Balloon
Bubbles in Bowl
Anthropologie

Giddy
Bubbles in Green Bowl
Anthropologie

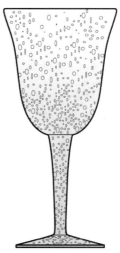

Fizzy
Wine Shown
Pink or Turquoise,
Bubbles in Bowl & Stem
Anthropologie

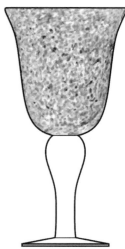

Afternoon Gambol
Multicolored Dots
Anthropologie

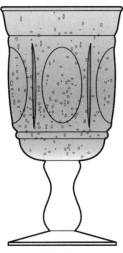

Evelina
Various Color Bowls
with Bubbles
Anthropologie

Vinifera
Moss or Olive Green,
Embossed
Anthropologie

Saintpaulia
Wine Shown
Purple Band on
Scalloped Bowl, Green Foot
Anthropologie

Tivoli
Various Colors,
Scrolls & Diamonds
Anthropologie

Mythic Glen
Gold & Pink Floral,
Pink Ball Stem
Anthropologie

Dappled
Champagne Flute Shown
Black, White & Brown Spots
Anthropologie

Colordrop
Footed Tumbler Shown
Multicolored Dots
Anthropologie

Sea Glass
Aqua Bowl,
Amber Foot with Bubbles
Anthropologie

Pebbled
Highball Shown
Amber, Textured Dots
Anthropologie

Nile Delta
Footed Tumbler Shown
Clear, Green or Turquoise,
Bubbles in Bowl & Stem
Anthropologie

Tulip
Tumbler Shown
Various Colors, Bubbles
in Bowl, Hobnail Base
Anthropologie

Ombre
Tumbler Shown
Blue, Green or Pink at
Top of Bowl
Anthropologie

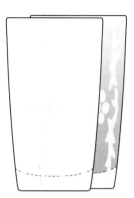

Freshly Squeezed
Tumbler Shown
Clear, Blue or Green,
Dripped White Stripes
Anthropologie

Frolicsome Coterie
Tumbler Shown
Clear or Plum,
Etched Fish & Dragonflies
Anthropologie

Nepenthean
Tumbler Shown
Blue, Green or Amber,
Gray Cut Floral
Anthropologie

Hushed
Tumbler Shown
Etched Floral Vines
Anthropologie

Cordata
Highball Shown
Green,
Textured Vertical Lines
Anthropologie

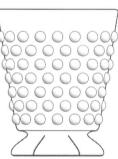

Hobnail
Juice Shown
Clear, Green or Turquoise
Anthropologie

Delta
Tumblers Shown
Clear or Green,
Pressed Quilt Design
Anthropologie

Opalescent
Tumbler Shown
Blue, Green or White,
Panels, Dots & Scrolls
Anthropologie

Fleur De Lis
Tumbler Shown; Clear or
Various Colors, Embossed
Floral & Bead Medallions
Anthropologie

Brasserie
Tumbler Shown
Clear, Amber or Green,
Embossed Dots & Bands
Anthropologie

Helianthus
Clear or Various Colors,
Embossed Floral & Beads
Anthropologie

Dutch Garden
Blue Bowl, Painted Floral
Anthropologie

Euro Milk
Tumbler Shown
Embossed Word Band
Anthropologie

Alphabet
Tumbler Shown
Various Color Letters
& Decals, Multi-Motif
Anthropologie

Let It Snow
Tumbler Shown
Various Colors,
Snowflakes & Child Decals
Anthropologie

Bookhand
Tumbler Shown
Light Green, Bubbles,
Green Medallions
Anthropologie

Life-At-Sea
Tumbler Shown
Painted Sea Items,
Multi-Motif
Anthropologie

Spring Showers
Tumbler Shown
Various Color Painted
Flowers, Gold Dots
Anthropologie

Nikau
Tumbler Shown
Various Color Painted
Flowers, Gold Dots
Anthropologie

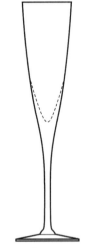

Aurora
Champagne Flute Shown
Plain
Arabia

Taika
Red Wine Shown
Black Raised Drip
Arabia

AC 2
Sherry Shown
Raised Drip
Arabia

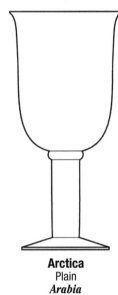

Arctica
Plain
Arabia

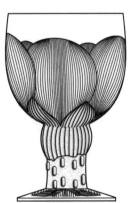

AC 1
Plain
Arabia

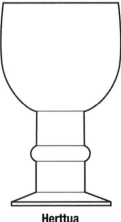

Pioni
Wine Shown
Textured Floral &
Leaf Design
Arabia

Herttua
Plain
Arabia

Silja
Raised Thistle
Arabia

Fauna
Iced Tea Shown
Various Animals,
Textured Design
Arabia

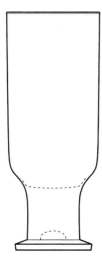

Helmi
Bubble in Stem
Arabia

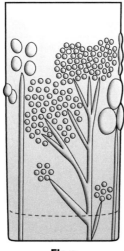

Flora
Highball Shown
Cobalt, Embossed Floral
Clear — see *"Iittala"*
Arabia

Nuutajarvi
Mug Shown
Plain
Arabia

Krouvi
Mug Shown
Embossed, 50cl
Arabia

Kastehelmi
Bread & Butter Plate Shown
Clear or Various Colors,
Beaded Bands, Pressed Glass
Arabia

ARE 14
Gray Cut,
Open Center Flower,
789
Arcadia

Orlean
Gray Cut Floral & Dots
Arcadia

Pine Cone
Gray Cut Pine Cones
Arcadia

ARE 9
Cut Floral
Arcadia

Laurette
Vertical & Laurel Cuts
Arcadia

Capri
Cut Floral
Arcadia

Electra
Gray Cut Floral & Dots
Arcadia

Duncan
Cut Floral & Stars
Arcadia

ARE 15
Gray Cut Floral
Arcadia

ARE 11
Fan & Circle Cuts
Arcadia

Starburst
Cut Starbursts,
Bubble in Stem
Arcadia

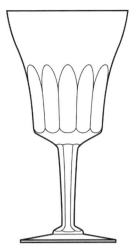

Lyric
Panel Cuts
Arcadia

Colonial
Gray Cut Thistle
Arcadia

Adriatic
Gray Cut Lines
Arcadia

Caesar
Gray Cut Floral,
Crisscross Cuts
Arcadia

ARE 16
Red Bowl, Gold Grapes &
Leaves, Gold Stem Accent,
Bowl & Foot Trim
Arcadia

ARE 12
Wine Shown
Amethyst Bowl
Arcadia

ARE 6
Floral & Dot Cuts,
Cut Ball Stem
Arcadia

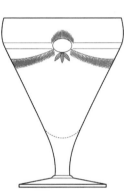

ARE 7
Gray Cut Swags
Arcadia

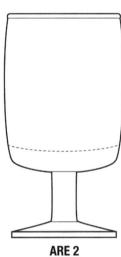

ARE 2
Plain
Arcadia

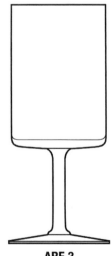

ARE 3
Plain
Arcadia

ARE 8
Bubble in Stem
Arcadia

Starlight
Gray Cut Stars
Arcadia

Aphrodite
Martini Shown
Clear Bowl & Foot,
Frosted Nude Stem
Arcadia

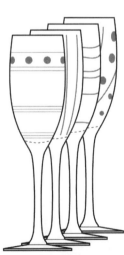

Metropolitan
Champagne Flute Shown
Gray Cut Dots, Rings &
Lines, Multi-Motif
Arcoroc

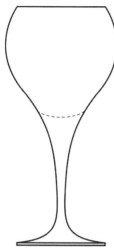

Sensation
Wine Shown
Plain
Arcoroc

Amelia
Plain
Arcoroc

Cervoise
Beer Glass Shown
Plain
Arcoroc

Octime
Multisided Bowl,
Black Stem
Arcoroc

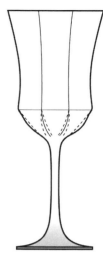

Octime
Multisided Bowl,
White Bowl & Stem
Arcoroc

Arcade/Bengale
Scalloped Panels,
Tempered Glass
Arcoroc

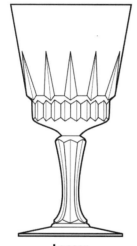

Lancer
Vertical Cuts
Arcoroc

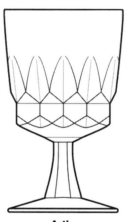

Artic
Optic Bowl
Arcoroc

Forum
Tumbler Shown
Horizontal Cut
Arcoroc

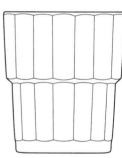

Norvege
On The Rocks Shown
Arcoroc

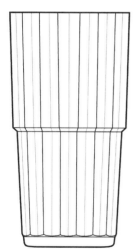

Stratford
Highball Shown
Optic, Barware
Arcoroc

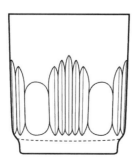

Aberdeen
Old Fashioned Shown
Vertical Cuts
Arcoroc

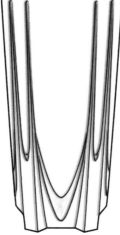

New Jersey
Highball Shown
Vertical Cuts to Top
Arcoroc

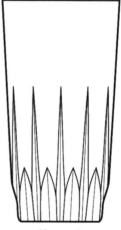

Hussard
Cooler Shown
Clear or Blue,
Vertical Cuts, Barware
Arcoroc

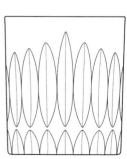

ACO 16
Double Old Fashioned Shown
Vertical Cuts
Arcoroc

Arcoroc

ACO 5
Tumbler Shown
Confetti, Christmas Tree
Arcoroc

Cocoon
Mug Shown
Clear or Various Colors,
Dinnerware & Accessories
Arcoroc

Classique
Mug Shown
Clear or Ruby,
Rim or Coupe Plates
Arcoroc

Directoire
Mug Shown
Clear or Blue,
Dinnerware
Arcoroc

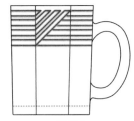

ACO 1
Mug Shown
Geometric Textured
Stripes on Edge
Arcoroc

Britannia
Beer Mug Shown
Thumbprint Design
Arcoroc

Jardiniere
Mug Shown
Turquoise, Embossed Rings
Arcoroc

Vercors
Mug Shown
Clear, Ruby or Sapphire,
Textured, Plain or Gold Trim
Arcoroc

ACO 3
Mug Shown
Holly & Ribbon Decal,
Gold Trim
Arcoroc

Holly Tree
Mug Shown
Christmas Tree & Holly
Arcoroc

Through The Woods
Mug Shown
Sleigh with Frosted
Tree Design
Arcoroc

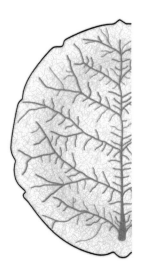

Aspen
Dinner Plate Shown
Clear, Blue or Turquoise,
Scalloped, Leaf Shaped
Arcoroc

Canterbury
Dinner Plate Shown
Embossed Floral
Arcoroc

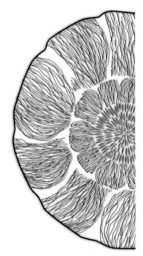

Fleur
Dinner Plate Shown
Clear or Cobalt,
Embossed Floral
Arcoroc

Rosa
Dinner Plate Shown
Clear, Blue, Pink or Smoke,
Embossed Floral
Arcoroc

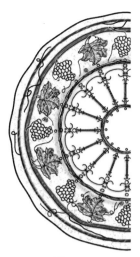

Minos
Dinner Plate Shown
Clear, Sapphire or Jade,
Grapes & Panels, Scalloped
Arcoroc

Seabreeze
Dinner Plate Shown
Swirled & Scalloped
Arcoroc

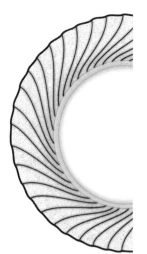

Clearbrook
Dinner Plate Shown
Textured/Swirled Rim,
No Stemware
Arcoroc

Teorama
Vertical Cuts,
Square Foot
Arnolfo di Cambio

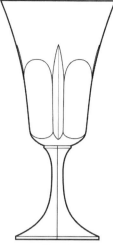

Royal
Wine Shown
Vertical & Panel Cuts,
Square Foot
Arnolfo di Cambio

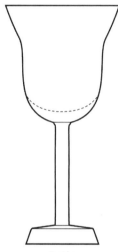

Delfo
Thick Round Foot
Arnolfo di Cambio

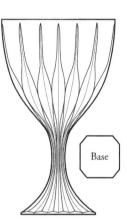

Artica
Vertical Cuts,
Multisided Foot
Arnolfo di Cambio

ACY 3
Cordial Shown
Panel Cuts,
Multisided Foot
Arnolfo di Cambio

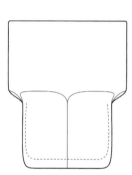

Mapan
Old Fashioned Shown
Square Base, Barware
Arnolfo di Cambio

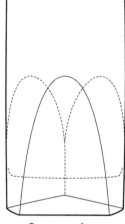

Conversazione
Highball Shown
3-Sided Arched Panels,
Barware
Arnolfo di Cambio

Deco
Old Fashioned Shown
Art Deco Arch Design,
Squarish Shape, Barware
Arnolfo di Cambio

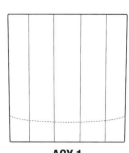

ACY 1
Double Old Fashioned Shown
12-Sided, Barware
Arnolfo di Cambio

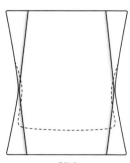

Cibi
Old Fashioned Shown
Square Shape, Bent Corners
Arnolfo di Cambio

AIZ 3
Various Color Bowls,
Gold Wreath & Swags,
Gold Trim
Arte Italica

AIZ 4
Wide Gold or Platinum
Encrusted Band & Swags
Arte Italica

AIZ 2
Various Color Bowls,
Wide Gold Encrusted Band
& Swags
Arte Italica

Medici
Clear or Various Color
Bowls, Gold Encrusted
Band & Swags
Arte Italica

Vetro
Clear, Frosted or Various
Color Bowls, Gold or
Platinum Encrusted Swags
Arte Italica

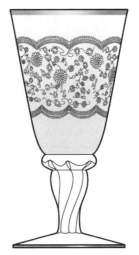

AIZ 6
Pink Bowl,
Gold Etched Floral,
Twisted Stem
Arte Italica

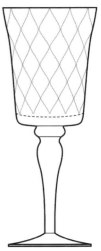

Bella Bianca
Diamond Optic Bowl
Arte Italica

Diamante
Optic Bowl,
Bubble in Stem,
6-Sided Foot
Arte Italica

Sofia
Ribbed Stem
Arte Italica

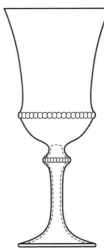

Sofia
Beaded Bowl & Stem
Hollow Stem
Arte Italica

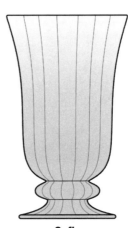

Sofia
Highball Shown
Cranberry, Mocha or Pink,
Optic Bowl
Arte Italica

Tulipani
Pewter Stem
Arte Italica

Regale
Black, Platinum Band
Arte Italica

Verona
Iced Tea Shown
Pewter Stem
Arte Italica

Baroque
Footed Tumbler Shown
Gold or Platinum Encrusted
Swags & Garland
Arte Italica

Milano
Tumbler Shown
Pewter Base, Oval Shape,
Barware
Arte Italica

Tesoro
Salad/Dessert Plate Shown
Pewter Beaded Edge
Arte Italica

Splendore
Dinner Plate Shown
White/Taupe Iridescent,
Pewter Beaded Edge
Arte Italica

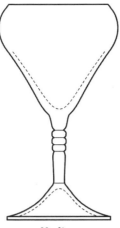

Veritas
Plain, Hollow Foot
Artel

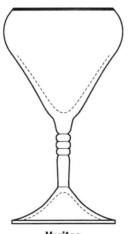

Veritas
Gold or Platinum Trim,
Hollow Foot
Artel

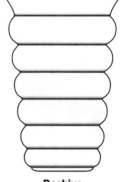

Beehive
Tumbler Shown
Clear or Various Opalescent
Colors, Rippled Body
Artel

Glacier
Double Old Fashioned Shown
Clear or Various Colors,
Multifaceted
Artel

Harlequin
Clear or Various Colors,
Etched Crisscross
Lines & Dots
Artel

Palace
Martini Shown
Clear or Various Colors,
Gray Cut Dots & Grid
Artel

Perla
Clear or Various Colors,
Cut Dots, Petals & Lines
Artel

Praha
Clear or Various Colors,
Etched Wavy Lines & Dots
Artel

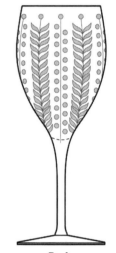

Pariz
Red Wine Shown
Clear or Various Colors,
Etched Leaves, Lines & Dots
Artel

Bublinka
Clear or Various Colors,
Etched Dots & Vertical Lines
Artel

Staro
Clear or Various Colors,
Stars, Dots & Laurel
Artel

Balloons
Clear or Various Colors,
Etched Dots & Curved Lines
Artel

Empire
Highball Shown
Clear or Various Colors,
Etched Diamonds & Stars
Artel

Herringbone
Tumbler Shown
Clear or Various Colors,
Etched Zigzag Bands
Artel

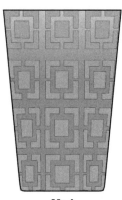

Mod
Tumbler Shown
Clear or Various Colors,
Etched Squares
Artel

Weave
Tumbler Shown
Clear or Various Colors,
Etched Basketweave
Artel

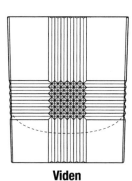

Viden
Double Old Fashioned Shown
Clear or Various Colors,
Horizontal & Vertical Cuts
Artel

Fireworks
Champagne Trumpet Flute Shown
Clear or Various Colors,
Etched Fireworks
Artel

Sprigs
Champagne Trumpet Flute Shown
Clear or Various Colors,
Etched Sprigs
Artel

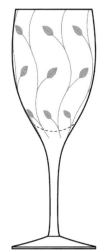

Novy Flora
White Wine Shown
Clear or Various Colors,
Gray Cut Leaves & Stems
Artel

Blue Bells
Clear or Various Colors,
Etched Floral
Artel

Daisy
Clear or Various Colors,
Etched Daisies
Artel

Water Lilies
Red Wine Shown
Clear or Various Colors,
Gray Cut Lily Pads & Vines
Artel

Willow
Clear or Various Colors,
Etched Willow Leaves
Artel

Narcissus
Clear or Various Colors,
Etched Flowers & Berries
Artel

Foliage
Clear or Various Colors,
Various Etched Leaves
Artel

Verdure
Clear or Various Colors,
Etched Floral
Artel

Baroko
Clear or Various Colors,
Etched Scrolls & Birds
Artel

Finch
Clear or Various Colors,
Etched Birds & Vines
Artel

Blackbirds
Stemless Goblet Shown
Black Painted Birds
Artel

Swans
Highball Shown
Clear or Various Colors,
Etched Swans & Scrolls
Artel

Poe
Martini Shown
Clear or Various Colors,
Etched Bird & Branch
Artel

Night Owl
Highball Shown
Clear or Various Colors,
Etched Owl & Branches
Artel

Bugs
Old Fashioned Shown
Etched Insects, Multi-Motif
Artel

Bugs
Champagne Trumpet Flute Shown
Painted Insects,
Multi-Motif
Artel

Fly Fusion
Various Gray Cut Insects
Artel

Fly Fusion
Various Painted Insects
Artel

Atlantis
Clear or Various Colors,
Etched Ocean Scene
Artel

Poseidon
Highball Shown
Clear or Various Colors,
Etched Seahorses & Scrolls
Artel

Frutti di Mare
Clear or Various Colors,
Etched Sea Life
Artel

Sea Life
Old Fashioned Shown
Clear or Various Colors,
Etched Sea Creatures
Artel

Fish L'Art Deco
Highball Shown
Clear or Various Colors,
Etched Fish, Dots & Lines
Artel

Sardinky
Highball Shown
Clear or Various Colors,
Etched Fish & Wavy Lines
Artel

Golden Age of Yachting
Highball Shown
Clear or Various Colors,
Etched Yachts & Birds
Artel

Safari
Old Fashioned Shown
Clear or Various Colors,
Etched Animals, Multi-Motif
Artel

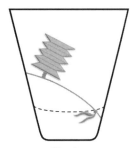

Cinska
Nite Set Tumbler Shown
Clear or Various Colors,
Etched Chinese Lanterns
Artel

Kentucky Derby
Mint Julep Shown
Gray Decoration
Arthur Court

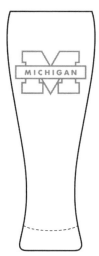

University Glassware
Pilsner Shown
Multi-Motif,
Various College Decals
Arthur Court

Safari
Pilsner Shown
Multi-Motif,
Platinum Animals on Stems
Arthur Court

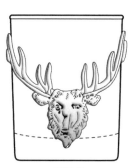

AUU 3
Double Old Fashioned Shown
Raised Reindeer
Arthur Court

Salute
Clear or Various
Color Bowls, Plain
Artland

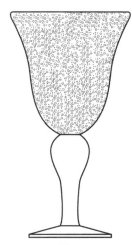

Fizz
Clear or Various Color
Textured Bowls
Artland

Iris
Clear or Various Color
Bowls with Bubbles
Artland

Bubble
Margarita Shown
Various Color Bowls
with Bubbles
Artland

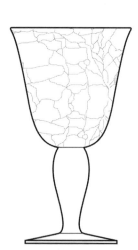

Crackle
Clear or Various Color
Crackled Bowls
Artland

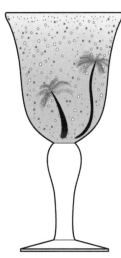

St. Croix
Palm Trees on Green Bowl
with Bubbles
Artland

Renaissance
Clear or Various Color
Bowls, Frosted Scrolls
Artland

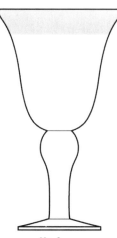

Horizon
Various Color Bands
Artland

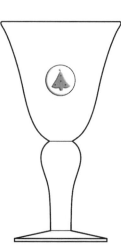

Tree Medallion
Green Tree Medallion
Artland

Gazebo
Clear or Various Color
Bowls, Etched Band
Artland

Filoli Terrace Collection
Iced Tea Shown
Clear, Blue & Yellow
Glass Flowers
Artland

Fiore
Clear, Amber or Turquoise
Bowl with Multicolor
Circles & Dots
Artland

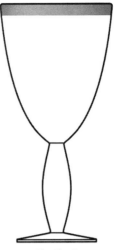

Festival
Various Color Bands
Artland

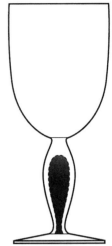

Hampton
Amethyst Bubble in Stem
Artland

Nassau
Clear, Gold or Platinum
Color Drop in Stem
Artland

Optic Bouquet
Light Green Optic Bowl
Artland

Bouquet
Blue, Green, Purple or
Yellow Tinted Bowls
Artland

Purple Passion
Purple Flowers,
Green Stem
Artland

Greetings
White Wine Shown
Red Bowl
Artland

Bijoux
Amber, Blue, Green
or Purple Bowl
Artland

Currents
Etched Wavy Lines
Artland

Midnight
Various Colors
Artland

Optic
Clear, Bue or Green,
Optic Bowl
Artland

Solo
Plain
Artland

Sommelier
Wine Shown
Plain
Artland

Oslo
Plain
Artland

Veritas
Plain
Artland

Braid
Clear or Various Color
Bowls, Air Twist Stem
Artland

Tuscan Villa
Frosted Leaf
Artland

Polka Dot
Clear or Various Color
Bowls, Cut Gray Dots
Artland

Holiday Stars
Balloon Wine Shown
Blue Bowl, White Star & Curl
Artland

Helios
Lines & Multicolor Shapes
Artland

Butterfly Breeze
Etched Butterfly & Scroll
Artland

Peppermint
Green & Red Swirled Lines
Artland

Snowflake
Frosted Snowflake
Artland

Leaf Collection
Frosted Leaves
Artland

Cherry Blossom
Clear or Various Color
Bowls, Etched Floral
Artland

Cosmopolitan
Plain
Artland

Concentrix
Etched Rings
Artland

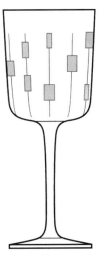

Alex
Gray Etched Rectangles
Artland

Soho
Clear or Various Color
Hourglass Shaped Bowls
Artland

Celebrations
Cordials Shown
Various Color &
Bowl Shapes
Artland

Legacy Black
Black Stem & Foot
Artland

Austin Collection
Wine Shown
Various Color Glass
Diamonds, Cut Lines
Artland

Love Bird
Champagne Flute Shown
Birds, Hearts
Artland

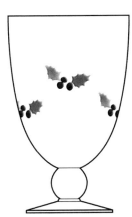

Holly Days
Iced Tea Shown
Green Holly, Red Berries
Artland

Luster Bell Optic
Green or Purple Optic Bowl
Artland

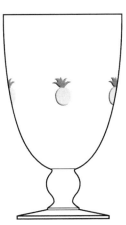

Pineapple Welcome
Iced Tea Shown
Yellow & Green Pineapples
Artland

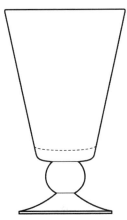

Season Cheer
Clear, Blue, Green
or Ruby Bowl
Artland

Wildwood
Various Gray Etched
Animals, Multi-Motif
Artland

Emory
Amber, Amethyst, Blue
or Green Bowl
Artland

Victoria
Blue or Green Stem
Artland

Olive
Martini Shown
Green & Red Olive Stems,
Hollow Foot
Artland

Veranda
Amber, Black, Ruby or
White Bowl, Hollow Stem
Artland

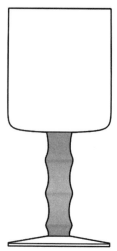

Bamboo
Frosted Bamboo
Shaped Stem
Artland

Radiance
Black & Gold Ball Stem
Artland

Christmas Splendor
Various Stem Shapes,
Multicolor Stem Accents
Artland

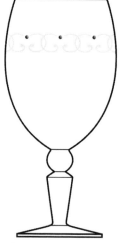

Oatlands Collection
Scrolls & Various Color Dots
Artland

Halo
Various Color Bowls,
Frosted Stem Accent
Artland

Venture
Optic Bowl,
Various Color Stems
Artland

Aldrich
Wine Shown
Optic Bowl
Artland

Drayton Hall Collection
Etched Garlands,
Colored Jeweled Dots
Artland

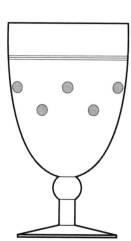

Decatur Collection
Gray Cut Dots &
Horizontal Lines
Artland

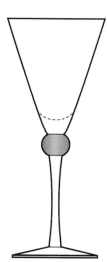

Top Hat
Wine Shown
Gold or Platinum Stem Accent
Artland

Megan's Garden
Handpainted,
Multicolor Flowers
Artland

Cactus
Margarita Shown
Green Cactus Stem
Artland

Catera
Crooked Stems
Artland

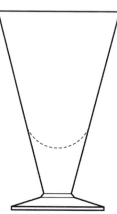

Shrub Collection
Footed Tumbler Shown
Clear, Blue or Red
Artland

Splash
Martini Shown
Various Color Stripes
Down Stem
Artland

Flamingo
Martini Shown
Painted Pink Birds
Artland

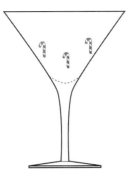

Candy Cane
Martini Shown
Red & White Candy Canes
Artland

Samba Blue
Martini Shown
Blue Stripe
Artland

Upstairs Martini
Martini Shown
Hollow Foot
Artland

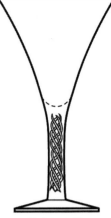

Twisted Air
Air Twist Stem
Artland

Metro
Martini Shown
Various Color Bowls,
Dots & Lines
Artland

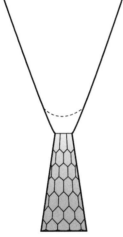

Presscott
Wine Shown
Various Color Frosted Stems
Artland

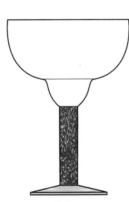

Salsa
Margarita Shown
Various Color Stems,
Yellow Foot
Artland

Twister
Shot Glasses Shown
Clear or Various Colors,
Multi-Motif
Artland

Sierra
Vodka Shown
Artland

Invitations
Vodka Shown
Artland

Tom Collins
Tom Collins Shown
Blue, Green, Pink or Yellow
Artland

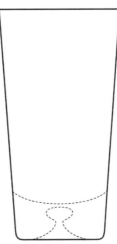

Rockwell
Highball Shown
Bubble in Base
Artland

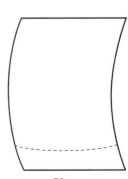

Disco
Shot Glass Shown
Clear or Various Colors
Artland

Elegance
Mini Martini Shown
Various Color Bowls,
Bubble in Base, Barware
Artland

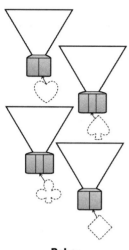

Poker
Martini Shown
Red Hearts & Diamonds,
Black Clubs & Spades on Base
Artland

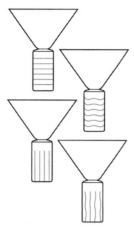

New Age
Wine Shown
Frosted Bases
Artland

Mojito
Mojito Shown
Black Swirls, Green Leaf
Artland

AZB 1
Wine Shown
Hollow Foot
Arzberg

Shine
Red Wine Shown
Plain
Arzberg

ACN 1
Arch & Fan Cuts
Ashford Castle Collection

Christina
Crisscross & Fan Cuts
Astral

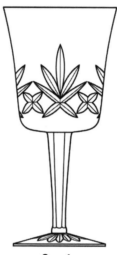

Questa
Crisscross & Fan Cuts
Astral

AST 1
Crisscross & Fan Cuts
Astral

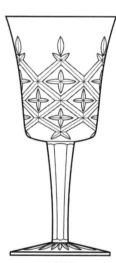

AST 6
Crisscross & Star Cuts
Astral

Willow
Vertical Cuts
Astral

Venus
Crisscross & Vertical Cuts
Astral

Peerage
Vertical Cuts
Astral

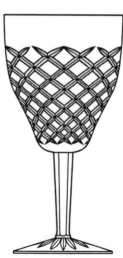

Starry
Crisscross Cuts
Astral

Celeste
Crisscross & Vertical Cuts
Astral

Fantasia Ice
Frosted Cuts
Astral

Fantasia
Clear Cuts
Astral

Joan
Diamond & Fan Cuts
Astral

Peerage
Vertical Cuts
Astral

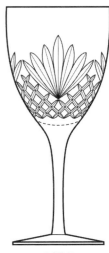

AST 5
Wine Shown
Crisscross & Fan Cuts
Astral

Diane
Crisscross & Fan Cuts
Astral

Mira
Crisscross Cuts
Astral

Pela
Wine Hock Shown
Vertical & Leaf Cuts
Astral

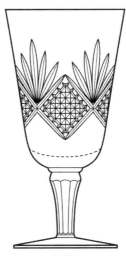

AST 2
Ice Tea Shown
Crisscross & Fan Cuts
Astral

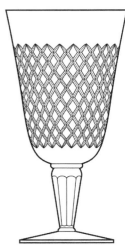

AST 3
Iced Tea Shown
Crisscross Cuts
Astral

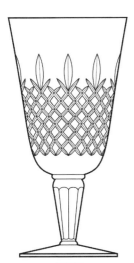

AST 7
Iced Tea Shown
Crisscross & Vertical Cuts
Astral

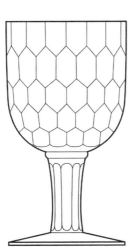

AST 4
Honeycomb Cuts
Astral

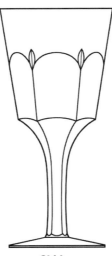

Obidos
Panel Cuts
Atlantis

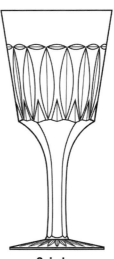

Coimbra
Vertical & Horizontal Cuts
Atlantis

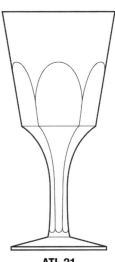

ATL 21
Panel Cuts
Atlantis

Atlantis

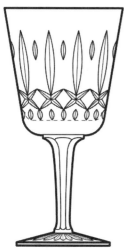

Fatima
Crisscross & Vertical Cuts
Atlantis

Santarem
Crisscross Cuts
Atlantis

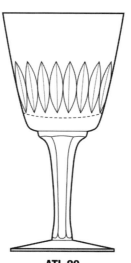

ATL 20
Wine Shown
Vertical Cuts
Atlantis

ATL 1
Vertical, Horizontal &
Thumbprint Cuts
Atlantis

Isabel
Crisscross & Vertical Cuts
Atlantis

Caldas
Vertical & Horizontal Cuts
Atlantis

Algarve
Vertical & Thumbprint Cuts
Atlantis

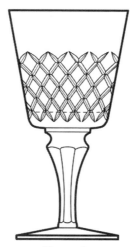

Diamante
Crisscross Cuts
Atlantis

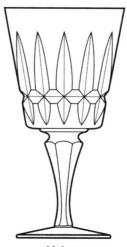

Lisbon
Vertical & Horizontal Cuts
Atlantis

Silves
Crisscross Cuts
Atlantis

Palacio
Panel Cuts
Atlantis

Moselle
Crisscross Cuts
Atlantis

Thames
Vertical Cuts
Atlantis

Marquise
Wine Shown
Fan & Leaf Cuts
Atlantis

Faro
Dot Cuts
Atlantis

Oporto
Vertical & Dot Cuts
Atlantis

Cascais
Vertical Cuts
Atlantis

Elvas
Crisscross Cuts
Atlantis

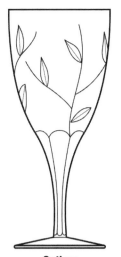

Cathay
Cut Plant
Atlantis

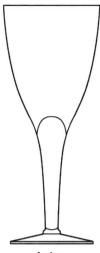

Lotus
Flat-Sided Stem
Atlantis

Fount
Fan Cuts, Flat-Sided Stem
Atlantis

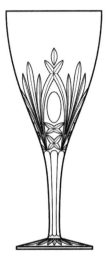

Anabella
Fan Cuts
Atlantis

Bel Air
White Wine Shown
Crisscross & Fan Cuts
Atlantis

Castelo
Vertical Cuts
Atlantis

ATL 9
Wine Shown
Crisscross & Vertical Cuts
Atlantis

Estrella
Crisscross Cuts
Atlantis

Magellan
Crisscross & Fan Cuts
Atlantis

Magellan Gold
Crisscross & Fan Cuts,
Gold Trim
Atlantis

Nazare
Crisscross & Vertical Cuts
Atlantis

Palmela
Floral & Arch Cuts
Atlantis

Estoril
Vertical Cuts
Atlantis

Setubal
Vertical Cuts
Atlantis

Azores
Vertical Cuts
Atlantis

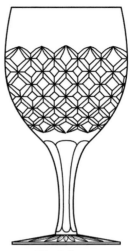

Montalegre
Crisscross Cuts
Atlantis

Tintern
Crisscross & Fan Cuts
Atlantis

ATL 18
Crisscross Cuts
Atlantis

ATL 4
Wine Shown
Vertical Cuts
Atlantis

Evora
Panel Cuts
Atlantis

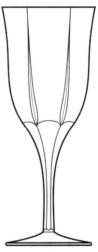

Lyric
Vertical Cuts
Atlantis

Diana
Crisscross Cuts
Atlantis

Stripes
Vertical Cuts
Atlantis

Chalice
Vertical Cuts,
Flat-Sided Stem
Atlantis

Pillar
Flat-Sided Stem
Atlantis

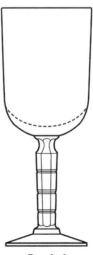

Pombal
Geometric Cut Stem
Atlantis

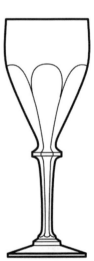

Arcadas
Panel Cuts
Atlantis

Sacavem
Vertical & Horizontal Cuts
Atlantis

Sintra
Vertical Cuts
Atlantis

Column
Cut Thumbprints on Stem
Atlantis

Grid
Vertical & Horizontal Cuts
Frosted Ball Stem Accent
Atlantis

Coliseum
Cut Rectangles
Atlantis

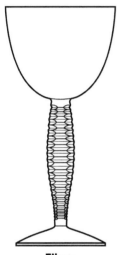

Eliane
Horizontally Cut Stem
Atlantis

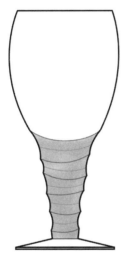

Alpha Satin
Frosted Cut Stem
Atlantis

Gala
Various Color Optic Bowls
Atlantis

Athena
Vertical Cuts
Atlantis

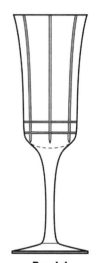

Rondel
Champagne Flute Shown
Vertical & Horizontal Cuts
Atlantis

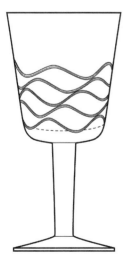

Synergy
Wavy Cuts
Atlantis

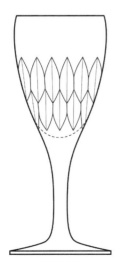

Madeira
Cordial Shown
Vertical Cuts
Atlantis

Nova
Wine Shown
Arch & Fan Cuts
Atlantis

ATL 17
Polished Arch Cuts
Atlantis

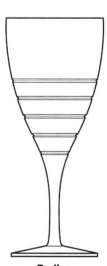

Radius
Wine Shown
Cut Rings
Atlantis

Atlantis

Elica
Cut Slanted Rings
Atlantis

Flight
Cut
Atlantis

Genesis
Clear Cut Arches
Atlantis

Genesis
Gray & Clear Cut Arches
Atlantis

Fantasy
Vertical Cuts
Atlantis

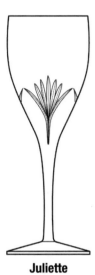

Juliette
Fan Cuts
Atlantis

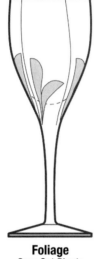

Foliage
Gray Cut Plants
Atlantis

Paris
Fan Cuts
Atlantis

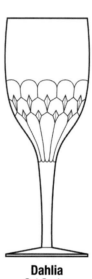

Dahlia
Cut Scales
Atlantis

ATL 15
Crisscross & Fan Cuts
Atlantis

ATL 30
Polished Cut Dots & Lines
Atlantis

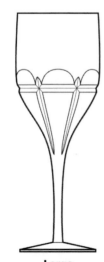

Largo
Vertical & Horizontal Cuts
Atlantis

Tara
Polished Cuts
Atlantis

Aria
Vertical & Arch Cuts
Atlantis

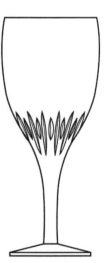

Sonnet
Vertical Cuts
Atlantis

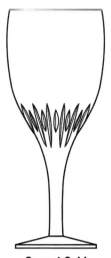

Sonnet Gold
Vertical Cuts, Gold Trim
Atlantis

Celebration
Crisscross & Arch Cuts
Atlantis

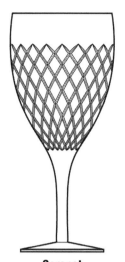

Coronet
Crisscross Cuts
Atlantis

Sara
Panel Cuts
Atlantis

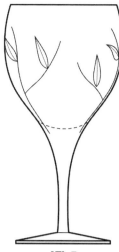

ATL 5
Cut Plants
Atlantis

Chartres
Vertical & Arch Cuts
Atlantis

Chartres Gold
Vertical & Arch Cuts,
Gold Trim
Atlantis

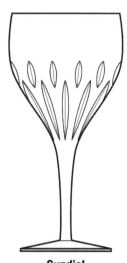

Sundial
Vertical Cuts
Atlantis

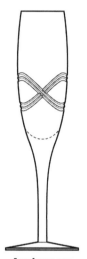

Anniversary
Champagne Flute Shown
Cut Intertwined Lines
Atlantis

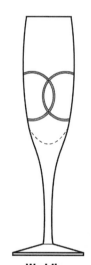

Wedding
Champagne Flute Shown
Cut Intertwined Circles
Atlantis

Connoisseur
Wine Shown
Plain
Atlantis

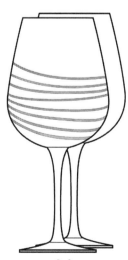

Axis
Wine Shown
Gray Cut Swirls or Plain
Atlantis

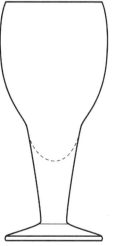

Alpha
Plain
Atlantis

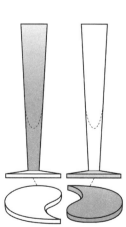

Millennium Duo
Champagne Flute Shown
Clear & Frosted,
Connecting Bases
Atlantis

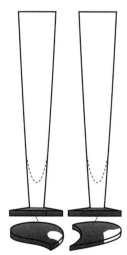

Heart Break
Champagne Flute Shown
Red Connecting Bases
Atlantis

Atlantis

Zephyr
Swirl Cuts
Atlantis

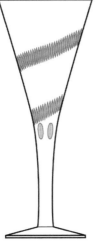

Quill
Small Vertical Cuts
Atlantis

Storm
Martini Shown
Gray or Polished Cut Leaves
Atlantis

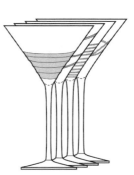

Tundra
Martinis Shown
Multi-Motif
Atlantis

ATL 8
Brandy Shown
Crisscross & Vertical Cuts
Atlantis

ATL 31
Brandy Shown
Crisscross & Vertical Cuts
Atlantis

Connoisseur
Cognac Shown
Cut Lines
Atlantis

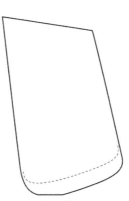

Zanzibar
Highball Shown
Plain, Slanted
Atlantis

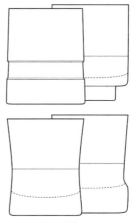

Pavillion
Double Old Fashioned Shown
Multi-Motif
Atlantis

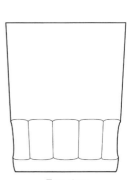

Equator
Whiskey Shown
Square Cuts
Atlantis

Arctic
Vodka Shown
Gray Cut Design
Atlantis

Medusa
Highball Shown
Gray Cut Lines
Atlantis

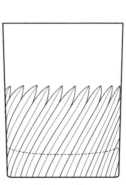

Amarante
Whiskey Shown
Diagonal Cuts, Barware
Atlantis

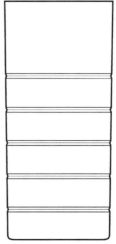

Oxford
Highball Shown
Cut Rings, Barware
Atlantis

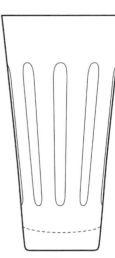

Max
Highball Shown
Vertical Cuts,
Barware
Atlantis

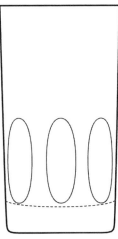

Fab
Highball Shown
Panel Cuts, Barware
Atlantis

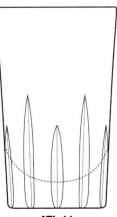

ATL 11
Highball Shown
Vertical Cuts to Base,
Barware
Atlantis

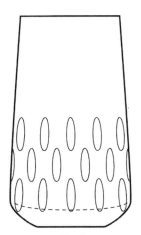

Nioni
Highball Shown
Vertical Cuts, Barware
Atlantis

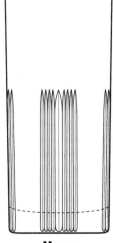

Manor
Highball Shown
Vertical Cuts, Barware
Atlantis

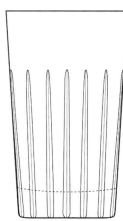

Dorchester
Highball Shown
Vertical Cuts, Barware
Atlantis

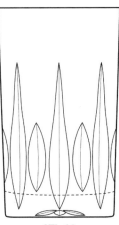

ATL 13
Tumbler Shown
Vertical Cuts
Atlantis

ATL 16
Tumbler Shown
Fan Cuts
Atlantis

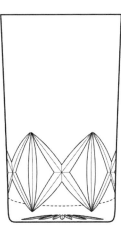

ATL 10
Highball Shown
Crisscross & Vertical Cuts
Atlantis

Fernando
Highball Shown
Crisscross & Vertical Cuts,
Barware
Atlantis

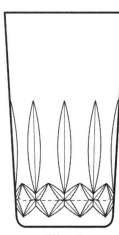

Miguel
Highball Shown
Crisscross & Vertical Cuts,
Barware
Atlantis

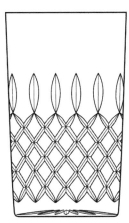

ATL 14
Highball Shown
Crisscross & Vertical Cuts
Atlantis

Jose
Old Fashioned Shown
Crisscross & Vertical Cuts,
Barware
Atlantis

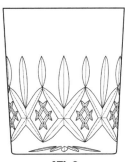

ATL 6
Double Old Fashioned Shown
Crisscross & Vertical Cuts,
Barware
Atlantis

Catalina
Double Old Fashioned Shown
Crisscross & Fan Cuts,
Barware
Atlantis

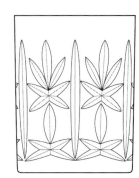

Delray
Double Old Fashioned Shown
Crisscross, Vertical &
Fan Cuts, Barware
Atlantis

Meridian
Double Old Fashioned Shown
Crisscross & Fan Cuts,
Barware
Atlantis

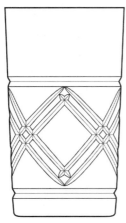

ATL 19
Tumbler Shown
Horizontal & Crisscross Cuts
Atlantis

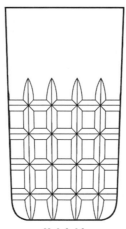

Helsinki
Vertical & Horizontal Cuts,
Barware
Atlantis

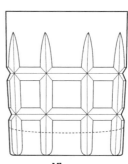

Viana
Old Fashioned Shown
Vertical & Horizontal Cuts,
Barware
Atlantis

AUR 1
Flowers & Leaves on Blue
Band, Gold Bands & Trim
Aurum

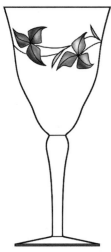

Bridal
Gray Cut 3-Petal Flowers
Avitra

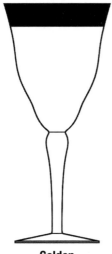

Golden
Wide Gold Trim
Avitra

Golden
Wide Gold Trim &
Verge Line
Avitra

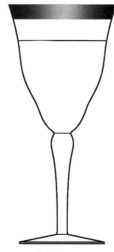

Platinum
Wide Platinum Trim &
Verge Line
Avitra

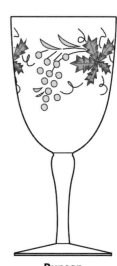

Duncan
Engraved Grapes & Leaves
Avitra

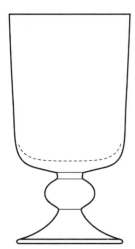

Leonardo
Plain
Avitra

Pinwheel
Pinwheel & Fan Cuts
Avitra

AVC 1
Champagne Flute Shown
Floral Design
Avon

Hummingbird
Etched Floral,
Frosted Stem
Avon

Rose Anniversary
Cut Rose
Avon

Classic Collection
Diamond & Fan Cuts
Avon

Golden Accents
Star & Fan Cuts,
Gold Trim
Avon

American Blue
Blue,
Fan & Circle Cuts
Avon

George & Martha Washington
Dark Blue, Frosted Cameos
Avon

Hearts & Diamond
Clear or Ruby,
Raised Hearts & Diamonds
Avon

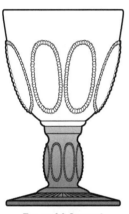

Emerald Accent
Green Stem
Avon

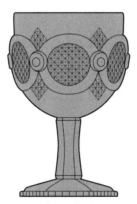

Cape Cod
Red or Blue
Avon

Royal Sapphire
Old Fashioned Shown
Blue, Molded Raised Design
Avon

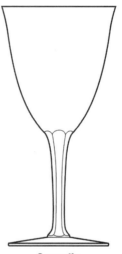

Coppelia
Plain
Baccarat

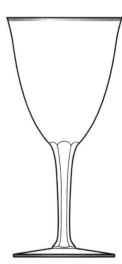

Directoire
Gold Trim
Baccarat

Zurich
Panel Cuts
Baccarat

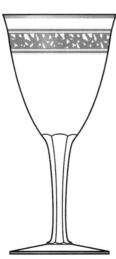

Colorado
Gold Trim
Baccarat

Bellinzona
Crisscross Cuts
Baccarat

Noyon
Crisscross & Fan Cuts
Baccarat

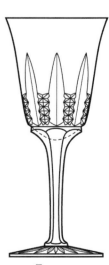

Turenne
Vertical Cuts
Baccarat

Baccarat

Burgos
Tall Goblet Shown
Crisscross Cuts
Baccarat

BAC 6
Port Wine Shown
Optic Bowl
Baccarat

BAC 21
Cordial Shown
Plain
Baccarat

Lafayette
Etched Scrolls,
Smooth Stem
Baccarat

Rochambeau
Etched Scrolls,
Multisided Stem
Baccarat

Toscane
Gold Scrolls,
Gold Bowl & Foot Trim
Baccarat

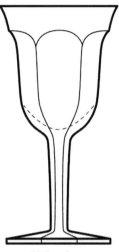

Malmaison
Panel Cuts,
Multisided Foot
Baccarat

BAC 49
Wine Shown
Red Bowl, Panel Cuts
Baccarat

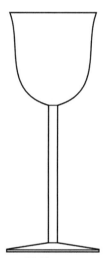

St. Exupery
Plain
Baccarat

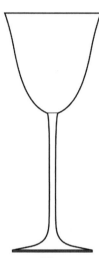

Filao
Plain
Baccarat

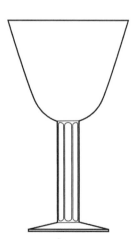

Lyra
Ribbed, Column Stem
Baccarat

100/192
Champagne Flute Shown
Plain
Baccarat

BAC 25
Blue Bowl, Etched Scrolls
Baccarat

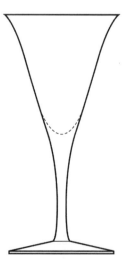

2933
Sherry Shown
Plain
Baccarat

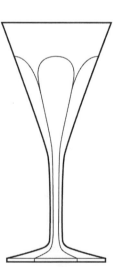

11454
Champagne Flute Shown
Panel Cuts,
Multisided Foot
Baccarat

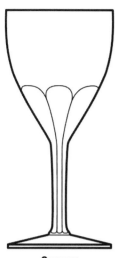

Genova
Panel Cuts
Baccarat

Auvergne/Perigold
Crisscross Cuts
Baccarat

Epron
Swag & Crisscross Cuts
Baccarat

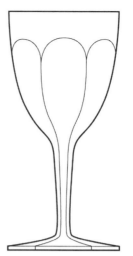

Compiegne
Panel Cuts,
Multisided Foot
Baccarat

Thorigny
Crisscross Cuts
Baccarat

Palerme
Honeycomb Cuts
Baccarat

Lagny
Elaborate Cut Star Design
Baccarat

Lagny
Cobalt Blue Bowl,
Elaborate Cut Star Design
Baccarat

Juigne
Crisscross Cuts
Baccarat

Bogota
Crisscross & Star Cuts
Baccarat

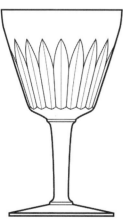

Val de Loire
Vertical Cuts,
Smooth Stem
Baccarat

Val d'Oise
Vertical Cuts,
Multisided Stem
Baccarat

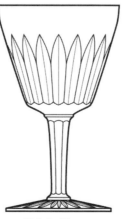

Val de Marne
Vertical Cuts,
Multisided Stem, Cut Foot
Baccarat

Amboise
Vertical & Horizontal Cuts,
Smooth Stem
Baccarat

BAC 4
Vertical & Horizontal Cuts,
Multisided Stem
Baccarat

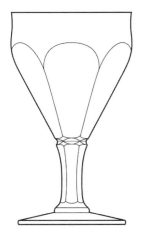

Duchesse de Dino
Panel Cuts
Baccarat

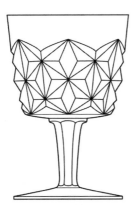

Bernadotte
Star Cuts
Baccarat

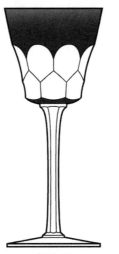

BAC 50
Wine Shown
Green Bowl,
Honeycomb Cuts
Baccarat

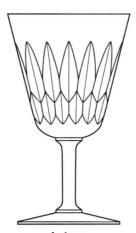

Lutece
Long & Short Vertical Cuts
Baccarat

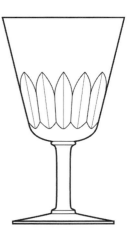

Cote d'Azur
Vertical Cuts,
Smooth Stem
Baccarat

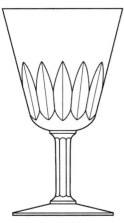

Lavandou
Vertical Cuts,
Multisided Stem
Baccarat

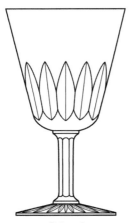

Esterel
Vertical Cuts,
Multisided Stem, Cut Foot
Baccarat

Orleans
Vertical Cuts
Baccarat

Riberac
Plain
Baccarat

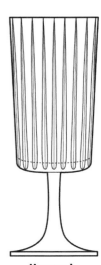

Harmonie
Vertical Cuts
Baccarat

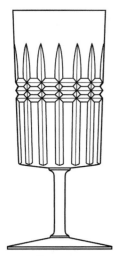

Sancerre
Vertical & Horizontal Cuts
Baccarat

Brantome
Plain
Baccarat

Bahrein
Gold Floral,
Horses & Birds
Baccarat

Leillah
Etched Floral,
Horses & Birds
Baccarat

Jasmina
Etched Floral,
Horses & Birds,
Gold Trim
Baccarat

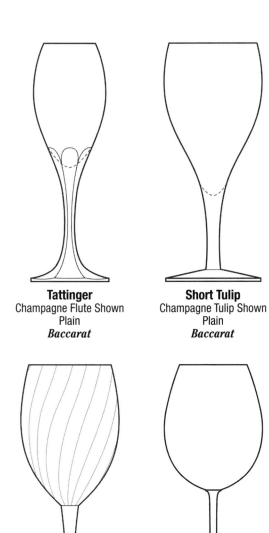

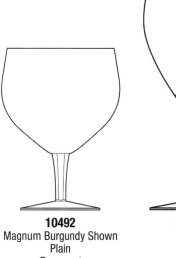
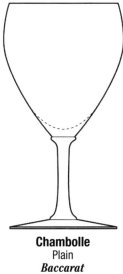

Tattinger
Champagne Flute Shown
Plain
Baccarat

Short Tulip
Champagne Tulip Shown
Plain
Baccarat

St. Remy
Plain
Baccarat

10492
Magnum Burgundy Shown
Plain
Baccarat

Chambolle
Plain
Baccarat

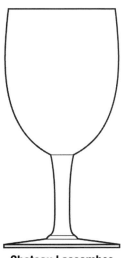

Livourne
Optic Bowl
Baccarat

Degustation
Bordeaux Grand Wine Shown
Plain
Baccarat

Chateau Lascombes
Plain
Baccarat

Francois Villon
Plain
Baccarat

Henri IV
Etched Vine
Baccarat

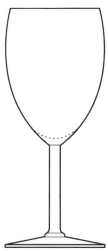

Haut Brion
Plain
Baccarat

Epicure
Plain
Baccarat

BAC 31
Wine Shown
Etched Floral & Scrolls
Baccarat

Perfection
Plain
15358
Baccarat

Oenologie
Great Wine Shown
Plain
Baccarat

Baccarat

Courviosier
Brandy Shown
Plain
3299
Baccarat

Big Ben
Oversize Wine Shown
Plain
Baccarat

Tastevin (Pommard)
Burgundy Wine Shown
Plain
15879
Baccarat

16652
Rhine Wine Shown
Various Color Bowls
Baccarat

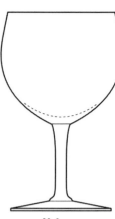

Volnay
Plain
Baccarat

Rabelais
Plain
Baccarat

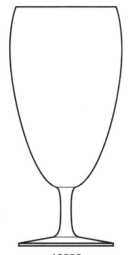

16806
Iced Tea Shown
Plain
Baccarat

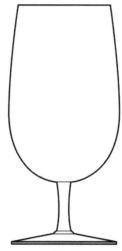

17641
Large Brandy Shown
Plain
Baccarat

Pavillon
Wine Shown
Plain
15880
Baccarat

Bacchus
Balloon Wine Shown
Plain
15992
Baccarat

Corton
Plain
Baccarat

Napoleon
Brandy Shown
Gold "N" & Crown,
Circled with Leaves
Baccarat

Napoleon
Brandy Shown
Gold "N" & Crown
Baccarat

BAC 40
Claret Wine Shown
Lattice & Oval Cuts
Baccarat

Montaigne
Plain
Baccarat

66

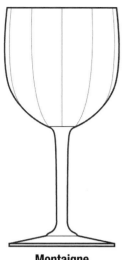

Montaigne
Optic Bowl
Baccarat

Montaigne
Optic Bowl, Gold Trim
Baccarat

Montaigne
Optic Bowl, Tall Stem
Baccarat

Clos de Vougeot
Multisided Cut Stem
Baccarat

Voltaire
Multisided Notched Stem
Baccarat

Avranches
Multisided Cut Stem
Baccarat

Brummel
Plain
Baccarat

Aquarelle
Blue, Green or Yellow Bowls
Baccarat

Tranquility
Gray Cut Ovals &
Vertical Lines
Baccarat

Paris
Vertical Cuts
Baccarat

BAC 33
Etched Floral,
Butterfly & Plants,
Cut Stem & Foot
Baccarat

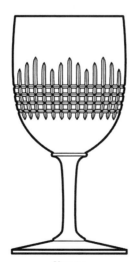

Nancy
Vertical & Horizontal Cuts,
Smooth Stem
Baccarat

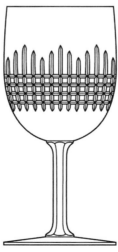

Colmar
Vertical & Horizontal Cuts,
Multisided Stem
Baccarat

Sevigne
Etched Leaves & Scrolls
Baccarat

Recamier
Etched Leaves & Scrolls,
Gold Bowl & Foot Trim
Baccarat

Baccarat

Comtesse de Paris
Plain
Baccarat

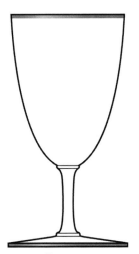

Regence
Gold Bowl & Foot Trim
Baccarat

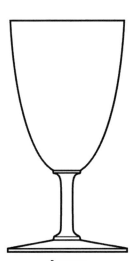

Angers
Plain
Baccarat

Ostende
Etched Fleur-de-lis
Baccarat

Madame Butterfly
Etched Floral,
Butterfly & Plants
Baccarat

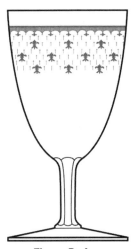

Fleurs De Lys
Etched Fleur-de-lis
Baccarat

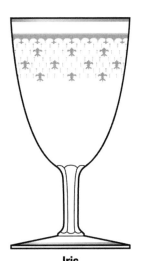

Iris
Gold Fleur-de-lis,
Gold Bowl & Foot Trim
Baccarat

BAC 7
Vertical & Arch Cuts
Baccarat

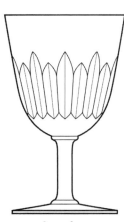

Lorraine
Vertical Cuts,
Smooth Stem
Baccarat

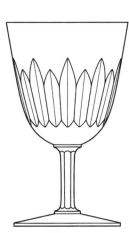

Verone
Vertical Cuts,
Multisided Stem
Baccarat

Florence
Etched Floral
Baccarat

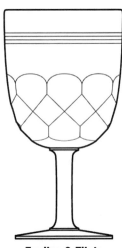

Ecailes & Filets
Honeycomb Cuts,
Horizontal Lines
Baccarat

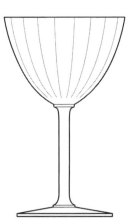

Asservillers
Optic Bowl
Baccarat

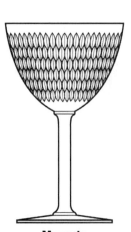

Magenta
Rows of Small Vertical Cuts
Baccarat

11433
Rhine Wine Shown
Ruby Bowl
Baccarat

11080
Rhine Wine Shown
Various Color Bowls
Baccarat

Dom Perignon
Plain
Baccarat

Laurent Perrier
Champagne Flute Shown
Plain
Baccarat

Athena
Horizontal Cuts,
Ribbed Stem
Baccarat

Scarlatti
Etched Floral & Vines
Baccarat

Capri
Optic Bowl
Baccarat

Capri Gold
Optic Bowl, Gold Trim
Baccarat

Capri
Optic Bowl, Tall Stem
Baccarat

Chimney
Brandy Shown
Plain
6477, 11981
Baccarat

Chimney
Brandy Shown
Gold Bowl & Foot Trim
Baccarat

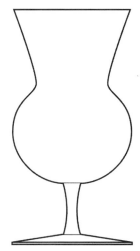

Thistle
Brandy Shown
Plain
10774
Baccarat

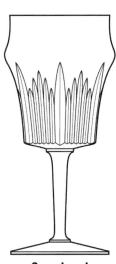

Courchevel
Vertical Cuts
Baccarat

Clara
Plain
Baccarat

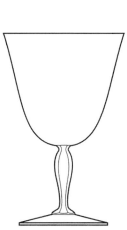

Clara
Plain, Small Stem
Baccarat

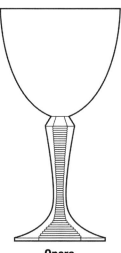

Opera
Multisided Cut Stem
Baccarat

Baccarat

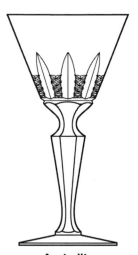

Austerlitz
Vertical & Crisscross Cuts
Baccarat

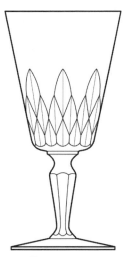

Carcassonne
Vertical Cuts
Baccarat

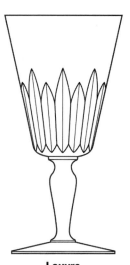

Louvre
Vertical Cuts
Baccarat

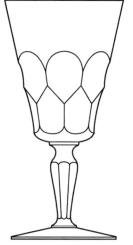

Belle de France
Panel Cuts
Baccarat

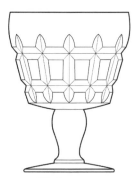

Marignanne
Vertical & Horizontal Cuts,
Smooth Stem
Baccarat

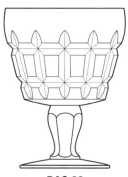

BAC 38
Vertical & Horizontal Cuts,
Multisided Stem
Baccarat

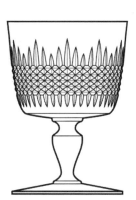

Alsace
Crisscross & Vertical Cuts
Baccarat

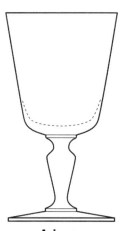

Avignon
Plain
Baccarat

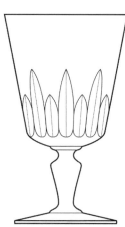

Biarritz
Vertical Cuts,
Smooth Stem
Baccarat

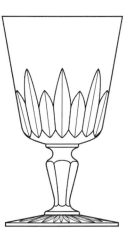

Bayonne
Vertical Cuts,
Multisided Stem, Cut Foot
Baccarat

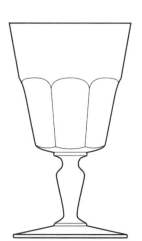

Bretagne
Panel Cuts
Baccarat

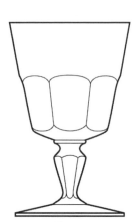

Texas
Panel Cuts
Baccarat

Ohio
Panel Cuts,
Multisided Stem, Cut Foot
Baccarat

Eldorado
Panel Cuts, Etched Scrolls,
Gold Bowl & Foot Trim
Baccarat

Orenoque
Panel Cuts,
Gold Etched Scrolls,
Gold Bowl & Foot Trim
Baccarat

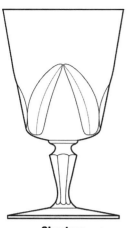

Chartres
Arch Cuts
Baccarat

Hossegor
Vertical Cuts
Baccarat

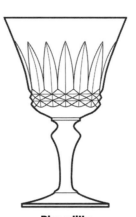

Piccadilly
Vertical & Horizontal Cuts
Smooth Stem
Baccarat

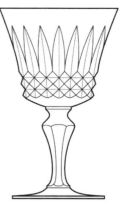

Balmoral
Vertical & Horizontal Cuts
Multisided Stem
Baccarat

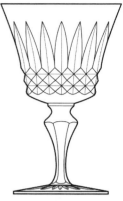

Buckingham
Vertical & Horizontal Cuts,
Multisided Stem, Cut Foot
Baccarat

Parme
Etched Birds & Scrolls,
Vertical Cuts
Smooth Stem
Baccarat

Bergame
Gold Birds & Scrolls,
Vertical Cuts,
Multisided Stem
Baccarat

Borromees
Gold Birds & Scrolls,
Vertical Cuts,
Smooth Stem
Baccarat

Normandie
Plain
Baccarat

Manon
Gold Bowl & Foot Trim
Baccarat

Norma
Platinum Bowl & Foot Trim
Baccarat

Naples
Optic Bowl
Baccarat

Turin
Vertical & Horizontal Cuts
Baccarat

Monte Carlo
Optic Bowl
Baccarat

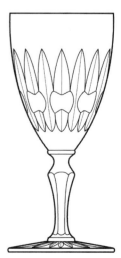

Enghein
Vertical & Panel Cuts,
Multisided Stem, Cut Foot
Baccarat

Baccarat

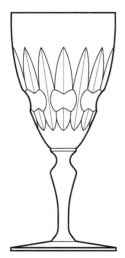

Auteuil
Vertical & Panel Cuts,
Smooth Stem
Baccarat

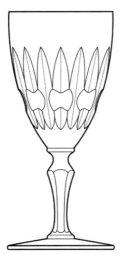

Deauville
Vertical & Panel Cuts,
Multisided Stem
Baccarat

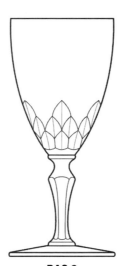

BAC 9
Vertical Cuts
Baccarat

Beaufort
Heavy Cut Diamond Design
Baccarat

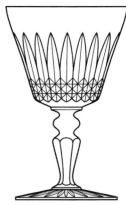

Pigalle
Vertical & Horizontal Cuts
Baccarat

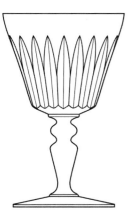

Rochechouart
Vertical Cuts
Baccarat

Ile Rousse
Crisscross & Vertical Cuts,
Multisided Stem
Baccarat

Ile d'Aix
Crisscross & Vertical Cuts,
Multisided Stem, Cut Foot
Baccarat

Ile de France
Crisscross & Vertical Cuts,
Smooth Stem
Baccarat

Nemours
Layered Vertical Cuts
Baccarat

Renaissance
Vertical Cuts
Baccarat

Marillon
Etched Scrolls
Baccarat

BAC 13
Claret Wine Shown
Crisscross & Arch Cuts
Baccarat

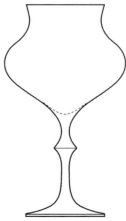

Cosmos
Plain
Baccarat

Damoiselles
Clear & Black, Floral & Dots,
Multi-Motif
Baccarat

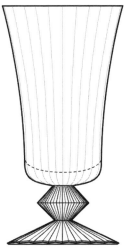

Mille Nuits
Optic Bowl,
Ribbed Stem & Foot
Baccarat

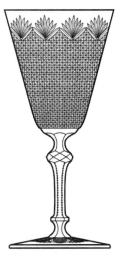

Nonancourt
Crosshatch & Fan Cuts
Baccarat

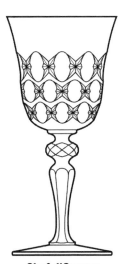

Chef d'Oeuvre
Cut
Baccarat

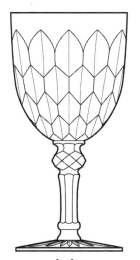

Juvisy
Vertical Cuts,
Starburst Foot
Baccarat

Nimes
Vertical Cuts,
Alternating Rays on Foot
Baccarat

SCE No. 35
Vertical Cuts,
Alternating Rays on Foot
Baccarat

BAC 22
Champagne Flute Shown
Crisscross & Vertical Cuts,
Square Foot
Baccarat

Annie
Gold Trim
Baccarat

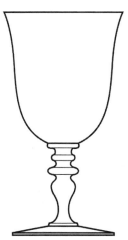

Provence
Plain
Baccarat

Beauvais
Hollow Stem
Baccarat

Bedarieux
Bubble in Stem
Baccarat

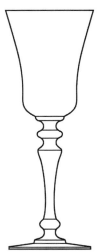

Vienne
Plain
Baccarat

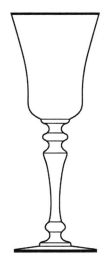

Vienne
Gold Trim
Baccarat

Prestige
Gold Encrusted Flowers,
Scrolls & Band,
Vertical Cuts, Gold Trim
Baccarat

Prestige
Etched Flowers,
Scrolls & Band,
Vertical Cuts, Gold Trim
Baccarat

Baccarat

BAC 26
Gray Cut Scrolls & Band,
Vertical Cuts, Gold Trim
Baccarat

Bellegarde
Bubble in Stem
Baccarat

Arcade
Optic Bowl,
Multisided Foot
Baccarat

Rivoli
Gold Encrusted Floral Band,
Multisided Foot
Baccarat

Czar
Various Color Bowls,
Crisscross & Fans Cuts,
Scalloped Foot
Baccarat

Perigueux
Crosshatch & Vertical Cuts,
Bubble in Stem
Baccarat

Libourne
Crisscross & Vertical Cuts,
Bubble in Stem
Baccarat

Marennes
Cut Scrolls,
Bubble in Stem
Baccarat

BAC 139
Ruby Bowl.
Gold Shells & Scrolls,
Multisided Foot
Baccarat

Armagnac
Vertical Cuts
Smooth Stem
Baccarat

Poitou
Vertical Cuts,
Multisided Stem, Cut Foot
Baccarat

Artois
Vertical Cuts
Multisided Stem
Baccarat

Bourgogne
Plain
Baccarat

Constantine
Cut
Baccarat

BAC 14
Wine Shown
Optic Bowl
Baccarat

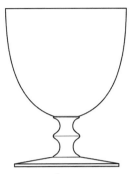

Azay
Plain
17171
Baccarat

Chinese Rose
Etched Floral
Baccarat

Blue Tower
Etched Floral
Baccarat

Flora
Gold Encrusted Floral
& Scrolls
Baccarat

Camilla
Etched Floral & Scrolls
Baccarat

Touraine
Crisscross & Horizontal Cuts
Baccarat

Rohan
Etched Scrolls
Baccarat

Retz
Gold Scrolls
Baccarat

Byzance
Gold Fleur-de-lis & Leaves,
Gold Trim
Baccarat

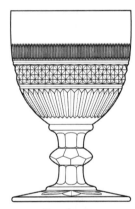

Kensington
Crosshatch & Vertical Cuts
Baccarat

BAC 44
Champagne/Tall Sherbet Shown
Honeycomb Cuts
Baccarat

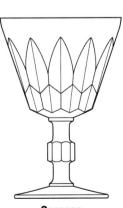

Caracas
Vertical Cuts
Baccarat

Harcourt
Panel Cuts,
Multisided Foot
Baccarat

Castiglione
Panel Cuts,
Multisided Foot
Baccarat

Enee
Panel Cuts, Multisided Foot,
Platinum Bowl & Foot Trim
Baccarat

Ems
Panel Cuts, Multisided Foot,
Gold Bowl & Foot Trim
Baccarat

Aie Harcourt
Various Color Embedded
Gems, Panel Cuts,
Multisided Foot
Baccarat

Jonzac
Laurel Band, Panel Cuts
Baccarat

Empire
Gold Etched Scrolls,
Panel Cuts, Multisided Foot,
Gold Bowl & Foot Trim
Baccarat

Embassy
Plain
Baccarat

BAC 20
Vertical & Horizontal Cuts
Baccarat

BAC 29
Panel Cuts
Baccarat

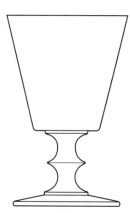

Sully
Plain
Baccarat

Charles X
Panel Cuts, Laurel Band
Baccarat

BAC 39
Iced Tea Shown
Gray Cut Grapes
Baccarat

Venise
Gold Etched Scrolls,
Panel Cuts,
Gold Bowl & Foot Trim
Baccarat

Lauzun
Panel Cuts
Baccarat

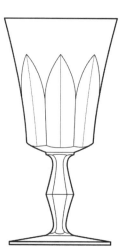

Polignac
Thick Vertical Cuts
Baccarat

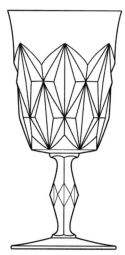

Choiseul
Crisscross Cuts
Baccarat

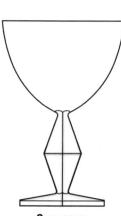

Guynemer
Diamond Stem,
Square Foot
Baccarat

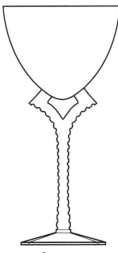

Oxygene
Notched Stem
Baccarat

Gascogne
Plain
Baccarat

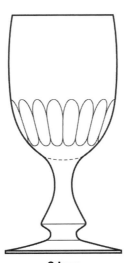

Odeon
Thumbprint Cuts
Baccarat

Passy
Vertical Cuts
Baccarat

Gascogne
Multisided Stem
Baccarat

Monaco
Panel Cuts
Baccarat

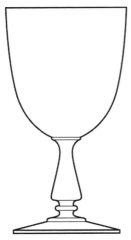

Angouleme
Plain
Baccarat

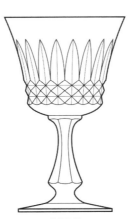

BAC 3
Vertical & Horizontal Cuts
Baccarat

Navarre
Vertical & Horizontal Cuts
Baccarat

Lucullus
Crisscross Cuts
Baccarat

Pasha
Star Cuts
Baccarat

Colbert
Crisscross & Swag Cuts
Baccarat

Harfleur
Large & Small
Crisscross Cuts
Baccarat

Lamartine
Crisscross & Star Cuts
Baccarat

Tourville
Crisscross & Vertical Cuts
Baccarat

Baccarat

Picardie
Vertical Cuts
Baccarat

BAC 1
Pressed Diamond Point
Baccarat

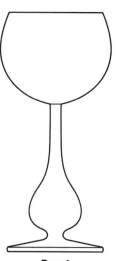

Pavot
Plain
Baccarat

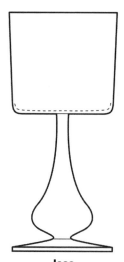

Jose
Plain
Baccarat

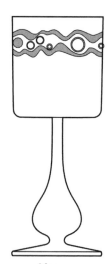

Liseron
Etched Band
Baccarat

Longchamps
Plain
Baccarat

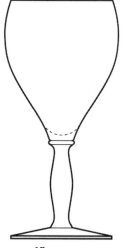

Vincennes
Plain
Baccarat

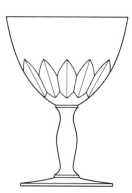

Longemer
Vertical Cuts
Baccarat

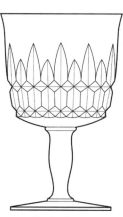

Canterbury
Uneven Vertical Cuts
Baccarat

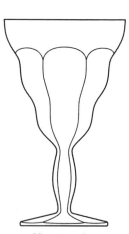

Montpensier
Panel Cuts
Baccarat

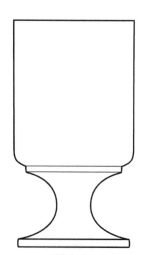

Diabolo
Plain
Baccarat

BAC 51
Wide Gold Band,
Multisided Foot
Baccarat

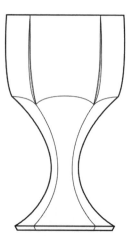

Mercure
Vertical Cuts,
Multisided Foot
Baccarat

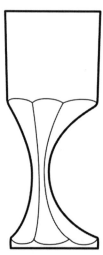

Narcisse
Cut, Offset Stem
Baccarat

Neptune
Cut
Baccarat

Louis XVIII
Panel Cuts,
Multisided Foot
Baccarat

Louis Philippe
Crisscross & Panel Cuts,
Multisided Foot
Baccarat

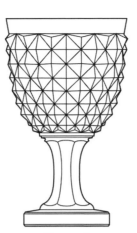

Kernevel
Diamond Cuts,
Square Foot
Baccarat

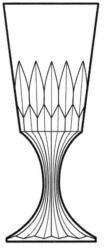

d'Assas
Vertical Cuts
Baccarat

Massena
Vertical Cuts, Plain
Baccarat

Massena
Vertical Cuts, Gold Trim
Baccarat

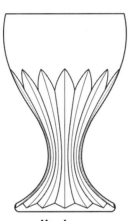

Vendome
Vertical Cuts
Baccarat

Orsay
Clear or Various Color
Bowls, Multisided Foot
Baccarat

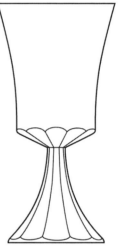

Sylvia
Panel Cuts
Baccarat

Mermoz
Multisided Stem & Foot
Baccarat

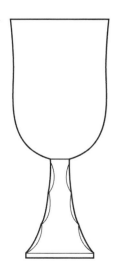

Maladetta
Square Foot
Baccarat

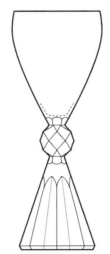

Brabant
Cut Ball Stem & Cut Base
Baccarat

Castellane
Arch Cuts,
Cut Stem & Foot
Baccarat

Etampes
Arch Cuts,
Cut Stem & Foot
Baccarat

Elbeuf
Crisscross & Arch Cuts,
Cut Stem & Foot
Baccarat

Baccarat

Conde
Crisscross Cuts,
Cut Stem, Scalloped Foot
Baccarat

Jets d'Eau
Gray Arches,
Frosted Floral Stem
Baccarat

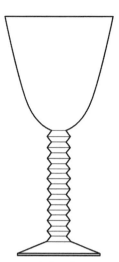

Lalande
Stacked Disk Stem
Baccarat

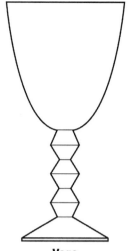

Vega
Clear or Various Color
Bowls, Diamond Shaped
Wafer Stem
Baccarat

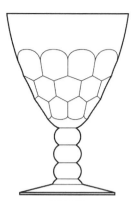

BAC 28
Wine Shown
Thumbprint Cuts
Baccarat

Onde
Multisided Stem
Baccarat

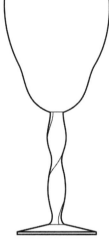

Stream
Twisted Stem
Baccarat

Bourbon
Panel Cuts,
Multisided Foot
Baccarat

BAC 30
Gold Filigree Design,
Panel Cuts, Multisided Foot,
Gold Bowl & Foot Trim
Baccarat

Savoie
Panel Cuts,
Cut Foot
Baccarat

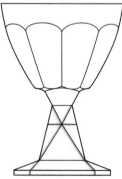

Latour Maubourg
Panel Cuts,
Multisided Foot
Baccarat

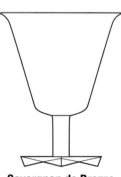

Savorgnan de Brazza
Square Cut Foot
Baccarat

La Tremoille
Cut Foot
Baccarat

Grenados
Cut Foot
Baccarat

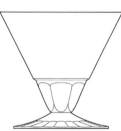

BAC 24
Panel Cuts,
Cut Foot
Baccarat

80

Albufera
Panel Cuts,
Square Foot
Baccarat

Abysse
Thick Multisided Foot
with Panel Cuts
Baccarat

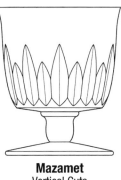

Mazamet
Vertical Cuts
Baccarat

Muret
Star Cuts
Baccarat

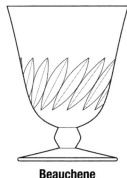

Beauchene
Diagonal Cuts
Baccarat

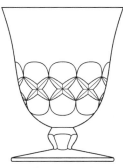

Beauregard
Crisscross & Round
Panel Cuts
Baccarat

Beaujeu
Arch & Star Cuts
Baccarat

Lulli
Etched Scrolls
Baccarat

Valancay
Panel Cuts
Baccarat

Tallyrand
Panel Cuts
Baccarat

Gilbert
Plain
Baccarat

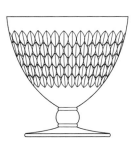

Lodi
Vertical Cuts
Baccarat

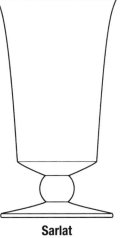

Sarlat
Plain
Baccarat

Djeddah
Etched Floral,
Horses & Birds
Baccarat

BAC 48
Footed Tumbler Shown
Plain
Baccarat

Lausanne
Etched Floral,
No Stem
Baccarat

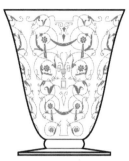

Michelangelo
Cordial Shown
Etched Scrolls & Swags
Baccarat

Charmes
Thumbprint Cuts
Baccarat

Chenonceaux
Connecting Oval Cuts
Baccarat

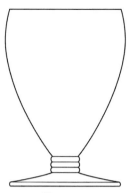

Cheverny
Plain
Baccarat

Flore
Optic Bowl, No Stem
Baccarat

Ronceveaux
Thumbprint & Panel Cuts
Baccarat

Rendezvous
Wine Shown
Etched Scrolls & Leaves
Baccarat

H2O
Flat Tumbler Shown
Plain, Barware
Baccarat

Mosaique
Tumbler Shown
Blue, Green or Yellow,
Barware
Baccarat

Alpha
Tumbler Shown
Plain, Barware
Baccarat

Beluga
Double Old Fashioned Shown
Cut Dots, Barware
Baccarat

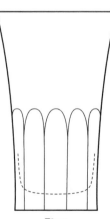

Etna
Highball Shown
Panel Cuts, Barware
Baccarat

Triade
Highball Shown
Vertical Cuts, Barware
Baccarat

Lola
Highball Shown
Horizontal Cuts
Baccarat

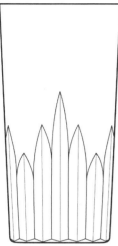

Spear Cut
Highball Shown
Vertical Cuts, Barware
Baccarat

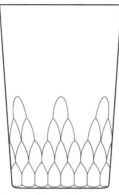

Deauville
Flat Tumbler Shown
Polished Vertical Cuts,
Barware
Baccarat

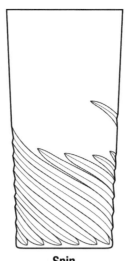

Spin
Highball Shown
Spiral Cuts, Barware
Baccarat

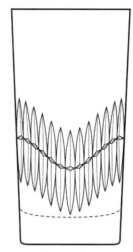

Serpentine
Highball Shown
Vertical Wave Cuts,
Barware
Baccarat

Smoke
Highball Shown
Cut Wavy Bands,
Barware
Baccarat

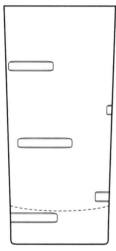

Horizon
Highball Shown
Horizontal Cuts,
Barware
Baccarat

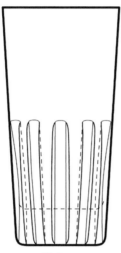

Rotary
Highball Shown
Vertical Cuts, Barware
Baccarat

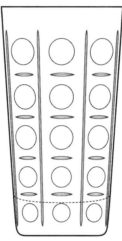

Equinox
Highball Shown
Horizontal Lines & Dots,
Barware
Baccarat

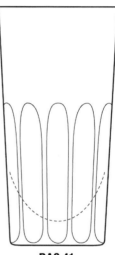

BAC 41
Highball Shown
Panel Cuts, Barware
Baccarat

Arlequin
Highball Shown
Vertical Cuts, Barware
Baccarat

Bali
Highball Shown
Vertical Cuts, Barware
Baccarat

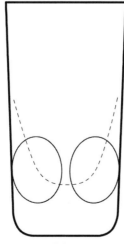

Orion
Highball Shown
Thumbprint Cuts, Barware
Baccarat

Apparat
Tumbler Shown
Gold Decoration,
Barware
Baccarat

Imperator
Double Old Fashioned Shown
Gold Encrusted, Vertical Cuts,
Optic Bowl, Barware
Baccarat

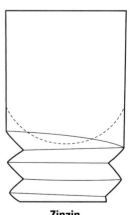

Zinzin
Tumbler Shown
Zigzag Horizontal Cuts,
Barware
Baccarat

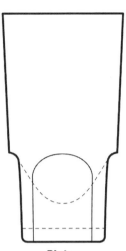

Pluton
Highball Shown
Square Base, Barware
Baccarat

Projection
Old Fashioned Shown
Angled, Various Colors
in Base, Barware
Baccarat

Arabesque
Luncheon Plate Shown
Scrolls, Diamonds & Flowers
Baccarat

Alice
Vertical & Horizontal Cuts
Badash

Oxford
Crisscross & Fan Cuts,
Smooth Stem
Badash

Oxford
Crisscross & Fan Cuts,
Multisided Stem
Badash

Galaxy
Highball Shown
Bubble in Base
Badash

Princess Feather
Scrolls & Diamonds,
Pressed Glass
Bakewell, Pears, Black

Frosted Ribbon
Clear & Frosted Panels,
Pattern Glass
Bakewell, Pears, Black

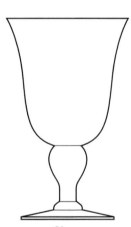

Siena
Clear or Various Color Bowls
Ballard Design

Savannah
Plain
Ballard Design

Curves
Martini Shown
Vertical Wavy Lines
Bar Essentials

Linear
Martini Shown
Cut Rings
Bar Essentials

Grappa
Martini Shown
Gray Cut Grapes
Bar Essentials

BGS 1
Champagne/Tall Sherbet Shown
Gray Cut Floral
Barth Art Glass

Parsifal
Panel Cuts
9418
Barthmann

Florenz
Panel Cuts
9150
Barthmann

Melodie
Circle Cuts
9155
Barthmann

Aida
Panel Cuts
Barthmann

Tosca
Vertical & Dot Cuts
9140
Barthmann

Palais
Vertical Cuts
9166
Barthmann

Trianon
Vertical Cuts
Barthmann

Julia
Thumbprint Cuts
9126
Barthmann

Pronto
Thumbprint Cuts
9129
Barthmann

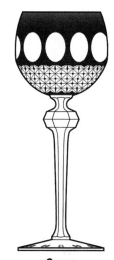

Casar
Wine Hock Shown
Various Color Bowls,
Crisscross & Thumbprint Cuts
Barthmann

Rom
Wine Hock Shown
Various Color Bowls,
Panel Cuts
Barthmann

Malmo
Optic Bowl
9165
Barthmann

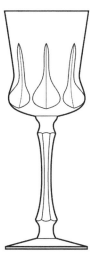

Karin
Vertical Cuts
9164
Barthmann

Madame
Vertical & Thumbprint Cuts
9151
Barthmann

Jet
Vertical Cuts
9105
Barthmann

Apollo
Vertical Cuts
9109
Barthmann

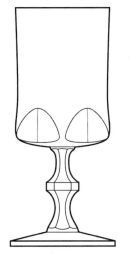

Luna
Thumbprint Cuts
9109
Barthmann

Nelson
Vertical Cuts
9072
Barthmann

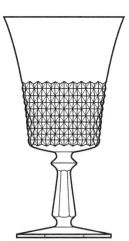

Consul
Crosshatch Cuts,
Multisided Foot
9030
Barthmann

Clarissa
Vertical Cuts
9157
Barthmann

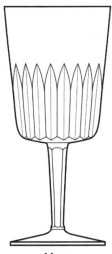

Liege
Vertical Cuts
Barthmann

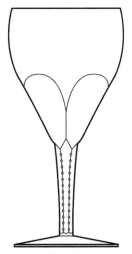

Narziss
Panel Cuts, Cut Stem
9070
Barthmann

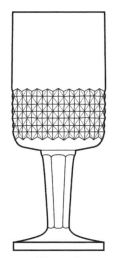

Diamant
Crosshatch Cuts
9007
Barthmann

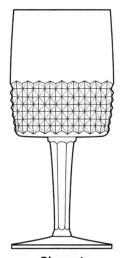

Diamant
Crosshatch Cuts
Barthmann

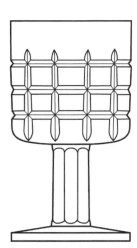

King Richard
Vertical & Horizontal Cuts
Barthmann

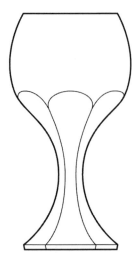

Kardinal
Goblet/Burgundy Wine Shown
Panel Cuts, Multisided Stem
9092
Barthmann

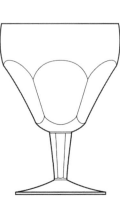

BRT 1
Panel Cuts, 6-Sided Stem
Barthmann

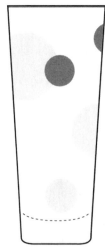

Eclipse
Tumbler Shown
Gold & Blue, Green, Red
or Yellow Dots, Multi-Motif
Bartlett Collins

BTC 1
Tumbler Shown
Green Holly, Red Berries
Bartlett Collins

Decoration 59
Cocktail Tumbler Shown
Three Red Cherries
Bartlett Collins

Cut 52
Clear or Green, Optic Bowl,
Cut Floral
Bartlett Collins

Manhattan
Various Colors,
Bullseye & Cane
Bartlett Collins

Decoration 806
Clear or Amber with
White Decal or
Clear with Blue Decal
Bartlett Collins

Decoration 806
Clear with White Decal,
Gold or Platinum Trim
Bartlett Collins

Royal
Crisscross & Fan Cuts
Barzel Glass

Rose
Cut Rose, Gold Trim
Bavarian

Blush Rose
Cut Rose
9040
Bavarian

Bacchante
Frosted Stem
Bayel

Bacchante
Frosted Stem,
Gold Plated Bowl & Foot
Bayel

BAY 5
Frosted Nude Stem
Bayel

BAY 5
Frosted Nude Stem,
Gold Plated Bowl & Foot
Bayel

Venus
Frosted Stem
Bayel

Napoleon
Frosted Stem
Bayel

Napoleon
Frosted Stem,
Gold Bowl & Foot Trim
Bayel

Napoleon
Frosted Stem,
"N" Etched on Bowl,
Gold Bowl & Foot Trim
Bayel

Sea Horse
Frosted Stem
Bayel

Owl
Frosted Stem
Bayel

Dolphin
Frosted Stem
Bayel

Bordeaux
Crisscross & Fan Cuts,
Thick Knob Stem
Bayel

Bordeaux
Crisscross & Fan Cuts,
Thin Knob Stem
Bayel

Orleans
Crisscross Cuts
Bayel

Strasbourg
Vertical & Horizontal Cuts
Bayel

Vineyard Grape
Clear or Various Color Bowls,
Grape, Leaf & Fan Cuts,
Cut Stem
Bayel

Paris Rose
Gray Cut Floral,
Clear Crisscross Cuts,
Cut Stem
Bayel

Dominique
Vertical & Horizontal Cuts
Bayel

Baguette
Vertical & Horizontal Cuts
Bayel

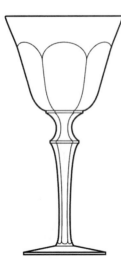

BAY 3
Wine Shown
Clear or Various Colors on
Top of Bowl, Panel Cuts
Bayel

Normandy
Crisscross & Fan Cuts
Bayel

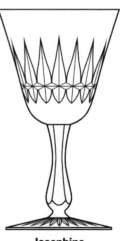

Josephine
Vertical Cuts
Bayel

Dubarry
Horizontal, Crisscross &
Crosshatch Cuts
Bayel

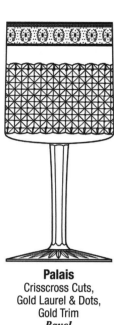

Palais
Crisscross Cuts,
Gold Laurel & Dots,
Gold Trim
Bayel

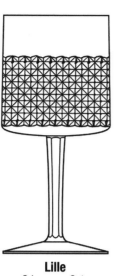

Lille
Crisscross Cuts
Bayel

Jeannine
Plain
Bayel

Antoinette
Vertical & Horizontal Cuts
Bayel

Trianon
Crisscross, Horizontal
& Vertical Cuts
Bayel

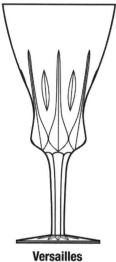

Versailles
Vertical Cuts
Bayel

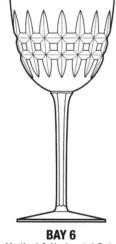

BAY 6
Vertical & Horizontal Cuts
Bayel

Lafayette
Crisscross Cuts
Bayel

Strawberry Diamond
Crosshatch & Fan Cuts
Bayel

Rochelle
Panel Cuts
Bayel

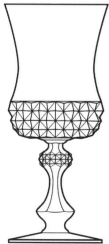

Pompadour
Crisscross Cuts
Bayel

BAY 2
Wine Shown
Fan Cuts
Bayel

Americana
Pressed Glass
Bayel

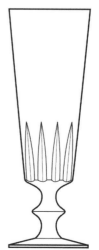

BAY 1
Champagne Flute Shown
Vertical Cuts
Bayel

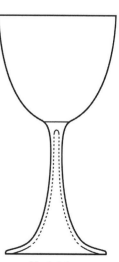

Madeleine
Hollow Stem
Bayel

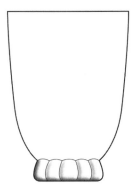

BAY 4
Highball Shown
Scalloped, Textured Foot
Bayel

Sun
Tumbler Shown
Various Colors,
Dots & Sun Medallion
Bed, Bath & Beyond

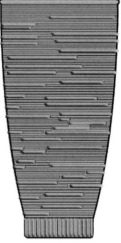

Illusion
Tumbler Shown
Various Colors,
Embossed Rings
Bed, Bath & Beyond

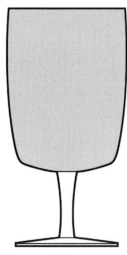

BCY 1
Smoke Bowl
Belcrest

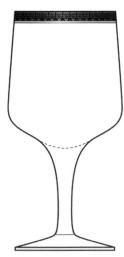

Renee
Platinum Encrusted Band
Belcrest

Majestic
Panel Cuts, Platinum Trim
Belcrest

Petit Rose
Wine Shown
Cut Rose
Belcrest

Moonglo
Smoke Bowl & Stem
Belcrest

Edelweiss
Gray/Clear Swirl Cuts
Belfor

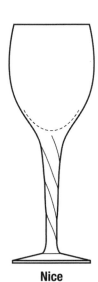

Nice
Twisted Stem
Belfor

Optic
Optic Bowl
Belfor

Heritage
Gray Cut Plants, Panel Cuts
Belfor

BFR 1
Optic Bowl
Belfor

Savannah
Gray Cut Plants
Belfor

Finesse
Swirl Optic Bowl
Belfor

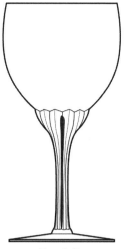

Exquisite
Black Core in Stem
Belfor

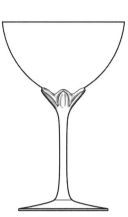

Rhapsody
Champagne/Tall Sherbet Shown
Plain
Belfor

Reflections
Panel Cuts
Belkraft

BK 1
Smoke Bowl
Belkraft

Beaded Rosette
Floral & Bead Design,
Pressed Glass
Bellaire Goblet Company

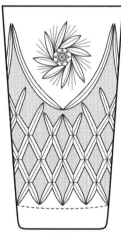

BCQ 1
Tumbler Shown
Pinwheel & Crisscross Cuts
Bereg

BDG 1
Champagne/Tall Sherbet Shown
Plain
Bergdala Glass

BEZ 1
Wine Hock Shown
Various Color Bowls,
Cut Stem
Beyer

BEZ 2
Crisscross, Arch,
& Floral Cuts
Beyer

Peanut Butter
Iced Tea Shown
Clear or Milk Glass,
Pressed Glass
Big Top

BJR 1
Cobalt, Plain
Bjorkshult

BFC 1
Gray Cut Floral,
Platinum Trim
Blefeld & Company

BFC 5
Wide Platinum Band,
Bubble in Stem
Blefeld & Company

BFC 6
Wide Platinum Band
Blefeld & Company

BFC 9
Blue Bowl & Foot
Blefeld & Company

Cive
Crisscross Cuts
Blefeld & Company

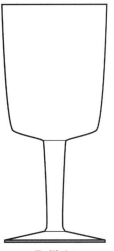

Twilight
Plain
Blefeld & Company

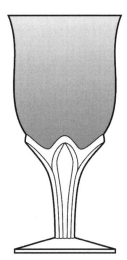

Leaf Fantasy
Lilac Bowl & Foot or
Green Bowl
Blefeld & Company

BFC 11
Bubble in Stem
Blefeld & Company

Eleanora
Iridescent Bowl
Blefeld & Company

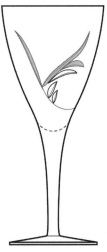

BFC 4
Gray/Clear Cut Plant
Blefeld & Company

BFC 4
Gray/Clear Cut Plant,
Platinum Trim
Blefeld & Company

BFC 2
Cut Floral
Blefeld & Company

BFC 12
Wine Shown
Various Bowl & Foot Colors,
Twisted Stem
Blefeld & Company

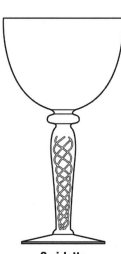

Swirlette
Air Twist Stem
Blefeld & Company

BFC 10
Pink Frosted Bowl,
Air Twist Stem
Blefeld & Company

BFC 7
Wine Shown
Blue Bowl
Blefeld & Company

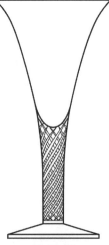

Air-Twist
Air Twist Stem
Blenko Glass

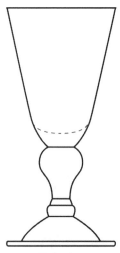

Baluster
Thick Shammed Bowl,
Wide Bulbous Stem
Blenko Glass

OLD FASHIONED HIGHBALL

Ringed
Various Color Rings
3749, 448
Blenko Glass

BLG 1
Tumbler Shown
Crackled Bowl,
Green Dot Base
Blenko Glass

1802
Tumbler Shown
Topaz, Ringed Base
1802, 1902
Blenko Glass

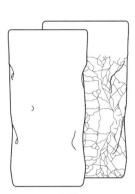

418
Tumbler Shown
Various Colors,
Plain or Crackled, Pinched
Blenko Glass

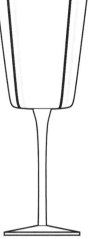

Firenze
Black & White Stripes
Block

Olympic
Crisscross & Vertical Cuts,
Square Bowl
Block

Rainbow
Arch Cuts
Block

Olympic
Crisscross & Vertical Cuts,
Round Bowl
Block

Dusk
Vertical Cuts
Block

BLC 11
Gold Trim
Block

Symphony
Vertical Cuts
Block

Lexington
Crisscross Cuts
Block

Gulfstream
Vertical & Panel Cuts
Block

Ribbons
Vertical Cuts
Block

Aura
Fan & Vertical Cuts
Block

Tulip Garden
Wine Shown
Vertical & Horizontal Cuts
Block

Block

Forum
Crisscross & Fan Cuts
Block

BLC 4
Fan Cuts
Block

BLC 18
Crisscross & Fan Cuts
Block

Contour
Champagne Flute Shown
Vertical Cuts
Block

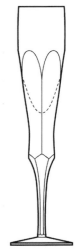

Embrace
Champagne Flute Shown
Panel Cuts
Block

Tiara
Vertical Cuts
Block

Radiance
Optic Bowl, Gold Trim
Block

Soul
Champagne Flute Shown
Vertical Cuts
Block

Oslo
Champagne Flute Shown
Blue Bowl
Block

Spellbound
Champagne Flute Shown
Panel Cuts
Block

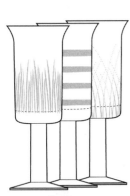

Synergy
Cordial Shown
Frosted Decor, Multi-Motif
Block

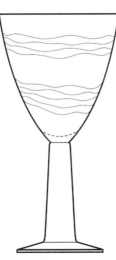

Ocean
Gray Cut Horizontal Waves
Block

Versailles
Iced Tea Shown
Arch & Horizontal Cuts
Block

Cote d'Argente
Thin Platinum Trim
Block

Cote d'Argent
Wide Optic Bowl,
Thick Platinum Trim
Block

BLC 7
Plain
Block

Cote d'Or
Optic Bowl,
Thick Gold Trim
Block

BLC 8
Optic Bowl, Platinum Trim
Block

Chateau Blanc
Plain
Block

Chateau d'Or (Gold Trim)
Chateau d'Argent (Plat. Trim)
Gold or Platinum
Bowl & Foot Trim
Block

WINE   GOBLET

Watercolors
Various Colors
Block

Transition
Black, Blue or Frosted (Clear)
Block

Capers
Clear or Various Colors
Block

GOBLET   WINE

Harmony
Clear or Various Color
Bowls & Stems
Block

GOBLET   WINE

Chromatics
Convex or Concave,
Various Colors
Block

Whisper
Crackle Bowl,
Various Color Stems
Block

Floral
Green Stem
Block

Montana Cobalt
Cobalt Bowl & Foot,
Green Stem
Block

Sutton
Optic Bowl
Block

York
White Wine Shown
Optic Bowl
Block

Block

Gramercy
Plain
Block

Manchester Gold
Gold Encrusted Laurel Band
Block

Espana Blanco (Clear)
Espana Noche (Smoke)
Hollow Foot
Block

Espana Oro (Gold Trim)
Espana Platine (Plat. Trim)
Hollow Foot
Block

Celebration
Wine Shown
Plain
Block

BLC 3
Black Stem & Foot
Block

BLC 5
Black, Plain
Block

BLC 1 (Pink Stem)
BLC 2 (Blue/Gray Stem)
Champagne Flute Shown
Block

GOBLET
ICED TEA

Kaleidoscope
Various Color Bowls
Block

WINE
BALLOON WINE

Carousel
Various Color Bowls
Block

Monterey
Wine Shown
Various Color Bowls
Block

Allegro Optic
Various Color Optic Bowls
Block

Festival
Amber or Blue Bowl with
Green Stem; Amethyst or
Green Bowl with Blue Stem
Block

Plasma
Various Color Bowls
Block

BLC 13
Optic Bowl, Amethyst,
Blue or Green Stem
Block

Market Basket
Blue, Green or Pink
Block

BLC 6
Aqua or Pale Pink Bowl
Block

Ole
Green Bowl,
Gray Cut Leaves
Block

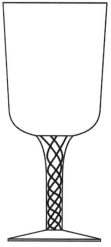

Airtwist
Clear, Blue, Black or Red
Line in Air Twist Stem
Block

Helix
Red Bowl,
Air Twist Stem
Block

Artesia
Martini Shown
Red Circle in Base
C2282
Block

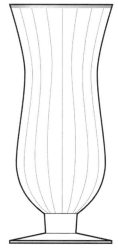

Celebration
Iced Tea Shown
Optic Bowl, Gold Trim
Block

Paradise Collection
Etched Floral
Block

Tulipa
Clear or Various Color
Tulip Embossed Bowls
Block

Granite
Optic Bowl,
Blue or Red Mottled
Stem & Foot
Block

Milano
Various Colors, Circle Design
Block

Tango
Various Color Stems
Block

Lagoon
Blue or Green
Block

Synergy
Cobalt or Plum
Rings on Stem
Block

Halo Gold
Optic Bowl,
Gold Ringed Stem
Block

Block

Carnival
Multicolored Ring Stem
Block

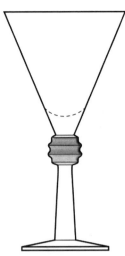

Mardi Gras
Pink, Green & Yellow
Wafers in Stem
Block

BLC 20
Wine Shown
Pink, Clear, & Blue
Balls in Stem
Block

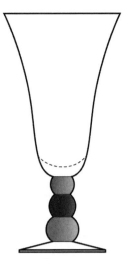

Rumors
Blue, Red & Yellow
Ball Stem
Block

Pillar
Amber Stem,
Amethyst Foot &
Rings on Stem
Block

Fire
Amber & Red Stem,
Blue Foot
Block

Water
Purple & Blue Stem,
Green Foot
Block

Vintage
Clear or Blue Bowl,
Wide Gold Trim,
Gold Ball Stem
Block

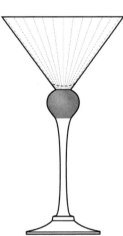

Vintage Optic
Martini Shown
Optic Bowl,
Gold Ball Top of Stem
Block

Artesia
Blue or Red Bubble
in Stem
Block

Manet
Red or Blue Swirl
Block

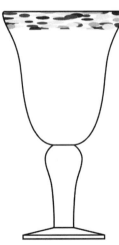

Eclipse
Multicolored Band
Block

Pimento
Martini Shown
Red & Green Stuffed Olives
Block

Sunset
Margarita Shown
Green, Orange, & Yellow Circles,
Red Bands, Green on Foot
Block

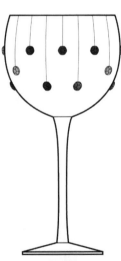

Jewel
Balloon Wine Shown
Colored Jewels on Bowl
Block

Confetti
Balloon Wine Shown
Multicolored Dots
Block

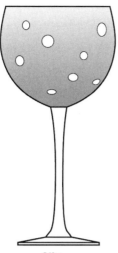

Glitter
Various Color Bowls,
Clear Dots
Block

Spring Meadow
Wine Shown
Clear or Various Color Bowls,
Etched Vine
Block

Isola
Blue Dots & Flecks
Block

Degas
Blue Swirls
Block

Mosaic
Blue, Green & Turquoise
Raised Design
Block

Tier
Blue or Red Bands
Block

Manhattan
Champagne Flute Shown
Blue, Red & Yellow Ribbons
Block

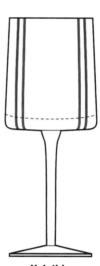

Yuletide
Red & Green Stripes
Block

Rainy Day
Blue Inside Bowl,
Clear Frosted Bowl & Stem
Block

Happy Hour
Margarita Shown
Green, Orange, Blue
& Yellow Bands
Block

Celebration
Champagne Flute Shown
Red & White Bands
Block

Snowmen
Iced Tea Shown
Various Color Snowmen,
Frosted Stem, Multi-Motif
Block

Silent Night
Iced Tea Shown
Christmas Trees & Snow,
Blue & Green Bands on Foot
Block

Daisy
Iced Tea Shown
Multicolor Painted Flowers,
Multi-Motif
Block

99

Block

Flower Shop
Multicolor Flowers,
Green Leaves, Multi-Motif
Block

Songs of the Season
Multicolor Handpainted
Christmas Symbols,
Multi-Motif
Block

Twelve Days of Christmas
Multicolor 12 Days of
Christmas Symbols,
Multi-Motif
Block

Spring Meadow
Multicolor Handpainted
Wildflowers, Multi-Motif
Block

BLC 21
Multicolor Handpainted
Flowers on Bowl & Foot
Block

Parallel
Balloon Wine Shown
Pink, Orange, Yellow
& Purple Bands
Block

Flower Power
Balloon Wine Shown
Multicolor Flowers
Block

Wildflowers
Multicolor Floral Decals,
Purple Bands on Stem &
Trim on Foot
Block

Loves Me
Balloon Wine Shown
Handpainted White Flowers,
Green Bands on Stem
Block

Poinsettia Toss
Balloon Wine Shown
Handpainted Pink Flowers,
Green Leaves, BG8505
Block

Splendor
White & Tan Flowers,
Red Berries,
Red Trim on Foot
Block

Full Bloom
Balloon Wine Shown
Multicolor Handpainted
Flowers, Multi-Motif
Block

Garden Rose
Balloon Wine Shown
Handpainted Pink Flowers,
Multi-Motif
Block

Vintage Rose
Balloon Wine Shown
Handpainted Roses,
Multi-Motif
Block

Handpicked
Balloon Wine Shown
Handpainted Flowers,
Multi-Motif
Block

Tropical Lillies
Multicolor Handpainted
Flowers, Multi-Motif
Block

Orchid
Balloon Wine Shown
Handpainted Pink &
Purple Flowers, Multi-Motif
Block

Palm Breeze
Green & Brown Palm Trees
Block

Orchard
Balloon Wine Shown
Multicolor Handpainted
Fruit, Multi-Motif
Block

Vineyard
Balloon Wine Shown
Multicolor Handpainted
Grapes, Multi-Motif
Block

Napa Valley
Balloon Wine Shown
Multicolor Handpainted
Grapes & Leaves, Multi-Motif
Block

Harvest Home
Balloon Wine Shown
Multicolor Handpainted
Fruit, Multi-Motif
Block

Berry Holiday
Balloon Wine Shown
Green Leaves, Red Berries
Block

Poinsettia
Balloon Wine Shown
Green Leaves, Red Berries
BG8501, BG8502
Block

Holiday Lights
Balloon Wine Shown
Christmas Lights
on Red String
Block

Holly & Berry
Green Holly, Red Berries
Block

Holiday
Iced Tea Shown
Green Leaves, Red Berries
Block

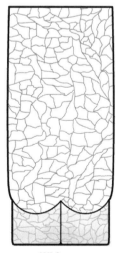

Whisper
Tumbler/Highball Shown
Square Purple & Clear Base,
Crackle Design
Block

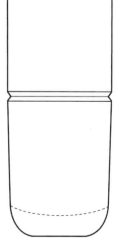

Zenith
Highball Shown
Single Cut Ring
Block

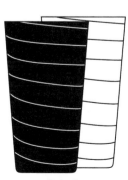

Spirals
Highball Shown
White on Black or Black
on White Spiral Design
Block

101

Block

Coil
Triple Old Fashioned Shown
Cut Spirals, Barware
Block

Northwinds
Cooler Shown
Curved Horizontal Cuts
Block

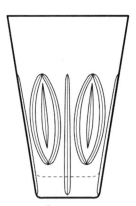

Crescent
Highball Shown
Vertical & Oval Cuts
Block

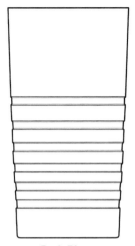

Park Place
Highball Shown
Cut Rings, Barware
Block

Wave
Highball Shown
Horizontal Cuts, Barware
Block

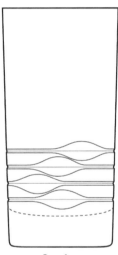

Camber
Highball Shown
Horizontal Cuts, Barware
Block

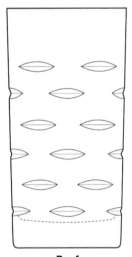

Reef
Highball Shown
Oval Cuts, Barware
Block

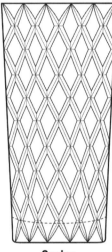

Casino
Highball Shown
Crisscross Cuts, Barware
Block

Galaxy
Highball Shown
Dot Cuts, Barware
Block

Linia
Highball Shown
Deep Vertical Cuts, Barware
Block

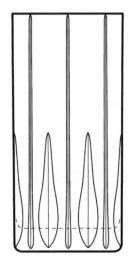

Parallel
Highball Shown
Vertical Cuts, Barware
Block

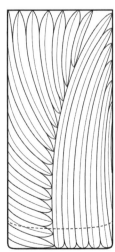

Deco
Highball Shown
Swirl Cuts, Barware
Block

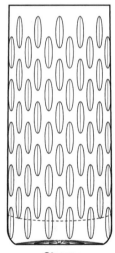

Storm
Highball Shown
Oval Cuts, Barware
Block

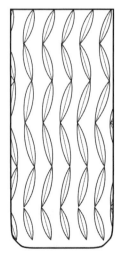

Vegas
Highball Shown
Zigzag Cuts, Barware
Block

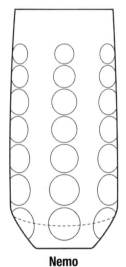

Nemo
Highball Shown
Dot Cuts, Barware
Block

Sunrise
Highball Shown
Plain
Block

Glacier
Highball Shown
Plain, Barware
Block

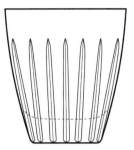

Rhapsody
Double Old Fashioned Shown
Vertical Cuts, Barware
Block

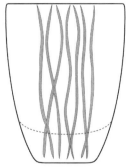

Paradox
Double Old Fashioned Shown
Curved Lines
Block

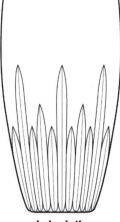

Labyrinth
Highball Shown
Vertical Cuts, Barware
Block

Victoria
Tumbler Shown
Crisscross & Fan Cuts,
Barware
Block

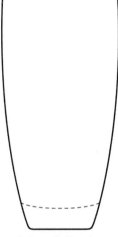

Galaxy Collection
Highball Shown
Opaque White/Clear
Barware
Block

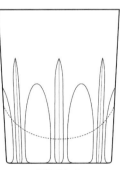

Trinidad
Highball Shown
Vertical Cuts
Block

Essex
Double Old Fashioned Shown
Crisscross & Fan Cuts,
Barware
Block

Ergo
Double Old Fashioned Shown
Cut Bands, Barware
Block

Starlight
Double Old Fashioned Shown
Heavy Sham Base
Block

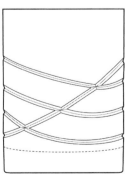

Alias
Double Old Fashioned Shown
Crisscross Cut Rings
Block

Innovation
Double Old Fashioned Shown
Bubble in Base, Barware
Block

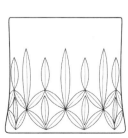

Newport
Tumbler Shown
Crisscross & Vertical Cuts
Block

Bella Vista
Double Old Fashioned Shown
Blue & Clear Body,
Vertical Cuts
Block

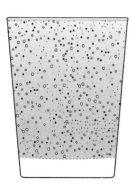

Baha
Double Old Fashioned Shown
Textured Bubbles, Cobalt
Amethyst, Aqua or Green
Block

Portfolio
Highball Shown
Amethyst or Blue,
Straight Optic
Block

Laser
Highball Shown
White with Clear Spiral or Blue,
Green, Orange with White Spiral
Block

Tao
Highball Shown
Amethyst or Smoke,
Bubble in Base
Block

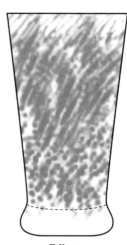

Trilogy
Highball Shown
Cobalt, Green or Lavender
Swirls, Barware
Block

Cabaret
Highball Shown
Yellow, Pink, Green &
Blue Cut Circles
Block

Riptide
Tumbler Shown
Cobalt Swirls
Block

Plasma
Highball Shown
Various Colors,
Swirls & Lines
Block

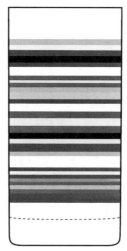

Salsa
Highball Shown
Multicolor Stripes
Block

Marilyn Monroe
Highball Shown
Various Colors,
Marilyn Monroe Motif
Block

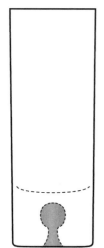

Crayon
Vodka Shown
Various Colors in Base
Block

Karlstadt
Bubble in Base
Block

Alborg (Smoky Blue)
Stockholm (Cobalt)
Bubble in Base
Block

Oasis
Highball Shown
Frosted Base, Barware
Block

BFZ 1
Highball Shown
Amber or Green,
Cut Floral
Bobby Flay

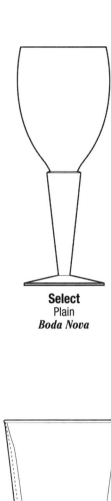

Select
Plain
Boda Nova

BNX 1
Tumbler Shown
Plain, Barware
Boda Nova

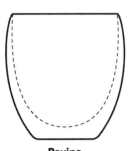

Pavina
Tumbler Shown
Two Layers, Handblown
Bodum

Bistro
Tumbler Shown
Two Layers
Bodum

Rigi
Tumbler Shown
Two Layers
Bodum

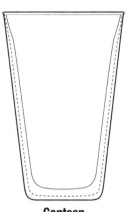

Canteen
Beer Shown
Two Layers, Straight Sides
Bodum

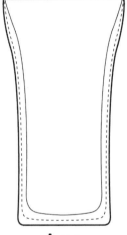

Assam
Beer Shown
Two Layers, Flared
Bodum

Manhattan
Wine Shown
Two Layers
Bodum

Derby
Honeycomb Cuts
Bohemia

BOC 71
Panel Cuts
Bohemia

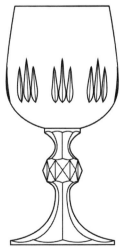

Edinburg
Vertical Cuts
Bohemia

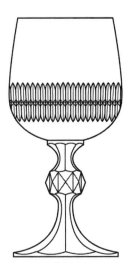

BOC 121
Vertical & Horizontal Cuts
Bohemia

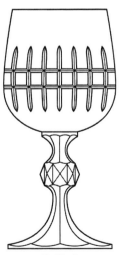

Belfast
Vertical & Horizontal Cuts
Bohemia

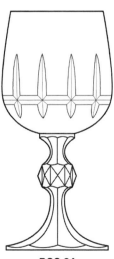

BOC 64
Wine Shown
Vertical & Horizontal Cuts
Bohemia

BOC 115
Crisscross Cuts
Bohemia

Bohemia

BOC 9
Crisscross Cuts
Bohemia

BOC 90
Pinwheel & Star Cuts
Bohemia

BOC 62
Wine Shown
Frosted/Etched Floral
Bohemia

BOC 122
Wine Shown
Frosted Bowl, Gold
Encrusted Floral & Trim
Bohemia

BOC 47
Wine Shown
Frosted Bowl, Gold Leaf,
Bands & Trim, Purple Dots
Bohemia

BOC 141
Wide Gold Band,
Etched Scrolls & Floral
Bohemia

BOC 118
Gold Encrusted Band,
Leaves, Gold Trim
Bohemia

Queen's Lace
Etched Floral, Gold Trim
Bohemia

BOC 101
Etched Floral
Bohemia

BOC 73
Etched Scrolls
Bohemia

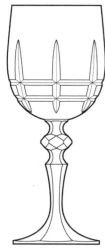

BOC 37
Wine Shown
Vertical & Horizontal Cuts
Bohemia

BOC 111
Wine Shown
Crisscross & Fan Cuts
Bohemia

BOC 94
Wine Shown
Crisscross & Fan Cuts
Bohemia

BOC 93
Wine Shown
Crisscross & Vertical Cuts
Bohemia

BOC 97
Wine Shown
Crisscross & Fan Cuts
Bohemia

BOC 142
Wine Shown
Crisscross & Fan Cuts
Bohemia

BOC 99
Wine Shown
Crisscross & Fan Cuts
Bohemia

Mirell
Wine Shown
Crisscross Cuts
Bohemia

BOC 144
Wine Shown
Fan Cuts
Bohemia

BOC 66
Wine Shown
Swirl & Dot Cuts
Bohemia

Harmony
Wine Shown
Pinwheel & Vertical Cuts
Bohemia

BOC 134
Wine Shown
Crisscross Cuts
Bohemia

BOC 36
Crisscross & Fan Cuts
Bohemia

BOC 124
Crisscross & Fan Cuts
Bohemia

BOC 136
Crisscross & Fan Cuts
Bohemia

BOC 26
Gold Trim
Bohemia

BOC 63
Gray Cut Floral
Bohemia

BOC 41
Gray Cut Floral,
Polished Cut Leaves
Bohemia

BOC 69
Wine Shown
Fan & Swirl Cuts
Bohemia

BOC 5
Pinwheel & Vertical Cuts
Bohemia

Marquis
Crisscross & Vertical Cuts
Bohemia

Stratford
Vertical Cuts
Bohemia

BOC 140
Crisscross Cuts
Bohemia

BOC 28
Thumbprint & Vertical Cuts
Bohemia

BOC 28
Thumbprint & Vertical Cuts
Gold Trim
Bohemia

BOC 30
Vertical Cuts
Bohemia

BOC 18
Crisscross Cuts
Bohemia

BOC 91
Crisscross & Vertical Cuts
Bohemia

BOC 16
Crisscross & Fan Cuts
Bohemia

BOC 17
Crisscross & Fan Cuts
Bohemia

BOC 68
Crisscross & Fan Cuts
Bohemia

BOC 32
Horizontal, Crisscross
& Fan Cuts
Bohemia

BOC 59
Crisscross, Vertical
& Fan Cuts
Bohemia

BOC 52
Horizontal, Vertical
& Star Cuts
Bohemia

BOC 149
Crisscross, Vertical
& Star Cuts
Bohemia

BOC 57
Star & Fan Cuts
Bohemia

BOC 24
Crisscross, Star & Fan Cuts
Bohemia

BOC 74
Pinwheel & Vertical Cuts
Bohemia

BOC 14
Pinwheel & Vertical Cuts,
6-Sided Foot
Bohemia

BOC 8
Vertical & Star Cuts,
Multisided Foot
Bohemia

BOC 10
Polished & Gray Cuts,
Round Foot
Bohemia

BOC 11
Polished & Gray Cuts,
6-Sided Foot
Bohemia

Riviera
Fan & Crosshatch Cuts,
Cut Stem
Bohemia

Nicole
Pinwheel Cuts
Bohemia

Nicole
Pinwheel & Arch Cuts
Bohemia

BOC 100
Wine Shown
Crisscross & Fan Cuts
Bohemia

Diana
Crisscross & Fan Cuts
2152
Bohemia

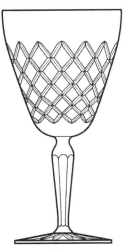

Karo
Crisscross Cuts
Bohemia

Lada
Horizontal, Fan & Star Cuts
Bohemia

BOC 39
Vertical & Star Cuts,
Cut Stem
Bohemia

Bohemia

BOC 49
Panel Cuts
Bohemia

BOC 120
Wine Shown
Crisscross & Fan Cuts
Bohemia

BOC 20
Wine Shown
Diamond & Fan Cuts
Bohemia

BOC 53
Champagne Flute Shown
Crisscross & Fan Cuts
Bohemia

BOC 6
Crisscross & Fan Cuts
Bohemia

BOC 113
Champagne Flute Shown
Crisscross, Arch
& Fan Cuts
Bohemia

BOC 127
Crisscross &
Crosshatch Cuts
Bohemia

BOC 22
Crisscross, Pinwheel
& Arch Cuts
Bohemia

BOC 82
Cordial Shown
Pinwheel Cuts
Bohemia

BOC 43
Crisscross & Fan Cuts
Bohemia

BOC 58
Crisscross & Fan Cuts
Bohemia

BOC 80
Wine Shown
Crisscross & Fan Cuts
Bohemia

BOC 76
Leaf & Swirl Cuts
Bohemia

BOC 114
Wine Shown
Swirl Cuts
Bohemia

BOC 85
Wine Shown
Crisscross & Vertical Cuts
Bohemia

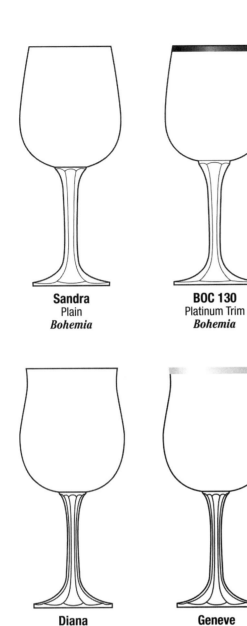

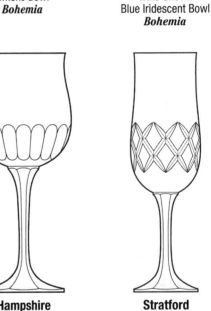

Sandra
Plain
Bohemia

BOC 130
Platinum Trim
Bohemia

Goldlace
Wine Shown
Etched Scrolls & Swags,
Gold Trim
Bohemia

Royal Smoke
Smoke Bowl
Bohemia

BOC 75
Wine Shown
Blue Iridescent Bowl
Bohemia

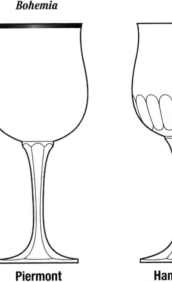

Diana
Plain
40157
Bohemia

Geneve
Gold Trim
Bohemia

Piermont
Platinum Trim
Bohemia

Hampshire
Claret Wine Shown
Polished Panel Cuts
Bohemia

Stratford
Champagne Flute Shown
Crisscross Cuts
Bohemia

Brighton
Vertical Cuts
Bohemia

BOC 15
Etched Floral,
Copper Tint Bands
Bohemia

BOC 126
Wine Shown
Etched Gold Band
Bohemia

BOC 116
Etched Floral & Scrolls,
Gold Trim
Bohemia

BOC 147
Etched Floral, Gold Trim
Bohemia

Bohemia

Romy
Plain
40301
Bohemia

BOC 105
Champagne Flute Shown
Cut Clover & Vertical Cuts
Bohemia

Simone
Vertical Cuts
Bohemia

Diamond
Clear or Frosted Stem
Bohemia

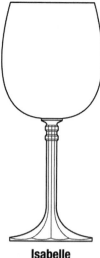

Isabelle
Plain
Bohemia

BOC 29
Red Wine Shown
Frosted Stem
Bohemia

Tulip
Pink Tulip Decal
Bohemia

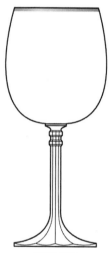

BOC 112
Gold Trim
Bohemia

Fleur
Leaf Shape in Stem
Bohemia

BOC 109
Heart Twist Stem
Bohemia

Victoria
Etched Swags & Bands
Bohemia

BOC 146
Iced Tea Shown
Frosted Ovals & Stem
Bohemia

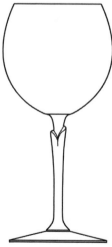

Brigitta
Plain
Bohemia

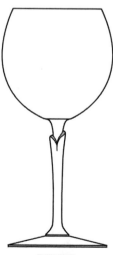

D27458
Gold Accent Stem
Bohemia

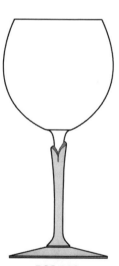

BOC 154
Frosted Stem & Foot,
Gold Accent
Bohemia

D27046
Gold Trim
Bohemia

D44031
Gold Encrusted Band
Bohemia

D44178
Geometric Etch,
Gold Trim
Bohemia

D37760
Gold Encrusted Band
& Gold Trim
Bohemia

D35861
Floral Decal
Bohemia

D35954
Floral Decal
Bohemia

D35976
Floral Decal
Bohemia

Savanna
Gray Cuts
Bohemia

BOC 81
Plant & Swirl Cuts
Bohemia

BOC 70
Etched Leaves
Bohemia

BOC 86
Crisscross Cuts
Bohemia

BOC 44
Gray/Clear Plant
& Swirl Cuts
Bohemia

BOC 119
Gray Swag, Fan Cuts
Bohemia

BOC 61
Wine Shown
Crisscross & Star Cuts
Bohemia

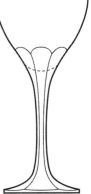

Manon
Panel Cuts
Bohemia

Bohemia

Dynasty
Panel Cuts
Bohemia

Belfor Carousel
Cordial Shown
Gray Cut Panels
Bohemia

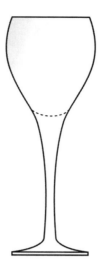

Fairlane
Iridescent Lustre Bowl
Bohemia

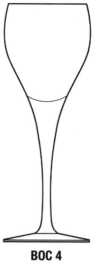

BOC 4
Plain
Bohemia

Canterbury
Fan Cuts
Bohemia

Cortina
Crisscross & Fan Cuts
Bohemia

BOC 65
Purple Bowl
Bohemia

BOC 38
Champagne Flute Shown
Cut Lines & Swirls
Bohemia

BOC 89
Crisscross & Fan Cuts
Bohemia

BOC 1
Crisscross & Fan Cuts
Bohemia

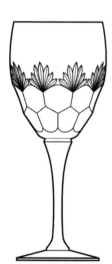

BOC 152
Cordial Shown
Panel & Fan Cuts
Bohemia

Sydney
Vertical Cuts
Bohemia

Concerto
Diamond & Fan Cuts
Bohemia

BOC 23
Wine Shown
Crisscross & Fan Cuts
Bohemia

BOC 21
Wine Shown
Crisscross & Fan Cuts
Bohemia

Gala
Cordial Shown
Plain
Bohemia

Inno
Red Wine Shown
Plain
Bohemia

Nancy
Plain
40300
Bohemia

Lara Collection
Plain
Bohemia

BOC 79
Plain
Bohemia

Sierra
Plain
Bohemia

BOC 25
Ruby, Plain
Bohemia

Degustation
Wine Shown
Plain
Bohemia

Forum
Red Wine Shown
Plain
Bohemia

Nana
Plain
Bohemia

Vino Classico
Plain, Oversized Stem
Bohemia

Lunar
Plain
Bohemia

Lisbet
Plain
Bohemia

Classic Platinum
Platiunum Trim
Bohemia

BOC 155
Vertical Cuts
Bohemia

Bohemia

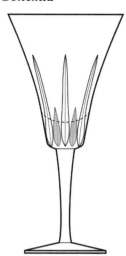

Princess
Clear & Frosted
Vertical Cuts
Bohemia

BOC 13
Liquor Cocktail Shown
Gray/Clear Swirl Cuts
Bohemia

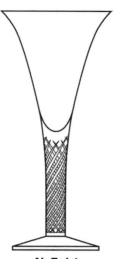

Air Twist
Air Twist Stem
Bohemia

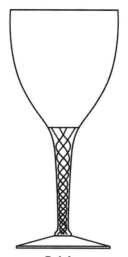

Belaire
Air Twist Stem
Bohemia

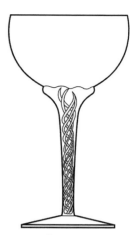

Suzanne
Champagne/Tall Sherbet Shown
Air Twist Stem
Bohemia

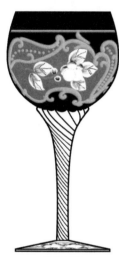

BOC 92
Ruby Bowl, Gold & Painted
Flower, Twisted Stem
Bohemia

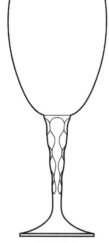

BOC 84
Molded Stem
Bohemia

BOC 12
Leaf Cuts on Gold or Platinum
Band with Trim on Foot;
or Gold Band with Plain Foot
Bohemia

BOC 78
Wine Shown
Gold Encrusted Ivy Leaves,
Gold Trim
Bohemia

Thistle
Etched Leaves
Bohemia

Marion
Geometric Etch
1554
Bohemia

BOC 72
Gold Encrusted Band,
Panel Cuts,
Frosted Ball in Stem
Bohemia

Piano Gold
Gold Ball in Stem
Bohemia

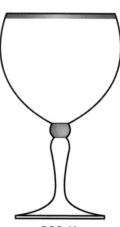

BOC 42
Wide Gold Band &
Gold Ball in Stem
Bohemia

BOC 83
Green Ball in Stem
Bohemia

116

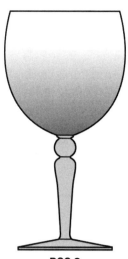

BOC 2
Orange Bowl, Green Stem
Bohemia

Olympia
Pinwheel Cuts, Square Foot
Bohemia

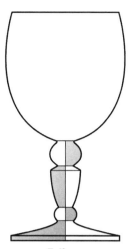

Eclipse
Frosted Stem, Square Foot
Bohemia

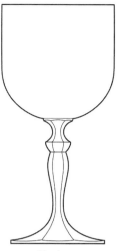

Mariana
Wine Shown
Plain
Bohemia

Ingrid/Andrea
Plain
Bohemia

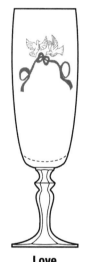

Love
Champagne Flute Shown
Etched Doves &
Ribbon/Bow
Bohemia

Angela
Hollow Foot
Bohemia

BOC 131
Etched Scrolls, Gold Trim
Bohemia

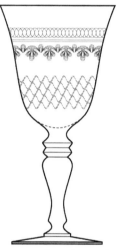

Lady Hamilton Collection
Geometric Etch
1114, 1214
Bohemia

Pinwheel
Pinwheel, Crisscross
& Fan Cuts
Bohemia

BOC 45
Wine Shown
Gold Etched Band,
Etched Plants
Bohemia

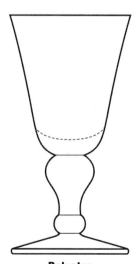

Baluster
Plain
Bohemia

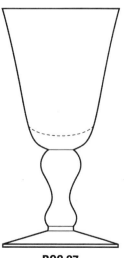

BOC 27
Plain
Bohemia

BOC 104
Wine Shown
Crisscross, Fan &
Horizontal Cuts
Bohemia

Etoile
Etched Floral,
Optic Bowl, Gold Trim
Bohemia

Bohemia

BOC 129
Gold Trim
Bohemia

Winchester
Frosted Arches
Bohemia

BOC 87
Blue Bowl,
Cut Floral
Bohemia

BOC 95
Wine Shown
Blue Bowl, Gold Etched
Floral, Gold Trim
Bohemia

BOC 67
Geometric Etch,
Gold Trim
Bohemia

BOC 103
Wine Shown
Amber, Gray Cut Floral
& Scrolls
Bohemia

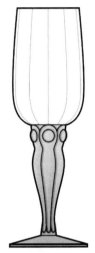

BOC 151
Cordial Shown
Various Color Stems,
Optic Bowl
Bohemia

BOC 48
Iced Tea Shown
Crisscross & Vertical Cuts
Bohemia

BOC 117
Iced Tea Shown
Gray/White Flower Decal
Bohemia

Fjord
Highball Shown
Square Base, Barware
Bohemia

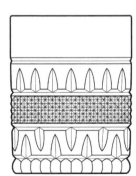

Glasgow
Old Fashioned Shown
Vertical, Horizontal
& Crosshatch Cuts
Bohemia

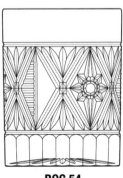

BOC 54
Old Fashioned Shown
Crisscross & Star Cuts,
Barware
Bohemia

Dominique
Cordial Shown
Crisscross & Diamond Cuts
Bohemia

BOC 150
Tumbler Shown
Applied Textured Ribbon
Bohemia

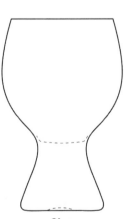

Gina
Plain
Bohemia

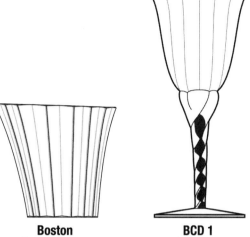

Boston
Tumbler Shown
Panel Cuts
Bohemia Jihlava

BCD 1
Optic Bowl,
Blue Air Twist Stem
Bohemian Crown Import

BBM 1
Champagne Flute Shown
Vertical Cuts
Bombay

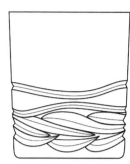

BBM 3
Wine Shown
Various Colors,
Gold Fleck Stem
Bombay

BBM 2
Double Old Fashioned Shown
Wavy Horizontal Cuts
Bombay

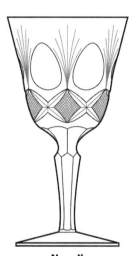

Wheat
Gray Cut Wheat
Borgfeldt

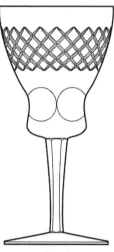

Napoli
Crosshatch, Fan, &
Thumbprint Cuts
Borgfeldt

Capri
Crisscross & Panel Cuts
Borgfeldt

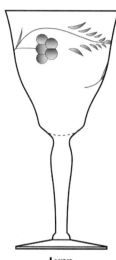

Ferndale
Gray Cut Plants
Borgfeldt

Lynn
Gray Cut Floral,
Bulbous Bowl & Stem
Borgfeldt

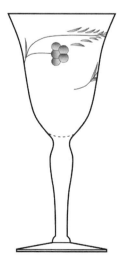

Lynn
Gray Cut Floral,
Bulbous Stem
Borgfeldt

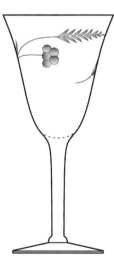

Lynn
Gray Cut Floral,
Straight Stem
Borgfeldt

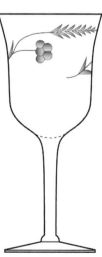

Lynn
Gray Cut Floral,
Straight Stem
Borgfeldt

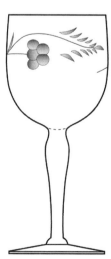

Lynn
Gray Cut Floral,
Bulbous Stem
Borgfeldt

Lynn
Polished Cut Floral,
Bulbous Stem
Borgfeldt

Regency
Floral & Plant Cuts
Borgfeldt

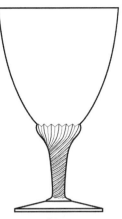

Lisa
Clear, Amber or Cranberry
Bowl, Twisted Stem
Borgfeldt

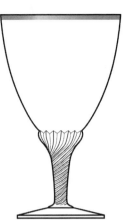

Lisa
Twisted Stem, Gold Trim
Borgfeldt

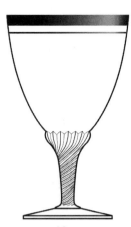

Lisa
Wide Platinum Band &
Verge, Twisted Stem
Borgfeldt

Lisa
Gray, Cranberry or Iridescent
Optic Bowl, Twisted Stem
Borgfeldt

Triennium
Swirl Cuts, Twisted Stem
Borgfeldt

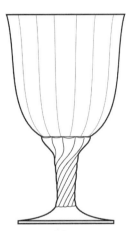

Liza
Clear, Cranberry, Green or
Iridescent Optic Bowl,
Twisted Stem
Borgfeldt

Darien
Gray Cut Floral,
Optic Bowl, Twisted Stem
Borgfeldt

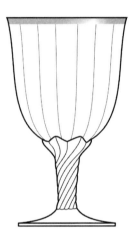

Liza
Optic Bowl,
Twisted Stem, Gold Trim
Borgfeldt

Premium
Merlot Wine Shown
Plain
Bormioli Rocco

Convivium
Burgundy Wine Shown
Plain
Bormioli Rocco

Aurum
Red Wine Shown
Plain
Bormioli Rocco

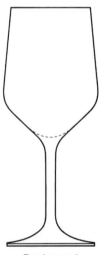

Restaurant
Clear or Blue
Bormioli Rocco

Magnesium
Plain
Bormioli Rocco

Aria
Plain
Bormioli Rocco

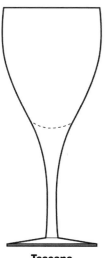

Toscana
Plain
Bormioli Rocco

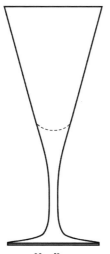

Ypsilon
Wine Shown
Plain
Bormioli Rocco

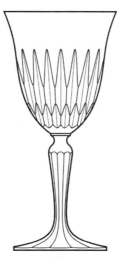

Aida
Vertical Cuts
Bormioli Rocco

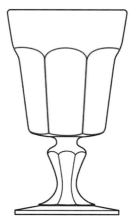

BCZ 1
Panel Cuts
Bormioli Rocco

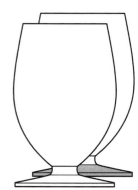

Tulip
Juice Shown
Clear or Various Foot Colors
Bormioli Rocco

Capri
Champagne Flute Shown
Blue Bowl
Bormioli Rocco

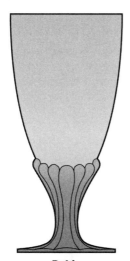

Bahia
Blue Bowl,
Green Stem
Bormioli Rocco

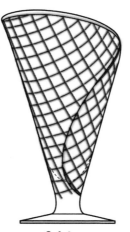

Gelato
Footed Dessert Shown
Clear or Various Colors,
Waffle Cone Shape
Bormioli Rocco

Murano
Tumbler Shown
Textured, Plain
Bormioli Rocco

Murano
Tumbler Shown
Textured, Blue Swirls
Bormioli Rocco

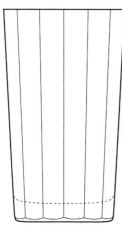

Oxford
Highball Shown
Multisided
Bormioli Rocco

Brio
Double Old Fashioned Shown
Optic Bowl,
Square Shape, Barware
Bormioli Rocco

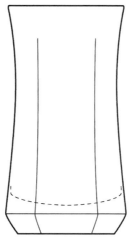

Capitol
Cooler Shown
Round Top,
Multisided Base, Barware
Bormioli Rocco

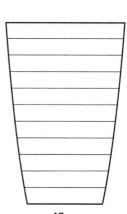

Viva
Tumbler Shown
Horizontal Rings
Bormioli Rocco

Luna
Cooler Shown
Clear, Blue or Green,
Bubble in Base, Barware
Bormioli Rocco

Bormioli Rocco, Boston

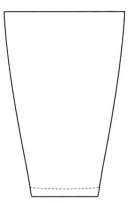

Zeno
Long Drink Shown
Clear or Various Colors,
Plain
Bormioli Rocco

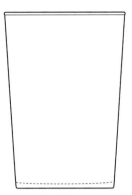

Bodega
Tumbler Shown
Plain
Bormioli Rocco

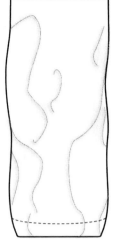

Sorgente
Cooler Shown
Clear or Various Colors,
Textured, Wavy Body
Bormioli Rocco

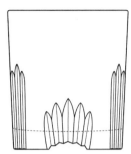

Selecta
Old Fashioned Shown
Fan & Vertical Cuts
Bormioli Rocco

Rock Bar
Double Old Fashioned Shown
Panel Cuts
Bormioli Rocco

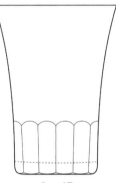

Amalfi
Tumbler Shown
Thumbprint Base
Bormioli Rocco

Galassia
Sherbet/Dessert Shown
Clear or Various Colors,
Textured Base
Bormioli Rocco

Rondo
Cup & Saucer Set Shown
Cobalt, Plain
Bormioli Rocco

Verdi-Oslo
Cappuccino Mug Shown
Glass with Metal Handles
Bormioli Rocco

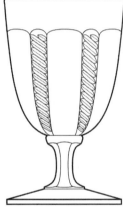

Cable
Cables & Panels,
Pressed Glass
Boston

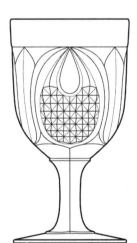

New England Pineapple
Vertical & Crosshatch Cuts,
Pressed Glass
Boston

Magnet & Grape
Frosted Grapes & Leaves,
Pressed Glass
Boston

Egyptian
Palm Trees/Buildings,
Pressed Glass
Boston

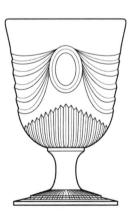

Lincoln Drape
Oval & Drape,
Pressed Glass
Boston

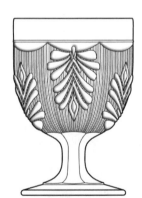

Inverted Fern
Egg Cup Shown
Ribbed, Ferns,
Pressed Glass
Boston

Beaded Grape Medallion
Grapes on Oval Medallion,
Pressed Glass
Boston Silver Glass

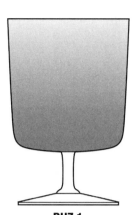

BUZ 1
Wine Shown
Smoke Bowl
Boussu

Lincoln
Amber, Plain
Boussu

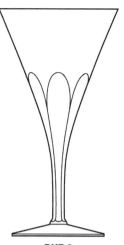

BUZ 3
Panel Cuts,
Multisided Stem
Boussu

BGD 3
Crisscross, Vertical
& Fan Cuts
Bridge

Leander
Crisscross & Fan Cuts
Bridge

BGD 2
Double Old Fashioned Shown
Crisscross & Fan Cuts
Bridge

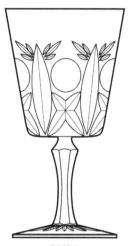

BLX 1
Wine Shown
Crisscross, Vertical
& Dot Cuts
Brier Glass

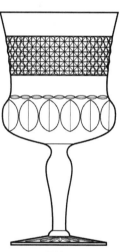

BHG 1
Crisscross &
Thumbprint Cuts
Brierly Hill Glass

Pinwheel
Pinwheel, Star & Fan Cuts
Brilliant

American Concord
Clear or Amber,
Textured, Pressed Glass
Brockway Glass

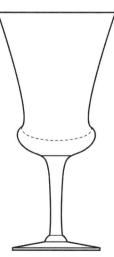

Benedict
Plain
Brodegaard

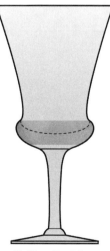

Golden Beatrice
Gold Tint, Gold Band
Brodegaard

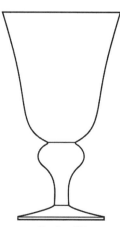

Gustav III
Plain
Brodegaard

Hamilton
Plain
Brodegaard

123

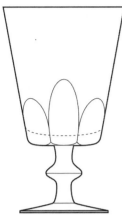

Viking
Panel Cuts
Brodegaard

Lorraine
Crisscross & Fan Cuts
Brodegaard

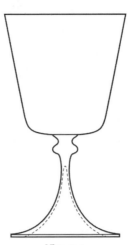

Vicenza
Hollow Stem
Brodegaard

Palazza
Clear or Cranberry Bowl,
Hollow Stem
Brodegaard

Freesia
Hollow Foot
Brodegaard

1776
Cobalt Bowl
Brodegaard

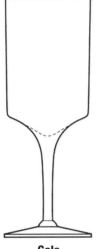

Gala
Plain
Brodegaard

Siri
Plain
Brodegaard

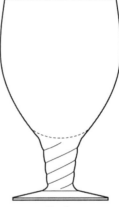

Greta
Twisted Stem
Brodegaard

Nordic
Plain
Brodegaard

Madison
Smoke, Plain
Brodegaard

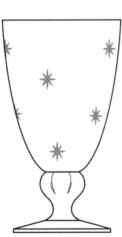

BR 1
Star Cuts
Brodegaard

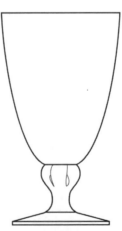

Kristine
Clear or Smoke Bowl
Brodegaard

Lisa
Plain
Brodegaard

Margrit
Panel Cuts,
Bubble in Stem
Brodegaard

Kungsholm
Plain, No Stem
Brodegaard

Bryce Shapes and Lines

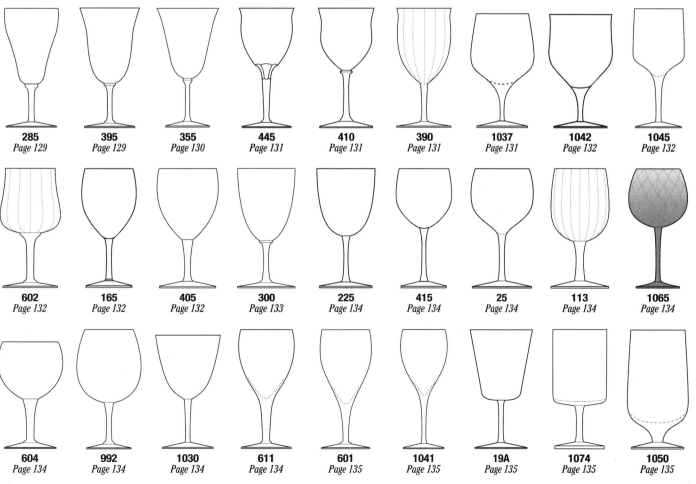

285
Page 129

395
Page 129

355
Page 130

445
Page 131

410
Page 131

390
Page 131

1037
Page 131

1042
Page 132

1045
Page 132

602
Page 132

165
Page 132

405
Page 132

300
Page 133

225
Page 134

415
Page 134

25
Page 134

113
Page 134

1065
Page 134

604
Page 134

992
Page 134

1030
Page 134

611
Page 134

601
Page 135

1041
Page 135

19A
Page 135

1074
Page 135

1050
Page 135

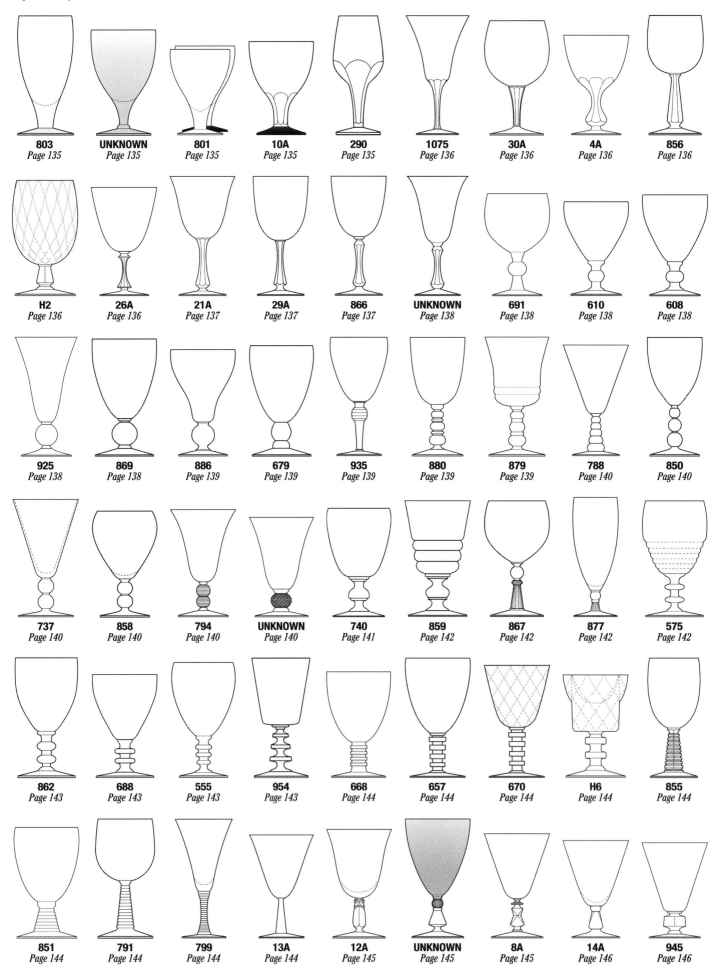

803
Page 135

UNKNOWN
Page 135

801
Page 135

10A
Page 135

290
Page 135

1075
Page 136

30A
Page 136

4A
Page 136

856
Page 136

H2
Page 136

26A
Page 136

21A
Page 137

29A
Page 137

866
Page 137

UNKNOWN
Page 138

691
Page 138

610
Page 138

608
Page 138

925
Page 138

869
Page 138

886
Page 139

679
Page 139

935
Page 139

880
Page 139

879
Page 139

788
Page 140

850
Page 140

737
Page 140

858
Page 140

794
Page 140

UNKNOWN
Page 140

740
Page 141

859
Page 142

867
Page 142

877
Page 142

575
Page 142

862
Page 143

688
Page 143

555
Page 143

954
Page 143

668
Page 144

657
Page 144

670
Page 144

H6
Page 144

855
Page 144

851
Page 144

791
Page 144

799
Page 144

13A
Page 144

12A
Page 145

UNKNOWN
Page 145

8A
Page 145

14A
Page 146

945
Page 146

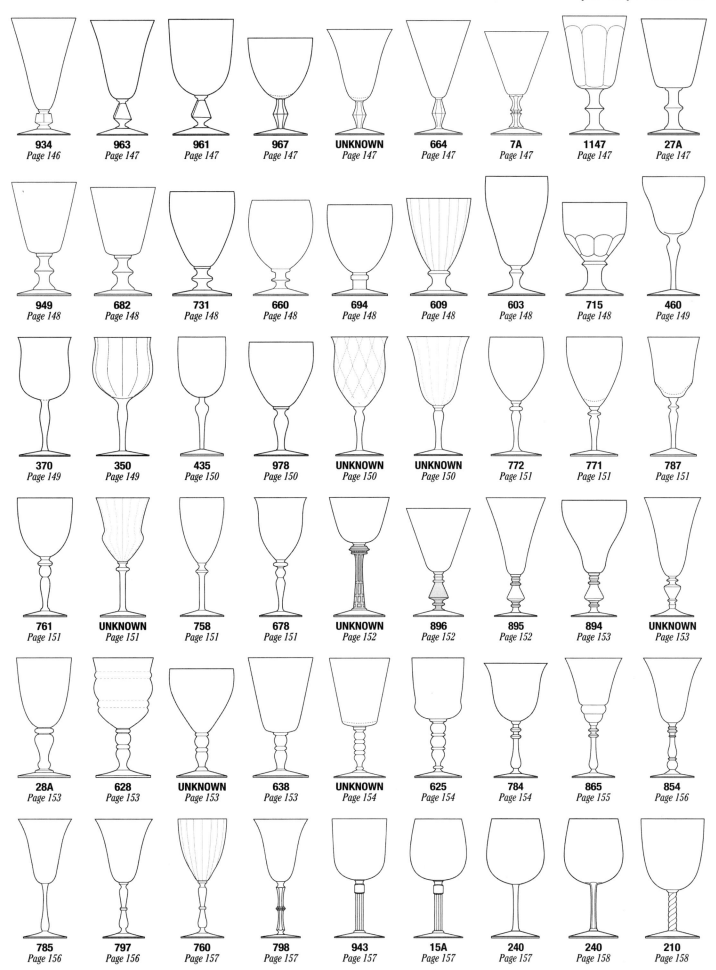

934
Page 146

963
Page 147

961
Page 147

967
Page 147

UNKNOWN
Page 147

664
Page 147

7A
Page 147

1147
Page 147

27A
Page 147

949
Page 148

682
Page 148

731
Page 148

660
Page 148

694
Page 148

609
Page 148

603
Page 148

715
Page 148

460
Page 149

370
Page 149

350
Page 149

435
Page 150

978
Page 150

UNKNOWN
Page 150

UNKNOWN
Page 150

772
Page 151

771
Page 151

787
Page 151

761
Page 151

UNKNOWN
Page 151

758
Page 151

678
Page 151

UNKNOWN
Page 152

896
Page 152

895
Page 152

894
Page 153

UNKNOWN
Page 153

28A
Page 153

628
Page 153

UNKNOWN
Page 153

638
Page 153

UNKNOWN
Page 154

625
Page 154

784
Page 154

865
Page 155

854
Page 156

785
Page 156

797
Page 156

760
Page 157

798
Page 157

943
Page 157

15A
Page 157

240
Page 157

240
Page 158

210
Page 158

Bryce Shapes and Lines

325	UNKNOWN	UNKNOWN	UNKNOWN	942	950	UNKNOWN	735	265
Page 158	Page 158	Page 158	Page 158	Page 158	Page 159	Page 159	Page 159	Page 159

235, 270	270	606	6A	22A	946	1A	11A	16A
Page 159	Page 159	Page 159	Page 159	Page 160	Page 160	Page 160	Page 161	Page 161

20A	2A	Atlas	Clear Circle	Beaded Oval & Scroll	Tulip with Sawtooth	Horn of Plenty	Grand	Hawaiian Lei
Page 161	Page 161	Page 161	Page 161	Page 161	Page 161	Page 162	Page 162	Page 162

Rope Bands	Rosette	Paneled Daisy	Paneled Forget Me Not	Fishscale	Paneled Thistle	Thistle	Teasel	Rose in the Snow
Page 162	Page 162	Page 162	Page 162	Page 162	Page 162	Page 162	Page 162	Page 162

Spirea Band	Yale	Filly	180	3A	5A	9A	761	763
Page 162	Page 162	Page 163	Page 163	Page 163	Page 163	Page 163	Page 163	Page 163

1137	1138	1325	1104	888	1139	1102	1104 1/4	294
Page 163	Page 163	Page 163	Page 163	Page 163	Page 163	Page 163	Page 163	Page 164

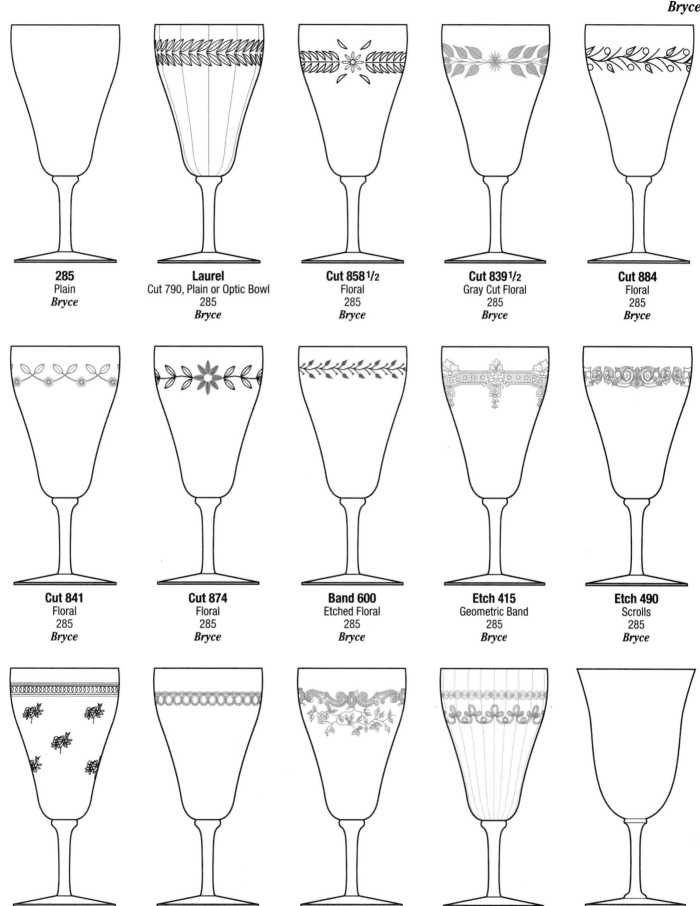

285
Plain
Bryce

Laurel
Cut 790, Plain or Optic Bowl
285
Bryce

Cut 858 1/2
Floral
285
Bryce

Cut 839 1/2
Gray Cut Floral
285
Bryce

Cut 884
Floral
285
Bryce

Cut 841
Floral
285
Bryce

Cut 874
Floral
285
Bryce

Band 600
Etched Floral
285
Bryce

Etch 415
Geometric Band
285
Bryce

Etch 490
Scrolls
285
Bryce

Etch 340
Floral
285
Bryce

Etch 341
Geometric Loops
285
Bryce

Etch 324
Floral
285
Bryce

Etch 374
Optic Bowl, Trefoils
285
Bryce

395
Plain
Bryce

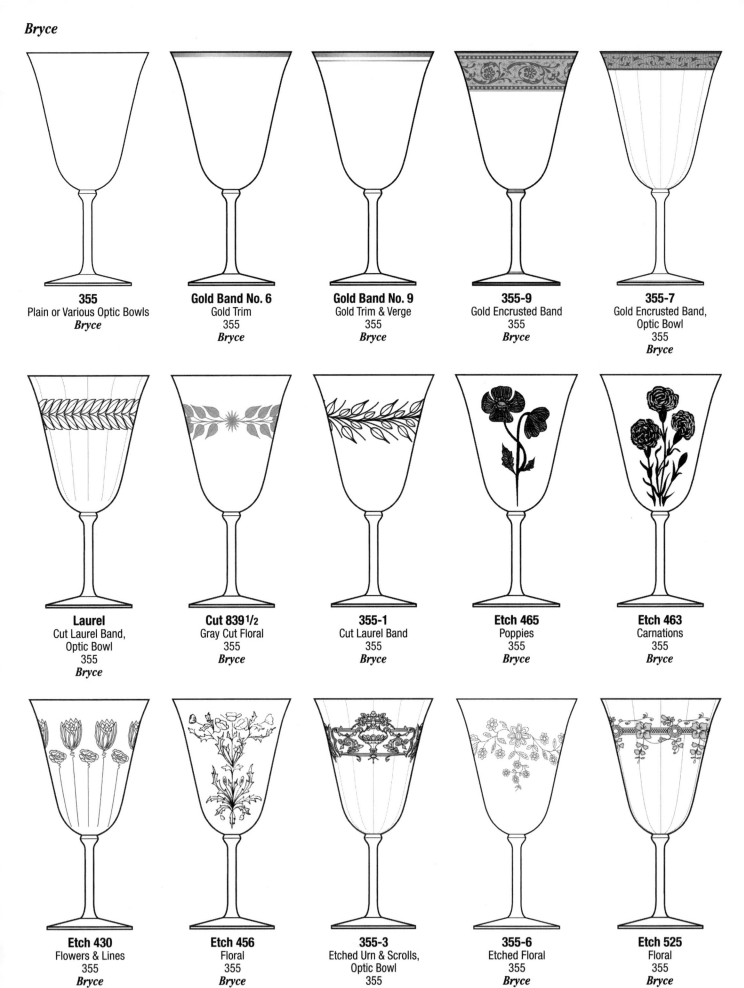

355
Plain or Various Optic Bowls
Bryce

Gold Band No. 6
Gold Trim
355
Bryce

Gold Band No. 9
Gold Trim & Verge
355
Bryce

355-9
Gold Encrusted Band
355
Bryce

355-7
Gold Encrusted Band,
Optic Bowl
355
Bryce

Laurel
Cut Laurel Band,
Optic Bowl
355
Bryce

Cut 839 1/2
Gray Cut Floral
355
Bryce

355-1
Cut Laurel Band
355
Bryce

Etch 465
Poppies
355
Bryce

Etch 463
Carnations
355
Bryce

Etch 430
Flowers & Lines
355
Bryce

Etch 456
Floral
355
Bryce

355-3
Etched Urn & Scrolls,
Optic Bowl
355
Bryce

355-6
Etched Floral
355
Bryce

Etch 525
Floral
355
Bryce

Etch 515
Floral
355
Bryce

Etch 410
Needle Etched Lilies
355
Bryce

Etch 305
Floral, Optic Bowl
355
Bryce

Etch 500
Floral Swags
355
Bryce

Etch 378
Geometric Loops
355
Bryce

Etch 382
Horizontal Cuts,
Etched Loops
355
Bryce

Engraving 95
Floral, Optic Bowl
355
Bryce

Engraving 90
Floral
355
Bryce

355-10
Multicolored Floral Basket,
Green Band, Gold Trim
355
Bryce

Etch 485
Floral Swags
445
Bryce

Etch 420
Floral Swags
410
Bryce

390
Various Optic Bowls
Bryce

Etch 375 1/2
Floral Swags,
Diamond Optic Bowl
390
Bryce

Minuet
Clear, Pink or Amethyst
1037
Bryce

1037-1
Platinum Bowl & Foot Trim
1037
Bryce

Ballet
Various Colors
1042
Bryce

Adonis
Amber, Clear,
Green or Smoke
1045
Bryce

**Tiara Gold
Tiara Platinum**
Gold or Platinum Trim
1045
Bryce

La Fontaine
Cut 1, Vertical Cuts
1045
Bryce

Biltmore
Optic Bowl
602
Bryce

165
Plain
Bryce

Etch 311
Geometric Bands
165
Bryce

405
Plain
Bryce

Cut 850
Vertical Cuts
405
Bryce

Etched Rye
Bundle of Grain
405
Bryce

Cut 868
Stars & Leaves
405
Bryce

Etch 500
Floral Swags
405
Bryce

Etch 495
Scrolls
405
Bryce

Etch 462
Floral Band
405
Bryce

Etch 334
Geometric Bands
405
Bryce

Etch 405
Floral Band
405
Bryce

Etch 480
Ribbon & Branch
405
Bryce

Etch 635
Floral Band
405
Bryce

Etch 633
Floral Band
405
Bryce

Etch 336
Geometric Band
405
Bryce

Etch 632
Geometric Band
405
Bryce

Etch 630
Geometric Band
405
Bryce

Etch 631
Geometric Band
405
Bryce

Etch 413
Geometric Band
405
Bryce

300
Plain
Bryce

Etch 236
Fleur-de-lis
300
Bryce

Etch 275
Floral Band
300
Bryce

Etch 325
Geometric Band
300
Bryce

Etch 329
Geometric Band
300
Bryce

Etch 327
Geometric Band
300
Bryce

Bryce

Etch 311
Geometric Band
300
Bryce

225
Plain
Bryce

Etch 520
Geometric Band
225
Bryce

Etch 330
Geometric Band
225
Bryce

415
Plain
Bryce

Etch 425
Floral Band
415
Bryce

Etch 445
Ribbons & Swags
415
Bryce

Etch 445
Ribbons & Swags
25
Bryce

113
Optic Bowl
Bryce

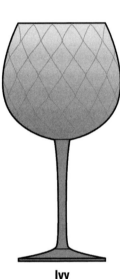

Ivy
Amethyst, Flame (Red) or
Green, Diamond Optic Bowl
1065
Bryce

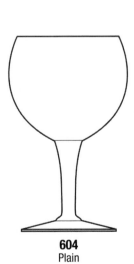

604
Plain
Bryce

Continental
Clear or Cerulean
Blue Stem & Foot
992
Bryce

Ascot (Gold Trim)
Madison (Platinum Trim)
992
Bryce

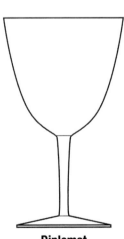

Diplomat
Clear or Green, or
Clear with Platinum Trim
1030
Bryce

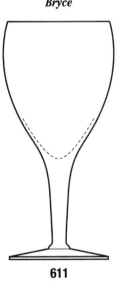

611
Plain
Bryce

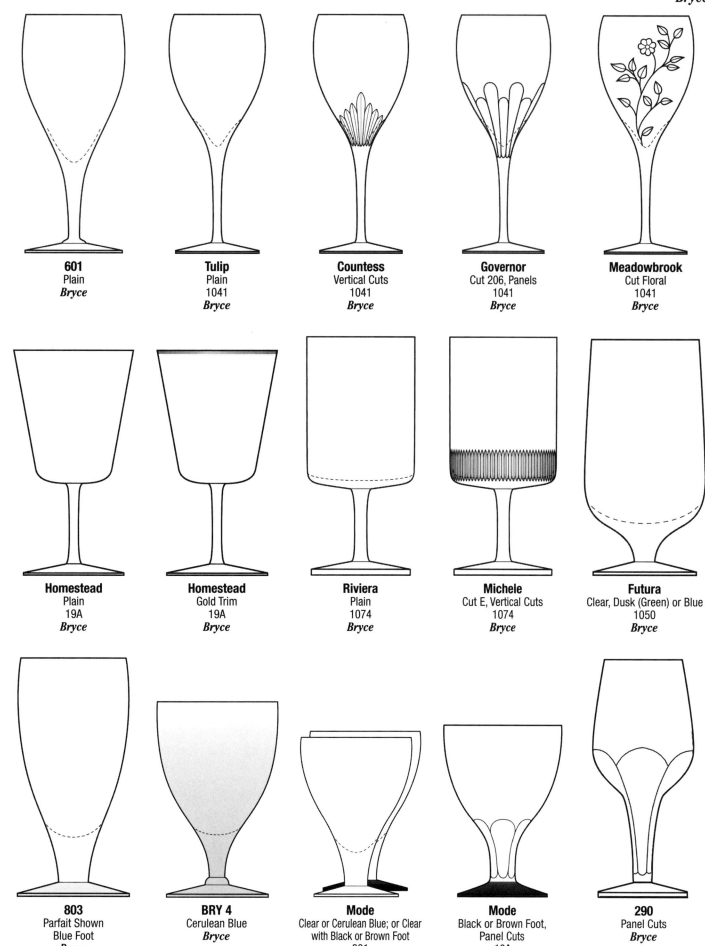

601
Plain
Bryce

Tulip
Plain
1041
Bryce

Countess
Vertical Cuts
1041
Bryce

Governor
Cut 206, Panels
1041
Bryce

Meadowbrook
Cut Floral
1041
Bryce

Homestead
Plain
19A
Bryce

Homestead
Gold Trim
19A
Bryce

Riviera
Plain
1074
Bryce

Michele
Cut E, Vertical Cuts
1074
Bryce

Futura
Clear, Dusk (Green) or Blue
1050
Bryce

803
Parfait Shown
Blue Foot
Bryce

BRY 4
Cerulean Blue
Bryce

Mode
Clear or Cerulean Blue; or Clear
with Black or Brown Foot
801
Bryce

Mode
Black or Brown Foot,
Panel Cuts
10A
Bryce

290
Panel Cuts
Bryce

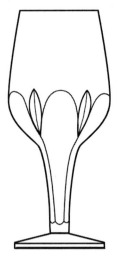

Cut 537
Vertical & Panel Cuts
290
Bryce

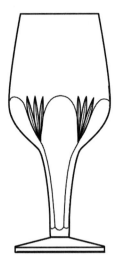

Cut 805
Fan & Panel Cuts
290
Bryce

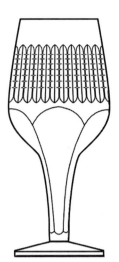

Cut 802
Crosshatch & Panel Cuts
290
Bryce

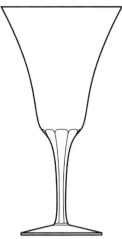

Regal
Plain
1075
Bryce

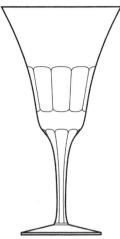

State
Panel Cuts
1075
Bryce

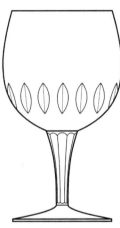

Moonlight
Cut 365, Vertical Cuts
30A
Bryce

Candlelight
Cut 363, Vertical Cuts
30A
Bryce

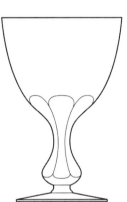

Heritage
Panel Cuts
4A
Bryce

Diadem
Cut 277,
Horizontal & Star Cuts
4A
Bryce

856
Clear or Blue Stem
Bryce

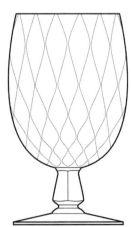

Holiday
Various Optic Bowls,
Stem & Foot Colors
H2
Bryce

Roslyn
Plain
26A
Bryce

Roslyn
Platinum Bowl & Foot Trim
26A
Bryce

Augusta
Cut 323, Laurel
26A
Bryce

Drexel
Vertical Cuts
26A
Bryce

Bristol
Cut 336, Vertical Cuts
26A
Bryce

Clinton
Cut 372, Vertical Cuts
26A
Bryce

Ferndale
Cut 371, Leaves & Vine
26A
Bryce

Avalon
Cut 369, Plant
26A
Bryce

21A
Plain
Bryce

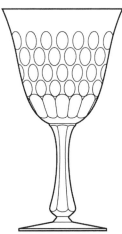

Ambassador
Cut 121,
Thumbprints & Panels
21A
Bryce

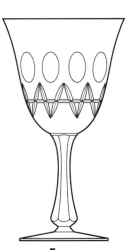

Essex
Cut 265,
Thumbprints & Archs
21A
Bryce

29A
Plain
Bryce

Royalty (Gold Trim)
Revere (Platinum Trim)
29A
Bryce

Coronation
Gold Band 35
29A
Bryce

Flirtation
Cut 374
29A
Bryce

Princess
Cut 374, Platinum Trim
29A
Bryce

Vine
Cut 269, Leaves & Vine
29A
Bryce

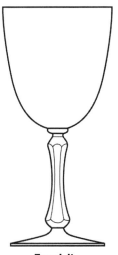

Exquisite
Plain
866
Bryce

Exquisite
Platinum Bands & Foot Trim
866
Bryce

Bryce

866-1
Vertical Cuts
866
Bryce

866-2
Crisscross & Fan Cuts
866
Bryce

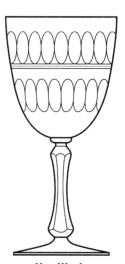

Van Wyck
Oval Cuts
866
Bryce

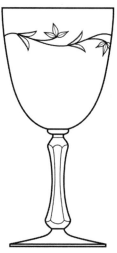

866-3
Cut Leaves & Vine
866
Bryce

BRY 3
Vertical Oval Cuts
Bryce

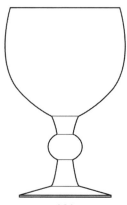

691
Clear or Black Bowl & Foot
Bryce

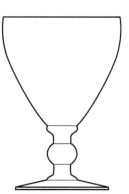

610
Plain
Bryce

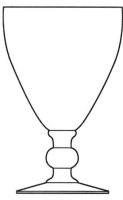

608
Plain or Clear Block Optic
Bowl & Green Stem
Bryce

Apollo
Various Colors; Plain, Swirl
or Block Optic Bowls
925
Bryce

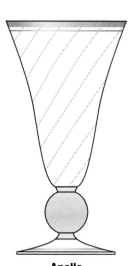

Apollo
Swirl Optic Bowl, Blue Stem,
Gold Bands & Foot Trim
925
Bryce

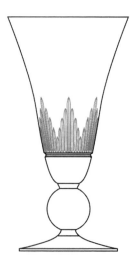

Parkside
Vertical & Horizontal Cuts
925
Bryce

925-1
Cut Wheat
925
Bryce

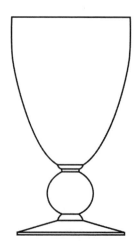

Contour
Various Colors; Plain, Swirl
or Block Optic Bowls
869
Bryce

Betsy Ross
Gray Cut Floral
869
Bryce

869-2
Crisscross & Dot Cuts
869
Bryce

138

869-3
Polished Laurel Cuts
869
Bryce

869-1
Cobalt, Gold Encrusted
Etched Floral, Gold Trim
869
Bryce

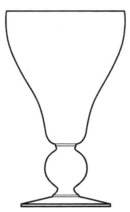

886
Various Bowl, Stem &
Foot Colors; Plain
Bryce

886-1
Panel Cuts
886
Bryce

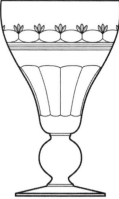

886-2
Fan & Panel Cuts
886
Bryce

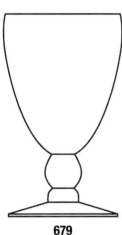

679
Plain
Bryce

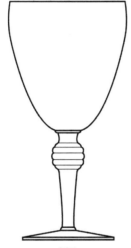

935
Clear or Various Color Bowls
Bryce

880
Plain
Bryce

Columbine
Gray Cut Leaves & Vine
880
Bryce

879
Plain
Bryce

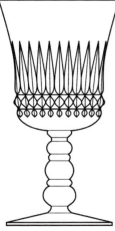

Wakefield
Cut 178, Vertical Cuts
879
Bryce

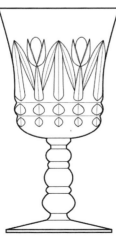

879-1
Vertical & Floral Cuts
879
Bryce

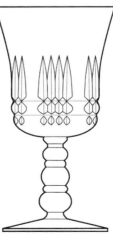

879-3
Vertical Cuts
879
Bryce

879-5
Vertical Cuts
879
Bryce

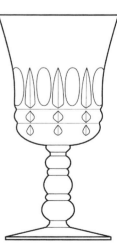

879-4
Thumbprint & Vertical Cuts
879
Bryce

788
Plain
Bryce

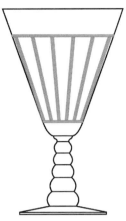

788-1
Gray Cut Lines & Bands
788
Bryce

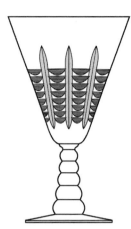

788-2
Vertical & Horizontal
Gray Cuts
788
Bryce

Aristocrat
Various Bowl, Stem
& Foot Colors
850
Bryce

850-6
Cut Stem
850
Bryce

850-7
Multicolored Handpainted
Floral, Gold Trim
850
Bryce

850-2
Gold Scrolls & Trim,
Aqua Stem
850
Bryce

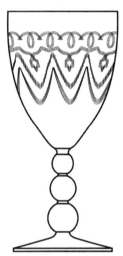

850-1
Geometric Etch
850
Bryce

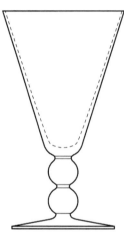

737
Various Bowl, Stem
& Foot Colors
Bryce

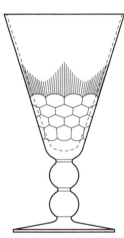

737-4
Vertical Lines &
Honeycomb Cuts
737
Bryce

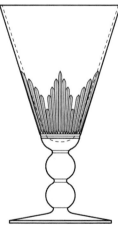

737-1
Vertical Cuts
737
Bryce

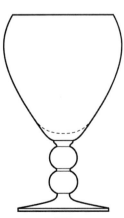

858
Plain
Bryce

794
Various Bowl, Stem
& Foot Colors
Bryce

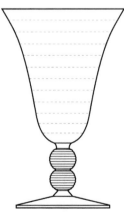

794-1
Saturn Optic Bowl
794
Bryce

Theodora
Amethyst Bowl & Foot
Bryce

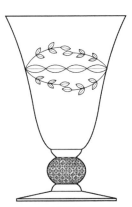

BRY 8
Plant & Horizontal Cuts
Bryce

Early American
Plain, Clear or Blue Stem
740
Bryce

Early American Laurel
Cut 790, Laurel
740
Bryce

Colonial
Wreath Cuts
740
Bryce

Brilliant
Cut 265, Clear or
Amethyst Bowl
740
Bryce

White House
Crisscross, Horizontal
& Vertical Cuts
740
Bryce

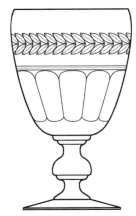

740-6
Horizontal, Laurel
& Panel Cuts
740
Bryce

740-2
Diamond & Fan Cuts
740
Bryce

740-10
Crisscross & Horizontal Cuts
740
Bryce

740-11
Gray Cut Floral
740
Bryce

740-1
Gray & Polished
Cut Sunflowers
740
Bryce

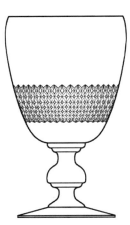

740-4
Diamond Cuts
740
Bryce

740-12
Horizontal & Dot Cuts
740
Bryce

740-8
Thumbprint & Vertical Cuts
740
Bryce

740-5
Diamond Cuts
740
Bryce

740-3
Oval Panel Cuts
740
Bryce

859
Plain
Bryce

859-3
Vertical Cuts
859
Bryce

859-6
Crisscross Cuts
859
Bryce

859-2
Laurel Cuts
859
Bryce

859-5
Groove Cuts
859
Bryce

859-4
Fan Cuts
859
Bryce

St. Moritz
Plain
867
Bryce

St. Moritz
Block Optic Bowl
867
Bryce

867-1
Laurel Cuts
867
Bryce

877
Plain or Block Optic Bowl
Bryce

Georgian
Plain, Various Colors
575
Bryce

575-1
Laurel Cuts
575
Bryce

575-5
Crisscross Cuts
575
Bryce

Etch 520
Geometric Band
575
Bryce

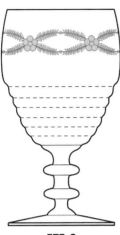

575-3
Gray Cut Floral Band
575
Bryce

575-6
Floral Cuts
575
Bryce

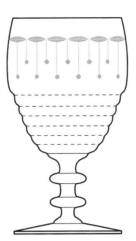

575-2
Gray Cut Ovals,
Lines & Dots
575
Bryce

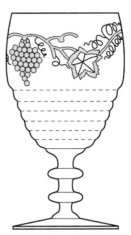

575-4
Gray Cut Grapes & Leaves
575
Bryce

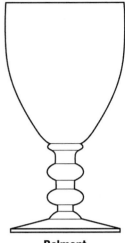

Belmont
Plain
862
Bryce

Williamsburg
Cut 167,
Vertical & Panel Cuts
862
Bryce

Concord
Crisscross, Horizontal,
& Panel Cuts
862
Bryce

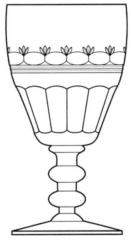

862-1
Horizontal, Fan
& Panel Cuts
862
Bryce

Park Lane
Plain
688
Bryce

Springtime
Various Color Bowls
688
Bryce

688-7
Gold Bowl & Foot Trim
688
Bryce

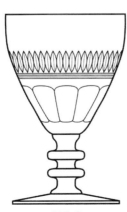

688-2
Panel & Vertical Cuts
688
Bryce

688-1
Red Bowl, Grape & Vine Etch
688
Bryce

555
Clear or Cobalt Bowl
Bryce

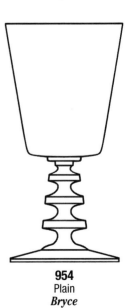

954
Plain
Bryce

143

Starlight
Cut 283, Stars
954
Bryce

Hampshire
Cut 300, Diagonal Cuts
954
Bryce

Kildare
Vertical & Dot Cuts
954
Bryce

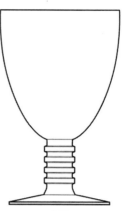

668
Clear, Cobalt or Ruby Bowl
Bryce

657
Clear or Various Color Bowls
Bryce

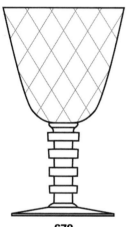

670
Port Wine Shown
Various Colors,
Diamond Optic Bowl
Bryce

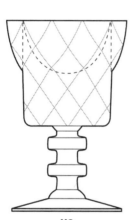

H6
Martini Shown
Diamond Optic Bowl
Bryce

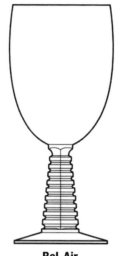

Bel-Air
Clear or Various Color Stems,
Plain or Block Optic Bowl
855
Bryce

851
Plain
Bryce

851-1
Geometric Etched Band
851
Bryce

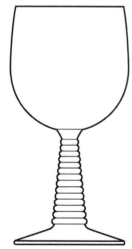

Ringmont
Plain or Various Optic Bowls,
Clear or Cerulean Blue Stem
791
Bryce

791
Panel Cuts
Bryce

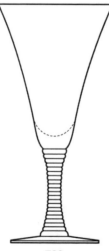

799
Clear or Amber Bowl
Bryce

Simplicity
All Milk Glass or Various
Color Bowls & Clear Stem
13A
Bryce

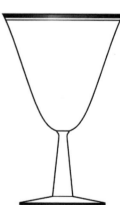

13A-1 (Clear)
13A-3 (Milk Glass)
Gold Bands & Foot Trim
13A
Bryce

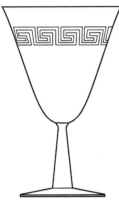

Cretan
Engraving 1100
13A
Bryce

Festival
Clear or Blue Bowl,
Star Cuts
13A
Bryce

Kingsley
Cut Floral
13A
Bryce

Fern Leaf
Cut 290
13A
Bryce

Starfire
Star Cuts
13A
Bryce

Cathay
Plain
12A
Bryce

Celeste
Leaf Cuts
12A
Bryce

Harmony
Cut 291, Leaf Cuts
12A
Bryce

Bridal Wreath
Leaf & Oval Cuts
12A
Bryce

Cathay
Etched Scrolls
12A
Bryce

BRY 16
Cerulean Blue Bowl
Bryce

Sharon
Clear or Yellow Bowl, Plain
8A
Bryce

8A-5
Platinum Bowl & Foot Trim
8A
Bryce

8A-3
Platinum Bands & Foot Trim
8A
Bryce

Starburst
Cut 283
8A
Bryce

8A-2
Yellow Bowl, Star Cuts
8A
Bryce

8A-6
Gray Cut Wheat
8A
Bryce

Arlington
Gray Cut Plant
8A
Bryce/Home Arts Crystal

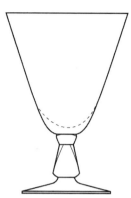

Cosmopolitan
All Clear or Various
Bowl & Foot Colors
14A
Bryce

Wilmington
All Clear or Various Bowl &
Foot Colors, Square Stem
945
Bryce

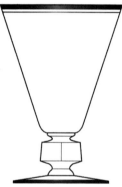

945-6 (Platinum Trim)
945-3 (Gold Trim)
Square Stem
945
Bryce

945-8
Gray Cut Rose,
Square Stem
945
Bryce

Wilmington Rose
Gray Cut Rose,
Square Stem
945
Bryce

945-9
Floral & Dot Cuts,
Square Stem
945
Bryce

945-2
Plant & Dot Cuts,
Square Stem
945
Bryce

945-5
Plant Cuts, Square Stem
945
Bryce

945-1
Gray Cut Snowflakes,
Square Stem
945
Bryce

Helenic
Clear or Various Color
Square Stems, Plain
934
Bryce

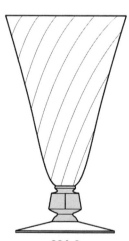

934-3
Swirl Optic Bowl,
Various Color Square Stems
934
Bryce

934-1
Platinum Band & Foot Trim,
Square Stem
934
Bryce

934-2
Platinum Bands & Foot Trim,
Square Stem
934
Bryce

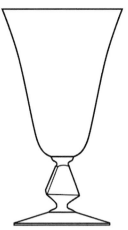

Tulip Aquarius
Clear or Amethyst
Bowl & Foot, Square Stem
963
Bryce

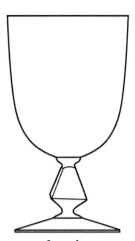

Aquarius
All Clear or Various Bowl,
Stem & Foot Colors
961
Bryce

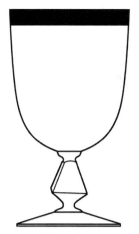

Aquarius
Platinum Band,
Square Stem
961
Bryce

Cretan
Gray Cut Greek Key,
Square Stem
961
Bryce

Kimberley
Plain
967
Bryce

BRY 17
Plain
Bryce

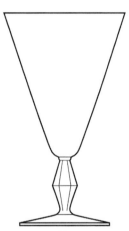

664
All Clear or Various
Bowl & Foot Colors
Bryce

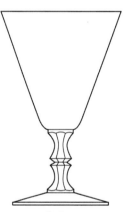

Debut
Clear or Cerulean Blue Bowl
7A
Bryce

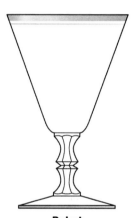

Debut
Gold or Platinum Bands
& Foot Trim
7A
Bryce

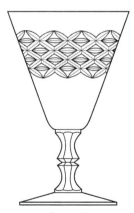

Coronet
Cut 20A, Crisscross & Ovals
7A
Bryce

Rowena
Cut 279, Floral
7A
Bryce

7A-1
Cut Rose
7A
Bryce

Antique
Clear or Various Colors,
Panels
1147
Bryce

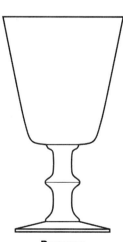

Regency
Plain
27A
Bryce

Lancaster
Cut 265, Panels & Arches
27A
Bryce

Ardmore
Cut 383,
Crisscross & Vertical Cuts
27A
Bryce

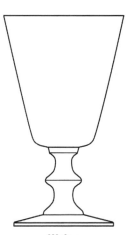

Wales
Clear or Blue Bowl & Foot
949
Bryce

Mayfair
Cut 319, Vertical Cuts
949
Bryce

Empire
Cut 7, Crisscross & Blocks
949
Bryce

Traditional
Cut 552C,
Crisscross & Fans
949
Bryce

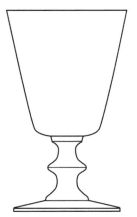

Wales
Plain
682
Bryce

Wales Laurel
Cut Laurel Band
682
Bryce

682-1
Crisscross & Panel Cuts
682
Bryce

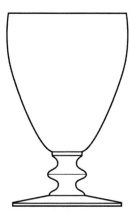

731
Clear or Various
Color Bowls, Plain
Bryce

660
Clear or Various
Color Bowls, Plain
Bryce

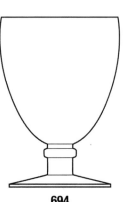

694
Plain
Bryce

609
Optic Bowl
Bryce

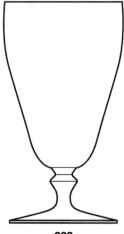

603
Plain
Bryce

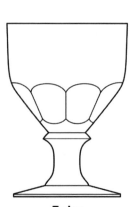

Tudor
Panel Cuts
715
Bryce

460
Plain
Bryce

Cut 887
Cut Laurel Band
460
Bryce

Etch 426
Geometric Band
460
Bryce

Cut 889
Geometric Band
460
Bryce

Etch 510
Geometric Band
460
Bryce

Etch 390
Scrolls
370
Bryce

350
Various Colors &
Various Optic Bowls
Bryce

Laurel
Cut 790, Laurel Band
350
Bryce

Laurel
Cut 790, Optic Bowl,
½" Cut Laurel Band
350
Bryce

Laurel
Cut 790, Optic Bowl,
¼" Cut Laurel Band
350
Bryce

Cut 839 ½
Floral
350
Bryce

Cut 834
Vertical & Horizontal Cuts
350
Bryce

Etch 535
Floral
350
Bryce

Etch 322
Butterfly & Swags,
Optic Bowl
350
Bryce

Etch 500
Floral Swags
350
Bryce

Bryce

Etch 375
Geometric Band,
Floral Swags, Optic Bowl
350
Bryce

Etch 375 1/2
Geometric Band,
Floral Swags, Optic Bowl
350
Bryce

Etch 490
Scrolls, Optic Bowl
350
Bryce

Etch 340 1/2
Floral, Optic Bowl
350
Bryce

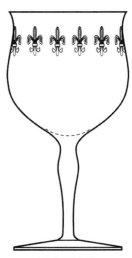

Etch 321 1/2
Fleur-de-lis
350
Bryce

435
Plain
Bryce

Cut 848
Vertical & Oval Cuts
435
Bryce

Etch 421
Geometric Band
435
Bryce

Etch 416
Geometric Band
435
Bryce

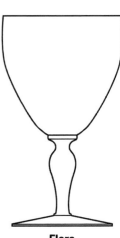

Flora
Plain
978
Bryce

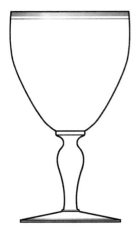

Andora Gold
Gold Bands & Foot Trim
978
Bryce

Andora
Cut 117,
Laurel & Dots
978
Bryce

Flora
Cut 241, Crisscross &
Leaves, Optic Bowl
978
Bryce

BRY 6
Clear or Blue,
Etched Floral Swags,
Diamond Optic Bowl
Bryce

BRY 23
Etched Butterfly & Swags,
Optic Bowl
Bryce

Regal
Plain
772
Bryce

772-1
Cut Floral
772
Bryce

771-1
Laurel & Dot Cuts
771
Bryce

771-2
Floral & Oval Cuts
771
Bryce

771-3
Oval & Dot Cuts
771
Bryce

771-4
Gray Crisscross &
Line Cuts, Cut Foot
771
Bryce

787
Plain
Bryce

Fern Leaf
Etched Floral
787
Bryce

761
Plain
Bryce

761-1
Oval & Dot Cuts
761
Bryce

Etch 525
Floral
Bryce

758
Plain
Bryce

758-2
Etched Fans
758
Bryce

758-1
Etched Floral & Basket
758
Bryce

678
Clear or Various Colors,
Plain or Optic Bowl
Bryce

Bryce

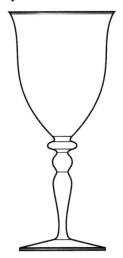

678-4
Gold Bowl & Foot Trim
678
Bryce

678-2
Etched Floral & Basket
678
Bryce

Etch 463C
Carnations
678
Bryce

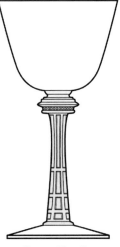

Space Needle
Topaz Space Needle Stem
Bryce

896
Various Bowl, Stem
& Foot Colors
Bryce

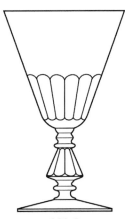

896-2
Panel Cuts
896
Bryce

896-1
Etched Urn & Scrolls
896
Bryce

896-5
Etched Floral & Scrolls
896
Bryce

895
Clear or Various Color
Bowls & Stems
Bryce

895
Ruby Bowl
Bryce

895-5
Cut Swirls
895
Bryce

895-4
Crisscross Cuts
895
Bryce

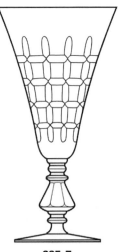

895-7
Vertical & Horizontal Cuts
895
Bryce

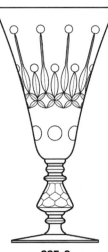

895-8
Crisscross, Vertical
& Dot Cuts
895
Bryce

895-3
Amber or Cranberry Flashed
Bowl, Gray Cut Grapes
895
Bryce

894
Clear or Various
Bowl & Stem Colors
Bryce

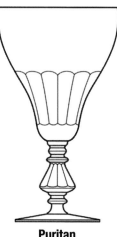

Puritan
Panel Cuts
894
Bryce

894-1
Horizontal, Oval
& Vertical Cuts
894
Bryce

Fern Leaf
Needle Etched Floral
894
Bryce

BRY 12
Iced Tea Shown
Gray Cut Floral
Bryce

Newport
Plain
28A
Bryce

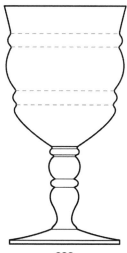

628
Plain
Bryce

BRY 1
Amethyst Bowl, Plain
Bryce

BRY 1
Cobalt, Plain
Bryce

BRY 1-2
Floral & Dot Cuts
Bryce

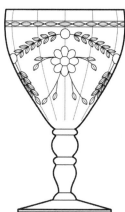

BRY 1-1
Floral & Oval Cuts,
Optic Bowl
Bryce

BRY 1
Etched Floral & Basket
Bryce

638
Clear or Various
Colors, Plain
Bryce

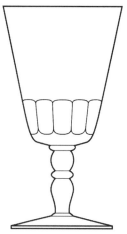

638-1
Panel Cuts
638
Bryce

638-2
Crisscross, Vertical
& Panel Cuts
638
Bryce

638-5
Crisscross & Vertical Cuts
638
Bryce

638-4
Vertical, Oval &
Floral Cuts
638
Bryce

638-6
Leaf & Panel Cuts
638
Bryce

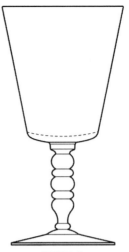

BRY 5-1
Plain
Bryce

BRY 5
Panel & Dot Cuts
Bryce

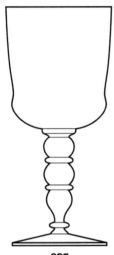

625
Various Color Bowls, Plain
Bryce

625-2
Gray Cut Floral, Cut Stem
625
Bryce

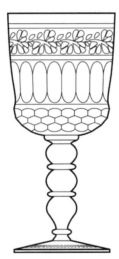

625-8
Floral, Honeycomb,
& Panel Cuts
625
Bryce

625-4
Gray Cut Floral
625
Bryce

625-3
Gray Cut Floral,
Cut Stem
625
Bryce

625-6
Gray Cut Floral,
Cut Stem
625
Bryce

625-1
Crisscross, Star
& Fan Cuts
625
Bryce

784
Plain
Bryce

Old Lace
Band 567,
Etched Geometric
784
Bryce

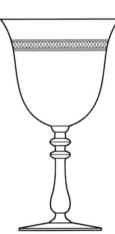

784-9
Etched Geometric Band
784
Bryce

784-4
Cut Laurel Band
784
Bryce

Columbine
Gray Cut Leaves & Vine
784
Bryce

784-5
Vertical Cuts
784
Bryce

784-1
Vertical Cuts
784
Bryce

Fern Leaf
Needle Etched Floral
784
Bryce

784-11
Gray Cut Floral &
Horizontal Bands
784
Bryce

784-6
Etched Floral & Scrolls
784
Bryce

784-3
Needle Etched Swags
784
Bryce

784-8
Gray Cut Floral
784
Bryce

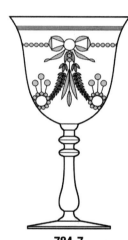

784-7
Gray Cut Floral & Bow
784
Bryce

784-2
Horizontal & Leaf Cuts
784
Bryce

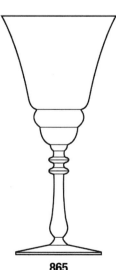

865
Plain
Bryce

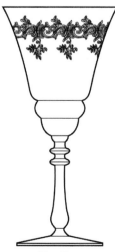

Charlene
Etched Scrolls
865
Bryce

865-2
Crisscross & Fan Cuts,
Gray Cut Stars
865
Bryce

865-6
Needle Etched Scrolls
865
Bryce

Bryce

865-4
Gray Cut Oval & Dot Cuts
865
Bryce

865-8
Crisscross, Vertical
& Dot Cuts
865
Bryce

854
Plain
Bryce

Fern Leaf
Needle Etched Floral,
Optic Bowl
854
Bryce

854-1
Needle Etched Scrolls,
Optic Bowl
854
Bryce

854-2
Needle Etched Swags,
Optic Bowl
854
Bryce

854-4
Etched Floral,
Optic Bowl
854
Bryce

854-6
Cut Stars
854
Bryce

854-3
Vertical & Leaf Cuts
854
Bryce

854-8
Cut Floral, Optic Bowl
854
Bryce

785
Plain
Bryce

Cascade
Gray Vertical Cuts
785
Bryce

785-1
Vertical & Star Cuts
785
Bryce

797
Plain
Bryce

797-1
Etched Floral & Basket
797
Bryce

760
Optic Bowl, Various
Color Bowls & Stems
Bryce

Etch 463D
Carnations, Optic Bowl
760
Bryce

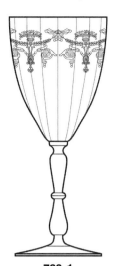

760-1
Etched Swags, Optic Bowl
760
Bryce

798
Plain
Bryce

798-2
Platinum Bands & Foot Trim
798
Bryce

798-1
Vertical Cuts
798
Bryce

798-4
Needle Etched Floral,
Plain & Optic Bowls
798
Bryce

798-3
Needle Etched Swags
798
Bryce

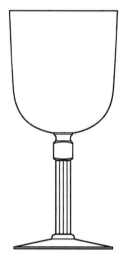

Colonnade
Clear or Various
Color Bowls, Plain
943
Bryce

Columbine
Clear or Various Color Bowls,
Gray Cut Leaves & Vine
943
Bryce

943-1
Gray Cut Leaves
943
Bryce

Modern Classic
Plain
15A
Bryce

240
Smooth Stem, Plain
Bryce

Elegance
Cut Stem, Gold Trim
240
Bryce

St. Regis
Gold Band 35,
Cut Stem, Gold Foot Trim
240
Bryce

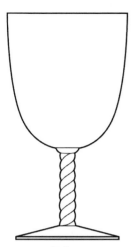

Bolero
Clear or Various Color
Bowls, Twisted Stem
210
Bryce

325
Various Optic Bowls,
Clear or Various Colors
Bryce

Etch 390
Scrolls, Green Stem
325
Bryce

325-1
Gray Cut Laurel Band
325
Bryce

325-3
Gray Cut Geometric Band
325
Bryce

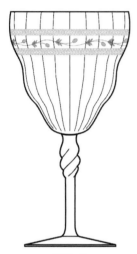

325-4
Gray Cut Geometric Band
325
Bryce

Etch 411
Geometric Band
325
Bryce

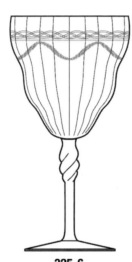

325-6
Clear or Yellow Iridescent,
Geometric Band & Swags
325
Bryce

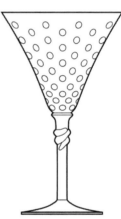

BRY 9
Oval Cuts, Twisted Stem
Bryce

BRY 21
Gray Cut Vines & Leaves,
Twisted Stem
Bryce

Columbine
Gray Cut Leaves & Vine,
Twisted Stem
Bryce

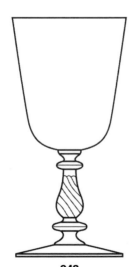

942
Clear or Various
Color Bowls
Bryce

942-1
Cut Laurel Band
942
Bryce

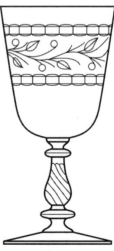

Regina
Cut Plants
942
Bryce

Prince Consort
Cut 1A,
Leaves & Thumbprints
942
Bryce

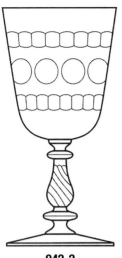

942-2
Dot & Panel Cuts
942
Bryce

942-3
Horizontal, Vertical
& Oval Cuts
942
Bryce

942-5
Gray Cut Wheat
942
Bryce

Lace
Etch 515, Floral
942
Bryce

942-4
Etched Floral & Scrolls
942
Bryce

Whitehall
Optic Bowl, Various Bowl
& Foot Colors
950
Bryce

BRY 2
Liquor Cocktail Shown
Plain
Bryce

735-2
Crisscross & Vertical Cuts
735
Bryce

265
Plain
Bryce

Etch 321
Fleur-de-lis
265
Bryce

Classic
Plain
235, 270
Bryce

235-2
Crisscross & Vertical Cuts
235
Bryce

Classic Platinum
Platinum Bands & Foot Trim
270
Bryce

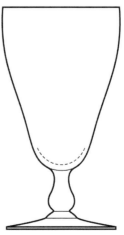

606
Plain
Bryce

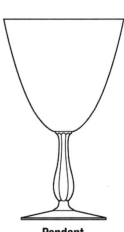

Pendant
Plain
6A
Bryce

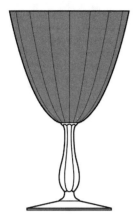

Pendant
Brown Optic Bowl
6A
Bryce

Harvest
Cut 267½, Gray Cut Leaves
6A
Bryce

Wreath
Cut Leaves
6A
Bryce

Rhythm
Cut 301½,
Floral Band
6A
Bryce

Snowflake
Cut 276½
6A
Bryce

6A-1
Gray Cut Floral
6A
Bryce

22A
Plain
Bryce

22A-3
Optic Bowl,
Gold Bowl & Foot Trim
22A
Bryce

22A-1
Platinum Bands
22A
Bryce

Spring Flower
Gray Cut Floral
22A
Bryce

22A-2
Thumbprint & Fan Cuts
22A
Bryce

Delhi
Clear or Various Color Bowls
946
Bryce

946-1
Gray Cut Floral,
Polished Dots
946
Bryce

Symphony
Plain
1A
Bryce

Symphony
Amethyst Bowl & Foot
1A
Bryce

Snowflower
Cut 299, Leaves
1A
Bryce

Autumn
Cut 267½, Gray Cut Leaves
1A
Bryce

Baroque
Leaf & Dot Cuts
1A
Bryce

Woodflower
Cut 266, Floral Cuts
1A
Bryce

1A
Gold Fleur-de-lis
Bryce

Trellis
Vertical & Oval Cuts
11A
Bryce

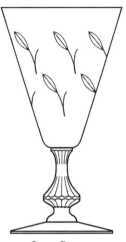

Snowflower
Cut 299, Leaves
16A
Bryce

20A
Plain
Bryce

20A-1
Gray Cut Wheat
20A
Bryce

Lenox
Cut 323, Laurel Band
20A
Bryce

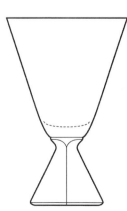

Lido
Clear, Green, or Yellow
Square Foot
2A
Bryce

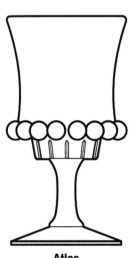

Atlas
Pressed Glass
Bryce

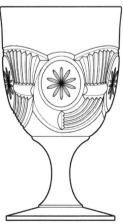

Clear Circle
Pressed Glass
Bryce

Beaded Oval & Scroll
Pressed Glass
Bryce

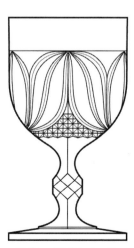

Tulip with Sawtooth
Pressed Glass
Bryce

Bryce

Horn of Plenty
Pressed Glass
Bryce

Grand
Pressed Glass
Bryce

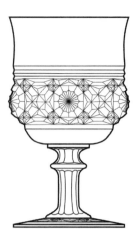

Hawaiian Lei
Pressed Glass
Bryce

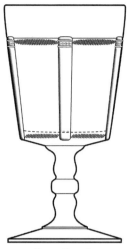

Rope Bands
Pressed Glass
Bryce

Rosette
Pressed Glass
Bryce

Paneled Daisy
Pressed Glass
Bryce

Paneled Forget Me Not
Pressed Glass
Bryce

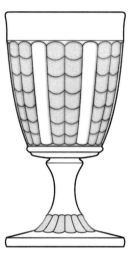

Fishscale
Pressed Glass
Bryce

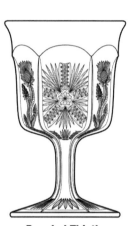

Paneled Thistle
Pressed Glass
Bryce

Thistle
Pressed Glass
Bryce

Teasel
Pressed Glass
Bryce

Rose in the Snow
Clear or Vaseline,
Pressed Glass
Bryce

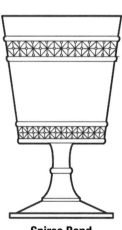

Spirea Band
Clear or Amber,
Pressed Glass
Bryce

Yale
Plain, Pressed Glass
Bryce

Yale
Gray Cut Leaves,
Pressed Glass
Bryce

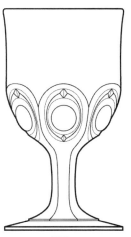

Filly
Pressed Glass
Bryce

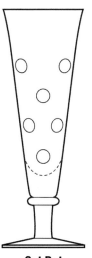

Cut Dot
Pilsner Shown
Polished Cut Dots
180
Bryce

Pirouette
Iced Tea Shown
Clear, Amethyst or Brown Bowl
3A
Bryce

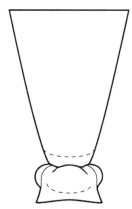

Tempo
Clear, Brown or Green Bowl
5A
Bryce

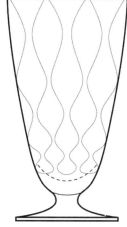

Monterey
Clear or Various Colors,
Diamond Optic Bowl
9A
Bryce

Modern
Iced Tea Shown
Various Color Bowls
761
Bryce

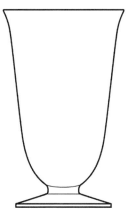

Classic Flared
Plain
763
Bryce

El Rancho
Clear or Various Colors,
Textured
1137
Bryce

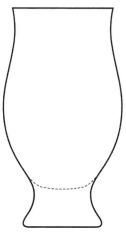

Silhouette
Clear or Various Colors, Plain
1138
Bryce

Patio
Tumbler Shown
Clear or Various Colors, Textured Panels
1325
Bryce

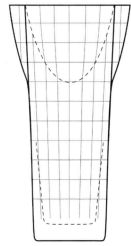

Ensenada
Highball Shown
Block Optic, Square Foot
1104
Bryce

888
Tumbler Shown
Cobalt, Plain
Bryce

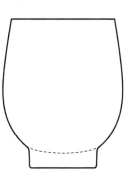

Holiday
Juice Shown
Clear, Green or Yellow, Plain
1139
Bryce

Turkey Eagle
Highball Shown
Smoke Eagle Emblem
1102
Bryce

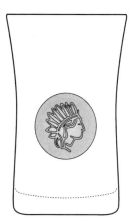

Indian Head
Tumbler Shown
Amber Emblem
1104 ¼
Bryce

Engraving 294
Tumbler Shown
Etched Fleur-de-lis
Bryce

Hobnail
Red
Brylane Home

Bubbly
Wine Shown
Bubbles in Bowl
Buzz

Janette
Amethyst Bowl,
Crisscross & Fan Cuts
76379
Caesar

Panache
Various Color Swirls
Caithness Glass

Tiara
Toasting Glass Shown
Crisscross & Swag Cuts
Caithness Glass

Diane
Plain
Caithness Glass

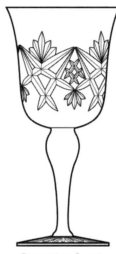

Brampton Court
Crisscross & Fan Cuts
Caithness Glass

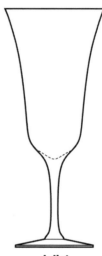

Juliet
Plain
Caithness Glass

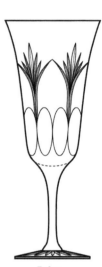

Priory
Panel & Fan Cuts
Caithness Glass

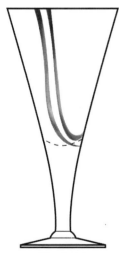

Charisma
Black & Gray Lines
Caithness Glass

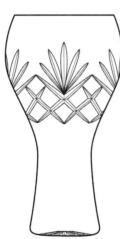

CTG 1
Crisscross & Fan Cuts
Caithness Glass

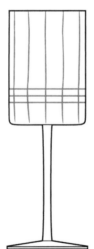

Graphic Weave
White Wine Shown
Gray Vertical &
Horizontal Cuts
Calvin Klein

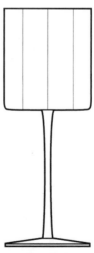

Faceted
Red Wine Shown
Octagonal Bowl
Calvin Klein

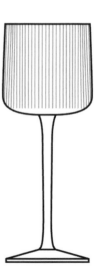

CKC 4
Optic Bowl
Calvin Klein

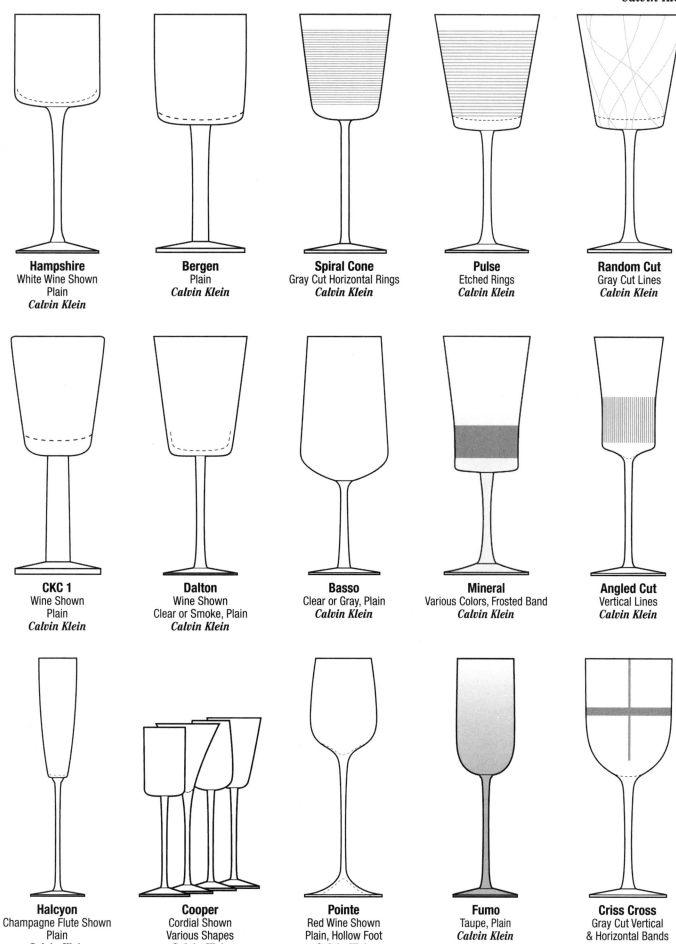

Hampshire
White Wine Shown
Plain
Calvin Klein

Bergen
Plain
Calvin Klein

Spiral Cone
Gray Cut Horizontal Rings
Calvin Klein

Pulse
Etched Rings
Calvin Klein

Random Cut
Gray Cut Lines
Calvin Klein

CKC 1
Wine Shown
Plain
Calvin Klein

Dalton
Wine Shown
Clear or Smoke, Plain
Calvin Klein

Basso
Clear or Gray, Plain
Calvin Klein

Mineral
Various Colors, Frosted Band
Calvin Klein

Angled Cut
Vertical Lines
Calvin Klein

Halcyon
Champagne Flute Shown
Plain
Calvin Klein

Cooper
Cordial Shown
Various Shapes
Calvin Klein

Pointe
Red Wine Shown
Plain, Hollow Foot
Calvin Klein

Fumo
Taupe, Plain
Calvin Klein

Criss Cross
Gray Cut Vertical
& Horizontal Bands
Calvin Klein

Calvin Klein

Beekman
Plain, Square Foot
Calvin Klein

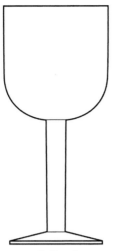

Bellport
Plain
Calvin Klein

Parker
Plain
Calvin Klein

Clinton
Lime Green or Blue Bowl
Calvin Klein

Caspian
Wine Shown
Gray Cut Rings
Calvin Klein

Enfield
Wine Shown
Plain
Calvin Klein

Tula
Plain
Calvin Klein

Scattered Flowers
Gray Cut Flower Petals
Calvin Klein

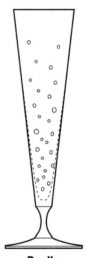

Boulle
Champagne Flute Shown
Bubbles in Bowl
Calvin Klein

Millbrook
Plain
Calvin Klein

Khaki
Various Colors, Plain
Calvin Klein

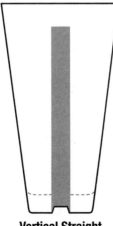

Vertical Straight
Highball Shown
Frosted Vertical Stripe
Calvin Klein

Gathered Lines
Double Old Fashioned Shown
Vertical Lines
Calvin Klein

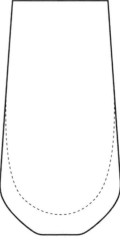

Gable
Highball Shown
Plain, Barware
Calvin Klein

166

Cambridge Shapes and Lines

3125 *Page 170*	**3104** *Page 170*	**3106** *Page 170*	**3114** *Page 171*	**3135** *Page 171*	**3134** *Page 171*	**3132** *Page 171*	**3035** *Page 172*	**3111** *Page 172*
3123 *Page 173*	**3120** *Page 173*	**3775** *Page 173*	**3725** *Page 174*	**3900** *Page 174*	**3700** *Page 174*	**3750** *Page 176*	**3675** *Page 176*	**3600** *Page 176*
3625 *Page 177*	**3650** *Page 177*	**3121** *Page 177*	**3126** *Page 178*	**3500** *Page 178*	**3776** *Page 179*	**3778** *Page 179*	**3777** *Page 180*	**3799** *Page 180*
3575 *Page 180*	**3779** *Page 181*	**3115** *Page 181*	**3144** *Page 182*	**3139** *Page 182*	**1958** *Page 183*	**3117** *Page 183*	**3116** *Page 183*	**3118** *Page 184*
300 *Page 184*	**3130** *Page 184*	**1936** *Page 185*	**3112** *Page 187*	**1402** *Page 187*	**1402/100** *Page 187*	**3122** *Page 188*	**3124** *Page 188*	**1066** *Page 188*

Cambridge Shapes and Lines

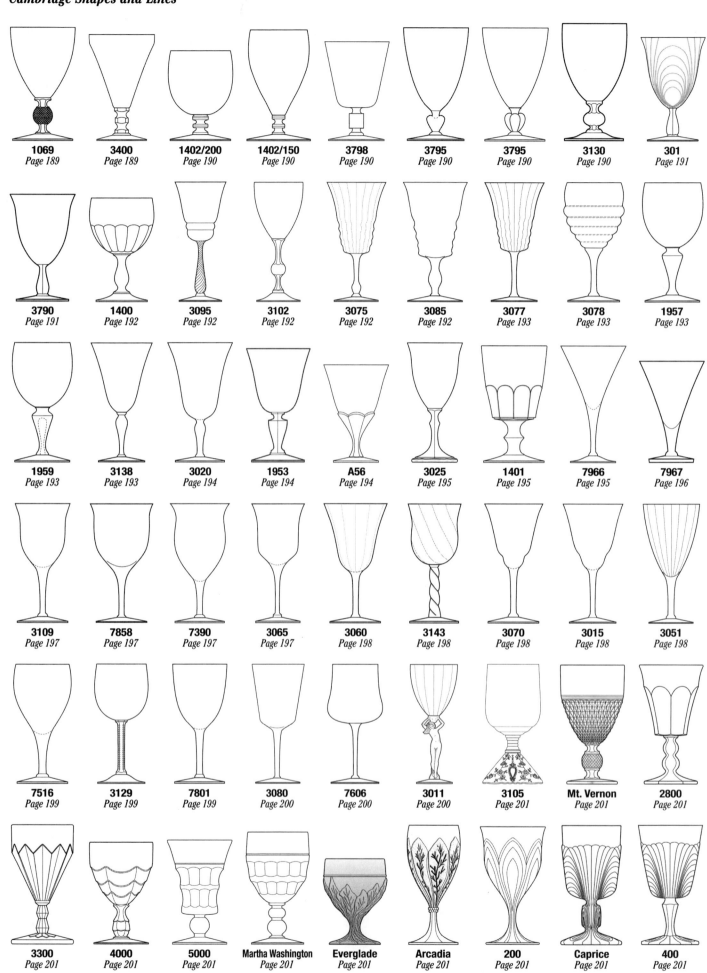

1069 *Page 189*	**3400** *Page 189*	**1402/200** *Page 190*	**1402/150** *Page 190*	**3798** *Page 190*	**3795** *Page 190*	**3795** *Page 190*	**3130** *Page 190*	**301** *Page 191*
3790 *Page 191*	**1400** *Page 192*	**3095** *Page 192*	**3102** *Page 192*	**3075** *Page 192*	**3085** *Page 192*	**3077** *Page 193*	**3078** *Page 193*	**1957** *Page 193*
1959 *Page 193*	**3138** *Page 193*	**3020** *Page 194*	**1953** *Page 194*	**A56** *Page 194*	**3025** *Page 195*	**1401** *Page 195*	**7966** *Page 195*	**7967** *Page 196*
3109 *Page 197*	**7858** *Page 197*	**7390** *Page 197*	**3065** *Page 197*	**3060** *Page 198*	**3143** *Page 198*	**3070** *Page 198*	**3015** *Page 198*	**3051** *Page 198*
7516 *Page 199*	**3129** *Page 199*	**7801** *Page 199*	**3080** *Page 200*	**7606** *Page 200*	**3011** *Page 200*	**3105** *Page 201*	**Mt. Vernon** *Page 201*	**2800** *Page 201*
3300 *Page 201*	**4000** *Page 201*	**5000** *Page 201*	**Martha Washington** *Page 201*	**Everglade** *Page 201*	**Arcadia** *Page 201*	**200** *Page 201*	**Caprice** *Page 201*	**400** *Page 201*

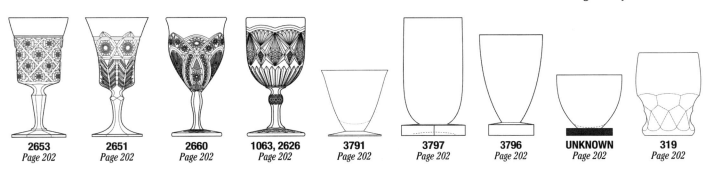

2653	2651	2660	1063, 2626	3791	3797	3796	UNKNOWN	319
Page 202	*Page 202*	*Page 202*	*Page 202*	*Page 202*	*Page 202*	*Page 202*	*Page 202*	*Page 202*

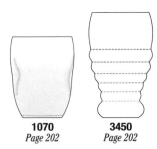

1070	3450
Page 202	*Page 202*

3400 Line
(with Gloria Pattern Shown)

Creamer	*Sugar*	*Dinner Plate*	*Cereal Bowl*	*Cup & Saucer*

3500 Gadroon Line

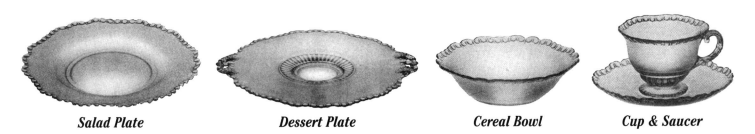

Salad Plate	*Dessert Plate*	*Cereal Bowl*	*Cup & Saucer*

Cambridge

Deauville
Yellow Bowl,
Etched Geometric
3125
Cambridge

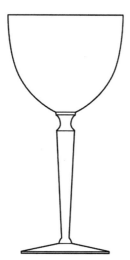

3104
Clear or Various Bowl
& Stem Colors, Plain
Cambridge

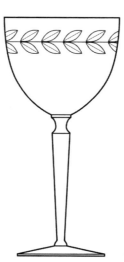

Laurel Wreath
Cut Laurel Band
3104
Cambridge

Diane
Etch 752, Floral
3104
Cambridge

Elaine
Etched Floral
3104
Cambridge

3106
Plain
Cambridge

Laurel Wreath
Cut Laurel Band
3106
Cambridge

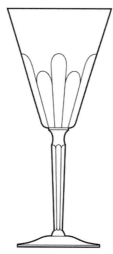

Sunnybrook
Panel Cuts
3106
Cambridge

Brentwood
Vertical Cuts
3106
Cambridge

Stafford
Cut 850, Crisscross & Fan
3106
Cambridge

Rose Point
Etched Floral,
Plain or Gold Trim
3106
Cambridge

Elaine
Etched Floral
3106
Cambridge

Diane
Etched Floral
3106
Cambridge

Lily of the Valley
Etched Floral
3106
Cambridge

Apple Blossom
Gold Floral Design D1036
3106
Cambridge

3114
Plain
Cambridge

Candlelight
Candle & Vertical Cuts
3114
Cambridge

Candlelight
Etch 897, Plain or
Gold Encrusted
3114
Cambridge

3135
Clear or Various Color
Optic Bowls
Cambridge

Apple Blossom
Etch 744, Clear or Various
Colors, Plain or Optic Bowls
3135
Cambridge

Gloria
Etch 746, Floral,
Clear or Various Colors
3135
Cambridge

Cleo
Etched Floral
3135
Cambridge

Broadmoor
Cut 951, Floral
3134
Cambridge

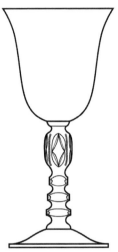

3132
Plain
Cambridge

Belfast
Cut 942, Crisscross
3132
Cambridge

Commodore
Cut Floral
3132
Cambridge

Mansard
Cut 906, Crisscross & Fan
3132
Cambridge

Neo Classic
Cut 907,
Thumbprints & Fans
3132
Cambridge

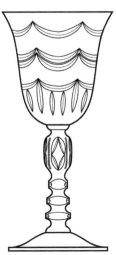

Rochelle
Cut 857, Verticals & Swags
3132
Cambridge

Sylvia
Cut 904, Leaves
3132
Cambridge

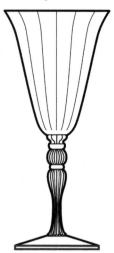

3035
Clear or Various Colors,
Plain or Optic Bowl
Cambridge

Cut 613
Floral
3035
Cambridge

Cut 614
Floral
3035
Cambridge

Cut 616
Floral
3035
Cambridge

Cut 621
Floral
3035
Cambridge

3035-2
Floral
3035
Cambridge

Gloria
Etch 746, Floral,
Clear or Various Colors
3035
Cambridge

Rosalie
Etch 731, Floral,
Clear or Various Colors
3035
Cambridge

Lorna
Etch 748, Floral,
Clear or Various Colors
3035
Cambridge

Elaine
Etched Floral
3035
Cambridge

Portia
Etched Floral
3035
Cambridge

Apple Blossom
Etch 744, Floral,
Clear or Various Colors
3035
Cambridge

3111
Clear or Various
Color Bowls, Plain
Cambridge

Candlelight
Candle & Floral Cuts
3111
Cambridge

Candlelight
Etch 897, Plain or
Gold Encrusted
3111
Cambridge

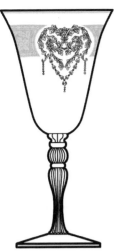

Bordero
Gold Etch D/1049
3111
Cambridge

Aero Optic
Clear or Various Colors,
Optic Bowl
3123
Cambridge

Rosalie
Etch 731, Floral, Clear or
Various Colors, Optic Bowl
3123
Cambridge

3120
Optic Bowl
Cambridge

Achilles
Cut 698, Floral
3120
Cambridge

Berkeley
Cut 85, Floral
3120
Cambridge

Rose Point
Cut 852, Floral
3120
Cambridge

Portia
Etched Floral
3120
Cambridge

Majestic
Etch 732, Scrolls,
Clear or Various Colors
3120
Cambridge

Diane
Etch 752, Floral
3120
Cambridge

Apple Blossom
Etch 744, Floral,
Clear or Various Colors
3120
Cambridge

Etch 733
Clear or Various Colors,
Birds & Urn
3120
Cambridge

Etch 739
Clear or Various Colors, Urn
3120
Cambridge

Gloria
Etch 746, Floral
3120
Cambridge

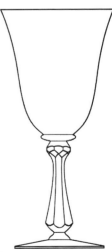

Arlington
Plain
3775
Cambridge

Roxbury
Cut 1030, Floral
3775
Cambridge

Chantilly
Etched Floral
3775
Cambridge

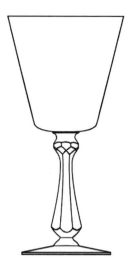

Castleton
Plain
3725
Cambridge

Bijou
Cut 1011, Vertical Cuts
3725
Cambridge

Cadet
Panel Cuts
3725
Cambridge

Lancelot
Crisscross & Vertical Cuts
3725
Cambridge

Laurel Wreath
Cut Laurel Band
3725
Cambridge

Plaza
Vertical Cuts
3725
Cambridge

Star
Cut 1016, Vertical
& Starbursts
3725
Cambridge

Wildflower
Etched Floral,
Plain or Gold Trim
3725
Cambridge

Corinth
Clear or Various Colors,
Optic Bowl
3900
Cambridge

Dunkirk
Plain
3700
Cambridge

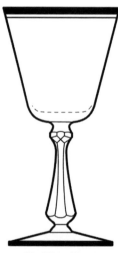

Wedding Band
Gold Bands & Foot Trim
3700
Cambridge

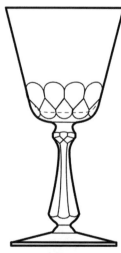

Ardsley
Panel Cuts
3700
Cambridge

Strathmore
Cut 1006, Panel Cuts
3700
Cambridge

Laurel Wreath
Cut Laurel Band
3700
Cambridge

Plymouth
Vertical & Horizontal Cuts
3700
Cambridge

Concord
Crisscross & Vertical Cuts
3700
Cambridge

King Edward
Cut 821, Crisscross & Dots
3700
Cambridge

Chesterfield
Vertical, Horizontal
& Oval Cuts
3700
Cambridge

3700-5
Crisscross & Oval Cuts
3700
Cambridge

Manor
Crisscross Cuts
3700
Cambridge

Empire
Cut 1010, Leaves
3700
Cambridge

3700-2
Cut Starbursts
3700
Cambridge

Cambridge Rose
Cut Floral
3700
Cambridge

Tempo
Cut 1029, Floral
3700
Cambridge

Montrose
Cut Floral
3700
Cambridge

3700-4
Cut Floral
3700
Cambridge

3700-1
Cut Abstract Pineapple
with Leaves
3700
Cambridge

3700-3
Cut Plant
3700
Cambridge

Cambridge

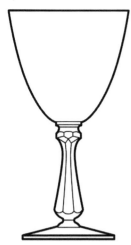

Charleston
Plain
3750
Cambridge

Wedding Band
Gold Trim
3750
Cambridge

3750-1
Gold Etch
Rose Point Medallion
3750
Cambridge

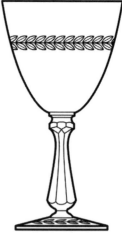

Minton Wreath
Cut Laurel Band
3750
Cambridge

Bexley
Cut 1014, Crisscross & Fans
3750
Cambridge

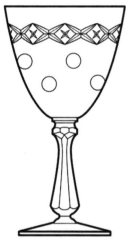

Hanover
Cut 1015,
Crisscross & Circles
3750
Cambridge

Ivy
Cut 1059, Leaves
3750
Cambridge

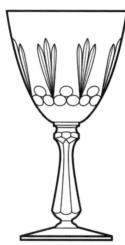

Euclid
Fans & Dot Cuts
3750
Cambridge

Harvest
Cut Wheat
3750
Cambridge

Fuchsia
Cut 1019, Floral
3750
Cambridge

Meadow Rose
Cut Floral
3750
Cambridge

3675
Plain, Optic Bowl
Cambridge

Blossom Time
Etched Floral, Plain,
Gold Trim or Encrusted
3675
Cambridge

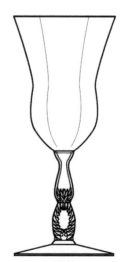

3600
Optic Bowl
Cambridge

Rose Marie
Cut 991, Rose
3600
Cambridge

Minuet
Cut 990, Floral
3600
Cambridge

Petite
Cut 988, Floral
3600
Cambridge

Chantilly
Etched Floral, Plain,
Gold Trim or Encrusted
3600
Cambridge

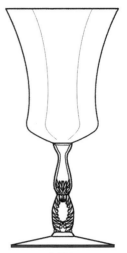

3625
Optic Bowl
Cambridge

Chantilly
Etched Floral
3625
Cambridge

3650
Plain
Cambridge

Astoria
Gold Trim
3650
Cambridge

Meadow Rose
Cut Floral
3650
Cambridge

Blossom Time
Gold Encrusted Floral
3650
Cambridge

3121
Plain or Optic Bowls,
Clear or Various Colors
Cambridge

Achilles
Cut 698, Floral
3121
Cambridge

Cut 640
Floral
3121
Cambridge

Cut 654
Floral
3121
Cambridge

Cut 655
Floral
3121
Cambridge

Rose Point
Etched Floral, Plain,
Gold Trim or Encrusted
3121
Cambridge

Portia
Etched Floral, Plain,
Gold Trim or Encrusted
3121
Cambridge

Wildflower
Etched Floral, Plain,
Gold Trim or Encrusted
3121
Cambridge

Elaine
Etched Floral, Plain
or Gold Encrusted
3121
Cambridge

3126
Clear or Various Colors,
Plain or Optic Bowl
Cambridge

3126
Platinum Bands &
Foot Trim, Optic Bowl
Cambridge

Elaine
Etched Floral
3126
Cambridge

Portia
Etched Floral,
Plain or Gold Encrusted
3126
Cambridge

Valencia
Etch 761, Floral
3126
Cambridge

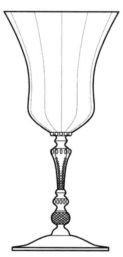

Gadroon
Clear or Various Colors,
Plain or Optic Bowl
3500
Cambridge

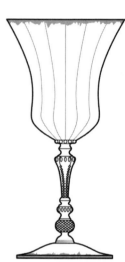

Gadroon
Gold or Platinum
Bowl & Foot Trim
3500
Cambridge

Adonis
Cut Floral
3500
Cambridge

Croesus
Cut Floral
3500
Cambridge

Harvest
Cut 1053, Wheat
3500
Cambridge

Victory Wreath
Cut Leaves
3500
Cambridge

Chintz
Etch 758, Floral
3500
Cambridge

Diane
Etch 752, Floral
3500
Cambridge

Elaine
Etched Floral, Plain,
Gold Trim or Encrusted
3500
Cambridge

Minerva
Etched Floral
3500
Cambridge

Rose Point
Clear or Red Bowl, Etched Floral,
Plain, Gold Trim or Encrusted
3500
Cambridge

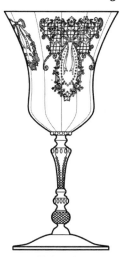

Valencia
Etched Floral, Plain
or Gold Encrusted
3500
Cambridge

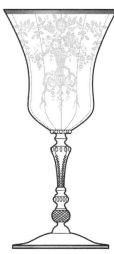

Decoration 1037
Clear, Cobalt or Ruby Bowl,
Gold Decoration 1037 & Trim
3500
Cambridge

Shelburne
Plain
3776
Cambridge

Minuet
Cut Floral
3776
Cambridge

Dover
Cut 1034, Floral
3776
Cambridge

Cortland
Cut 1037, Floral
3776
Cambridge

Maryland
Cut Floral
3776
Cambridge

Garland
Cut 1044, Floral
3776
Cambridge

Candlelight
Etched, Optic Bowl
3776
Cambridge

Century
Plain
3778
Cambridge

Ambassador
Cut 1038, Floral
3778
Cambridge

Cascade
Cut 1046, Swirls
3778
Cambridge

Deerfield
Cut 1033, Floral
3778
Cambridge

Fleurette
Cut 1032, Floral
3778
Cambridge

Larchmont
Cut 1036,
Laurel & Floral
3778
Cambridge

Winsor
Plain
3777
Cambridge

Fleurette
Cut 1032, Floral
3777
Cambridge

Melody
Cut 1035, Swags
3777
Cambridge

Patrician
Cut 1037, Floral
3777
Cambridge

Southgate
Cut 1045
3777
Cambridge

3799
Plain
Cambridge

Vogue
Cut Arches
3799
Cambridge

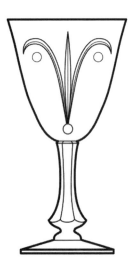

Jo Ann
Cut Dots & Lines
3799
Cambridge

Buttercup
Cut Floral
3799
Cambridge

Maytime
Cut Floral
3799
Cambridge

Regency (Stradivari)
Clear or Various Color Bowls
3575
Cambridge

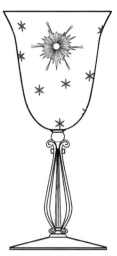

Celestial
Cut 930, Stars
3575
Cambridge

Symphony
Cut 929, Floral
3575
Cambridge

Diane
Etched Floral
3575
Cambridge

Portia
Etched Floral
3575
Cambridge

3779
Plain
Cambridge

Chantilly
Etched Floral
3779
Cambridge

Daffodil
Etched Floral
3779
Cambridge

Roselyn
Etched Floral
3779
Cambridge

3115
Clear or Various Colors,
Plain or Optic Bowls
Cambridge

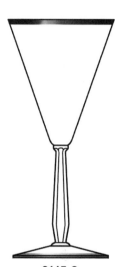

3115-2
Platinum Trim on Bowl,
Gold Band on Foot
3115
Cambridge

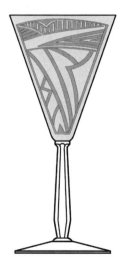

Etch 730
Pink Bowl
3115
Cambridge

Etch 733
Birds & Urn
3115
Cambridge

Etch 742
Wreath & Floral
3115
Cambridge

Cleo
Etched Swags
3115
Cambridge

Diane
Etch 752, Floral
3115
Cambridge

Majestic
Etch 732, Scrolls
3115
Cambridge

Rosalie
Etch 731, Floral,
Clear or Various Colors
3115
Cambridge

Virginian
Diamond Optic Bowl
3144
Cambridge

Sierra
Diamond Optic Bowl,
Frosted Stem
3144
Cambridge

3139
Plain
Cambridge

Triumph
Platinum Bowl
& Foot Trim
3139
Cambridge

Wedding Band
Gold Bowl & Foot Trim
3139
Cambridge

Laurel Wreath
Cut Laurel Band
3139
Cambridge

Lancelot
Cut Dots & Diamonds
3139
Cambridge

Juliana
Cut 997, Fans
3139
Cambridge

King George
Cut 1027, Leaves
3139
Cambridge

Buckingham
Vertical & Dot Cuts
3139
Cambridge

Regent
Cut 992, Crisscross & Dots
3139
Cambridge

Cranston
Cut 960, Crisscross & Floral
3139
Cambridge

Lyric
Cut 995, Floral
3139
Cambridge

Granada
Cut 1068, Floral & Thistle
3139
Cambridge

Maryland
Cut Floral
3139
Cambridge

Sicily
Cut 984, Floral
3139
Cambridge

Queen Mary
Plain
1958
Cambridge

Laurel Wreath
Cut Laurel Band
1958
Cambridge

Elite
Cut Swags
1958
Cambridge

1958-1
Crisscross & Dot Cuts
1958
Cambridge

Radiant Rose
Cut Rose
1958
Cambridge

3117
Plain
Cambridge

3116
Plain
Cambridge

Candlelight
Cut 897, Candle & Floral
3116
Cambridge

Corsage
Cut 107, Floral
3116
Cambridge

Glenmont
Cut 863, Floral
3116
Cambridge

Lucia
Cut 824, Floral
3116
Cambridge

Maryland
Cut Floral
3116
Cambridge

Sonora
Cut 895, Floral
3116
Cambridge

Wildflower
Etched Floral
3116
Cambridge

3118
Plain
Cambridge

Carnation
Cut 732, Floral
3118
Cambridge

Caprice
Clear or Various Colors,
Optic Bowl
300
Cambridge

Alpine
Clear or Blue Frosted Stem,
Optic Bowl
300
Cambridge

3130
Clear or Various Colors,
Optic Bowl
Cambridge

Auburn
Cut 867, Floral
3130
Cambridge

Cordelia
Cut 812, Floral
3130
Cambridge

Cut 538
Floral
3130
Cambridge

Cut 541
Floral
3130
Cambridge

Cut 652
Spirals & Stars
3130
Cambridge

Cut 656
Floral
3130
Cambridge

Cut 657
Dots & Stars
3130
Cambridge

Glendale
Cut 1028, Floral
3130
Cambridge

Ravenna
Cut Floral
3130
Cambridge

Wedding Rose
Vertical & Floral Cuts
3130
Cambridge

Winthrop
Cut 983, Floral
3130
Cambridge

3130-1
Yellow, Cut Floral
3130
Cambridge

Apple Blossom
Etch 744, Floral,
Clear or Various Colors
3130
Cambridge

Diane
Etch 752, Floral
3130
Cambridge

Elaine
Etched Floral
3130
Cambridge

Etch 739
Various Colors, Urn
3130
Cambridge

Gloria
Etch 726, Floral,
Clear or Various Colors
3130
Cambridge

Lorna
Etch 784, Floral
3130
Cambridge

Majestic
Etch 732, Scrolls,
Clear or Various Colors
3130
Cambridge

Portia
Etched Floral
3130
Cambridge

Rosalie
Etch 731, Floral,
Clear or Various Colors
3130
Cambridge

Pristine
Plain
1936
Cambridge

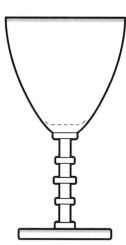

Astoria
Decoration 450,
Gold Bowl & Foot Trim
1936
Cambridge

Cambridge

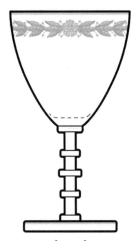

Laurel
Decoration 1050,
Gold Encrusted
1936
Cambridge

American Star
Crisscross, Vertical
& Star Cuts
1936
Cambridge

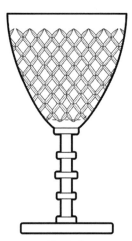

Belfast
Cut 942, Crisscross
1936
Cambridge

Broadmoor
Crisscross & Floral Cuts
1936
Cambridge

Chesterfield
Vertical, Horizontal
& Dot Cuts
1936
Cambridge

Courtship
Cut 939, Floral
1936
Cambridge

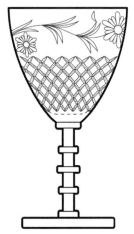

Cranston
Cut 960, Crisscross & Floral
1936
Cambridge

Grecian
Cut 936, Laurel & Circles
1936
Cambridge

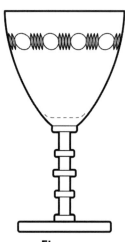

Etruscan
Cut 935, Vertical & Circles
1936
Cambridge

Fantasy
Cut 921, Plants
1936
Cambridge

Killarney
Cut 920, Dots & Lines
1936
Cambridge

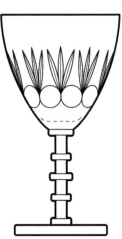

Neo Classic
Cut 907, Fans & Dots
1936
Cambridge

The Pines
Cut 919, Plants & Circles
1936
Cambridge

Strawflower
Cut 922, Floral
1936
Cambridge

Firenze
Etch 775, Scrolls
1936
Cambridge

186

Wildflower
Etched Floral
1936
Cambridge

Daffodil
Etched Floral,
Gold Encrusted
1936
Cambridge

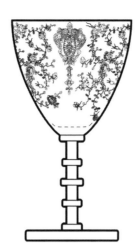

Rose Point
Etched Floral,
Plain or Gold Trim
1936
Cambridge

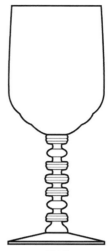

3112
Clear or Blue Bowl & Foot
Cambridge

Ye Olde Ivy
Etched Leaves
3112
Cambridge

Yukon
Frosted Bands
3112
Cambridge

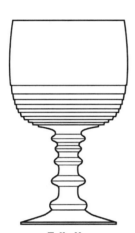

Tally Ho
Clear or Various Colors,
Plain
1402
Cambridge

1402-1
Crisscross & Fan Cuts
1402
Cambridge

Grape
Etched Grapes & Leaves
1402
Cambridge

Imperial Hunt
Etched Landscape
1402
Cambridge

Tally Ho
Clear or Various
Color Bowls, Plain
1402/100
Cambridge

1402/100-4
Crosshatch & Fan Cuts
1402/100
Cambridge

Elaine
Etched Floral,
Plain or Gold Encrusted
1402/100
Cambridge

Minerva
Gold Encrusted Floral
1402/100
Cambridge

Valencia
Etch 761, Floral
1402/100
Cambridge

Cambridge

Yukon
Frosted Bands
1402/100
Cambridge

3122
Clear or Various Colors,
Plain or Optic Bowl
Cambridge

Wedding Band
Gold or Platinum Trim
3122
Cambridge

3122-1
Cut Floral
3122
Cambridge

Gloria
Etch 746, Floral,
Yellow Bowl
3122
Cambridge

Diane
Clear or Various Colors,
Plain or Gold Encrusted
3122
Cambridge

Portia
Etched Floral
3122
Cambridge

3124
Clear or Various Colors,
Plain or Optic Bowl
Cambridge

Apple Blossom
Etch 744, Floral
3124
Cambridge

Gloria
Etch 746, Floral
3124
Cambridge

Minerva
Etch 763, Floral
3124
Cambridge

Portia
Etched Floral
3124
Cambridge

Aurora
Clear or Various Colors,
Plain or Optic Bowl
1066
Cambridge

1066
Gold Bands & Foot Trim,
Optic Bowl
Cambridge

Laurel Wreath
Cut Laurel Band
1066
Cambridge

Newport
Cut 762, Floral
1066
Cambridge

Cut 622
Crisscross & Floral
1066
Cambridge

Cut 629
Crisscross & Vertical
1066
Cambridge

Cut 690
Crisscross & Fans
1066
Cambridge

Apple Blossom
Etch 744, Floral,
Clear or Green Bowl
1066
Cambridge

Diane
Etch 752, Floral,
Clear or Various Colors
1066
Cambridge

Elaine
Etched Floral
1066
Cambridge

Gloria
Etch 746, Floral,
Clear or Various Colors
1066
Cambridge

Portia
Etched Floral
1066
Cambridge

Bretton
Ruby Bowl, Etched Floral
1066
Cambridge

1069
Plain
Cambridge

Apple Blossom
Etch 744, Floral,
Black Stem
1069
Cambridge

3400
Clear or Various Color Bowls
Cambridge

Apple Blossom
Etch 744, Floral,
Clear or Various Colors
3400
Cambridge

Gloria
Etch 746, Floral
3400
Cambridge

1402/200
Plain
Cambridge

Chintz
Etch 766, Floral
1402/200
Cambridge

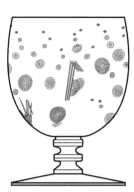

Vichy
Etch 765, Geometric
1402/200
Cambridge

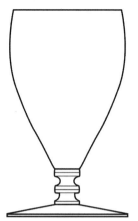

Tally Ho
Plain
1402/150
Cambridge

Elaine
Etched Floral
1402/150
Cambridge

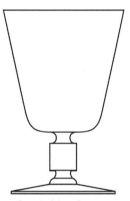

Cambridge Square
Plain
3798
Cambridge

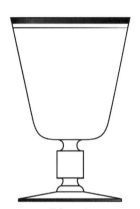

Triumph
Platinum Bowl & Foot Trim
3798
Cambridge

Sweetheart
Sculpted Heart Stem
3795
Cambridge

Allegro
4 Lobe Stem
3795
Cambridge

Paisley
Cut P125, Swirls & Leaves
3795
Cambridge

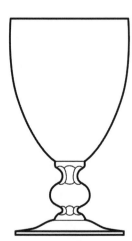

3103
Clear or Various Colors,
Plain
Cambridge

Laurel Wreath
Cut Laurel Band
3103
Cambridge

3103-1
Crisscross & Fan Cuts
3103
Cambridge

Buckingham
Cut 937,
Crisscross & Dots
3103
Cambridge

Exeter
Crisscross Cuts
3103
Cambridge

King Edward
Cut 821,
Crisscross & Circles
3103
Cambridge

3103-2
Crisscross & Dot Cuts
3103
Cambridge

Marlene
Etched Floral
3103
Cambridge

Ye Olde Ivy
Etched Ivy
3103
Cambridge

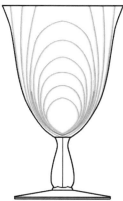

Caprice
Plain, Optic Bowl
301
Cambridge

Simplicity
Clear or Smoke Bowl
3790
Cambridge

Victory
Platinum Trim
3790
Cambridge

Blue Danube
Crosshatch Cuts
3790
Cambridge

Crown
Crisscross Cuts
3790
Cambridge

Flight
Cut Swirls
3790
Cambridge

Orion
Cut Stars & Arches
3790
Cambridge

Festoon
Cut 1071, Plants
3790
Cambridge

Lynbrook
Cut 1070, Floral
3790
Cambridge

Autumn
Cut Leaves
3790
Cambridge

Starburst
Cut 4P, Stars
3790
Cambridge

Starlite
Cut 10P, Stars
3790
Cambridge

Lily of the Valley
Cut 1069, Floral
3790
Cambridge

Tropical
Cut Palm Tree
3790
Cambridge

Magnolia
Etched Floral
3790
Cambridge

1400
Clear or Various Colors,
Panel Cuts
Cambridge

Cut 643
Panels & Crisscross
1400
Cambridge

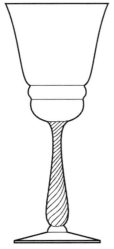

3095
Clear or Various Colors,
Plain
Cambridge

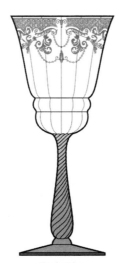

Etch 520
All Pink or Clear Bowl
& Green Stem
3095
Cambridge

3102
Plain
Cambridge

Marlene
Etched Floral
3102
Cambridge

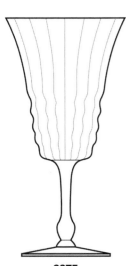

3075
Clear or Various Colors,
Optic Bowl
Cambridge

Imperial Hunt
Various Colors, Etched,
Plain or Gold Encrusted
3075
Cambridge

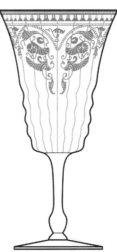

Etch 704
Various Colors
3075
Cambridge

3085
Plain
Cambridge

Imperial Hunt
Etch 718, Landscape,
Clear or Various Colors
3085
Cambridge

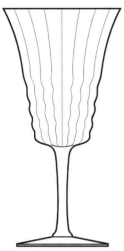

3077
Clear or Various Colors,
Optic Bowl
Cambridge

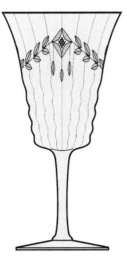

3077-1
Light Blue, Cut Plant
3077
Cambridge

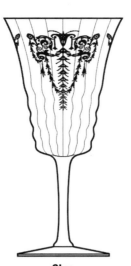

Cleo
Clear or Various Colors,
Etched Swags
3077
Cambridge

3078
Various Colors
Cambridge

Sonata
Plain
1957
Cambridge

Charm
Cut Swirls & Circles
1957
Cambridge

Leaves
Gray Cut Autumn Leaves
1957
Cambridge

Spring
Cut Floral
1957
Cambridge

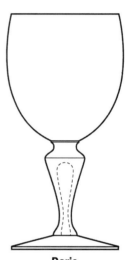

Doric
Plain, Bubble in Stem
1959
Cambridge

1959-1
Cut Leaves,
Bubble in Stem
1959
Cambridge

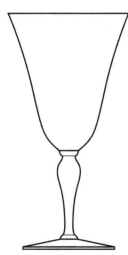

3138
Plain
Cambridge

Carnation
Cut 732, Floral
3138
Cambridge

Spring Beauty
Cut 999, Floral
3138
Cambridge

Chantilly
Etched Floral
3138
Cambridge

Portia
Etched Floral
3138
Cambridge

Cambridge

Rose Marie
Etch 755, Roses
3138
Cambridge

3020
Plain
Cambridge

Cut 4074
Floral, Optic Bowl
3020
Cambridge

Chrysanthemum
Etched Floral
3020
Cambridge

Etch 521
Grapes & Leaves
3020
Cambridge

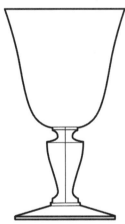

Cathedral
Plain
1953
Cambridge

Ambassador
Vertical & Swag Cuts
1953
Cambridge

Joan of Arc
Cut
1953
Cambridge

Old English
Cut 10, Fans & Stars
1953
Cambridge

Old Master
Crisscross & Horizontal Cuts
1953
Cambridge

Silver Wheat
Gray Cut Plant
1953
Cambridge

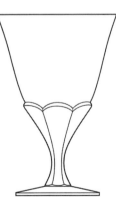

Today
Plain
A56
Cambridge

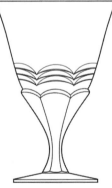

Formal
Cut Arches
A56
Cambridge

Roses
Cut 2P, Floral
A56
Cambridge

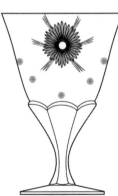

Starlite
Cut 10P, Stars
A56
Cambridge

194

Tomorrow
Cut Sprigs
A56
Cambridge

3025
Clear or Various Colors, Plain
Cambridge

Apple Blossom
Etch 744, Floral
3025
Cambridge

Gloria
Etch 746, Floral
3025
Cambridge

Etch 405
Various Color Stems
3025
Cambridge

Jefferson
Clear or Various Colors,
Pressed Glass
1401
Cambridge

Trumpet
Plain
7966
Cambridge

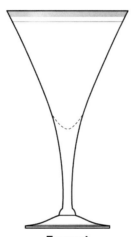

Trumpet
Gold Bands & Foot Trim
7966
Cambridge

Rondo
Cut Swirls
7966
Cambridge

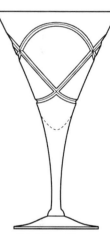

Wedding Rings
Cut Arches
7966
Cambridge

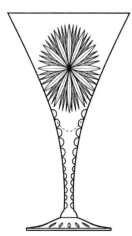

Sunburst
Cut 1002, Stars & Ovals
7966
Cambridge

Laurel Wreath
Cut Laurel Band
7966
Cambridge

Flame
Cut Flames
7966
Cambridge

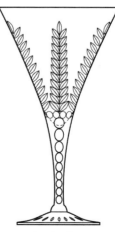

Lexington
Cut Plants
7966
Cambridge

Vichy
Etch 765, Geometric
7966
Cambridge

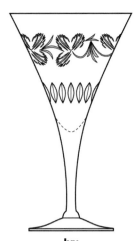

Ivy
Cut 1059, Ivy Leaves
7966
Cambridge

Delhi
Cut 1078, Floral
7966
Cambridge

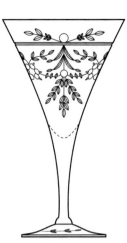

Avalon
Cut 806, Floral
7966
Cambridge

Lily of the Valley
Cut Floral
7966
Cambridge

Bacchus
Etched Grapevine
7966
Cambridge

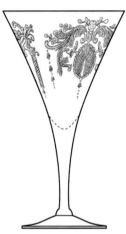

Candlelight
Etched Scrolls & Candle
7966
Cambridge

Chantilly
Etched Floral
7966
Cambridge

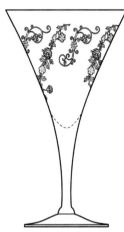

Elaine
Etched Floral
7966
Cambridge

Portia
Etched Floral
7966
Cambridge

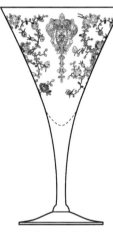

Rose Point
Etched Floral
7966
Cambridge

Golden Wheat
Decoration 1065,
Gold Wheat & Trim
7966
Cambridge

Apple Blossom
Decoration 1036,
Gold Floral
7966
Cambridge

Talisman Rose
Decoration 1063,
Gold Roses & Trim
7966
Cambridge

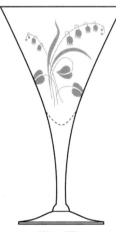

Woodlily
Gold Floral
7966
Cambridge

Melody
Plain
7967
Cambridge

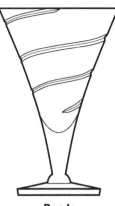

Rondo
Cut Swirls
7967
Cambridge

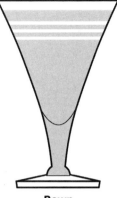

Dawn
Frosted
7967
Cambridge

Magnolia
Etched Floral
7967
Cambridge

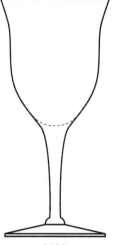

3109
Plain
Cambridge

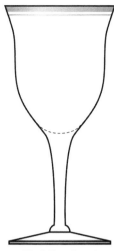

Wedding Band
Gold Bands & Foot Trim
3109
Cambridge

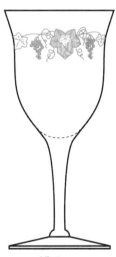

Vintage
Etched Grapes & Leaves
3109
Cambridge

Wedgewood
Etch 408, Wreath
3109
Cambridge

Ye Olde Ivy
Etched Ivy
3109
Cambridge

7858
Plain
Cambridge

Grape
Etched Grapes & Leaves
7858
Cambridge

Martha
Etched Grapes & Leaves
7858
Cambridge

Chrysanthemum
Etched Floral
7858
Cambridge

Adams
Etched Urn
7390
Cambridge

Chrysanthemum
Etched Floral
7390
Cambridge

Majestic
Etch 732, Pink
3065
Cambridge

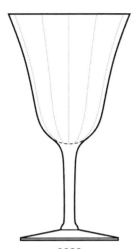

3060
Various Colors, Optic Bowl
Cambridge

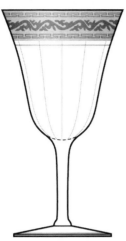

Etch 700
Gold Encrusted Band
3060
Cambridge

Etch 704
Clear or Various Colors,
Plain or Gold Encrusted
3060
Cambridge

Etch 702
Gold Encrusted
3060
Cambridge

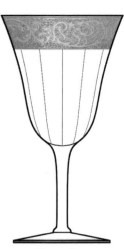

Florentine
Etch 703, Various Colors,
Plain or Gold Encrusted
3060
Cambridge

3060-1
Etch 703, Dark Amber,
Gold Encrusted
3060
Cambridge

Dresden Rose
Etch 722, Floral,
Pink or Green
3060
Cambridge

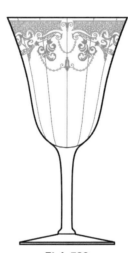

Etch 520
Clear or Various Colors,
Scrolls
3060
Cambridge

Cleo
Clear or Various Colors,
Etched Swags
3060
Cambridge

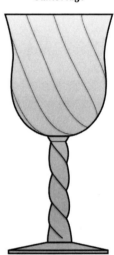

Gyro Optic
Various Colors,
Swirl Optic Bowl
3143
Cambridge

Beverly
Cut 843, Floral
3070
Cambridge

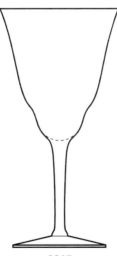

3015
Plain
Cambridge

Lorna
Etch 748, Floral,
Clear or Various Colors
3015
Cambridge

3051
Various Colors,
Optic Bowl
Cambridge

Florentine
Etch 703, Various Colors,
Plain or Gold Encrusted
3051
Cambridge

Etch 700
Gold Encrusted Band
3051
Cambridge

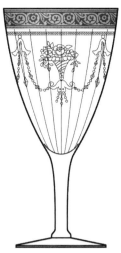

3051-3
Etched Urn,
Gold Encrusted Band
3051
Cambridge

Decoration 1
Various Colors, Gold
Encrusted Band, Etched Scrolls
3051
Cambridge

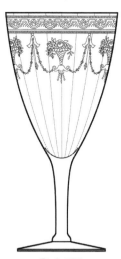

Etch 701
Various Colors, Plain,
Gold Trim or Gold Encrusted
3051
Cambridge

Wild Rose
Etched Rose
3051
Cambridge

Etch 408
Etched Wreath
7516
Cambridge

Wedgewood
Etched Wreath & Band
7516
Cambridge

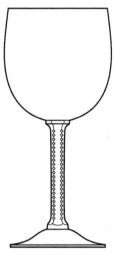

3129
Plain
Cambridge

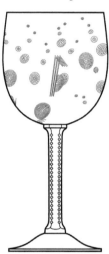

Vichy
Etch 765, Geometric
3129
Cambridge

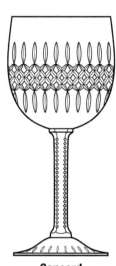

Concord
Crisscross & Vertical Cuts
3129
Cambridge

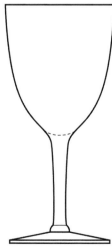

7801
Plain
Cambridge

Vichy
Etch 765, Geometric
7801
Cambridge

Swirl
Cut 791, Swirls & Dots
7801
Cambridge

Blossom Time
Etched Floral
7801
Cambridge

Chantilly
Etched Floral
7801
Cambridge

Cambridge

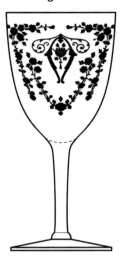

Diane
Etch 752, Floral
7801
Cambridge

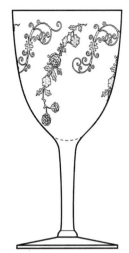

Elaine
Etched Floral
7801
Cambridge

Portia
Etched Floral
7801
Cambridge

Wildflower
Etched Floral
7801
Cambridge

3080
Plain
Cambridge

Chantilly
Etched Floral
3080
Cambridge

Hermosa
Cut 894, Floral
3080
Cambridge

7606
Plain
Cambridge

7606-1
Gray Cut Geometric & Floral
7606
Cambridge

Bordeaux
Etched Basket
7606
Cambridge

Cleo
Etched Floral
7606
Cambridge

Marjorie
Etched Floral
7606
Cambridge

Martha
Clear or Various Colors,
Etched Grapes & Leaves
7606
Cambridge

Old Fashioned Grape
Etch 401, Grapes
7606
Cambridge

Nude Stems
Clear or Various Colors
3011
Cambridge

Apple Blossom
Etch 744, Floral
3011
Cambridge

Rose Point
Gold Encrusted Floral
3011
Cambridge

Rose Point
Various Colors, Embossed
Floral Stem, Pressed Glass
3105
Cambridge

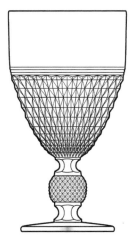

Mt. Vernon
Clear or Various Colors,
Pressed Glass
Cambridge

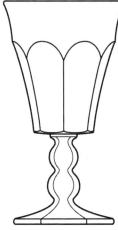

Colonial
Panels, Pressed Glass
2800
Cambridge

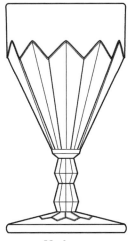

Moderne
Clear or Various Colors,
Panels, Pressed Glass
3300
Cambridge

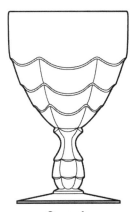

Cascade
Clear or Various Colors,
Pressed Glass
4000
Cambridge

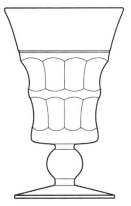

Heirloom
Clear or Various Colors,
Thumbprints, Pressed Glass
5000
Cambridge

Martha Washington
Clear or Various Colors,
Thumbprints,
Pressed Glass
Cambridge

Everglade
Clear or Blue,
Embossed Leaves,
Pressed Glass
Cambridge

Arcadia
Frosted Embossed Leaves,
Pressed Glass
Cambridge

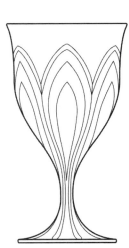

Caprice
Clear or Blue, Arches,
Pressed Glass
200
Cambridge

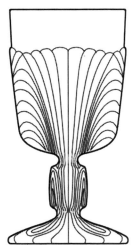

Caprice
Clear or Blue,
Pressed Glass
Cambridge

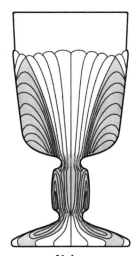

Alpine
Clear or Blue,
Partially Frosted,
Pressed Glass
Cambridge

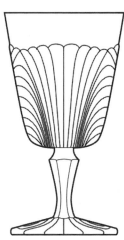

Caprice
Pressed Glass
400
Cambridge

Ribbon Candy
Blocks & Stars,
Pressed Glass
2653
Cambridge

Inverted Feather
Feathers & Stars,
Pressed Glass
2651
Cambridge

Wheat Sheaf
Stars & Arches,
Pressed Glass
2660
Cambridge

2626
Fans & Arches,
Pressed Glass
1063, 2626
Cambridge

Invitation
Plain
3791
Cambridge

Modern
Clear or Pink, Platinum Trim
3791
Cambridge

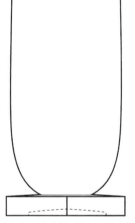

Cambridge Square
Plain, Square Foot
3797
Cambridge

Cambridge Circle
Plain, Round Foot
3796
Cambridge

Tuxedo
Various Foot Colors,
Round Foot
Cambridge

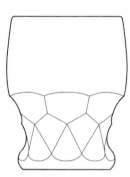

Georgian
Clear or Various Colors,
Honeycomb, Pressed Glass
319
Cambridge

1070
Various Colors, Pinched
Cambridge

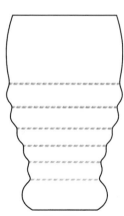

Nautilus
Clear or Various Colors
3450
Cambridge

Dahlia
Pressed Glass
Canton Glass

Chantilly
Optic Bowl
Carico

Elegante
Vertical Cuts
Carico

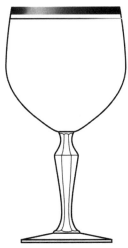

Reflections
Platinum Bands
Carico

Renaissance
Vertical & Horizontal Cuts
Carico

Tivoli
Blue/Gray, Black or
Green/Gray
Carico

La Maison du Roi
Gold Scrolls & Trim, Panels
Cartier

CTC 1
Plain
Cartier

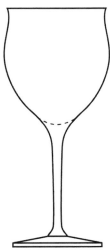

CTC 4
Plain
Cartier

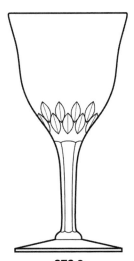

CTC 2
Cordial Shown
Vertical Cuts
Cartier

Du Prince
Vertical Cuts
Cartier

Des Must de Cartier
Gray & Clear Vertical Cuts
Cartier

Danse de Feu
Cut Swirls
Cartier

Des Must
Twisted Band
Stem Accents
Cartier

Bijoux
Champagne Flute Shown
Vertical & Panel Cuts
Cartier

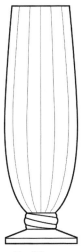

Venitienne
Champagne Flute Shown
Optic Bowl, Twisted Stem
Cartier

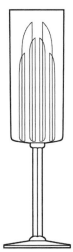

La Maison
Champagne Flute Shown
Vertical Cuts,
Flat Sided Stem
Cartier

De Louis Cartier
Vertical Cuts
Cartier

Cartier, Casa Cristina, Casafina

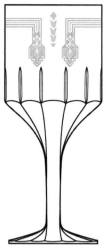

Des Ballets Russes
Etched Geometric,
Vertical Cuts
Cartier

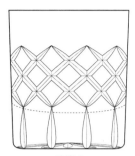

CTC 3
Tumbler Shown
Crisscross & Vertical Cuts
Cartier

Talavera
Cooler Shown
Gray Cut Diagonals
& Floral
Casa Cristina

CF1 2
Clear or Various Color Bowls
Casafina

Luster
Amber Bowl, Green Stem
Casafina

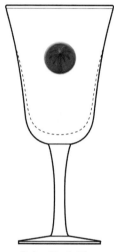

Palm Medallion
Amber or Green Medallion
Casafina

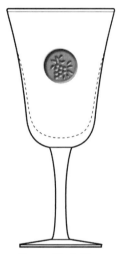

Grape Medallion
Amber or Green Medallion
Casafina

Meridian
Floral Medallion
Casafina

Red Dots
Champagne Flute Shown
Red Dots
Casafina

Square Base
Square Foot
Casafina

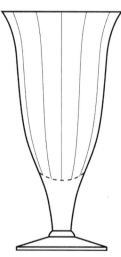

Optic
Optic Bowl
Casafina

Sandblast Stripes
Frosted Stripes
Casafina

Stripes
Green or Amber Stripes
Casafina

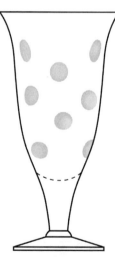

Dots
Gray Cut Dots
Casafina

Fish
Cut Fish
Casafina

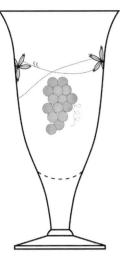

Grapes
Gray Cut Grapes & Leaves
Casafina

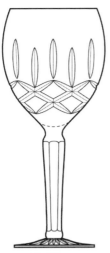

Kathleen
Red Wine Shown
Crisscross & Vertical Cuts
Cavan

Royal Cavan
Crosshatch Cuts
Cavan

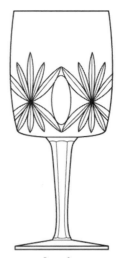

Annalee
Fan Cuts
Cavan

Shannon
Crisscross & Vertical Cuts
Cavan

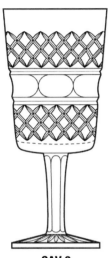

CAV 3
Crisscross & Oval Cuts
Cavan

Ramor
Crisscross & Vertical Cuts
Cavan

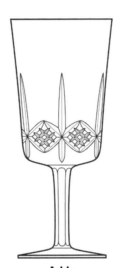

Arkle
Wine Shown
Crisscross & Vertical Cuts
Cavan

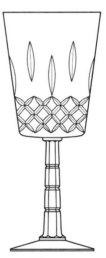

Killykeen
Crisscross & Vertical Cuts
Cavan

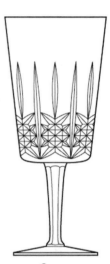

Cavan
Crisscross & Vertical Cuts
Cavan

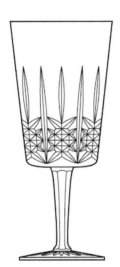

Cavan
Crisscross & Vertical Cuts,
Cut Foot
Cavan

Clontarf
Cut Harps
Cavan

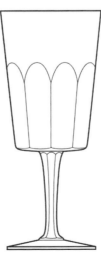

CAV 4
Wine Shown
Panel Cuts
Cavan

Sheelin
Crisscross & Fan Cuts
Cavan

Innisfree
Wine Large Shown
Crisscross & Vertical Cuts
Cavan

Bordeaux (Clear),
Andover (Gray),
Christiane (Lt. Blue)
Jacqueline (Pink), **Shannon** (Green)
Celebrity

Allegro
Optic Bowl, Platinum Trim
Celebrity

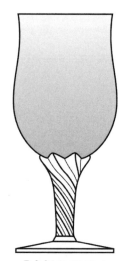

Brighton (Lt. Blue)
Cambridge (Cobalt),
Coco (Brown), **Hampton** (Smoke),
Stratford (Green)
Celebrity

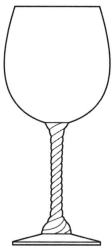

Kensington
Twisted Stem
Celebrity

Interlude
Black Bowl,
Twisted Stem
Celebrity

Wedding Band
Platinum Trim
Celebrity

Ebony
Black, Plain
Celebrity

Rhapsody
Black, Plain
Celebrity

Golden Rhapsody
Black, Gold Trim
Celebrity

Dynasty
Vertical Cuts
Celebrity

CEC 1
Smoke Bowl
Celebrity

CEC 2
Platinum Trim
Celebrity

Premium Krosno
White Wine Shown
Plain
The Cellar

Everyday
White Wine Shown
Plain
The Cellar

Victorian
Black, Panels
The Cellar

Serene
Highball Shown
Plain
The Cellar

Talia Ombre
Highball Shown
Clear/Blue, Barware
The Cellar

Classic
Highball Shown
Plain
The Cellar

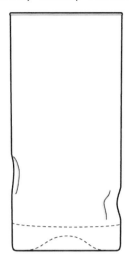

Silhouettes
Highball Shown
Clear or Blue,
Indented Base
The Cellar

Whiteware–Floral
Cooler Shown
Red, Yellow & Green Floral
The Cellar

C9N 1
Etched Floral, Gold Band
Cellini

C9N 2
Wine Shown
Etched Floral, Gold Band
Cellini

Balloton
Various Colors,
Diamond Optic Bowl
Cenedese

Murrine
Highball Shown
Multicolored Beads
Cenedese

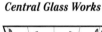

Veninga
Etch 421, Scrolls; Clear, Pink
or Green Stem, Optic Bowl
1447
Central Glass Works

Morgan
Etch 412, Pink Stem,
Optic Bowl
Central Glass Works

Morgan
Etch 412, Clear or
Various Colors, Optic Bowl
22
Central Glass Works

Pamela
Clear, Amber or Cobalt Bowl
Central Glass Works

Hester
Etch 432, Clear, Amber,
Pink or Topaz Bowl
1470
Central Glass Works

1470-3
Cut Floral & Dots
1470
Central Glass Works

207

Central Glass Works

Grigg's
Clear, Amber or Topaz Bowl,
Etched Lattice & Ovals
1470
Central Glass Works

1440
Various Colors
& Various Optic Bowls
Central Glass Works

Balda
Etch 410, Pink or Green
Stem, or All Pink
1440
Central Glass Works

Morgan
Etch 412, Blue
1440
Central Glass Works

Moderne
Black Stem & Foot
1446
Central Glass Works

24
Various Color Optic
Bowls & Stems
Central Glass Works

Balda
Etch 410, Scrolls,
Clear or Various Colors
24
Central Glass Works

Morgan
Etch 412, Various Colors
24
Central Glass Works

Harding
Etch 401, Blue Bowl
24
Central Glass Works

Veninga
Etch 421, Scrolls,
Clear, Green or Pink
24
Central Glass Works

CGL 1
Etched, Blue Optic Bowl
24
Central Glass Works

Morgan
Etch 412
750
Central Glass Works

Harding
Etch 401
780
Central Glass Works

1428
Various Colors,
Optic Bowl
Central Glass Works

Morgan
Etch 412, Purple/Orchid Tint
1428
Central Glass Works

Balda
Etch 410, Clear
or Various Colors
1428
Central Glass Works

1426
Various Colors,
Straight Optic Bowl
Central Glass Works

1426
Various Colors,
Diamond Optic Bowl
Central Glass Works

Morgan
Etch 412, Various Colors,
Optic Bowl
1426
Central Glass Works

Balda
Etch 410, Various Colors,
Diamond Optic Bowl
1426
Central Glass Works

Harding
Etch 401, Green Stem,
Diamond Optic Bowl
1426
Central Glass Works

1426-1
Pink, Cut Floral
1426
Central Glass Works

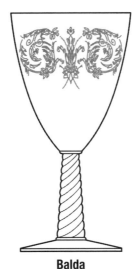

Balda
Etch 410, Twisted Stem
1900
Central Glass Works

1434
Various Colors,
Festoon Optic Bowl
Central Glass Works

Harding
Etch 401, Optic Bowl,
Green Stem
1434
Central Glass Works

1450
Various Colors, Optic Bowl,
Square Foot
Central Glass Works

David
Etched Fan, Black Stem
Central Glass Works

Etch 14
Wreath & Swags
Central Glass Works

Etch 6
Grapes & Leaves
112
Central Glass Works

Etch 6
Grapes & Leaves
Central Glass Works

Greek
Etch 7, Floral
1241
Central Glass Works

Greek
Etch 7, Floral
1236
Central Glass Works

Thistle
Etched Thistle
Central Glass Works

Etch 11
Floral
Central Glass Works

Balda
Etch 410, Amber
Central Glass Works

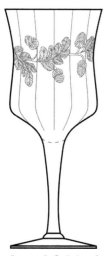

Acorn & Oak Leaf
Etch 19
528
Central Glass Works

Etch 6
Grapes & Leaves
7809
Central Glass Works

Cabbage Rose
Wine Shown
Pressed Glass
Central Glass Works

Krystol
Liquor Cocktail Shown
Panels, Pressed Glass
Central Glass Works

Allegro
Panel Cuts
Ceska

Suzanna
Vertical Cuts
Ceska

Tiara
Panel Cuts, Bubble in Stem
Ceska

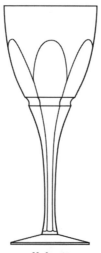

Helene
Panel Cuts
Ceska

Etude
Panel Cuts
Ceska

Galaxie
Crosshatch & Panel Cuts
Ceska

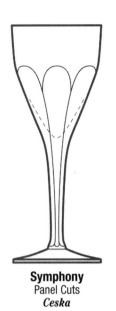

Symphony
Panel Cuts
Ceska

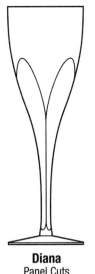

Diana
Panel Cuts
Ceska

Solitaire
Vertical & Horizontal Cuts
Ceska

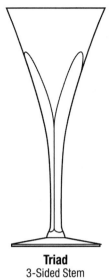

Triad
3-Sided Stem
Ceska

Brilliance
Crisscross Cuts
Ceska

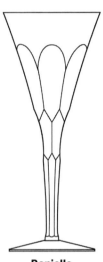

Danielle
Panel Cuts
Ceska

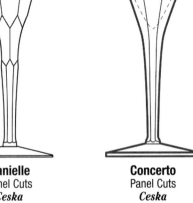

Concerto
Panel Cuts
Ceska

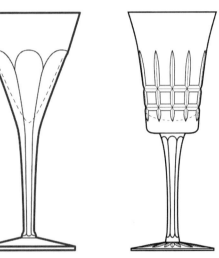

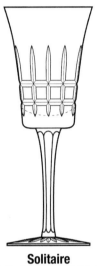

Solitaire
Vertical & Horizontal Cuts,
Flared Bowl
Ceska

St. Moritz
Vertical & Panel Cuts
Ceska

Canterbury
Crisscross Cuts,
Straight Stem
Ceska

Prague
Vertical & Horizontal Cuts,
Straight Stem
Ceska

Prague
Vertical & Horizontal Cuts,
Flared Stem
Ceska

Canterbury
Crisscross Cuts,
Flared Stem
Ceska

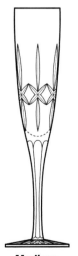

Madison
Champagne Flute Shown
Crisscross & Vertical Cuts
Ceska

CSK 5
Vertical & Horizontal Cuts
Ceska

Tradition
Crisscross & Fan Cuts
Ceska

Ascot
Crisscross Cuts
Ceska

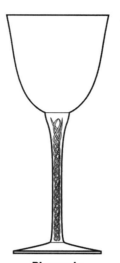

Rhapsody
Air Twist Stem
Ceska

Grand Renaissance
Fan, Star &
Crosshatch Cuts
Ceska

Day Lily
Plain
Ceska

Zenith
Wine Shown
6-Sided Base,
Bubble in Stem
Ceska

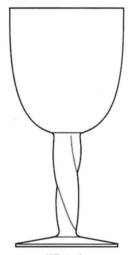

Wisteria
Twisted Stem
Ceska

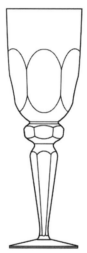

Regency
Thumbprint Cuts
Ceska

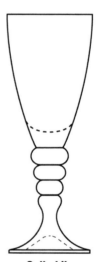

Calla Lily
Hollow Foot
Ceska

Tiger Lily
Square Bowl,
Hollow Foot
Ceska

Golf
Beer Mug Shown
Golf Motif, Barware
Ceska

Capri
Crisscross & Fan Cuts
Chalfonte

Maribel
Amber or Green,
Hollow Stem
Charter Club

C4H 2
Clear or Various
Color Optic Bowls
Charter Club

Grand Buffet–Silhouette
Wine Shown
Platinum Floral
Charter Club

Grand Buffet
Wine Shown
Gold or Platinum Scroll Band
Charter Club

Gold Double Band
Platinum Double Band
Balloon Wine Shown
Gold or Platinum Bands
Charter Club

Simone
Wine Shown
Burgundy & Gold Lustre
on Bowl, Burgundy Stem
Chele

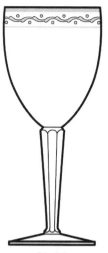

Cholet
Frosted Scrolls & Dots,
Gold Trim
Christian Dior

Dolce Vita
Cut Circles & Bubbles
Christian Dior

Casablanca
Black Cat Stem
Christian Dior

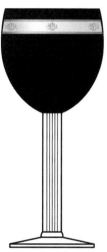

Ebony Dior
Gold Encrusted Band,
Black Bowl
Christian Dior

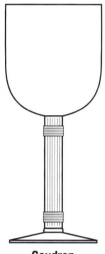

Gaudron
Gold or Frosted
Stem Accent
Christian Dior

Bijoux
Gold Rings
Stem Accent
Christian Dior

Dior Bow
Frosted Bow
Stem Accent
Christian Dior

Triomphe
Gold Trim on Bowl,
Stem & Foot
Christian Dior

Azure Royal
Swirl Optic Bowl,
Azure Stem, Gold Trim
Christian Dior

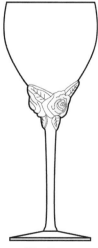

Dior Rose
Frosted Rose
Stem Accent
Christian Dior

Magnifique
Panel Cuts
Christian Dior

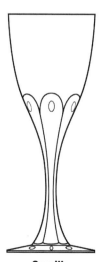

Camille
Oval Cuts
Christian Dior

213

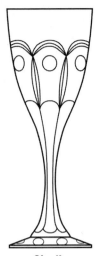

Giselle
Vertical, Arch & Dot Cuts
Christian Dior

Richelieu
Horizontal, Vertical
& Dot Cuts
Christian Dior

Casablanca
Highball Shown
Etched Animals & Trees
Christian Dior

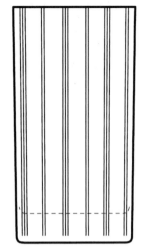

Ligne
Highball Shown
Vertical Cut Lines, Barware
Christian Dior

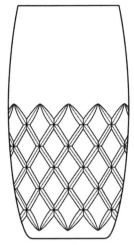

Paris
Highball Shown
Crisscross Cuts
Christian Dior

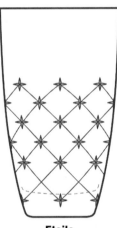

Etoile
Highball Shown
Crisscross & Star Cuts
Christian Dior

CHX 1
Tumbler Shown
Green, Panel Cuts
Christian Lacroix

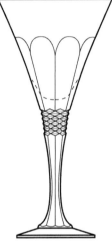

Pamela
Panel Cuts,
Cut Stem
*Christinenhutte/
Schott-Zwiesel*

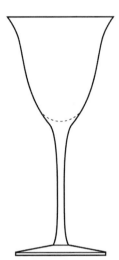

CRH 1
Wine Shown
Plain
Christinenhutte

CRH 6
Optic Bowl
Christinenhutte

Jeunesse
Vertical Cuts
Christinenhutte

CRH 7
Swirl Cuts
Christinenhutte

Calla
Frosted Petal Stem
Christinenhutte

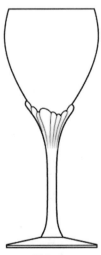

Valerie
Petal Stem
Christinenhutte

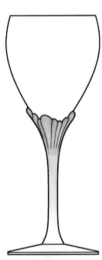

Vanessa
Frosted Petal Stem
Christinenhutte

Miramare
Plain
Christinenhutte

CRH 3
Wine Shown
Plain
Christinenhutte

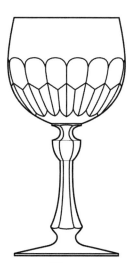

Allegro
Panel Cuts
4900
Christinenhutte

CRH 2
Vertical Cuts
Christinenhutte

Victoria
Red Wine Shown
Panel Cuts
Christinenhutte

CRH 8
Panel Cuts
Christinenhutte

Albi
Plain
Christofle

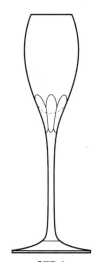

CTE 4
Champagne Flute Shown
Panel Cuts
Christofle

Alizes
Panel & Fan Cuts
Christofle

Vinea
Tasting Glass Shown
Plain
Christofle

Iriana
Vertical Cuts
Christofle

Basilique
Wine Shown
Vertical Cuts
Christofle

Cathedrale
Plain, Vertical Cuts
Christofle

Cathedrale Or
Vertical Cuts, Gold Trim,
Gold Bands on Stem
Christofle

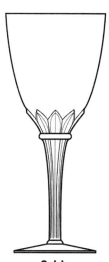

Osiris
Molded Stem
Christofle

Christofle, Christopher Stuart

Babylone
Panel Cuts,
Multisided Foot
Christofle

Kawali
Clear or Various
Color Bowls, Plain
Christofle

Kawali
Platinum Trim
Christofle

Roemer Collection
Rhine Wine Shown
Various Color Bowls
Christofle

Symphonie
Red Wine Shown
Horizontal Rings
Christofle

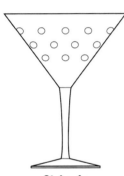

St. Louis
Martini Shown
Bubbles
Christofle

Iriana
Plain
Christofle

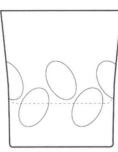

Cluny
Old Fashioned Shown
Oval Cuts, Barware
Christofle

Collection 3000
Highball Shown
Etched Checkered Base
Christofle

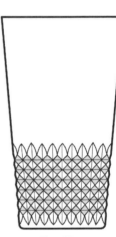

Facettes
Highball Shown
Diamond Cuts, Barware
Christofle

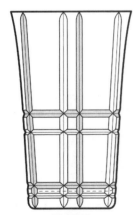

Scottish
Highball Shown
Polished/Gray Horizontal
& Vertical Cuts
Christofle

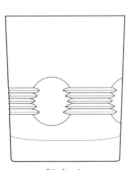

Atalante
Double Old Fashioned Shown
Horizontal & Circle Cuts,
Barware
Christofle

Carnegie
Plain or with
Gold Trim
Christopher Stuart

Opus
Curved Stem
Christopher Stuart

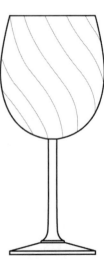

Optic Essence
Swirl Optic Bowl
Christopher Stuart

216

Talia
Plain or with
Gold Trim
Christopher Stuart

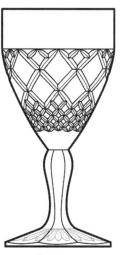

Regency
Crisscross Cuts
Christopher Stuart

Regency
Crisscross Cuts, Gold Trim
Christopher Stuart

Regency Ruby
Crisscross Cuts, Ruby Band
Christopher Stuart

Cameo
Crisscross & Oval Cuts
Christopher Stuart

Inspiration
Red Wine Shown
Swirl Cuts
Circleware

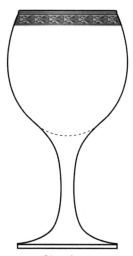

Classique
Wine Shown
Gold Encrusted Trim
Circleware

Tulip Gold
Wine Shown
Gold Trim
Circleware

Trieste
Various Color Bowls
Circleware

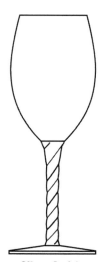

Silver Swirls
Platinum Spirals on Stem
Circleware

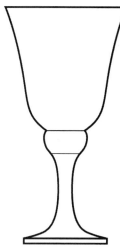

Capri
Plain
Circleware

White Diamond
Optic Bowl,
Crisscross Cuts on Stem
Circleware

Black Diamond
Plain Black Bowl,
Crisscross Cuts on Stem
Circleware

Luscious
Champagne Flute Shown
Various Stem Shapes
& Colors, Multi-Motif
Circleware

CRZ 1
Panel Cuts,
Pressed Glass
Circleware

217

Circleware

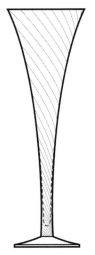

Fizz
Champagne Flute Shown
Swirl Optic
Circleware

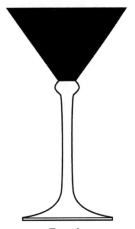

Tuxedo
Martini Shown
Black Bowl
Circleware

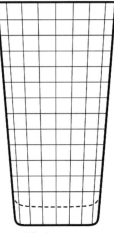

Windowpane
Tumbler Shown
Clear or Blue,
Textured Blocks
Circleware

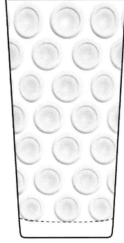

Circle
Highball Shown
Clear or Blue,
Indented Circles
Circleware

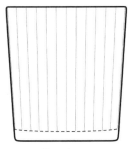

Spectrum
Double Old Fashioned Shown
Straight Optic
Circleware

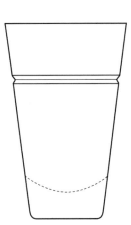

Signature
Cooler Shown
Single Indented Band
Circleware

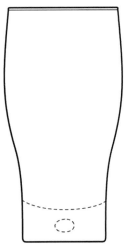

Moondrop
Highball Shown
Bubble in Base
Circleware

Oslo
Mojito Shown
Bubble in Base,
Barware
Circleware

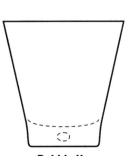

Bubble Up
Double Old Fashioned Shown
Bubble in Base
Circleware

Bentley
Cooler Shown
Thick Base, Dimpled
Circleware

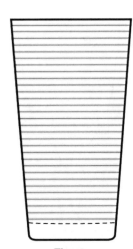

Theory
Cooler Shown
Horizontal Rings
Circleware

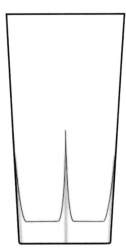

Ice Cube
Highball Shown
Square Base
Circleware

Copenhagen
Highball Shown
Square Shape,
Cut Band at Base
Circleware

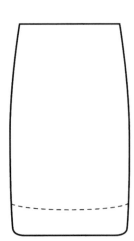

Chadwick
Highball Shown
Plain, Barware
Circleware

Sweden
Cooler Shown
Curved Vertical Cuts,
Barware
Circleware

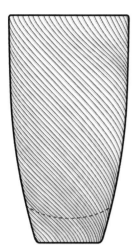

Excite
Highball Shown
Spiral Optic
Circleware

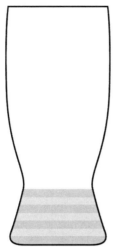

Colore Stripe
Highball Shown
Frosted Rings on Various
Color Bases, Multi-Motif
Circleware

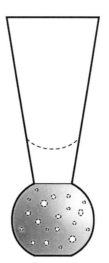

Fireball
Shot Glass Shown
Various Colors, Bubbles
on Ball Foot, Multi-Motif
Circleware

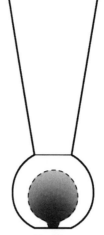

Bonfire
Shot Glass Shown
Various Color Bubbles
in Ball Foot, Multi-Motif
Circleware

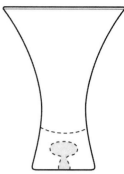

Intensity
Martini Shown
Various Color Bubbles
in Base, Multi-Motif
Circleware

Crosstown Tower
Cordial Shown
Various Shapes & Bubble
Colors in Base, Multi-Motif
Circleware

Dance
Shot Glass Shown
Various Colors,
Curved Bowls, Multi-Motif
Circleware

Buzz
Star & Pinwheel Cuts
Clapperton's

Beaumont
Diagonal & Oval Cuts
Clapperton's

Coronation
Fleur-de-lis,
Crisscross Cuts
Clapperton's

Nelson
Crisscross & Vertical Cuts
Clapperton's

Windsor
Crisscross & Vertical Cuts
Clapperton's

Block Diamond
Crisscross Cuts
Clapperton's

Sussex
Crisscross & Fan Cuts
Clapperton's

Norfolk
Crisscross &
Thumbprint Cuts
Clapperton's

Sherwood
Swirl Cuts
Clapperton's

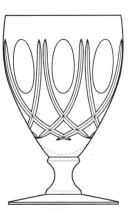

Carlton
Crisscross &
Thumbprint Cuts
Clapperton's

Colonial
Panel Cuts
Clapperton's

Festoon
Polished & Gray
Cut Floral
Clapperton's

CLY 2
Crisscross & Vertical Cuts,
Gold Trim
Clarenbridge

CLY 1
Crisscross Cuts
Clarenbridge

Sunk Daisy
Clear or Green,
Daisy & Cane,
Pressed Glass
Co-Operative Flint

Imperial
Crosshatch & Stars,
Pressed Glass
Co-Operative Flint

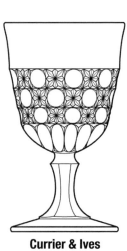

Currier & Ives
Stars & Dots,
Pressed Glass
130
Co-Operative Flint

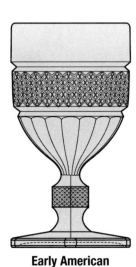

Early American
Clear or Various Colors, Crisscross
& Panels, Pressed Glass
587
Co-Operative Flint

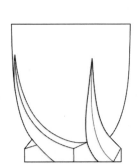

CFV 1
Double Old Fashioned Shown
Twisted Square Base, Barware
Cofrac Art Verrier

Golden Glam (Gold Trim)
Silver Chic (Platinum Trim)
Wine Shown
Colin Cowie

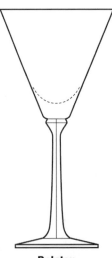

Balaton
4-Sided Stem
Colle

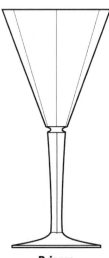

Prisma
Red Wine Shown
Octagon Shaped Bowl,
4-Sided Stem
Colle

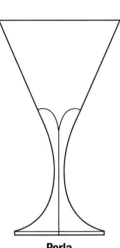

Perla
Plain, Square Foot
Colle

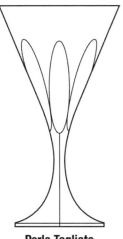

Perla Tagliato
Oval Cuts, Square Foot
Colle

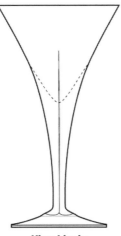

King Liscio
4-Sided Stem
Colle

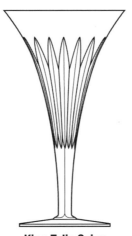

King Talio Svisu
White Wine Shown
Vertical Cuts
Colle

Berlino Calice
Panel Cuts,
Multisided Foot
Colle

CCO 2
Vertical Cuts,
Multisided Foot
Colle

Princeps
Plain
Colle

Professionali
Champagne Flute Shown
Plain
Colle

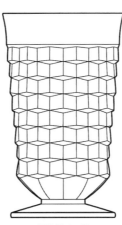

Whitehall
Iced Tea Shown
Various Colors,
Stacked Cubes
Colony

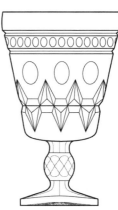

Park Lane
Various Colors,
Arches & Dots,
Pressed Glass
Colony

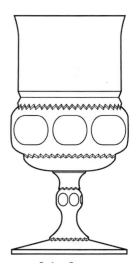

Color Crown
Various Colors, Zigzag &
Oval Thumbprint Cuts,
Pressed Glass
Colony

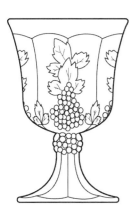

Harvest
Various Colors, Grapes,
Pressed Glass
Colony

Sandwich
Various Colors,
Scrolls, Pressed Glass
Colony

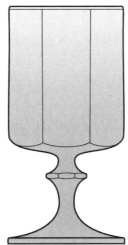

Nouveau
Various Colors,
Panels, Pressed Glass
Colony

Bern
Plain
Colony

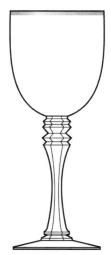

San Francisco (Gold Trim)
New York (Platinum Trim)
Colony

Colony

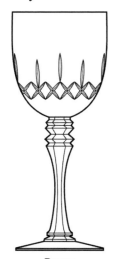

Roma
Crisscross & Vertical Cuts
Colony

Dublin
Crisscross & Fan Cuts
Colony

Frederica
Plain
Colony

Liszt
Pinwheel Cuts
Colony

Kara
Crisscross Cuts
Colony

Mozart
Wine Shown
Crisscross & Plant Cuts
Colony

Royal Ornate
Crisscross & Vertical Cuts,
Gold Trim
Colony

Kilkenny
Crisscross & Vertical Cuts
Colony

Aurora
Laurel, Crisscross
& Vertical Cuts
Colony

COL 3
Crisscross & Oval Cuts
Colony

Paris
Leaf & Dot Cuts
Colony

Amaryllis
Clear or Various Color
Frosted or Glossy Stems
Colony

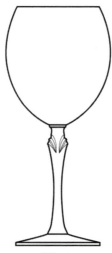

Bijoux
Clear or Various
Bowl & Stem Colors
Colony

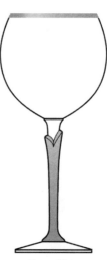

Versailles
Gold Stem & Trim
Colony

Brigitte
Various Color Iridescent
Bowls & Stems
Colony

Duo
Clear & Cobalt Stem
Colony

Provincial
Various Colors, Plain
Colony

COL 13
Various Colors, Plain
Colony

COL 24
Red Bowl
Colony

Krista
Plain
Colony

Picardo
Clear or Various Colors,
Hollow Foot
Colony

Richmond
Various Colors,
Plain
Colony

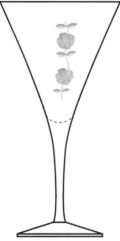

Sandra
Cut Floral
Colony

Lovebird
Champagne Flute Shown
Etched Birds & Hearts
Colony

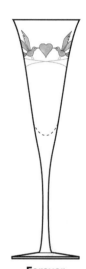

Forever
Champagne Flute Shown
Gray/Frosted
Birds & Heart
Colony

Imperial
Champagne Flute Shown
Crisscross Cuts
Colony

Celebration
Champagne Flute Shown
Hollow Stem
Colony

Solitude
Champagne Flute Shown
Gold Trim
Colony

Airflow
Champagne Flute Shown
Air Twist Stem
Colony

Tropez Gold Band
Champagne Flute Shown
Gold Spiral Band
Colony

Colony

Strata (Gold)
Confetti (Colors)
Spiral Band
Colony

Table Delight
Plain
Colony

Chateau
Plain
Colony

Caterina Black
Black, Plain
Colony

Diane
Blue, Red or Green
Bubble in Stem
Colony

COL 10
Black Stem & Foot
Colony

Wine Keepers
Plain
Colony

d'Anita
Plain
Colony

Optic
Optic Bowl
Colony

Bon Vivant
Plain
Colony

Galleria
Pink, Green, Blue & Yellow
Abstract Swirls
Colony

Vagueros
Various Colors,
Bubbles
Colony

Neel
Plain
Colony

Monet
Gray Cut Floral
Colony

Charlotte
Gray Cut Floral
Colony

224

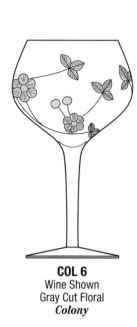

COL 6
Wine Shown
Gray Cut Floral
Colony

Chantilly
Gray Cut Floral
Colony

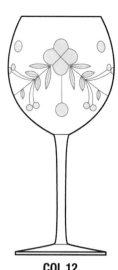

Sara
Gray Cut Floral
Colony

COL 12
Gray Cut Floral
Colony

Napa
Gray Cut Grapes
& Leaves
Colony

Astor
Gray Cut Floral
Colony

Sonora
Gray Cut Grapes
& Leaves
Colony

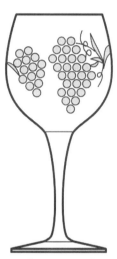

Grape & Leaf
Gray Cut Grapes
& Leaves
Colony

Classic Grape
Gray Cut Grapes
& Leaves
Colony

Classic Danube
Gray Cut Floral
Colony

Claridge
Gray Cut Plant
Colony

COL 28
Gray Cut Floral
Colony

New Hartsdale
Gray Cut Floral
Colony

COL 2
Gray Cut Floral
Colony

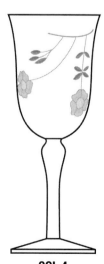

COL 4
Gray Cut Floral
Colony

Colony

Consara
Gray Cut Floral
Colony

COL 1
Gray Cut Floral
Colony

Retrospect
Optic Bowl
Colony

Joy
Optic Bowl
Colony

Lily of the Valley
Gray Cut Floral
Colony

Danube
Gray Cut Floral
Colony

Crocus
Gray Cut Floral
Colony

COL 11
Cut Floral
Colony

Lline
Gray Cut Floral
Colony

Elegance
Bubble in Stem
Colony

Mirage
Optic Bowl
Colony

Classic Gold
Gold Trim &
Stem Accent
Colony

Charleston
Plain
Colony

Kristina
Frosted Stem Accent
Colony

Anniversary
Champagne Flute Shown
Heart Stem Accent
Colony

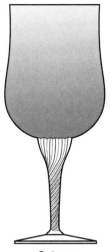

Saturn
Blue, Green or Red Bowl,
Twisted Stem
Colony

Regency Ruby
Red Bowl, Twisted Stem
Colony

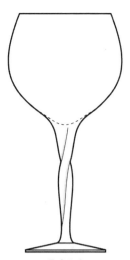

Bristol
Twisted Stem
Colony

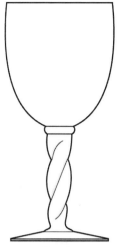

Rondo
Twisted Stem
Colony

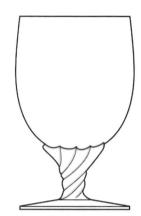

Splendor
Twisted Stem
Colony

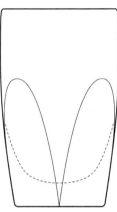

Vanity
Tumbler Shown
Amber or Clear,
Arch Panels, Barware
Colony

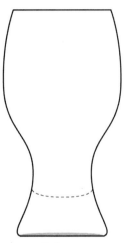

Calypso
Iced Tea Shown
Various Colors in Base
Colony

COL 20
Soda Tumbler Shown
Avocado Green, Panels,
Pressed Glass
Colony

Dogwood
Punch Cup Shown
Various Colors,
Dogwood Blossoms
Colony

Newport
Cup & Saucer Shown
Various Colors,
Scalloped Edge, Ribs
Colony

Starlight
Punch Cup Shown
Vertical Ribbed Cuts
Colony

Regency
Snack Set Shown
Vertical & Dot Cuts
Colony

CCR 1
Green Stem & Foot
Community

Deauville
Gray Cut Floral, Clear
or with Green Stem
Community

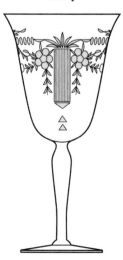

Grosvenor
Gray Cut Floral
Community

Community, Consolidated Glass, Corcoran

King Cedric
Gray Cut Floral
& Fruit
Community

Lady Hamilton
Gray Cut Tulips
Community

Noblesse
Gray Cut Floral,
Blue Stem
Community

Martele
Sherbet Shown
Jade Green,
Embossed Fruit
Consolidated Glass

Martele
Sherbet Shown
Frosted,
Embossed Dancing Nudes
Consolidated Glass

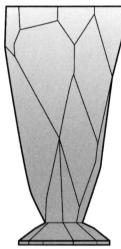

Ruba Rombic
Various Colors,
Multisided Foot
Consolidated Glass

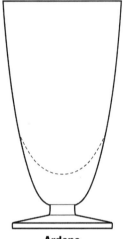

Ardene
Plain
Corcoran

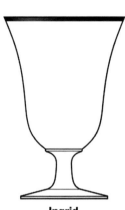

Ingrid
Platinum Trim
Corcoran

Lisa
Plain
Corcoran

Lisa
Wide Platinum Trim
Corcoran

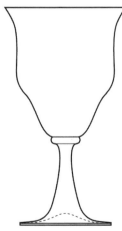

Greta
Plain, Hollow Foot
Corcoran

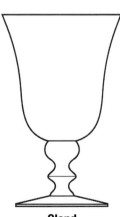

Oland
Plain
Corcoran

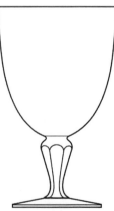

Olof
Plain
Corcoran

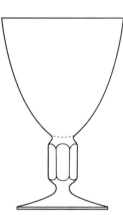

Alvesta
Panel Cut Stem
Corcoran

Downing
Oval Cuts
Corcoran

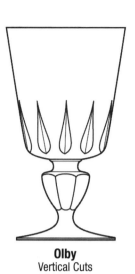

Olby
Vertical Cuts
Corcoran

Christina
Plain
Corcoran

CRC 1 (Gold Band)
Svea (Platinum Band)
Hollow Foot
Corcoran

Lund
Square Stem
Corcoran

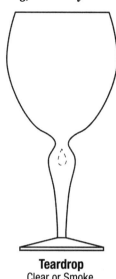

Teardrop
Clear or Smoke,
Bubble in Stem
Corcoran

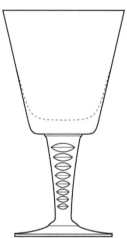

Karen
Cut Stem
Corcoran

Remi
Leaf Cuts,
Cut Stem
Corcoran

Air Twist
Air Twist Stem
Corcoran

Ebony
Black, Plain
7136
Cordon Bleu

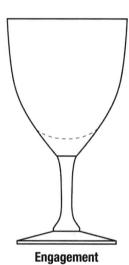

Engagement
Plain
Cordon Bleu

CBC 1
Smoke, Plain
Cordon Bleu

CXR 1
Wine Shown
Optic Bowl, Gold Trim
& Stem Accent
Corning

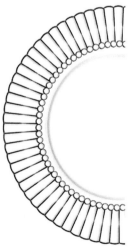

Sensation
Dinner Plate Shown
Ribbed
Corning

CXR 2
Salad Plate Shown
Swirl Rim, Scalloped
Corning

Verdant
Highball Shown
Vines, Crisscross Cuts,
Ribbed
Country Living

229

CQC 1
Old Fashioned Shown
Orange & Gold Floral,
Green Leaves
Couroc

CFS 1
Gray Cut Wheat
Craftsman Stemware

Old Bamboo
Gray Cut Bamboo
1920
Craftsman Stemware

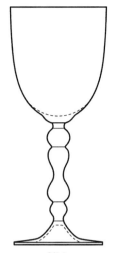

Gilda
Wine Shown
Plain, Hollow Foot
Crate & Barrel

Claudette
Optic Bowl & Stem
Crate & Barrel

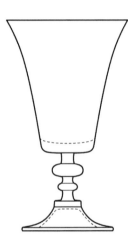

Marcel
Plain, Hollow Foot
Crate & Barrel

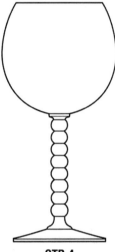

CTB 4
Plain
Crate & Barrel

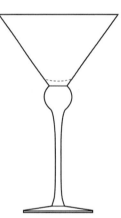

Roz
Martini Shown
Clear or with
Platinum Stem Accent
Crate & Barrel

CTB 15
Green Ball
Stem Accent
Crate & Barrel

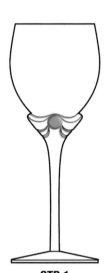

CTB 1
Wine Shown
Gold Ball Stem Accent
Crate & Barrel

Cluny
Clear or with
Gold or Platinum Stem
Crate & Barrel

CTB 20
Blue Stem
Crate & Barrel

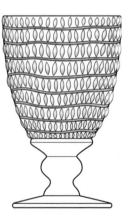

Palma
Embossed Dots & Rings
Crate & Barrel

CTB 41
Plain
Crate & Barrel

CTB 2
Yellow Bowl,
Green Stem, Red Foot
Crate & Barrel

CTB 18
Gold Stem
Crate & Barrel

Calypso
Aqua Textured Glass
Crate & Barrel

Santiago
Beverage Shown
Cobalt with Bubbles,
Handblown
Crate & Barrel

Cabo
Green, Plain
Crate & Barrel

Mendoza
Plain
Crate & Barrel

Kate
Plain
Crate & Barrel

Stella
Beverage Shown
Plain
Crate & Barrel

Belle
Wine Shown
Plain
Crate & Barrel

Leo
Plain
Crate & Barrel

CTB 34
Plain
Crate & Barrel

Viva
Clear or with
Black Stem & Foot
Crate & Barrel

Metro
Martini Shown
Plain
Crate & Barrel

CTB 29
Plain
Crate & Barrel

Payton
White Wine Shown
Plain
Crate & Barrel

Clyde
Plain
Crate & Barrel

Carlos
Margarita Shown
Plain
Crate & Barrel

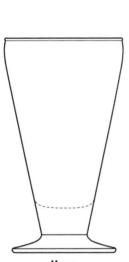

Miguel
Margarita Shown
Green Hue, Handblown
Crate & Barrel

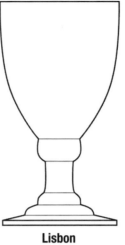

Lisbon
Plain
Crate & Barrel

Barcelona
Spanish Green, Plain
Crate & Barrel

Smoke
Gray Bowl,
Darker Stem, Plain
Crate & Barrel

CTB 16
Beer Shown
Green Bowl & Stem,
Blue Foot
Crate & Barrel

Hugo
Beverage Shown
Plain
Crate & Barrel

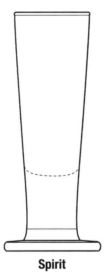

Spirit
Cordial Shown
Plain
Crate & Barrel

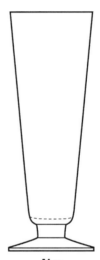

Alan
Pilsner Shown
Plain
Crate & Barrel

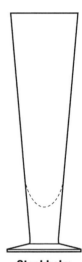

Stockholm
Pilsner Shown
Plain
Crate & Barrel

Rita
Wine Shown
Plain
Crate & Barrel

Tryst
Champagne Flute Shown
Plain, Hollow Foot
Crate & Barrel

Trumpet Flutes
Champagne Flute Shown
Trumpet Shaped,
Hollow Stem
Crate & Barrel

Paloma
Champagne Flute Shown
Plain
Crate & Barrel

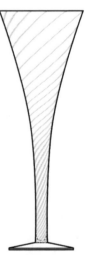

Renoir
Champagne Flute Shown
Swirl Optic Bowl & Stem
Crate & Barrel

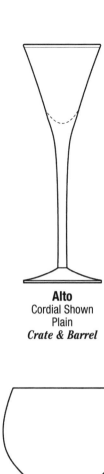

Alto
Cordial Shown
Plain
Crate & Barrel

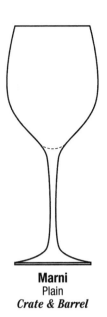

Marni
Plain
Crate & Barrel

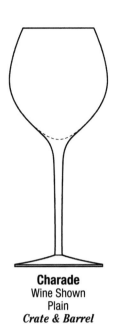

Charade
Wine Shown
Plain
Crate & Barrel

Aria
Champagne Flute Shown
Plain, Hollow Foot
Crate & Barrel

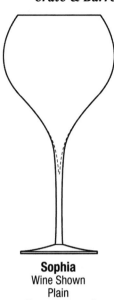

Sophia
Wine Shown
Plain
Crate & Barrel

Otis
Wine Shown
Plain
Crate & Barrel

Elite
Burgundy Wine Shown
Plain
Crate & Barrel

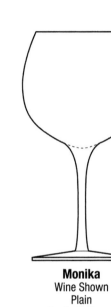

Monika
Wine Shown
Plain
Crate & Barrel

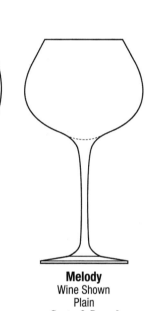

Melody
Wine Shown
Plain
Crate & Barrel

Isabella
Plain
Crate & Barrel

Liv
Wine Shown
Plain
Crate & Barrel

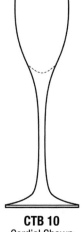

Balboa
Wine Shown
Plain
Crate & Barrel

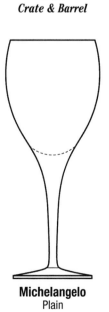

CTB 10
Cordial Shown
Plain
Crate & Barrel

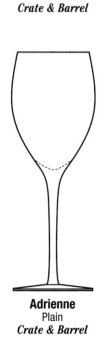

Michelangelo
Plain
Crate & Barrel

Adrienne
Plain
Crate & Barrel

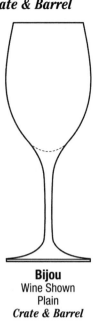

Bijou
Wine Shown
Plain
Crate & Barrel

Jordan
Wine Shown
Plain
Crate & Barrel

Carson
Plain, Oversized
Crate & Barrel

Coco
Wine Shown
Plain
Crate & Barrel

Marlet
Wine Shown
Plain
Crate & Barrel

Nora
Plain
Crate & Barrel

Solo
Port Wine Shown
Plain
Crate & Barrel

Duet
Red Wine Shown
Plain
Crate & Barrel

Vineyard
Bordeaux Wine Shown
Plain
Crate & Barrel

Gina
Wine Shown
Plain
Crate & Barrel

Elizabeth
Wine Shown
Plain
Crate & Barrel

Viv
Wine Shown
Plain
Crate & Barrel

Volo
Wine Shown
Plain
Crate & Barrel

Vivien
Wine Shown
Plain
Crate & Barrel

Silhouette
Wine Shown
Plain
Crate & Barrel

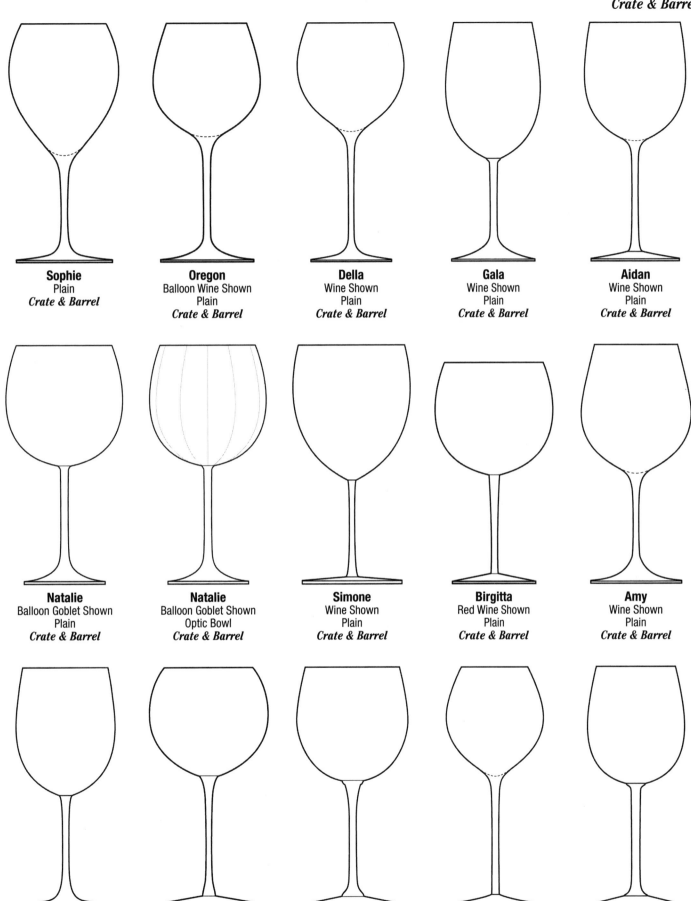

Sophie
Plain
Crate & Barrel

Oregon
Balloon Wine Shown
Plain
Crate & Barrel

Della
Wine Shown
Plain
Crate & Barrel

Gala
Wine Shown
Plain
Crate & Barrel

Aidan
Wine Shown
Plain
Crate & Barrel

Natalie
Balloon Goblet Shown
Plain
Crate & Barrel

Natalie
Balloon Goblet Shown
Optic Bowl
Crate & Barrel

Simone
Wine Shown
Plain
Crate & Barrel

Birgitta
Red Wine Shown
Plain
Crate & Barrel

Amy
Wine Shown
Plain
Crate & Barrel

Estate
Wine Shown
Plain, Oversized
Crate & Barrel

Karin
Balloon Wine Shown
Plain
Crate & Barrel

Annie
Plain
Crate & Barrel

Bryn
Wine Shown
Plain
Crate & Barrel

CTB 35
Plain
Crate & Barrel

Meg
Wine Shown
Plain
Crate & Barrel

CTB 13
Wine Shown
Swirl Optic Bowl
Crate & Barrel

Ollie
Wine Shown
Plain
Crate & Barrel

Grand
Plain
Crate & Barrel

Fay
Wine Shown
Plain
Crate & Barrel

Exquisite
Plain, Elongated Stem
Crate & Barrel

Casa
Wine Shown
Plain
Crate & Barrel

Picnic
Wine Shown
Plain
Crate & Barrel

Cheers
Wine Shown
Clear or Various Colors, Plain
Crate & Barrel

Jane
Plain
Crate & Barrel

CTB 24
Frosted Stem
Crate & Barrel

CTB 33
Plain
Crate & Barrel

Inga
Plain
Crate & Barrel

Gigi
Wine Shown
Plain
Crate & Barrel

Lira
Plain
Crate & Barrel

Edge
Wine Shown
Plain
Crate & Barrel

CTB 12
Wine Shown
Optic Bowl
Crate & Barrel

Ada
Wine Shown
Clear or Smoke
Crate & Barrel

Pops
Champagne Flute Shown
Plain
Crate & Barrel

Celia
Champagne Flute Shown
Plain
Crate & Barrel

Simplicity
Champagne Flute Shown
Plain
Crate & Barrel

Greta
Red Wine Shown
Plain
Crate & Barrel

Basic
Champagne Flute Shown
Plain
Crate & Barrel

Chloe
Wine Shown
Plain
Crate & Barrel

Jo
Wine Shown
Plain
Crate & Barrel

Rona
Plain
Crate & Barrel

Victoria
Red Wine Shown
Plain, Hollow Foot
Crate & Barrel

Arc
Wine Shown
Plain
Crate & Barrel

Basic
Plain
Crate & Barrel

Tate
Martini Shown
Plain
Crate & Barrel

Maude
Martini Shown
Plain
Crate & Barrel

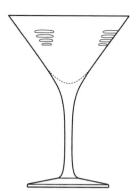

CTB 6
Martini Shown
Horizontal Cuts
Crate & Barrel

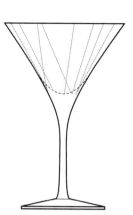

Park Avenue
Martini Shown
Vertical Lines
Crate & Barrel

Buzz
Martini Shown
Horizontal Ribs, Barware
Crate & Barrel

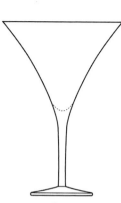

Gem
Martini Shown
Clear or Various Color Bowls
Crate & Barrel

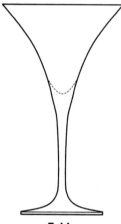

Zelda
Martini Shown
Plain
Crate & Barrel

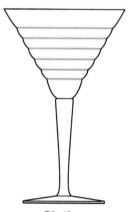

Rhythm
Martini Shown
Horizontal Ribs
Crate & Barrel

Felix
Martini Shown
Plain
Crate & Barrel

Vamp
Martini Shown
Amber Bowl
Crate & Barrel

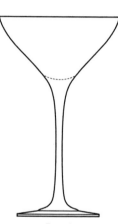

Bond
Martini Shown
Plain
Crate & Barrel

Mara
Wine Shown
Plain, Slanted Bowl
Crate & Barrel

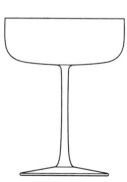

Posh
Champagne/Tall Sherbet Shown
Plain
Crate & Barrel

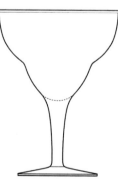

Mini
Margarita Shown
Plain
Crate & Barrel

Plaza
Wine Shown
Horizontal Cuts
Crate & Barrel

Scala
Wine Shown
Gray Cut Spiral Lines
Crate & Barrel

CTB 37
Line & Dot Cuts
Crate & Barrel

Spruce
Etched Pine Cones
& Boughs
Crate & Barrel

Savoy
Wine Shown
Wide Platinum Band
Crate & Barrel

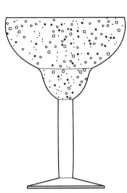

Zing
Margarita Shown
Bubbles in Thick Glass,
Handblown
Crate & Barrel

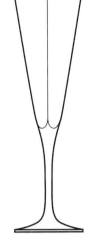

Zara
Champagne Flute Shown
Plain, Square Bowl
Crate & Barrel

Callaway
Champagne Flute Shown
Horizontal Cut Ring
Crate & Barrel

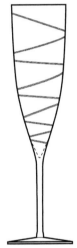

Pirouette
Champagne Flute Shown
Unpolished Spiral Cuts
Crate & Barrel

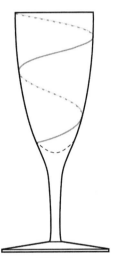

CTB 19
Champagne Flute Shown
Gold Swirl Line
Crate & Barrel

CTB 3
Light Blue,
Gray Cut Plants
Crate & Barrel

Calistoga
Wine Shown
Grape & Leaf Cuts,
Barware
Crate & Barrel

Metropolitan
Gray Cut Squares & Lines
Crate & Barrel / Krosno

Wisteria
Martini Shown
Etched Flowers & Birds
Crate & Barrel

Venezia
Red, Blue, Green & Gold
Bands on Stem
Crate & Barrel

Caprice
Multicolored Bands on Stem
Crate & Barrel

Moxie
Blue Stem with
Cobalt Stripes
Crate & Barrel

Silver Stem
Platinum Stem
Crate & Barrel

Party
Red Wine Shown
Various Color Stems
Crate & Barrel

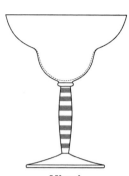

Miami
Margarita Shown
Green Striped Stem
Crate & Barrel

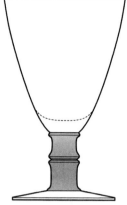

CTB 5
Yellow Stem
Crate & Barrel

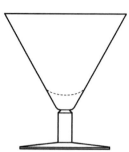

Shortinis
Martini Shown
Various Stem &
Foot Colors
Crate & Barrel

Samba
Red Bowl
Crate & Barrel

Temptation
Martini Shown
Aqua Bowl
Crate & Barrel

Rhapsody
Martini Shown
Cobalt Bowl
Crate & Barrel

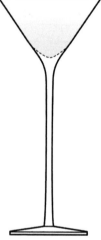

Tall Tini
Martini Shown
Various Color Bowls,
Elongaged Stem
Crate & Barrel

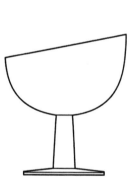

Satellite Dish
Champagne/Tall Sherbet Shown
Various Color
Slanted Bowls
Crate & Barrel

Slice
Green Bowl,
Etched Citrus Slices
Crate & Barrel

Tallritas
Margarita Shown
Various Color Bowls
Crate & Barrel

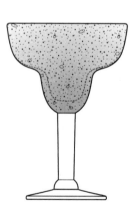

Copa
Margarita Shown
Blue Bowl with Bubbles
Crate & Barrel

Fiesta
Iced Tea Shown
Blue, Yellow, Red
& Green Specks
Crate & Barrel

Kira
Wine Shown
Lilac or Aqua
Crate & Barrel

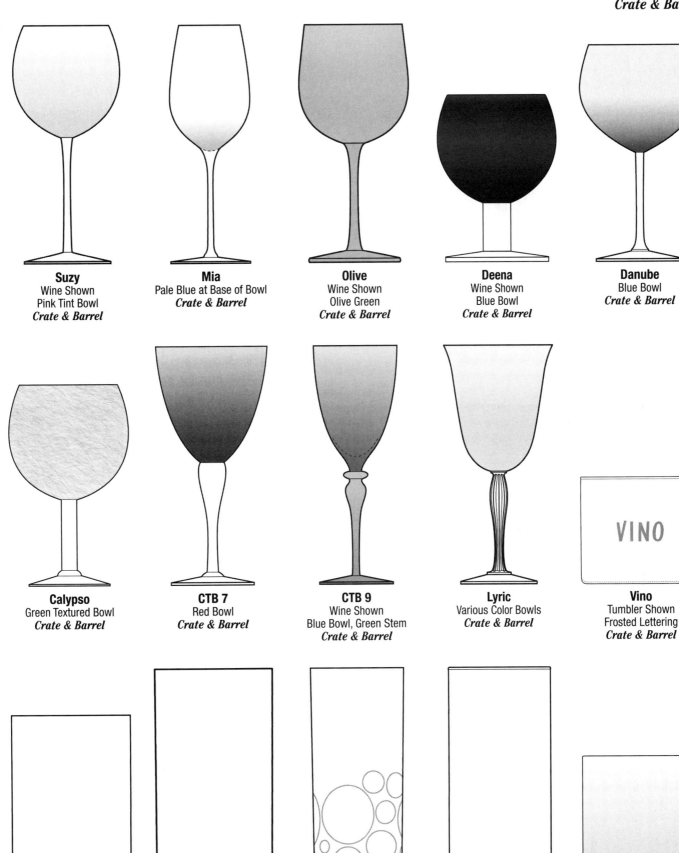

Suzy
Wine Shown
Pink Tint Bowl
Crate & Barrel

Mia
Pale Blue at Base of Bowl
Crate & Barrel

Olive
Wine Shown
Olive Green
Crate & Barrel

Deena
Wine Shown
Blue Bowl
Crate & Barrel

Danube
Blue Bowl
Crate & Barrel

Calypso
Green Textured Bowl
Crate & Barrel

CTB 7
Red Bowl
Crate & Barrel

CTB 9
Wine Shown
Blue Bowl, Green Stem
Crate & Barrel

Lyric
Various Color Bowls
Crate & Barrel

Vino
Tumbler Shown
Frosted Lettering
Crate & Barrel

Haute
Highball Shown
Bubble in Base
Crate & Barrel

Crescent
Highball Shown
Plain, Barware
Crate & Barrel

Circ
Highball Shown
Circles, Barware
Crate & Barrel

Tambien
Cooler Shown
Clear or Smoke, Barware
Crate & Barrel

Thriller
Double Old Fashioned Shown
Green or Orange, Barware
Crate & Barrel

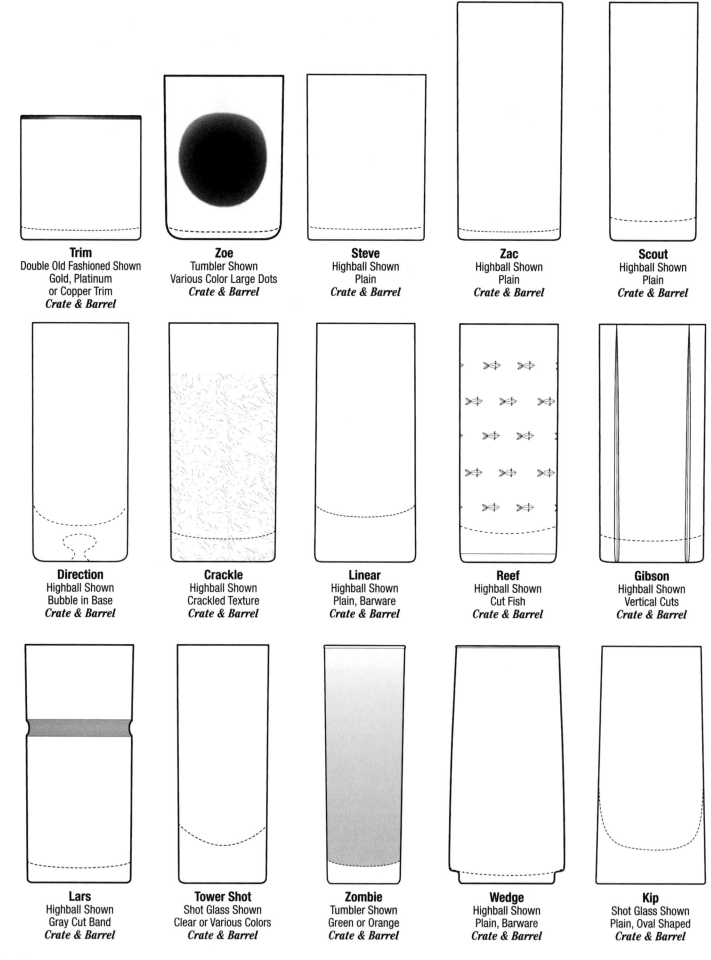

Trim
Double Old Fashioned Shown
Gold, Platinum
or Copper Trim
Crate & Barrel

Zoe
Tumbler Shown
Various Color Large Dots
Crate & Barrel

Steve
Highball Shown
Plain
Crate & Barrel

Zac
Highball Shown
Plain
Crate & Barrel

Scout
Highball Shown
Plain
Crate & Barrel

Direction
Highball Shown
Bubble in Base
Crate & Barrel

Crackle
Highball Shown
Crackled Texture
Crate & Barrel

Linear
Highball Shown
Plain, Barware
Crate & Barrel

Reef
Highball Shown
Cut Fish
Crate & Barrel

Gibson
Highball Shown
Vertical Cuts
Crate & Barrel

Lars
Highball Shown
Gray Cut Band
Crate & Barrel

Tower Shot
Shot Glass Shown
Clear or Various Colors
Crate & Barrel

Zombie
Tumbler Shown
Green or Orange
Crate & Barrel

Wedge
Highball Shown
Plain, Barware
Crate & Barrel

Kip
Shot Glass Shown
Plain, Oval Shaped
Crate & Barrel

Dave
Shot Glass Shown
White Band, Ribbed Base
Crate & Barrel

Gibraltar
Cooler Shown
Panel Cuts, Barware
Crate & Barrel

Winston
Tumbler Shown
Plain, Barware
Crate & Barrel

Ethan
Highball Shown
Plain
Crate & Barrel

Dylan
Highball Shown
Plain
Crate & Barrel

York
Highball Shown
Plain, Barware
Crate & Barrel

Dakota
Highball Shown
Plain
Crate & Barrel

Josh
Highball Shown
Plain
Crate & Barrel

Donatello
Highball Shown
Bubble in Base
Crate & Barrel

Ambi
Tumbler Shown
Plain
Crate & Barrel

Polly
Highball Shown
Plain
Crate & Barrel

Oola
Highball Shown
Plain
Crate & Barrel

Marta
Cooler Shown
Plain
Crate & Barrel

City
Highball Shown
Plain, Barware
Crate & Barrel

CTB 30
Tumbler Shown
Various Shaped Bubbles
Crate & Barrel

Surf
Highball Shown
Pale Blue, Plain
Crate & Barrel

Linden
Highball Shown
Olive Green, Plain
Crate & Barrel

Madrid
Double Old Fashioned Shown
Plain
Crate & Barrel

Swirl
Double Old Fashioned Shown
Orange or Green Band
Crate & Barrel

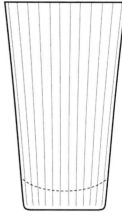

Candice
Highball Shown
Optic
Crate & Barrel

Rings
Double Old Fashioned Shown
Concentric Rings, Barware
Crate & Barrel

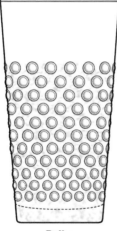

Polka
Highball Shown
Textured Dots
Crate & Barrel

CTB 17
Highball Shown
White Vertical Lines
Crate & Barrel

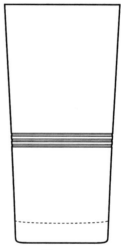

Bergen
Highball Shown
Horizontal Cut Lines
Crate & Barrel

CTB 26
Tumbler Shown
Various Color Stripes
Crate & Barrel

Zip
Highball Shown
Multicolored Curved Bands
Crate & Barrel

Stix
Highball Shown
Blue, Purple
& Green Bands
Crate & Barrel

CTB 27
Highball Shown
Goldfish
Crate & Barrel

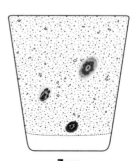

Zazz
Double Old Fashioned Shown
Bubbles & Colored Circles
Crate & Barrel

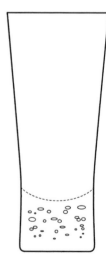

Verve
Highball Shown
Bubbles in Base
Crate & Barrel

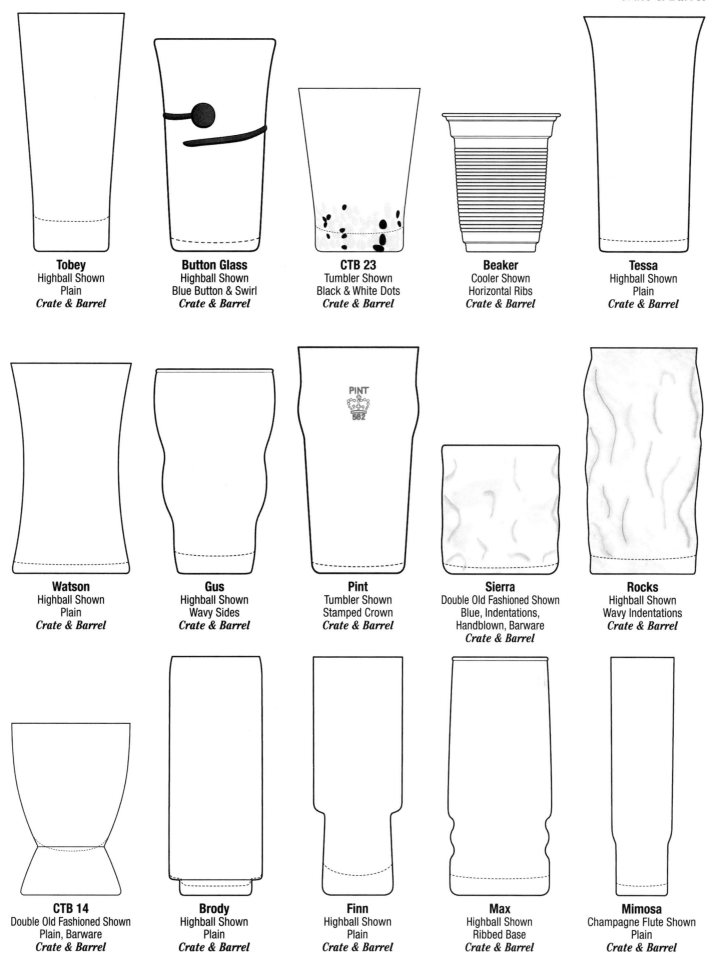

Tobey
Highball Shown
Plain
Crate & Barrel

Button Glass
Highball Shown
Blue Button & Swirl
Crate & Barrel

CTB 23
Tumbler Shown
Black & White Dots
Crate & Barrel

Beaker
Cooler Shown
Horizontal Ribs
Crate & Barrel

Tessa
Highball Shown
Plain
Crate & Barrel

Watson
Highball Shown
Plain
Crate & Barrel

Gus
Highball Shown
Wavy Sides
Crate & Barrel

Pint
Tumbler Shown
Stamped Crown
Crate & Barrel

Sierra
Double Old Fashioned Shown
Blue, Indentations,
Handblown, Barware
Crate & Barrel

Rocks
Highball Shown
Wavy Indentations
Crate & Barrel

CTB 14
Double Old Fashioned Shown
Plain, Barware
Crate & Barrel

Brody
Highball Shown
Plain
Crate & Barrel

Finn
Highball Shown
Plain
Crate & Barrel

Max
Highball Shown
Ribbed Base
Crate & Barrel

Mimosa
Champagne Flute Shown
Plain
Crate & Barrel

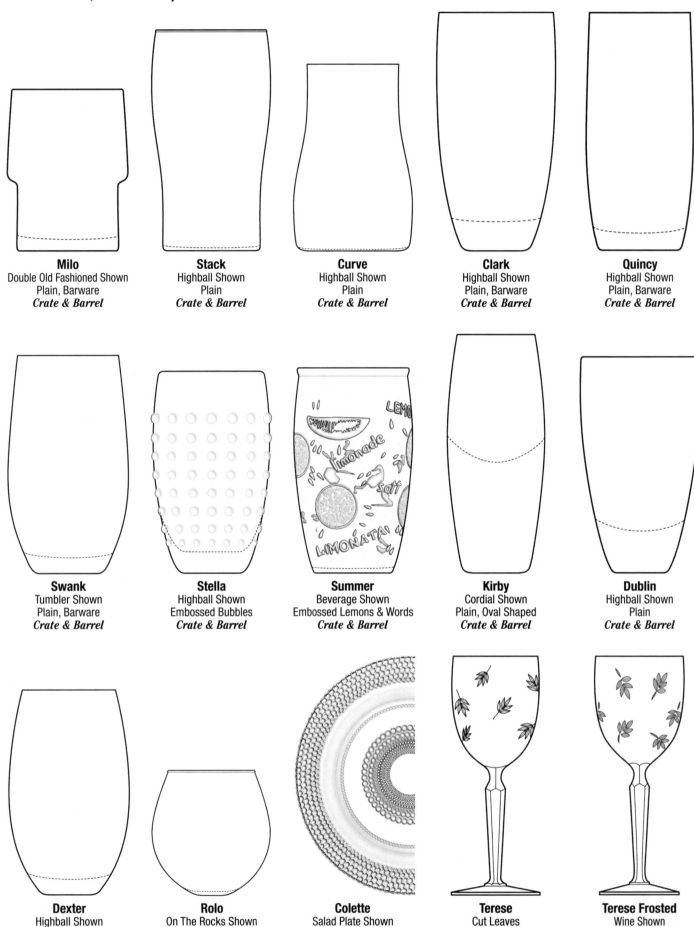

Milo
Double Old Fashioned Shown
Plain, Barware
Crate & Barrel

Stack
Highball Shown
Plain
Crate & Barrel

Curve
Highball Shown
Plain
Crate & Barrel

Clark
Highball Shown
Plain, Barware
Crate & Barrel

Quincy
Highball Shown
Plain, Barware
Crate & Barrel

Swank
Tumbler Shown
Plain, Barware
Crate & Barrel

Stella
Highball Shown
Embossed Bubbles
Crate & Barrel

Summer
Beverage Shown
Embossed Lemons & Words
Crate & Barrel

Kirby
Cordial Shown
Plain, Oval Shaped
Crate & Barrel

Dublin
Highball Shown
Plain
Crate & Barrel

Dexter
Highball Shown
Plain
Crate & Barrel

Rolo
On The Rocks Shown
Plain
Crate & Barrel

Colette
Salad Plate Shown
Beaded Border & Center
Crate & Barrel

Terese
Cut Leaves
Cristal d'Arques/Durand

Terese Frosted
Wine Shown
Cut Frosted Leaves
Cristal d'Arques/Durand

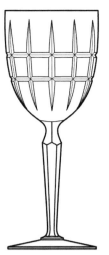

Glenellen
Horizonal & Vertical Cuts
Cristal d'Arques/Durand

Stacatto
Vertical Cuts
Cristal d'Arques/Durand

Resonance
Vertical Cuts
Cristal d'Arques/Durand

Resonance Gold
Vertical Cuts,
Gold Trim
Cristal d'Arques/Durand

Classic
Vertical Cuts
Cristal d'Arques/Durand

Provence
Crisscross & Fan Cuts
Cristal d'Arques/Durand

Monterey
Vertical Cuts
Cristal d'Arques/Durand

Diamant
Wine Shown
Vertical & Diamond Cuts
Cristal d'Arques/Durand

Dauphine
Multisided Lip,
Crisscross Cuts
Cristal d'Arques/Durand

Antique
Crosshatch, Arch & Fan Cuts,
6-Sided Stem
Cristal d'Arques/Durand

Antique
Crosshatch, Arch & Fan Cuts,
6-Sided Stem, Gold Trim
Cristal d'Arques/Durand

Constance
Vertical & Crisscross Cuts
Cristal d'Arques/Durand

Constance
Vertical & Crisscross Cuts,
Gold or Platinum Trim
Cristal d'Arques/Durand

Bergerac
Vertical & Panel Cuts
Cristal d'Arques/Durand

Bergerac
Vertical & Panel Cuts,
Gold Trim
Cristal d'Arques/Durand

247

Bergerac
Gold Encrusted Band,
Ruby Flash Bowl, Vertical &
Panel Cuts, Gold Foot Trim
Cristal d'Arques/Durand

Washington
Panel Cuts
Cristal d'Arques/Durand

Masquerade
Crisscross & Fan Cuts
Cristal d'Arques/Durand

Heritage/Hannon
Floral & Geometric,
Pressed Glass
Cristal d'Arques/Durand

Altesse
Crisscross, Floral,
& Arch Cuts
Cristal d'Arques/Durand

Carthage
Vertical & Fan Cuts
Cristal d'Arques/Durand

Anet
Vertical Cuts
Cristal d'Arques/Durand

CRA 59
Vertical Cuts
Cristal d'Arques/Durand

Azay Taille Luynes
Crisscross & Fan Cuts
Cristal d'Arques/Durand

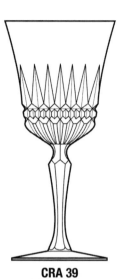

CRA 39
Wine Shown
Vertical Cuts
Cristal d'Arques/Durand

Baron
Vertical Cuts
Cristal d'Arques/Durand

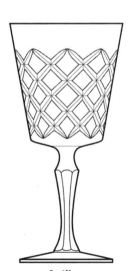

Antibes
Crisscross Cuts
Cristal d'Arques/Durand

Monte Carlo
Crisscross Cuts
Cristal d'Arques/Durand

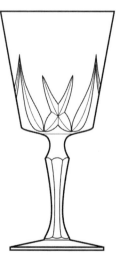

Launau
Crisscross & Vertical Cuts
Cristal d'Arques/Durand

Cannes
Crisscross & Fan Cuts
Cristal d'Arques/Durand

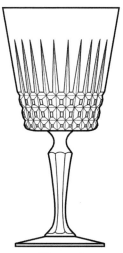

Diamant
Vertical & Horizontal Cuts
Cristal d'Arques/Durand

St. Maxime
Crisscross & Fan Cuts
Cristal d'Arques/Durand

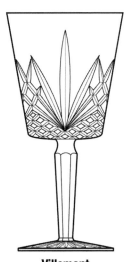

Villemont
Crisscross & Vertical Cuts
Cristal d'Arques/Durand

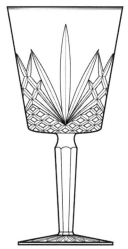

Villemont Gold
Crisscross & Vertical Cuts,
Gold Trim
Cristal d'Arques/Durand

Venice
Crisscross & Fan Cuts
Cristal d'Arques/Durand

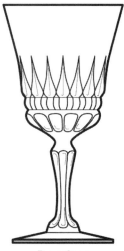

Barcelona
Vertical & Panel Cuts
Cristal d'Arques/Durand

Chateaudun
Vertical & Horizontal Cuts
Cristal d'Arques/Durand

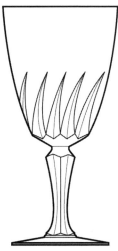

Flamenco
Curved Vertical Cuts
Cristal d'Arques/Durand

Palmes
Fan Cuts
Cristal d'Arques/Durand

Flammes
Diagonal Cuts
Cristal d'Arques/Durand

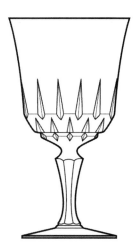

St. Germain
Vertical Cuts
Cristal d'Arques/Durand

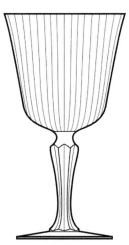

Meridien
Optic Bowl
Cristal d'Arques/Durand

Ambassade
Plain
Cristal d'Arques/Durand

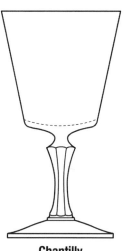

Chantilly
Plain
Cristal d'Arques/Durand

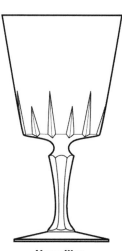

Versailles
Vertical Cuts
Cristal d'Arques/Durand

Cristal d'Arques/Durand

CRA 8
Crisscross Cuts
Cristal d'Arques/Durand

Saumur
Crisscross Cuts
Cristal d'Arques/Durand

Chantilly/Taille/Beaugency
Crisscross, Fan
& Star Cuts
Cristal d'Arques/Durand

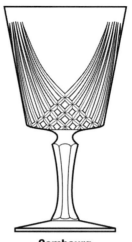

Combourg
Curved Vertical &
Crisscross Cuts
Cristal d'Arques/Durand

Matignon
Etched Floral
Cristal d'Arques/Durand

Riviera
Plain
Cristal d'Arques/Durand

Sogaro
Embossed Plant on
Clear or Frosted Stem
Cristal d'Arques/Durand

Castel
Vertical Cuts
Cristal d'Arques/Durand

Madrigal
Fan Cuts
Cristal d'Arques/Durand

Saga
Martini Shown
Indented Horizontal Band
Cristal d'Arques/Durand

Fuseau
Polished Wavy Cuts
Cristal d'Arques/Durand

Fuseau Satin
Frosted Wavy Cuts
Cristal d'Arques/Durand

Celina
Panel Cuts, Gold Trim
Cristal d'Arques/Durand

Alicia
Vertical & Panel Cuts
Cristal d'Arques/Durand

Moondance
Cut Blocks
Cristal d'Arques/Durand

Cascade
Vertical Oval Cuts
Cristal d'Arques/Durand

Sirius
Gray & Polished
Cut Floral
Cristal d'Arques/Durand

Fiama
Vertical Cuts
Cristal d'Arques/Durand

Majesty
Wine Shown
Vertical, Fan & Star Cuts
Cristal d'Arques/Durand

St. Moritz
Crisscross, Fan
& Crosshatch Cuts
Cristal d'Arques/Durand

Petale
Panel Cuts
Cristal d'Arques/Durand

Megeve Taille Genet
Vertical Cuts
Cristal d'Arques/Durand

Feuille
Vertical Cuts
Cristal d'Arques/Durand

Pistil
Vertical Plant Cuts
Cristal d'Arques/Durand

Diamant
Vertical & Crosshatch Cuts
Cristal d'Arques/Durand

Megeve Taille Corolle
Frosted Cuts
Cristal d'Arques/Durand

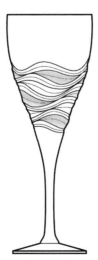

Crescendo
Wave Cuts with
Gray Accents
Cristal d'Arques/Durand

Celebration
Cut Dots
Cristal d'Arques/Durand

Courchevel
Dot, Line & Panel Cuts
Cristal d'Arques/Durand

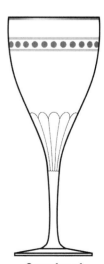

Courchevel
Dot, Line & Panel Cuts,
Gold Trim
Cristal d'Arques/Durand

Cassandra
Cut Plants
Cristal d'Arques/Durand

**Cassandra Gold
Cassandra Platinum**
Cut Plants,
Gold or Platinum Trim
Cristal d'Arques/Durand

William
Crisscross & Fan Cuts
Cristal d'Arques/Durand

William Gold
Crisscross & Fan Cuts,
Gold Trim
Cristal d'Arques/Durand

Natura
Gray Cut Leaves
Cristal d'Arques/Durand

Spa
Wavy Glass
Cristal d'Arques/Durand

Cubic
Inset Squares
Cristal d'Arques/Durand

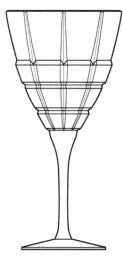

Facettes
Cut Squares
Cristal d'Arques/Durand

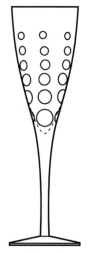

Tweed
Champagne Flute Shown
Polished Dots
Cristal d'Arques/Durand

Sorrento
Fan & Arch Cuts
Cristal d'Arques/Durand

Radiance
Vertical & Swag Cuts
Cristal d'Arques/Durand

Radiance Frosted
Frosted Vertical &
Swag Cuts
Cristal d'Arques/Durand

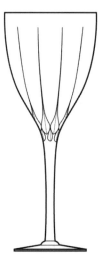

Elise
Vertical Cuts
Cristal d'Arques/Durand

Meribel
Vertical Cuts
Cristal d'Arques/Durand

Juliette
Crisscross & Vertical Cuts
Cristal d'Arques/Durand

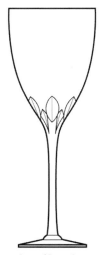

Lara/Angeles
Vertical Cuts
Cristal d'Arques/Durand

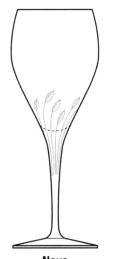

Nova
Gray Cut Plants
Cristal d'Arques/Durand

Orion
Crisscross & Fan Cuts
Cristal d'Arques/Durand

Orion
Crisscross & Fan Cuts,
Gold or Platinum Trim
Cristal d'Arques/Durand

Eternelle
Cut Plants
Cristal d'Arques/Durand

Eternelle Gold
Cut Plants, Gold Trim
Cristal d'Arques/Durand

Chamonix
Gray Vertical Cuts
Cristal d'Arques/Durand

Enchante
Vertical Cuts
Cristal d'Arques/Durand

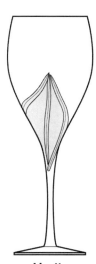

Linette
Frosted Petals
Cristal d'Arques/Durand

Alstaire
Vertical Cuts
Cristal d'Arques/Durand

Agena
Vertical Swirl Cuts
Cristal d'Arques/Durand

Agena Gold
Vertical Swirl Cuts,
Gold Trim
Cristal d'Arques/Durand

Callisto
Gray Vertical Cuts
Cristal d'Arques/Durand

Capella
Oval Cuts
Cristal d'Arques/Durand

Capella Gold
Capella Platinum
Oval Cuts,
Gold or Platinum Trim
Cristal d'Arques/Durand

Cristal d'Arques/Durand

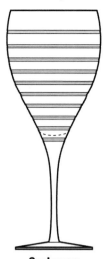

Cyclamen
Horizontal Cut Rings
Cristal d'Arques/Durand

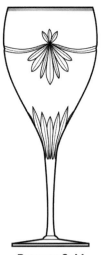

Rowena Gold
Swag & Fan Cuts,
Gold Trim
Cristal d'Arques/Durand

Sarlat
Crisscross, Fan,
& Crosshatch Cuts
Cristal d'Arques/Durand

Chatel
Etched Swags
Cristal d'Arques/Durand

Chatel Gold
Etched Swags,
Gold Trim
Cristal d'Arques/Durand

Valloire
Gold Encrusted
Etched Band, Gold Trim
Cristal d'Arques/Durand

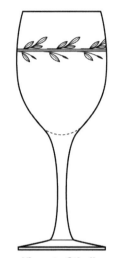

Vicomte Othello
Horizontal Line
& Leaf Cuts
Cristal d'Arques/Durand

Valinco
Leaf Cuts
Cristal d'Arques/Durand

Esterele
Vertical Cuts
Cristal d'Arques/Durand

Juan
Oval Cuts
Cristal d'Arques/Durand

Vicomte Vannie
Crisscross Cuts
Cristal d'Arques/Durand

Junon
Swirl Cuts
Cristal d'Arques/Durand

Farandole
Gray & Clear Swirl Cuts
Cristal d'Arques/Durand

Spirale Mate
Gray Cut Swirls
Cristal d'Arques/Durand

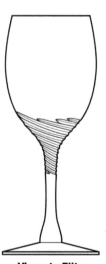

Vicomte Elite
Swirl Cuts
Cristal d'Arques/Durand

Vicomte Grape
Grape Leaves & Vine
Cristal d'Arques/Durand

Eleana
Gray Cut Leaves
Cristal d'Arques/Durand

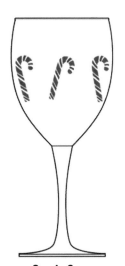

Candy Cane
Red & Green Candy Canes
Cristal d'Arques/Durand

Uptown
Balloon Wine Shown
Various Color Bowls,
Multi-Motif
Cristal d'Arques/Durand

Brush Rainbow
Iced Tea Shown
Multicolored
Horizontal Bands
Cristal d'Arques/Durand

CRA 36
Multicolored Geometric
Band, Blue Stem
Cristal d'Arques/Durand

Cachemire
Frosted Leaves
Cristal d'Arques/Durand

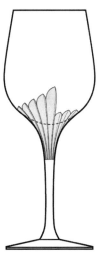

Cervione
Frosted Vertical Cuts
Cristal d'Arques/Durand

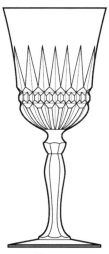

Villeneuve
Horizontal & Vertical Cuts
Cristal d'Arques/Durand

Ales
Fan Cuts
Cristal d'Arques/Durand

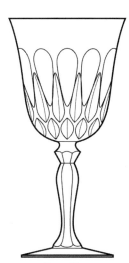

Beaulieu
Vertical & Panel Cuts
Cristal d'Arques/Durand

Ventoux
Etched Floral, Gold Trim
Cristal d'Arques/Durand

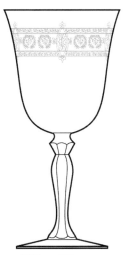

Villiers Miramar
Etched Wreaths & Scrolls
Cristal d'Arques/Durand

Villiers Magnolia
Gray Cut Floral
Cristal d'Arques/Durand

Villiers Epidaure
Cut Wheat
Cristal d'Arques/Durand

Cristal d'Arques/Durand

Issambres
Etched Floral
Cristal d'Arques/Durand

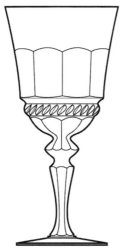

Fontainebleau
Panel Cuts
Cristal d'Arques/Durand

Menuet
Blue Bowl & Foot,
Crisscross & Leaf Cuts
Cristal d'Arques/Durand

Valse
Blue Bowl & Foot,
Swirl Cuts
Cristal d'Arques/Durand

Pavane
Blue Bowl & Foot, Clear
Vertical & Horizontal Cuts
Cristal d'Arques/Durand

CRA 38
Blue Bowl & Foot, Gray
Vertical & Horizontal Cuts
Cristal d'Arques/Durand

Annecy
Optic Bowl,
Crosshatch Cuts
Cristal d'Arques/Durand

Antique
Clear or Various Color Bowls,
Crosshatch & Fan Cuts
Cristal d'Arques/Durand

Antique
Clear or Various Color Bowls,
Crosshatch & Fan Cuts,
Gold Trim
Cristal d'Arques/Durand

Fidelio
Blue Bowl,
Vertical & Panel Cuts
Cristal d'Arques/Durand

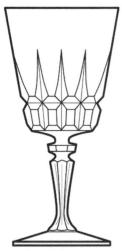

Chantelle/Lady Victoria
Vertical & Horizontal Cuts
Cristal d'Arques/Durand

Joanna
Horizontal, Fan &
Crisscross Cuts
Cristal 'Arques/Durand

Traditions Gold
Horizontal, Fan &
Crisscross Cuts, Gold Trim
Cristal d'Arques/Durand

Maria
Plain
Cristal d'Arques/Durand

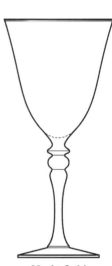

**Maria Gold
Maria Platinum**
Gold or Platinum Trim
Cristal d'Arques/Durand

Maria
Swirl Optic Bowl
Cristal d'Arques/Durand

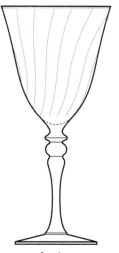

Lystra
Swirl Optic Bowl,
Gold Trim
Cristal d'Arques/Durand

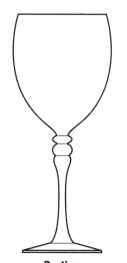

Cortina
Plain
Cristal d'Arques/Durand

Cortina
Various Color
Stem Accents
Cristal d'Arques/Durand

Dampierre
Etched Floral
Cristal d'Arques/Durand

Orly Satine
Frosted Stem
Cristal d'Arques/Durand

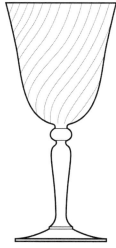

Angelique
Swirl Optic Bowl
Cristal d'Arques/Durand

Onyx
Swirl Optic Bowl,
Black Stem
Cristal d'Arques/Durand

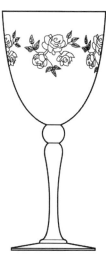

Roseraie
Etched Roses
Cristal d'Arques/Durand

Mystique
Crisscross & Fan Cuts
Cristal d'Arques/Durand

Dots
Cut Dots
Cristal d'Arques/Durand

Presence
Frosted Stem Accent
or Bases, Platinum Trim
Cristal d'Arques/Durand

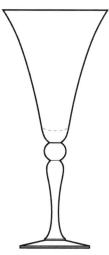

Harmony
Red Wine Shown
Plain
Cristal d'Arques/Durand

Emerald Glamour
Wine Shown
Green Optic Bowl
Cristal d'Arques/Durand

Flora
Frosted Embossed
Floral Stem Accent
Cristal d'Arques/Durand

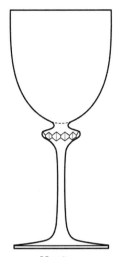

Mantova
Plain
Cristal d'Arques/Durand

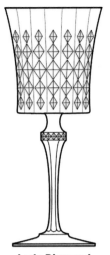

Lady Diamond
Diamond Cuts
Cristal d'Arques/Durand

Chesnay
Star, Fan &
Crosshatch Cuts
Cristal d'Arques/Durand

Fontenay
Crisscross, Crosshatch
Oval & Fan Cuts
Cristal d'Arques/Durand

Fontenay
Crisscross, Crosshatch
Oval & Fan Cuts, Gold Trim
Cristal d'Arques/Durand

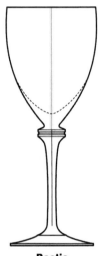

Bastia
Wine Shown
Plain, Square Bowl & Stem
Cristal d'Arques/Durand

Laser
Optic Bowl
Cristal d'Arques/Durand

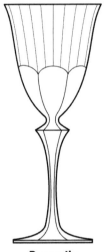

Damantis
Optic Bowl, Panel Cuts
Cristal d'Arques/Durand

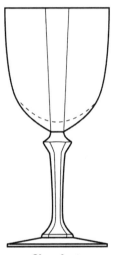

Chambery
Multisided Bowl
Cristal d'Arques/Durand

Alesia
Optic Bowl
Cristal d'Arques/Durand

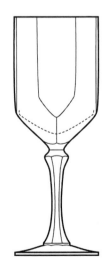

Nantes
Multisided Bowl
Cristal d'Arques/Durand

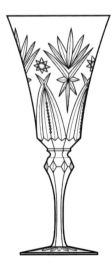

Vincennes
Star, Fan & Arch Cuts
Cristal d'Arques/Durand

Lude Lilas
Lilac Stem
Cristal d'Arques/Durand

St. Cloud
Vertical & Crisscross Cuts
Cristal d'Arques/Durand

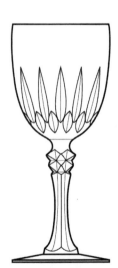

Lavandou
Oval Cuts
Cristal d'Arques/Durand

Deauville
Fan & Crisscross Cuts
Cristal d'Arques/Durand

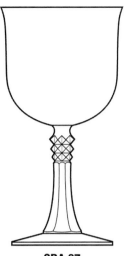

CRA 37
Clear or Frosted Stem
Cristal d'Arques/Durand

CRA 35
Pink or Blue Stem
Cristal d'Arques/Durand

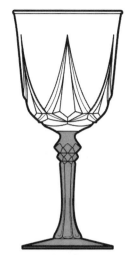

Auteuil Lilas
Vertical Cuts,
Purple Stem
Cristal d'Arques/Durand

Auteuil
Vertical Cuts
Cristal d'Arques/Durand

Avignon
Vertical Cuts
Cristal d'Arques/Durand

Elysee Taille
Vertical & Horizontal Cuts
Cristal d'Arques/Durand

Danube
Crisscross & Fan Cuts,
Optic Bowl
Cristal d'Arques/Durand

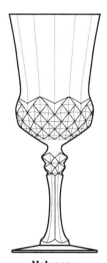

Valencay
Crisscross Cuts, Plain
Cristal d'Arques/Durand

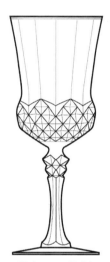

Valencay Gold
Crisscross Cuts,
Gold Trim
Cristal d'Arques/Durand

Longchamp
Various Solid Colors, or Various
Color Bowls with Clear Stem,
Vertical & Crosshatch Cuts
Cristal d'Arques/Durand

**Longchamp Gold
Longchamp Platinum**
Vertical & Crosshatch Cuts,
Gold or Platinum Trim
Cristal d'Arques/Durand

CRA 49
Fan, Star &
Crisscross Cuts
Cristal d'Arques/Durand

Gothic
Ruby Bowl,
Arch Cuts
Cristal d'Arques/Durand

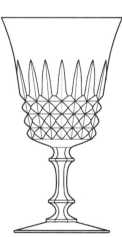

Tuilleries/Villandry
Vertical & Crisscross Cuts
Cristal d'Arques/Durand

259

Cristal d'Arques/Durand

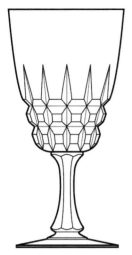

Pompadour
Vertical & Horizontal Cuts
Cristal d'Arques/Durand

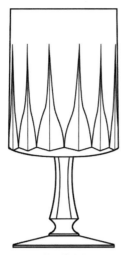

Bedford
Vertical Cuts
Cristal d'Arques/Durand

Louvre
Vertical Cuts
Cristal d'Arques/Durand

CRA 44
Crisscross & Fan Cuts
Cristal d'Arques/Durand

Diamond
Crisscross & Diamond Cuts
Cristal d'Arques/Durand

Luxemburg
Vertical Cuts
Cristal d'Arques/Durand

Palais
Crisscross, Vertical
& Crosshatch Cuts
Cristal d'Arques/Durand

Neuville
Crisscross, Arch
& Star Cuts
Cristal d'Arques/Durand

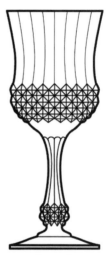

Ancenis
Vertical & Crisscross Cuts,
Optic Bowl
Cristal d'Arques/Durand

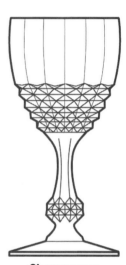

Chenonceaux
Vertical & Crisscross Cuts,
Optic Bowl
Cristal d'Arques/Durand

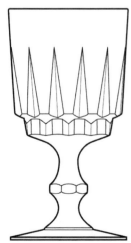

CRA 33
Vertical Cuts
Cristal d'Arques/Durand

Rambouillet
Panel Cuts,
Plain
Cristal d'Arques/Durand

Rambouillet
Panel Cuts,
Gold Trim
Cristal d'Arques/Durand

Rivoli
Panel Cuts
Cristal d'Arques/Durand

Paris Royal
Plain
Cristal d'Arques/Durand

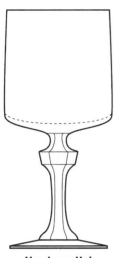

Vendome Uni
Plain
Cristal d'Arques/Durand

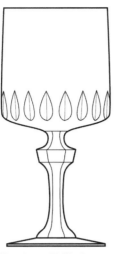

Vendome Taille Lance
Vertical Cuts
Cristal d'Arques/Durand

CRA 5
Crisscross Cuts
Cristal d'Arques/Durand

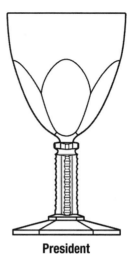

President
Panel Cuts,
Cut Stem, Multisided Foot
Cristal d'Arques/Durand

Imagination
Plain
Cristal d'Arques/Durand

Imagination Taille Lance
Vertical Cuts
Cristal d'Arques/Durand

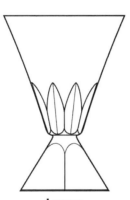

Lances
Vertical Cuts, Square Foot
Cristal d'Arques/Durand

Pyramid
Multisided Bowl,
Square Hollow Foot
Cristal d'Arques/Durand

Bretagne
Multisided Bowl,
Vertical Cuts
Cristal d'Arques/Durand

Bretagne Gold
Multisided Bowl,
Vertical Cuts, Gold Trim
Cristal d'Arques/Durand

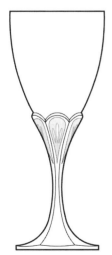

Granville
Frosted Panels on Stem
Cristal d'Arques/Durand

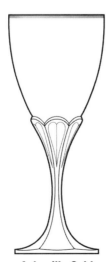

Asheville Gold
Gold Trim
Cristal d'Arques/Durand

Tornade
Swirl Cuts,
Multisided Foot
Cristal d'Arques/Durand

Orsay
Swirl Cuts,
Multisided Hollow Foot
Cristal d'Arques/Durand

Chaumont
Vertical Cuts,
Multisided Hollow Foot
Cristal d'Arques/Durand

Cristal d'Arques/Durand

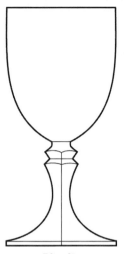

Biarritz
Plain, Square Foot
Cristal d'Arques/Durand

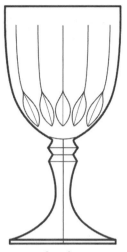

Argeles
Vertical Cuts,
Square Foot
Cristal d'Arques/Durand

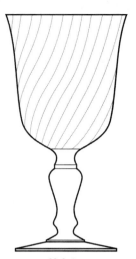

Volute
Swirl Optic Bowl
Cristal d'Arques/Durand

Rosaline
Pink, Swirl Optic Bowl
Cristal d'Arques/Durand

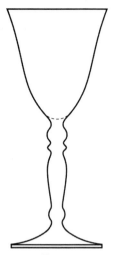

Baroc
Plain
Cristal d'Arques/Durand

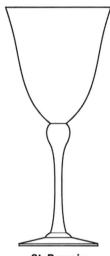

St. Romain
Plain
Cristal d'Arques/Durand

Venise Saphir (Blue)
Venise Emerald (Green)
Blue or Green Bubble
in Stem
Cristal d'Arques/Durand

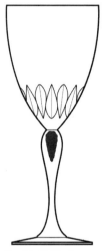

Saphir Taille Lance
Vertical Cuts,
Blue Bubble in Stem
Cristal d'Arques/Durand

Chateauneuf
Plain
Cristal d'Arques/Durand

Symphonie Taille Lunel
Gray & Clear Swirl Cuts
Cristal d'Arques/Durand

Byzance
Blue Twist Stem Accent
Cristal d'Arques/Durand

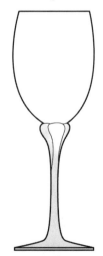

Uzes Satine
Frosted Stem
Cristal d'Arques/Durand

Veronese
Clear, Black, Blue
or Pink Stem
Cristal d'Arques/Durand

Nimes
Plain
Cristal d'Arques/Durand

Tourbillon
Wine Shown
Clear & Frosted Swirls
Cristal d'Arques/Durand

Penelope
Frosted Horizontal
& Leaf Cuts
Cristal d'Arques/Durand

Artemis
Arch Cuts
Cristal d'Arques/Durand

Florence
Frosted Petals
Cristal d'Arques/Durand

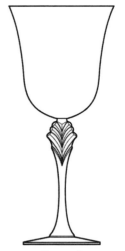

Verneuil
Plain
Cristal d'Arques/Durand

Noblesse
Plain
Cristal d'Arques/Durand

Cabourg
Optic Bowl
Cristal d'Arques/Durand

Grands Vins Cabourg
Burgundy Wine Shown
Optic Bowl
Cristal d'Arques/Durand

Nemours
Swirl Optic Bowl,
Twisted Stem
Cristal d'Arques/Durand

Sophia
Plain, Twisted Stem
Cristal d'Arques/Durand

Fleury Taille Epi
Cut Wheat, Twisted Stem
Cristal d'Arques/Durand

Fleury Gravure Venise
Etched Floral,
Twisted Stem
Cristal d'Arques/Durand

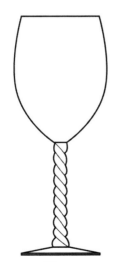

Fleury
Twisted Stem
Cristal d'Arques/Durand

Angelique
Clear, Aqua or Cobalt
Twisted Stem, Plain
Cristal d'Arques/Durand

Angelique
Twisted Stem, Gold Trim
Cristal d'Arques/Durand

Elegance
Plain
Cristal d'Arques/Durand

263

Cristal d'Arques/Durand

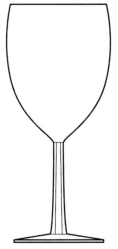

Grand Noblesse
Plain
Cristal d'Arques/Durand

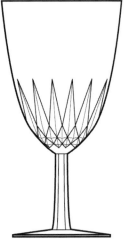

Diamant
Vertical Cuts, Plain
Cristal d'Arques/Durand

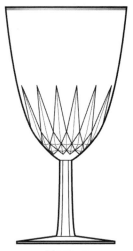

Diamant
Vertical Cuts, Gold Trim
Cristal d'Arques/Durand

Regency
Vertical Cuts
Cristal d'Arques/Durand

Petale
Panel Cuts
Cristal d'Arques/Durand

Taffetas
Champagne Flute Shown
Frosted Scrolls
Cristal d'Arques/Durand

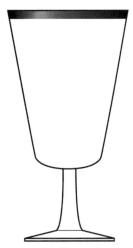

Parisienne
Wide Platinum Band
Cristal d'Arques/Durand

Carousel
Swirl Optic Bowl
Cristal d'Arques/Durand

Grand Meridian
Optic Bowl,
Clear or Black Stem
Cristal d'Arques/Durand

Tahiti
White, Blue or Amethyst
Frosted Stem
Cristal d'Arques/Durand

Americana
Clear or Various
Color Stems
Cristal d'Arques/Durand

Signature
Plain
Cristal d'Arques/Durand

Domino/Signature Black
Black Stem & Foot
Cristal d'Arques/Durand

Emerald
Green Stem & Foot
Cristal d'Arques/Durand

Perle
Gray Stem & Foot
Cristal d'Arques/Durand

Neptune
Blue Stem & Foot
Cristal d'Arques/Durand

Turquoise
Turquoise Stem & Foot
Cristal d'Arques/Durand

Azur
Blue Stem & Foot
Cristal d'Arques/Durand

Cherry
Red Stem & Foot
Cristal d'Arques/Durand

Rose
Pink Stem & Foot
Cristal d'Arques/Durand

Jade
Light Green Stem & Foot
Cristal d'Arques/Durand

CRA 31
Cobalt, Plain
Cristal d'Arques/Durand

Viva
Wine Shown
Black Stem & Foot
Cristal d'Arques/Durand

Color Program Ruby
Red Stem & Foot
Cristal d'Arques/Durand

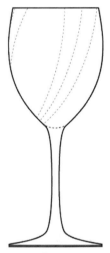

Astra
Swirl Optic Bowl, Plain
Cristal d'Arques/Durand

Astra
Swirl Optic Bowl,
Gold Trim
Cristal d'Arques/Durand

Shade
Black, White, Blue
or Green Bowl
Cristal d'Arques/Durand

Montego Gold
Wine Shown
Plain, Gold Trim
Cristal d'Arques/Durand

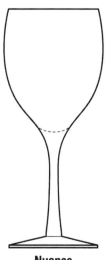

Nuance
Plain
Cristal d'Arques/Durand

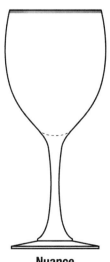

Nuance
Gold Trim
Cristal d'Arques/Durand

265

Cristal d'Arques/Durand

Monaco
Plain
Cristal d'Arques/Durand

Monaco
Clear or Purple
Optic Bowl
Cristal d'Arques/Durand

Festival
Swirl Optic Bowl
Cristal d'Arques/Durand

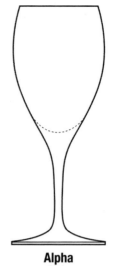

Alpha
Plain
Cristal d'Arques/Durand

Vicomte
Plain
Cristal d'Arques/Durand

Vigne
Plain
Cristal d'Arques/Durand

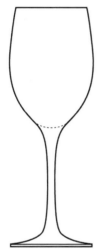

Invitation
Plain
Cristal d'Arques/Durand

Padova
Plain
Cristal d'Arques/Durand

Montlouis Gold
Swirl Optic Bowl,
Gold Trim
Cristal d'Arques/Durand

Clarisse
Optic Bowl, Plain
Cristal d'Arques/Durand

Clarisse Gold
Optic Bowl, Gold Trim
Cristal d'Arques/Durand

Connoisseur
White Wine Shown
Plain
Cristal d'Arques/Durand

Wine For Dummies
White Wine Shown
Plain
Cristal d'Arques/Durand

Oenologue/Connoisseur
Wine Shown
Plain
Cristal d'Arques/Durand

Chardonnay Ballon
Plain
Cristal d'Arques/Durand

Mendocino
Balloon Wine Shown
Plain
Cristal d'Arques/Durand

Selection
Balloon Wine Shown
Plain
Cristal d'Arques/Durand

Chardonnay
Plain
Cristal d'Arques/Durand

Chateau
Burgundy Wine Shown
Plain
Cristal d'Arques/Durand

Epitome
Red Wine Shown
Plain
Cristal d'Arques/Durand

Alto
Plain
Cristal d'Arques/Durand

Super Noblesse
Balloon Wine Shown
Plain
Cristal d'Arques/Durand

CRA 54
Wine Shown
Plain
Cristal d'Arques/Durand

Briancon Decor Fleur
Etched Flower
Cristal d'Arques/Durand

Ambassade
Plain
Cristal d'Arques/Durand

Sterling
Plain
Cristal d'Arques/Durand

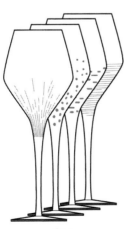

Ose
Various Gray Cut
Geometric Designs
Cristal d'Arques/Durand

Pearlescence
Martini Shown
Frosted, Barware
Cristal d'Arques/Durand

Grands Vins
White Wine Shown
Plain
Cristal d'Arques/Durand

CRA 55
Plain
Cristal d'Arques/Durand

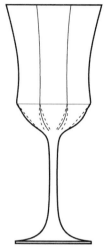

Octime
Clear, Black or White,
Octagonal Bowl
Cristal d'Arques/Durand

Stretch
White Rings on Stem
Cristal d'Arques/Durand

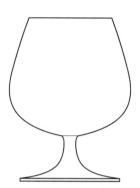

Cannes
Plain
Cristal d'Arques/Durand

Cavalier
Clear, Amber, Green
or Ruby Bowl
Cristal d'Arques/Durand

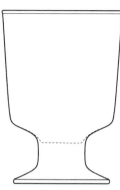

Mekano
Footed Tumbler Shown
Plain
Cristal d'Arques/Durand

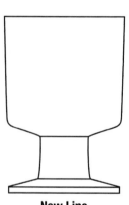

New Line
Plain
Cristal 'Arques/Durand

CRA 3
Ruby Bowl
Cristal d'Arques/Durand

Courtyard
Clear, Cobalt or
Turquoise Stem, Plain
Cristal d'Arques/Durand

Country Manor
Clear, Cobalt or Turquoise
Stem, Swirl Optic Bowl
Cristal d'Arques/Durand

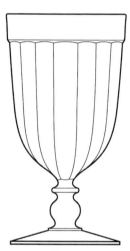

Kavya
Panel Cuts
Cristal d'Arques/Durand

Wine

Goblet

Casual Settings
Clear, Amethyst, Blue,
Green or Ruby Bowl
Cristal d'Arques/Durand

Quadro
Milkshake Tumbler Shown
Clear or Amethyst
Paneled Bowl
Cristal d'Arques/Durand

Ajaccio
White Wine Shown
Frosted Swirl Stem Accent
Cristal d'Arques/Durand

CRA 52
Iced Tea Shown
Red Stem
Cristal d'Arques/Durand

Organdi
Scrolls in Foot
Cristal d'Arques/Durand

CRA 53
Optic Bowl, Frosted Stem
Cristal d'Arques/Durand

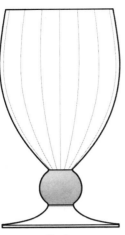

Corte
Optic Bowl, Frosted Stem
Cristal d'Arques/Durand

CRA 42
Wine Shown
Multisided Black Foot
Cristal d'Arques/Durand

Monceaux
Paneled Bowl
Cristal d'Arques/Durand

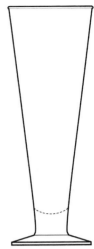

Classic Pilsner
Pilsner Shown
Plain
Cristal d'Arques/Durand

Kyoto
Clear, Red or Black Foot
Cristal d'Arques/Durand

Sombrero
Margarita Shown
Vertical & Arch Cuts,
Green Stem
Cristal d'Arques/Durand

Roemer
Turquoise or Green
Ring Stem
Cristal d'Arques/Durand

CRA 41
Gray Cut Grapes,
Green Ring Stem
Cristal d'Arques/Durand

Millennium 2001
Sculpted Stem
Cristal d'Arques/Durand

Millennium 2000
Champagne Flute Shown
Sculpted Stem or Foot
Cristal d'Arques/Durand

Noel
Red or Green Bowl,
Sculpted Stem
Cristal d'Arques/Durand

Forever
Champagne Flute Shown
Optic Bowl, Clear or Frosted
Sculpted Heart Stem
Cristal d'Arques/Durand

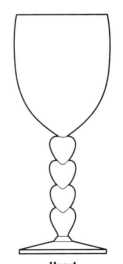

Heart
Sculpted Heart Stem
Cristal d'Arques/Durand

Abaca
Frosted Bambo
Shaped Stem
Cristal d'Arques/Durand

Lucia
Clear or Frosted
Rose Stem
Cristal d'Arques/Durand

Gaufrette
Champagne/Tall Sherbet Shown
Clear or Cobalt
Cristal d'Arques/Durand

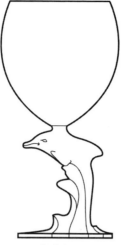

Dolphy
Wine Shown
Clear or Frosted
Dolphin Shaped Stem
Cristal d'Arques/Durand

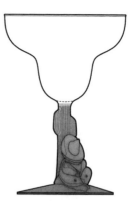

Siesta
Margarita Shown
Green Stem
Cristal d'Arques/Durand

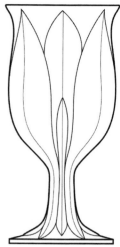

Pompano/Tulip
Embossed Leaves
Cristal d'Arques/Durand

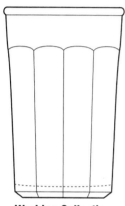

Working Collection
Highball Shown
Clear, Cobalt & Turquoise,
Paneled
Cristal d'Arques/Durand

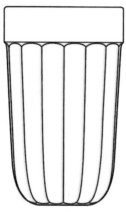

Rustic
Highball Shown
Paneled
Cristal d'Arques/Durand

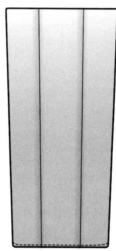

Octime
Tumbler Shown
Clear or Smoke, Multisided
Cristal d'Arques/Durand

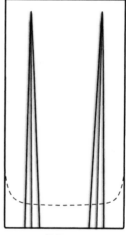

Tribute
Cooler Shown
Vertical Cuts
Cristal d'Arques/Durand

Victoria
Double Old Fashioned Shown
Vertical & Diamond Cuts
Cristal d'Arques/Durand

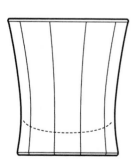

Temptation
On The Rocks Shown
Multisided, Barware
Cristal d'Arques/Durand

Stanford
Old Fashioned Shown
Vertical Cuts
Cristal d'Arques/Durand

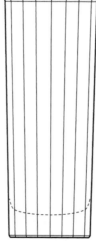

Quadrille
Highball Shown
Vertical Cuts
Cristal d'Arques/Durand

Diplomat
Tumbler Shown
Vertical Cuts
Cristal d'Arques/Durand

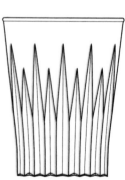

Derby/Danbury
Double Old Fashioned Shown
Vertical Cuts
Cristal d'Arques/Durand

Ginsing
Old Fashioned Shown
Stripes
Cristal d'Arques/Durand

Spiral
Double Old Fashioned Shown
Etched Rings
Cristal d'Arques/Durand

Ashley
Highball Shown
Vertical & Crisscross Cuts
Cristal d'Arques/Durand

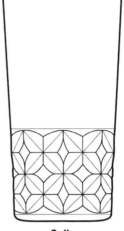

Sully
Highball Shown
Geometric Cuts, Barware
Cristal d'Arques/Durand

Tartan
Double Old Fashioned Shown
Vertical & Horizontal Cuts
Cristal d'Arques/Durand

Carrolton
Cooler Shown
Vertical & Horizontal Cuts
Cristal d'Arques/Durand

Diamant
Whiskey Shown
Diagonal & Crosshatch Cuts,
Barware
Cristal d'Arques/Durand

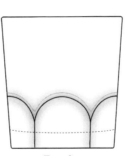

Esquire
Old Fashioned Shown
Panel Cuts
Cristal d'Arques/Durand

Cheverny
Highball Shown
Vertical Cuts
Cristal d'Arques/Durand

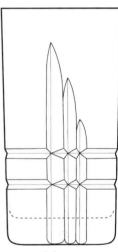

Arizona
Highball Shown
Vertical & Horizontal Cuts
Cristal d'Arques/Durand

Oasis
Old Fashioned Shown
Cut Wavy Rings
Cristal d'Arques/Durand

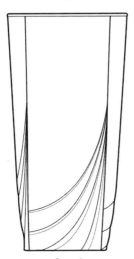

Ascot
Cooler Shown
Clear, Blue or Pink,
Cut Swirls, Barware
Cristal d'Arques/Durand

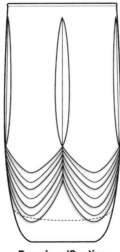

Premiere/Ovation
Cooler Shown
Vertical & Swag Cuts
Cristal d'Arques/Durand

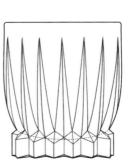

Spectrum
Double Old Fashioned Shown
Vertical Cuts
Cristal d'Arques/Durand

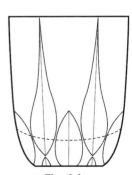

Fire & Ice
Double Old Fashioned Shown
Clear or Blue, Vertical Cuts
Cristal d'Arques/Durand

Cristal d'Arques/Durand

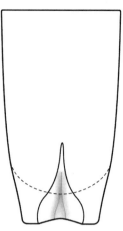

Lisbonne
Highball Shown
Vertical Cut
Cristal d'Arques/Durand

Sculptra
Highball Shown
Geometric Cuts, Barware
Cristal d'Arques/Durand

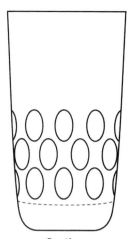

Ovation
Highball Shown
Oval Cuts
Cristal d'Arques/Durand

Orbits Etched
Cooler Shown
Gray Circles
Cristal d'Arques/Durand

Botanic
Cooler Shown
Embossed Leaves
Cristal d'Arques/Durand

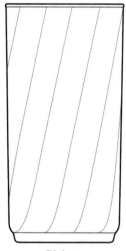

Riviera
Tumbler Shown
Optic, Barware
Cristal d'Arques/Durand

Aristocrat
Double Old Fashioned Shown
Plain
Cristal d'Arques/Durand

Amboise
Highball Shown
Plain
Cristal d'Arques/Durand

Etna
Tumbler Shown
Various Color Bases
Cristal d'Arques/Durand

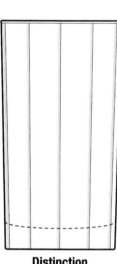

Distinction
Cooler Shown
Panels, Multisided
Cristal d'Arques/Durand

Stratus
Highball Shown
Plain, Barware
Cristal d'Arques/Durand

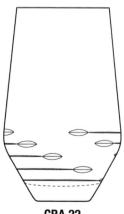

CRA 22
Highball Shown
Horizontal Cuts
Cristal d'Arques/Durand

Shetland
Old Fashioned Shown
Clear or Bluish/Purple
Plain, Barware
Cristal d'Arques/Durand

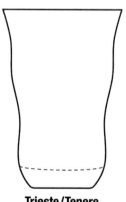

Trieste/Tenere
Cooler Shown
Clear or Amethyst
Plain
Cristal d'Arques/Durand

Curl
Cooler Shown
Plain
Cristal d'Arques/Durand

272

Coca Cola
Tumbler Shown
Clear or Red, Embossed
Logo, Multi-Motif
Cristal d'Arques/Durand

Holly Cheer
Highball Shown
Holly & Berries,
Red Vertical Lines
Cristal d'Arques/Durand

Spring Garden
Cooler Shown
Multicolored Flowers,
Green Stems
Cristal d'Arques/Durand

Heritage Rooster Collection
Mug Shown
Panels, Rooster Medallion
Cristal d'Arques/Durand

Floral Bouquet
Dinner Plate Shown
Panels & Beaded Bands
Cristal d'Arques/Durand

Country Wheat
Round Platter Shown
Wheat Stalks, Textured
Cristal d'Arques/Durand

Santa Fe
Dinner Plate Shown
Ridged Rings
Cristal d'Arques/Durand

Romance
Dessert Plate Shown
Frosted Flower
Cristal d'Arques/Durand

Soho
Dinner Plate Shown
Clear or Frosted,
Textured Rim
Cristal d'Arques/Durand

Mallory
Dinner Plate Shown
Embossed Leaves & Grapes
Cristal d'Arques/Durand

Plenitude
Dinner Plate Shown
Blue, Green or Red,
Scrolls & Vines
Cristal d'Arques/Durand

Matys
Salad Plate Shown
Blue, Green, Orange,
or Yellow Rim, Tulip Center
Cristal d'Arques/Durand

Tulip Ciel
Salad Plate Shown
Yellow Tulips on Blue
Cristal d'Arques/Durand

Roc
Dinner Plate Shown
Thumbprints
Cristal d'Arques/Durand

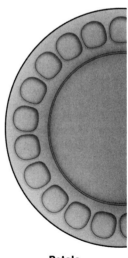

Petale
Plate Shown
Amber, Thumbprints
Cristal d'Arques/Durand

Boston
Cooler Shown
Clear, Cobalt or Light Blue,
Panel Cuts
Crisa

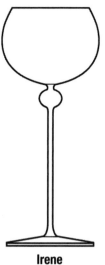

Irene
Plain
Cristais Hering

Karina
Red Wine Shown
Green Rings in Stem
Cristais Hering

Anna
Aqua Stem
Cristais Hering

Martina
Plain
Cristais Hering

CIH 3
Crisscross, Fan &
Star Cuts
Cristais Hering

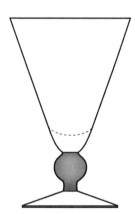

Juana
Red Wine Shown
Blue Ball Stem
Cristais Hering

PLZ 2
Crisscross Cuts
Cristal au Plomb

PLZ 1
Crisscross Cuts
Cristal au Plomb

CR7 1
Crisscross Cuts
Cristal d'Argental

Austria
Vertical Cuts
Cristal de Flandre

Salzburg
Crosshatch & Fan Cuts
Cristal de Flandre

Salzburg Gold
Crosshatch & Fan Cuts,
Gold Trim
Cristal de Flandre

CFL 1
Wine Shown
Crisscross, Fan & Star Cuts,
Optic Bowl
Cristal de Flandre

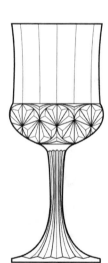

Fascination
Geometric Cuts
Cristal de Flandre

CDN 1
Laurel & Panel Cuts
Cristal de France

Nirvana
Vertical & Crisscross Cuts
Cristal de France

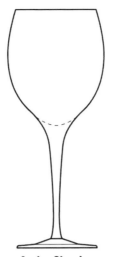

Andre Chenier
Plain
Cristal de Sevres

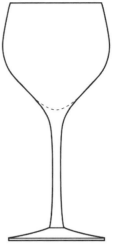

Sophie
Plain
Cristal de Sevres

Arpeges
Plain
Cristal de Sevres

Attitudes
Bordeaux Wine Shown
Plain
Cristal de Sevres

Degustation
Brandy Glass Shown
Plain
Cristal de Sevres

Sologne
Plain
Cristal de Sevres

Sologne
Gold Trim
Cristal de Sevres

Beaubourg
Plain
Cristal de Sevres

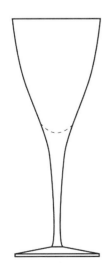

Florian
Plain
Cristal de Sevres

Florian
Platinum Trim
Cristal de Sevres

Gran Crus
Plain
Cristal de Sevres

Cepages
Tasting Glass Shown
Plain
Cristal de Sevres

St. Germain
Plain
Cristal de Sevres

Riviera
Plain
Cristal de Sevres

Lorelei
Wine Shown
Amethyst, Cobalt, Green, Gray,
Yellow or Turquoise Bowl
Cristal de Sevres

Tuileries
Vertical Cuts
Cristal de Sevres

Corinthe
Vertical Cuts
Cristal de Sevres

President
Vertical Cuts
Cristal de Sevres

Brissac
Thumbprint Cuts
Cristal de Sevres

Bareges
Vertical Cuts
Cristal de Sevres

Avril
Plain
Cristal de Sevres

Seudre
Plain
Cristal de Sevres

Fleville
Vertical Oval Cuts
Cristal de Sevres

Neufchateau
Vertical Cuts
Cristal de Sevres

Ritz
Optic Bowl, Gold Trim &
Stem Accent; also Plain with
Clear or Blue Bowl
Cristal de Sevres

Marienbad
Plain
Cristal de Sevres

Savannah
Red Wine Shown
Crisscross & Vertical Cuts
Cristal de Sevres

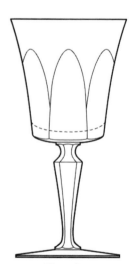

Marquise
Panel Cuts
T5166
Cristal de Sevres

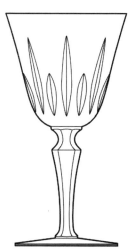

Colorado
Vertical Cuts
Cristal de Sevres

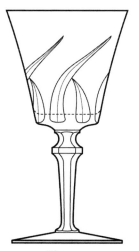

Niagara
Slanted Vertical Cuts
Cristal de Sevres

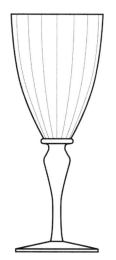

Iris
Optic Bowl
Cristal de Sevres

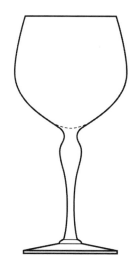

Pailly
Plain
Cristal de Sevres

Orpheo Noir
Black Core in Square Stem
Cristal de Sevres

Titien
Optic Bowl
Cristal de Sevres

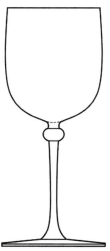

Albinoni
Plain
Cristal de Sevres

Corelli
Optic Bowl, Hollow Stem
Cristal de Sevres

Primavera
Vertical Cuts in
Gray Cut Panels
Cristal de Sevres

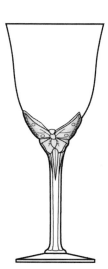

Crystal Butterfly
Frosted Butterfly
Cristal de Sevres

Swing
Champagne Flute Shown
Plain
Cristal de Sevres

Spirale
Air Twist Stem
Cristal de Sevres

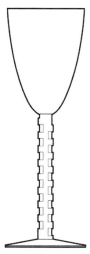

Totem
Cut Stem
Cristal de Sevres

Nevada
Crisscross & Fan Cuts
Cristal de Sevres

Norma
Twisted Stem
Cristal de Sevres

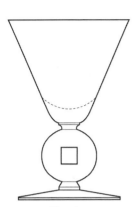

Rumba
Cut Square in
Round Disk Stem
Cristal de Sevres

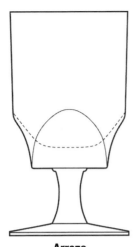

Arrezo
Panel Cuts, Square Bowl
Cristal de Sevres

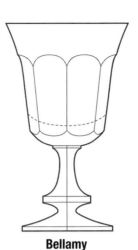

Bellamy
Panel Cuts, Square Foot
Cristal de Sevres

Montesquieu
Vertical & Crisscross Cuts,
Multisided Foot
T5512
Cristal de Sevres

Montesquieu
Panel Cuts,
Multisided Foot
Cristal de Sevres

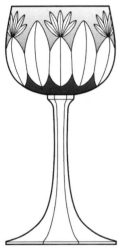

Bingen
Various Color Bowls,
Vertical & Fan Cuts,
Multisided Foot
Cristal de Sevres

Chenonceaux
Clear, Red or Blue Bowl,
Multisided Foot
Cristal de Sevres

Diane
Multisided Bowl & Foot
Cristal de Sevres

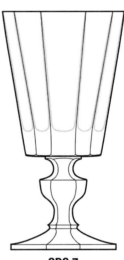

CDS 7
Multisided Bowl & Foot,
Optic Bowl
Cristal de Sevres

Mirande
Champagne Flute Shown
Optic Bowl, Twisted Stem,
Multisided Foot
Cristal de Sevres

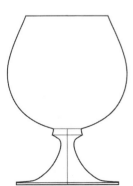

Jonzac
Brandy Glass Shown
Square Foot
Cristal de Sevres

Luna
Optic Bowl,
Blue Square Foot
Cristal de Sevres

Mila
Highball Shown
Twisted Base, Barware
Cristal de Sevres

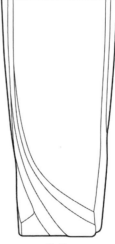

Sully
Highball Shown
Twisted Base, Barware
Cristal de Sevres

Arlay
Highball Shown
6-Sided, Barware
Cristal de Sevres

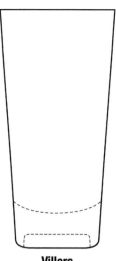

Villers
Highball Shown
Square Shape, Barware
Cristal de Sevres

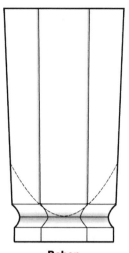

Rohan
Highball Shown
Multisided, Barware
Cristal de Sevres

CDS 5
Highball Shown
Vertical Cuts, Barware
Cristal de Sevres

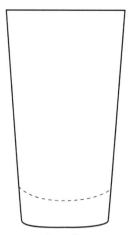

Rapallo
Highball Shown
Oval Shape, Barware
Cristal de Sevres

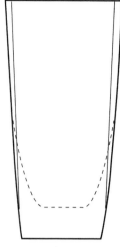

Keos
Highball Shown
Square Shape, Barware
Cristal de Sevres

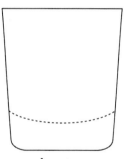

Laennec
Double Old Fashioned Shown
Plain
Cristal de Sevres

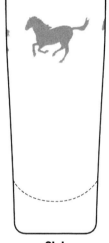

Club
Highball Shown
Gray Cut Horses
Cristal de Sevres

CTL 2
Gray Cut Swirl
Cristalleria

CEU 1
Wine Shown
Gray Cut Floral & Scrolls
Cristalleria Europa

Alexia Gambo Oro
Wine Shown
Gold Stem Accent,
Hollow Foot
Cristalleria Europa

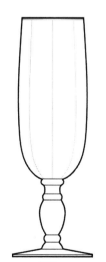

CZB 1
Champagne Flute Shown
Optic Bowl, Gold Trim
Cristallin Boussu

Provence
Optic Bowl,
Plain or Gold Trim
Crystal Clear Industries

Expressions
Plain or Gold Trim
Crystal Clear Industries

Romy
Optic Bowl, Gold Trim
Crystal Clear Industries

Jasmine
Gold Trim
Crystal Clear Industries

279

Regent Gold
Regent Platinum
Swirl Optic Bowl,
Gold or Platinum Trim
Crystal Clear Industries

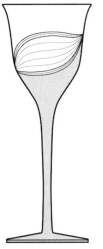

Melinda
Wine Shown
Swirl Cuts, Clear or
Pink Frosted Stem
Crystal Clear Industries

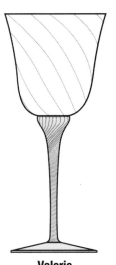

Valerie
Swirl Optic Bowl,
Clear, Dark Blue or
Peach Frosted Stem
Crystal Clear Industries

Aurora
Optic Iridescent Bowl
Crystal Clear Industries

Palazzo
Plain
Crystal Clear Industries

Mirage
Blue, Green, Red
or Yellow Ball in Stem
Crystal Clear Industries

Sara Gold
Gold Trim & Ball in Stem
Crystal Clear Industries

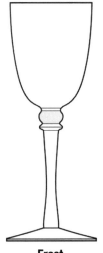

Frost
Frosted Stem Accent
Crystal Clear Industries

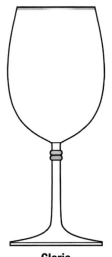

Gloria
Gold Trim & Bands on Stem
Crystal Clear Industries

CCI 8
Optic Bowl
Crystal Clear Industries

Malaga
Gray Cut Floral & Grapes
2726
Crystal Clear Industries

Kathy
Gray Cut Floral
Crystal Clear Industries

2690
Gray Cut Floral
Crystal Clear Industries

Lisa
Gray Cut Floral
Crystal Clear Industries

Star
Fan, Star & Crisscross Cuts
Crystal Clear Industries

Monica Pinwheel
Vertical, Star &
Pinwheel Cuts
Crystal Clear Industries

Elise
Vertical Cuts
Crystal Clear Industries

Celine
Crisscross, Vertical
& Floral Cuts
Crystal Clear Industries

Portico
Horizontal, Vertical
& Fan Cuts
Crystal Clear Industries

Camelia
Crosshatch, Fan &
Star Cuts
Crystal Clear Industries

CCI 2
Cut Floral
Crystal Clear Industries

133
Floral & Crosshatch Cuts
Crystal Clear Industries

132
Vertical, Fan, Star
& Oval Cuts
Crystal Clear Industries

Essex
Crisscross & Fan Cuts
Crystal Clear Industries

2704
Cut Floral, Multisided Foot
Crystal Clear Industries

Elegance
Vertical, Crisscross
& Floral Cuts
Crystal Clear Industries

3573
Fan, Star & Crosshatch Cuts
Crystal Clear Industries

Chardonney Grape
Gray Cut Grapes & Leaves
Crystal Clear Industries

CCI 7
Wine Hock Shown
Various Color Bowls,
Cut Fruit & Leaves
Crystal Clear Industries

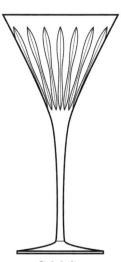

Celebrity
Vertical Cuts
Crystal Clear Industries

Crystal Clear Industries, *Crystal d'Adriana*

Linear Frost
Clear & Gray Vertical Cuts
Crystal Clear Industries

Elegance
Vertical Cuts,
Multisided Foot
2701
Crystal Clear Industries

Chardoney
Crosshatch & Floral Cuts
Crystal Clear Industries

Adria Pinwheel
Pinwheel, Fan & Swag Cuts
Crystal Clear Industries

CCI 4
Pinwheel & Vertical Cuts
Crystal Clear Industries

2696
Pinwheel & Vertical Cuts
Crystal Clear Industries

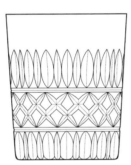

Versailles
Old Fashioned Shown
Vertical & Crisscross Cuts,
Barware
Crystal Clear Industries

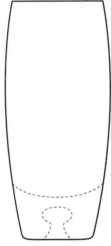

Nouveau
Highball Shown
Bubble in Base, Barware
Crystal Clear Industries

Artic
Tumbler Shown
Frosted Floral
Crystal Clear Industries

Athens
Mug Shown
Frosted Plumes, Panels
Crystal Clear Industries

York
Large Mug Shown
Indented Base, Barware
Crystal Clear Industries

Amber Bead
Dinner Plate Shown
Amber, Beaded Bands
Crystal Clear Industries

Trellis
Dinner Plate Shown
Clear, Pink or Blue,
Scrolls & Beaded Bands
Crystal Clear Industries

CDR 1
Crisscross & Fan Cuts
Crystal d'Adriana

Luna
Horizontal, Vertical, Fan
& Star Cuts
Crystal d'Adriana

Kimberly
Crisscross & Fan Cuts
Crystal Guild

Monte Carlo
Crosshatch & Star Cuts
Crystal Import Corp.

Monaco
Floral & Crisscross Cuts
Crystal Import Corp.

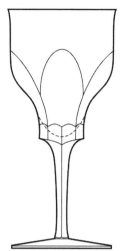

CXH 1
Wine Shown
Panel Cuts
Crystalex

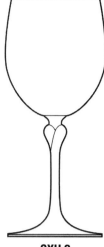

CXH 2
Plain
Crystalex

Valencia
Wine Shown
Green & Gold Filigree Band
Culver Ltd.

Valencia
Highball Shown
Wide Green & Gold
Filligree Band
Culver Ltd.

Cranberry Scroll
Cordial Shown
Gold Scrolls, Red Panels
Culver Ltd.

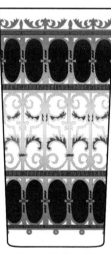

Emerald Scroll
Highball Shown
Gold Scrolls, Green Panels
Culver Ltd.

Toledo (Green)
Ebony Baroque (Black)
Highball Shown
Gold Scrolls on Green or Black
Culver Ltd.

CUV 11
Double Old Fashioned Shown
Gold & White Filigree, Ovals
Culver Ltd.

Tyrol
Old Fashioned Shown
Gold Encrusted Band,
Etched Vertical Lines
Culver Ltd.

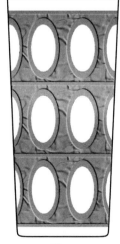

Piza
Highball Shown
Gold Grackle, Ovals
Culver Ltd.

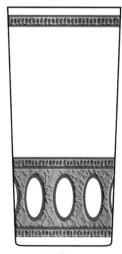

Antigua
Highball Shown
Gold Crackle, Ovals
Culver Ltd.

Images Gold
Tumbler Shown
Thin & Wide Gold
Diagonal Lines
Culver Ltd.

283

Culver Ltd.

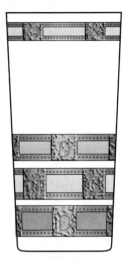

CUV 22
Highball Shown
Gold Crackle, Blue,
Green & Gold Rectangles
Culver Ltd.

Prado
Highball Shown
Green or Turquoise Squares,
Gold Scrolls, Barware
Culver Ltd.

CUV 23
Highball Shown
Platinum Scrolls
with Blue Accents
Culver Ltd.

Devon Black
Double Old Fashioned Shown
Gold Lines,
Wide Black Band
Culver Ltd.

CUV 32
Tumbler Shown
Green & Gold Bands,
Greek Key
Culver Ltd.

Saratoga
Double Old Fashioned Shown
Gold Design
Culver Ltd.

Gold Chantilly
Tumbler Shown
Gold Floral & Band
Culver Ltd.

Paisley
Double Old Fashioned Shown
Red & Gold Paisley,
Barware
Culver Ltd.

Florentine
Tumbler Shown
Gold Fruit Decals
Culver Ltd.

Sculptured Daisy
Highball Shown
White & Yellow Daisies,
Green Stems
Culver Ltd.

CUV 7
Highball Shown
Maroon, Blue & Gold Floral
Culver Ltd.

Owls
Highball Shown
Gold Encrusted Band, Owls
Culver Ltd.

CUV 39
Tumbler Shown
Cobalt, Various Gold
Astrological Signs
Culver Ltd.

Crockery
Tumbler Shown
Yellow, Blue, Gray & Orange
Lines & Fiestaware
Culver Ltd.

CUV 24
Double Old Fashioned Shown
Multicolor Halloween
Images on Frosted Squares
Culver Ltd.

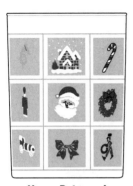

Xmas Potpourri
Double Old Fashioned Shown
Multicolor Christmas Images
on Frosted Squares
Culver Ltd.

Yule Horn
Old Fashioned Shown
Green & Red Plaid Ribbon,
Green Bough, Gold Horn
Culver Ltd.

Poinsettia
Double Old Fashioned Shown
Red Poinsettia,
Silver Leaves
Culver Ltd.

CUV 17
Double Old Fashioned Shown
Red Panels, Christmas
Geese, Gold & Green Lines
Culver Ltd.

Coniston
Plain
Cumbria

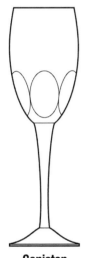

Coniston
Panel Cuts
Cumbria

Eksdale
Vertical & Panel Cuts
Cumbria

Langdale
Fan & Crisscross Cuts
Cumbria

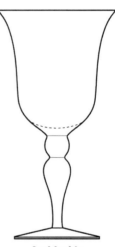

Ambleside
Plain
Cumbria

Grasmere
Oval & Crisscross Cuts
Cumbria

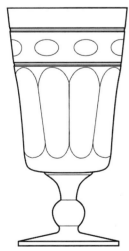

Helvellyn
Horizontal, Oval
& Panel Cuts
Cumbria

Atlas
Gold or Platinum Trim
& Stem Accent
Czechoslovakia

Atlas
Various Color Bowls,
Gold Stem Accent
Czechoslovakia

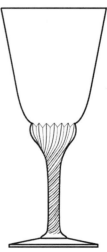

Flair
Clear or Various Color
Twisted Stems
Czechoslovakia

CZC 2
Star, Pinwheel &
Crisscross Cuts
Czechoslovakia

Adela
Wine Shown
Clear & Gray Swirl Cuts
Czechoslovakia

Pinwheel
Vertical, Crisscross, Star
& Pinwheel Cuts
Czechoslovakia

CZC 1
Etched Floral Band
& Swags, Optic Bowl
Czechoslovakia

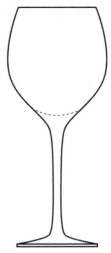

Leonardo da Vinci
Plain
da Vinci

Medici
Gray Cut Leaves & Berries
da Vinci

Caterina
Plain
da Vinci

Break-Line
Frosted Lines
da Vinci

Lucca
Panel Cuts
da Vinci

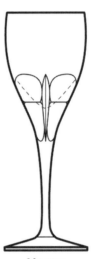

Livorno
Vertical & Panel Cuts
da Vinci

Apuania
Frosted Ovals
da Vinci

Carrara
Vertical & Horizontal Cuts
da Vinci

Siena
Vertical, Horizontal
& Crisscross Cuts
da Vinci

Firenze
Crisscross & Fan Cuts
da Vinci

Grosseto
Gray & Clear Crisscross
& Swirl Cuts
da Vinci

Arezzo
Wine Shown
Curved Vertical Cuts
da Vinci

Volterra
Diagonal Swirl Cuts
da Vinci

Pisa
Gray & Clear Cut Floral
da Vinci

Pistoia
Swirl Cuts
da Vinci

Prato
Vertical Cuts
da Vinci

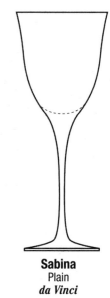

Sabina
Plain
da Vinci

Sabina Gold
Sabina Platinum
Gold or Platinum Trim
da Vinci

Saturna
Vertical Cuts
da Vinci

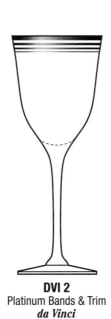

DVI 2
Platinum Bands & Trim
da Vinci

DVI 1
Gray Cut Floral
da Vinci

Cetona
Clear & Gray Swirl Cuts
da Vinci

Trevi
Panel Cuts
da Vinci

Tivoli
Panel & Crosshatch Cuts
da Vinci

Cortona
Vertical Cuts
da Vinci

Alba
Plain
da Vinci

Nuvola
Plain
da Vinci

Design
Wine Shown
Plain
da Vinci

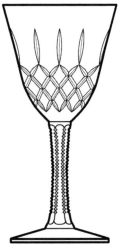

Camilla
Vertical & Crisscross Cuts,
Cut Stem
da Vinci

Adagio
Optic Bowl, Vertical Cuts
da Vinci

Isabella
Oval & Crisscross Cuts
da Vinci

Madame
Leaf & Swirl Cuts
da Vinci

Dolce Vita
Crooked Ring Cuts
da Vinci

Imperiale
Crisscross Cuts
da Vinci

Arctic
Frosted Stem
da Vinci

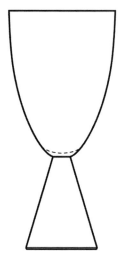

Antares
Plain
da Vinci

Viareggio
Plain
da Vinci

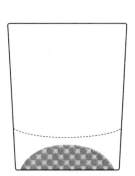

Golf
Double Old Fashioned Shown
Golf Ball Textured Base
da Vinci

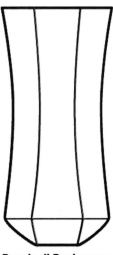

Duccio di Boninsegna
Highball Shown
Multisided, Barware
da Vinci

Hospitality
Frosted Pineapple
Stem Accent
Danbury Mint

White Floral
Wine Shown
White Floral Vine Decal
Daniel Cremieux

Isle of White
Frosted Flowers,
Optic Bowl
Daniel Cremieux

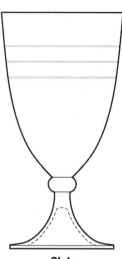

Club
Frosted Rings,
Hollow Foot
Daniel Cremieux

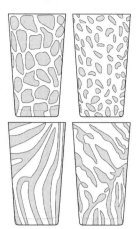

Expedition
Highball Shown
Frosted Animal Print Motifs
Daniel Cremieux

DHC 1
Various Color
Accents & Stems
Daniel Hechter

DHC 2
Frosted Gray or Black Stem
Daniel Hechter

DHC 3
Blue Bowl, Frosted Stem
Daniel Hechter

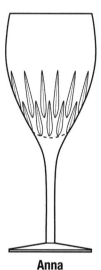

Anna
Vertical Cuts
Dansk

Glace
Red Wine Shown
Spiraling Rings
Dansk

Flora
Gray Cut Plant
Dansk

Tivoli
Gray Cut Floral
Dansk

Centro
Frosted Horizontal Cuts
Dansk

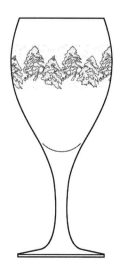

White Pine
White Pine Trees
& Snow Decal
Dansk

DAC 11
Swirl Optic Bowl
Dansk

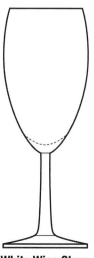

White Wine Glass
White Wine Shown
Plain
Dansk

Ursula
Multisided Optic Bowl
Dansk

Summerhouse
Plain, Barware
Dansk

Tapestries
Gray Cut Swirls
Dansk

DAC 4
Plain
Dansk

Elise
Clear or Light Blue Bowl
Dansk

Tjorn
Clear, Blue, Green
or Pink Bowl
Dansk

Dancing Roses
Pale Pink
Dansk

Fano
Optic Bowl
Dansk

Bottoms Up
Cordials Shown
Various Bowl Shapes
Dansk

Rio
Blue, Lime Green, Orange,
White or Yellow Bowl
Dansk

Cirrus
Indented Bowl
Dansk

Elegant
Plain
Dansk

Baltic
Red Wine Shown
Etched Rings
Dansk

Wild Willow
Cut Willow Tree Branch
Dansk

DAC 13
Wine Shown
Plain
Dansk

Nicole
Twisted Stem & Bowl
Dansk

DAC 16
Plain
Dansk

Anna
Plain, Hollow Foot
Dansk

Lisa
Plain
Dansk

Edesia
Frosted Woven Band
Dansk

Cozumel
Green or Blue
Dansk

Niels
Plain
Dansk

DAC 21
Twisted Stem
Dansk

Tivoli Garden
Twisted Stem
Dansk

Mix & Mingle
White Wine Shown
Frosted Words & Stem
Dansk

Reactic
Clear, Khaki, Plum
or Slate Stem
Dansk

Alborg
Plain
Dansk

Bistro
Blue Rings
Dansk

Caribe
Wine Shown
Various Stem & Foot Colors
Dansk

DAC 12
Blue Bowl, Blue/Green
Stem, Green Foot
Dansk

Ribe
Plain
Dansk

Kolby
Cut Stem
Dansk

Dansk

Adrianna
Plain
Dansk

Rondure
Wine Shown
Frosted Stem & Foot
Dansk

Keri
Optic Bowl
Dansk

Karin
Plain
Dansk

Karin Grafix
Frosted & Clear Bowls
& Line Motifs
Dansk

Karin Organix
Frosted & Clear Bowls
& Leaf Motifs
Dansk

Felicia
Textured Stem
Dansk

Greta
Plain
Dansk

Althea
Plain
Dansk

Kirsten
Plain
Dansk

Carla
Plain
Dansk

Sonya
Embossed Stem
Dansk

Erika
Plain
Dansk

Pia
Optic Bowl
Dansk

Bistro
Gray Cut Floral & Line
Dansk

Bistro
Cobalt Stem & Foot
Dansk

Annelise
Plain
Dansk

DAC 7
Plain
Dansk

Encore
Plain
Dansk

Vetro
Clear or Frosted Stem
Dansk

Mesa
Clear or Blue
Dansk

Belle
Plain
Dansk

Julien
Plain
Dansk

Rienna
Plain
Dansk

Nordic Knits
Green Tree Design
Dansk

Fredericia
Blue or Green Stem
Dansk

Christina
Plain
Dansk

Arabesque
Cobalt Stem
Dansk

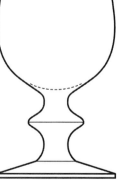

Sage Song
Blue & Green
Handpainted Floral
Dansk

Berries
Handpainted Fruit
Dansk

Dansk

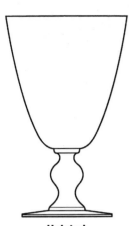

Holsted
Plain
Dansk

Amazon
Blue Bubble in Stem
Dansk

Floating Leaves
Frosted Leaves & Stem
Dansk

Hanna
All Clear or Various
Color Bowls or Stems
Dansk

Shine
Etched Snowflakes
Dansk

Britt
Plain
Dansk

Michel
Plain
Dansk

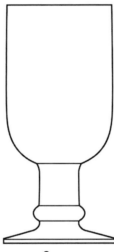

Genna
All Clear or Various
Color Bowls or Stems
Dansk

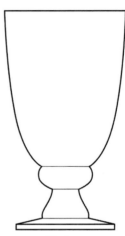

Madras
All Clear or Various
Color Bowls or Stems
Dansk

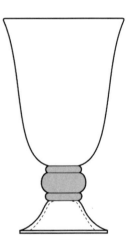

Tiberon Metallics
Gold or Silver Stem,
Hollow Foot
Dansk

Tiberon
Plain, Hollow Foot
Dansk

Burchetta
Wine Shown
Multicolored Leaves,
Hollow Foot
Dansk

Neptune
Shell Stem Accent
Dansk

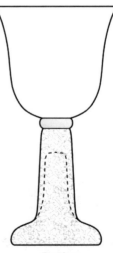

Portia
Frosted Stem Accent,
Textured Hollow Stem
Dansk

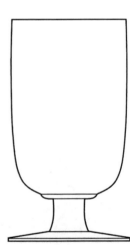

Regan
Plain
Dansk

Cobalt
Footed Tumbler Shown
Blue
Dansk

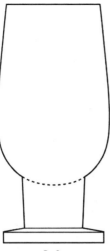

Cafe
Beverage Shown
Plain
Dansk

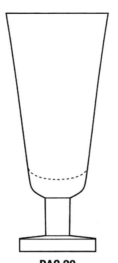

DAC 20
Pilsner Shown
Plain
Dansk

Tronada
Iced Tea Shown
Spiral Lines
Dansk

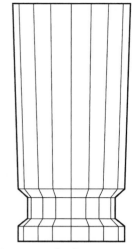

Gustav
Highball Shown
Ribbed, Barware
Dansk

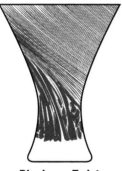

Blueberry Twist
Orange Twist
Cocktail Tumbler Shown
Blue or Orange, Clear Swirl
Dansk

Vivacious
Liquor Cocktail Shown
Various Color
Flecked Bases
Dansk

Ditto
Tumbler Shown
Multicolored Shapes
Dansk

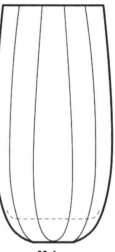

Melon
Highball Shown
Vertical Cuts
Dansk

Glasscapes
Tumbler Shown
Amber, Amethyst, Blue,
Lime Green or Teal
Dansk

Precision
Tumbler Shown
Etched Rings, Barware
Dansk

Solara
Tumbler Shown
Frosted Bottom, Barware
Dansk

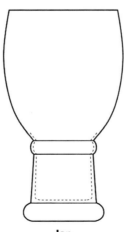

Ian
Highball Shown
Clear, Blue Lustre or Green
Lustre Foot & Stem Accents
Dansk

Clari. T
Cooler Shown
Horizontal Frosted Rings
Dansk

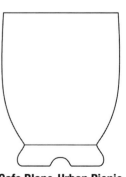

Cafe Blanc-Urban Picnic
Double Old Fashioned Shown
Plain
Dansk

Craftmark
Double Old Fashioned Shown
Frosted Leaf in Base
Dansk

Tip. C
Highball Shown
Plain
Dansk

Craft Colors
Tumbler Shown
Clear or Various Colors
Dansk

Swirl
Tumbler Shown
Vertical Swirl Cuts
Dansk

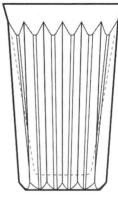

Prism
Highball Shown
Vertical Cuts, Barware
Dansk

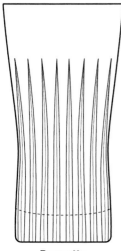

Baguette
Highball Shown
Vertical Cuts, Barware
Dansk

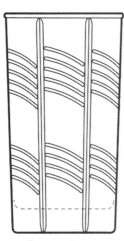

Summerhouse
Tumbler Shown
Vertical & Curved Cuts,
Barware
Dansk

Aqua
Tumbler Shown
Rippled Sides
Dansk

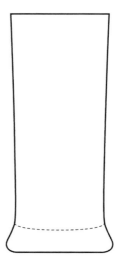

DAC 5
Highball Shown
Plain, Barware
Dansk

DAC 8
Tumbler Shown
Plain, Barware
Dansk

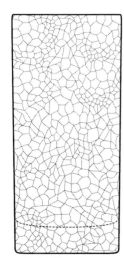

DAC 14
Highball Shown
Textured, Barware
Dansk

DAC 6
Highball Shown
Bubble in Base, Barware
Dansk

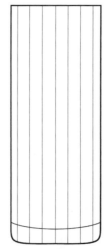

Facette
Highball Shown
Round Shape,
Panels, Barware
Dansk

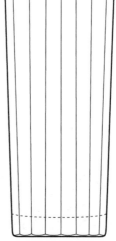

Oval Facette
Highball Shown
Oval Shape,
Panels, Barware
Dansk

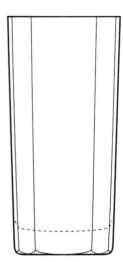

Scroll
Highball Shown
Multisided
Dansk

Thirst
Double Old Fashioned Shown
Horizontal Rings
Dansk

Borderline
Double Old Fashioned Shown
Various Colored
Bowls & Rims
Dansk

Spectra
Double Old Fashioned Shown
Various Colors in Bases
Dansk

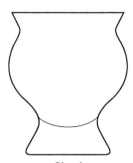

Cloud
Double Old Fashioned Shown
Plain
Dansk

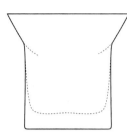

Forum
Tumbler Shown
Plain, Square Base
Dansk

Simplicity
Double Old Fashioned Shown
Plain
Dansk

Droplet
Flat Iced Tea Shown
Plain, Barware
Dansk

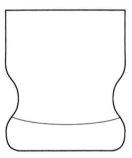

Advent
Old Fashioned Shown
Plain, Barware
Dansk

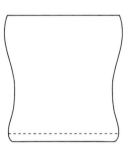

Feels Good
Tumbler Shown
Plain, Barware
Dansk

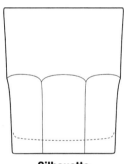

Silhouette
Double Old Fashioned Shown
Panels, Barware
Dansk

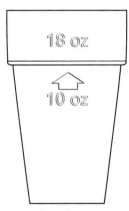

Sure Stack
Tumbler Shown
Embossed Numbers
Dansk

Bistro Cafe
Round Platter Shown
Blue, Ribbed
Dansk

Crocus
Optic Bowl
Dartington

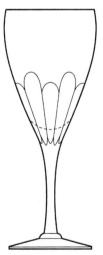

Chelsea
Panel Cuts
Dartington

Ascot
Wine Shown
Vertical Cuts
Dartington

297

Dartington

Mayfair
Crisscross Cuts
Dartington

Richmond
Vertical & Round Cuts
Dartington

Kensington
Vertical & Oval Cuts
Dartington

Windsor
Vertical & Crisscross Cuts
Dartington

Rachael
Plain
Dartington

Wine Master
White Wine Shown
Plain
Dartington

Marlowe
Plain
Dartington

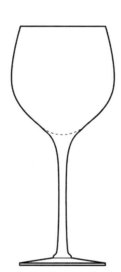

Chateauneuf
Plain
Dartington

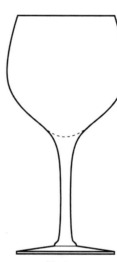

Chateau
Plain
Dartington

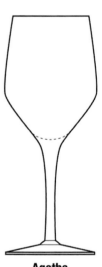

Agatha
Plain
Dartington

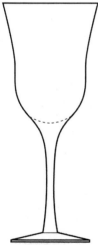

Shelley
Plain
Dartington

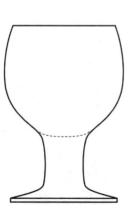

Compleat Imbiber
Plain
Dartington

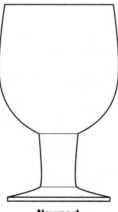

Newport
Plain
Dartington

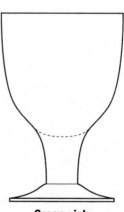

Greenwich
Plain
Dartington

Chalice
Clear, Blue or Green Stem
Dartington

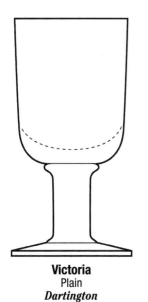

Victoria
Plain
Dartington

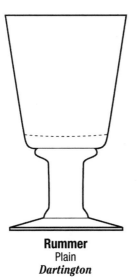

Rummer
Plain
Dartington

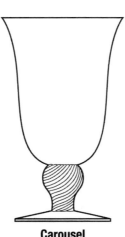

Carousel
Twisted Stem
Dartington

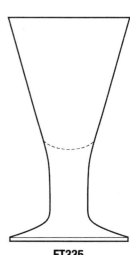

Sharon
Bubble in Stem
Dartington

FT335
Plain
Dartington

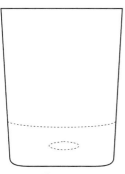

Exmoor
Double Old Fashioned Shown
Bubble in Base, Barware
Dartington

DAR 5
Old Fashioned Shown
Black Zoo Animals on
Frosted Glass, Multi-Motif
Dartington

Wildflowers
Double Old Fashioned Shown
Painted Flowers on
Frosted Glass, Multi-Motif
Dartington

DAR 2
Highball Shown
Large Painted Flower on
Frosted Glass, Multi-Motif
Dartington

Segur
Plain
Daum

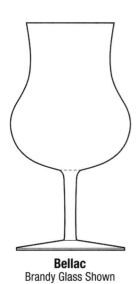

Bellac
Brandy Glass Shown
Plain
Daum

Iroise
Wine Shown
Plain
Daum

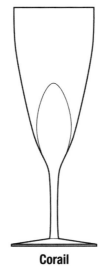

Corail
Plain
Daum

DAU 1
Wine Shown
Vertical Cuts
Daum

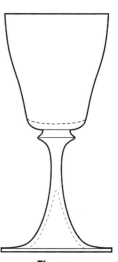

Fleurus
Plain, Hollow Stem
Daum

Daum

Saumur
Plain
Daum

Verone
Optic Bowl, Hollow Stem
Daum

Floralie
Optic Bowl
Daum

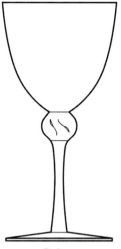

Bolero
Twisted Stem Accent
Daum

Boissy
Crisscross Cuts
Daum

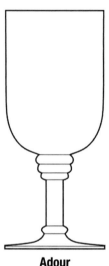

Adour
Plain
Daum

Beaugency
Vertical & Crisscross Cuts
Daum

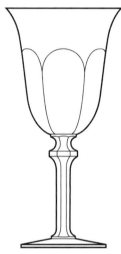

Gange
Wine Shown
Panel Cuts
Daum

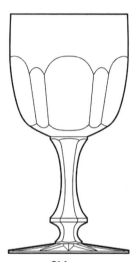

Chinon
Panel Cuts
Daum

Orval
Twisted Stem
Daum

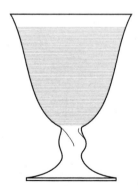

DAU 2
Thin Line Cuts,
Twisted Stem
Daum

Fontoy
Wine Shown
Plain
Daum

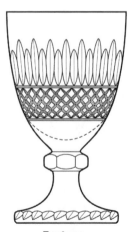

Fontenay
Wine Shown
Vertical, Horizontal
& Crisscross Cuts
Daum

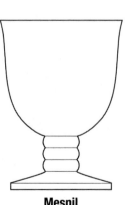

Mesnil
Plain
Daum

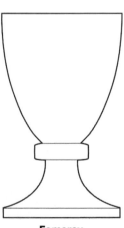

Fomerey
Plain
Daum

Beaune
Plain
Daum

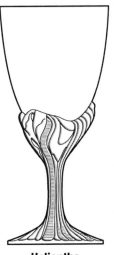

Helianthe
Wine Shown
Textured Stem & Foot
Daum

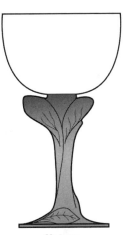

Nature
Claret Wine Shown
Green Tree Trunk Stem
Daum

Tea Rose Pink
Pink Frosted Stem
Daum

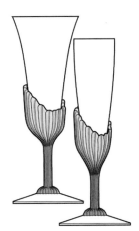

Fuchsia
Champagne Flutes Shown
Frosted Ribbed Stem
Daum

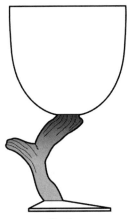

Cactus
Green Plant Stem,
Multi-Motif
Daum

Preval
Footed Tumbler Shown
Plain, Square Foot
Daum

Blanzey
Vodka Chiller Shown
Swirl Cut Base, Barware
Daum

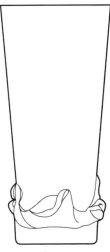

Sorcy
Beer Glass Shown
Textured Base
Daum

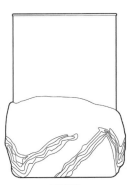

DAU 6
Tumbler Shown
Textured Base
Daum

Colori
Textured Gold Rectangles
T. Davlin

Buzz Saw
Wine Shown
Cobalt or Peach Iridescent,
Pressed Glass
Degenhart Glass Company

Daisy & Button
Wine Shown
Various Colors,
Pressed Glass
Degenhart Glass Company

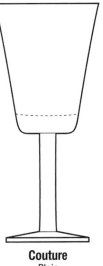

Couture
Plain
Denby

Drama
Smoke Bowl
Denby

Denby

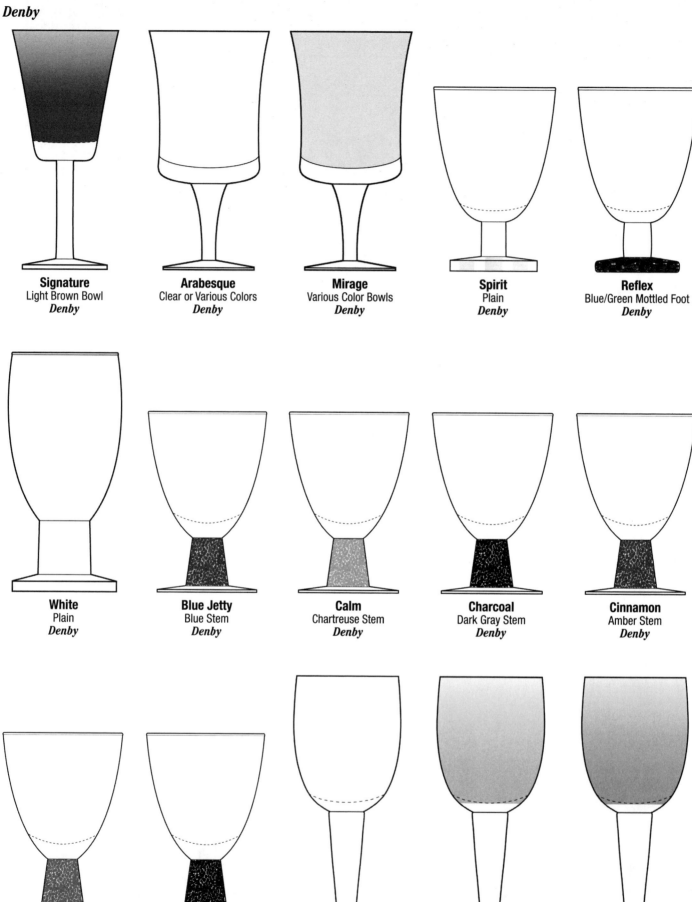

Signature
Light Brown Bowl
Denby

Arabesque
Clear or Various Colors
Denby

Mirage
Various Color Bowls
Denby

Spirit
Plain
Denby

Reflex
Blue/Green Mottled Foot
Denby

White
Plain
Denby

Blue Jetty
Blue Stem
Denby

Calm
Chartreuse Stem
Denby

Charcoal
Dark Gray Stem
Denby

Cinnamon
Amber Stem
Denby

Cranberry
Red Stem
Denby

Storm
Purple Stem
Denby

Flavours
Plain
Denby

Smokestone
Amber Bowl
Denby

Azure
Blue Bowl
Denby

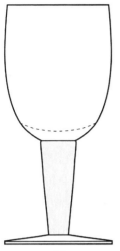

Jet
White Stem
Denby

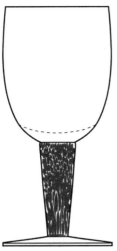

Fire
Orange/Amber Stem
Denby

Amethyst
Red Wine Shown
Purple Stem
Denby

Jet
Red Wine Shown
Black Stem
Denby

Imperial Blue
White Wine Shown
Blue Speckled Stem
Denby

Greenwich
White Wine Shown
Green Speckled Stem
Denby

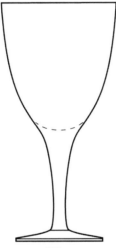

China
Plain
Denby

Vista
Wine Shown
Spice Brown or Green
Denby

Oyster
White Wine Shown
Plain
Denby

Olympia
Clear or Various Colors
Denby

Avanti
Clear, Blue, Brown,
Green or Smoke
Denby

Flare
Clear, Black, Blue, Lavender,
Pink or Green
Denby

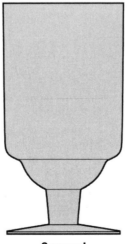

Carousel
Blue, Spice Brown
or Dusk Gray
Denby

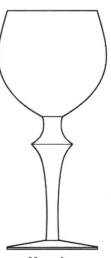

Moonrise
Clear, Blue or Smoke Bowl
Denby

Aurora
Clear or Various Color Bowls
Denby

Denby

DE 1
Blue or Pink Bowl
Denby

Chateau Rose
Pink Bowl
Denby

Stirling
Crisscross & Fan Cuts
Denby

Summer Smoke
Smoke Optic Bowl
Denby

Renaissance
Wine Shown
Optic Bowl
Denby

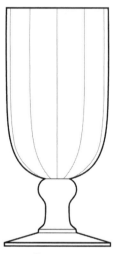

Provence
Wine Shown
Optic Bowl
Denby

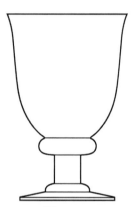

Magnum
Clear, Green or Blue Stem
Denby

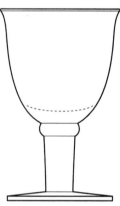

Linen
Plain
Denby

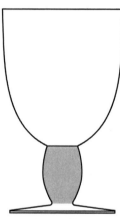

Energy/Zest
Frosted Stem
Denby

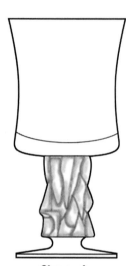

Chamonix
Clear or Various
Color Bowls
Denby

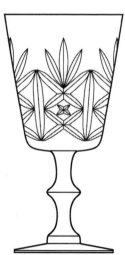

Guildford
Vertical, Crisscross
& Fan Cuts
Denby

Washington
Vertical Cuts
Denby

Lincoln
Vertical & Diamond Cuts
Denby

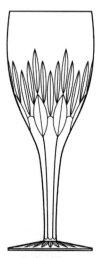

Reflections
Vertical Cuts
Denby

Elizabethan
Crisscross & Fan Cuts,
Cut Stem
Denby

Glastonbury
Vertical, Oval & Fan Cuts
Denby

Chatham
Crisscross & Fan Cuts
Denby

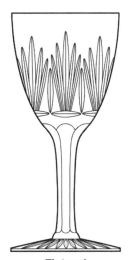

Tintagel
Horizontal & Fan Cuts
Denby

Frederick
Plain
Denby

Gustav
Plain
Denby

Starlight
Crisscross & Oval Cuts
Denby

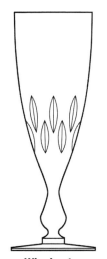

Winchester
Oval Cuts
Denby

Exeter
Vertical, Crisscross
& Star Cuts
Denby

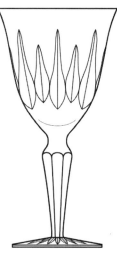

Fanfare
Vertical Cuts
Denby

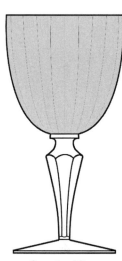

Country Lilac
Lilac Optic Bowl
Denby

DE 5
Highball Shown
Vertical & Crisscross Cuts,
Barware
Denby

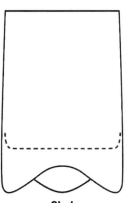

Skol
Old Fashioned Shown
Clear, Amber, Blue
or Plum Body, Barware
Denby

D1G 1
Sprayed Orange Bowl,
Black & Platinum Foot
Design Guild

Wine

Highball

Granite
Various Colors,
Speckled Base & Trim
di Sciacca

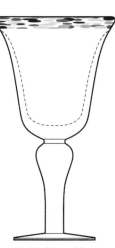

Multi Color Rim
Multicolor Dot Band
di Sciacca

Diamond Glass, Dorflinger, Dorothy Thorpe

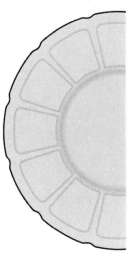

Victory
Various Colors, Panels,
Plain or Gold Trim
Diamond Glass

99
Salad Plate Shown
Various Colors,
Multisided
Diamond Glass

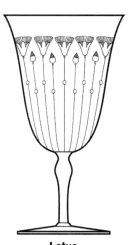

Lotus
Etched Geometric
Dorflinger

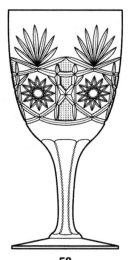

50
Star, Fan & Crisscross Cuts
Dorflinger

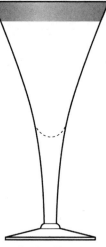

**Golden Band
Silver Band**
1" Wide Gold
or Platinum Band
Dorothy Thorpe

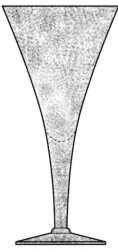

**Gold Fleck
Silver Fleck**
Gold or Silver Flecks
Dorothy Thorpe

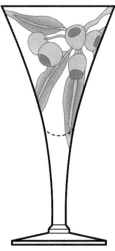

DTC 13
Frosted Olives & Leaves
Dorothy Thorpe

DTC 1
Handpainted Pink Roses
Dorothy Thorpe

DTC 8
White Lily of the Valley,
Green Leaves
Dorothy Thorpe

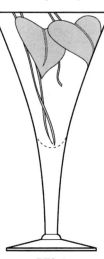

DTC 4
Frosted Floral
Dorothy Thorpe

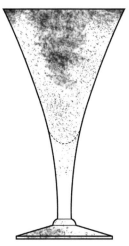

Sirl
Purple Iridescent
Dorothy Thorpe

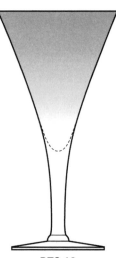

DTC 16
Green Frosted Bowl
Dorothy Thorpe

DTC 20
Powder Blue
Frosted Bowl
Dorothy Thorpe

DTC 7
White Laurel Leaves,
Frosted Bowl & Stem
Dorothy Thorpe

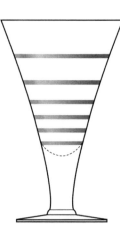

DTC 24
6 Platinum Bands
Dorothy Thorpe

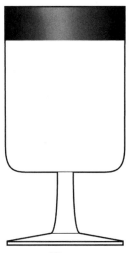

Allegro
Wide Platinum Band
Dorothy Thorpe

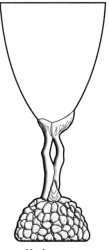

Hydrangea
Purple Frosted, Frosted
or Clear Stem
Dorothy Thorpe

Gold Dot
Champagne/Tall Sherbet Shown
Line of Gold Dots
Dorothy Thorpe

Bubble
Clear or Iridescent
Dorothy Thorpe

**Topaz Lustre
Blue Lustre**
Amber or Blue
Dorothy Thorpe

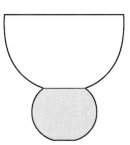

DTC 2
Champagne/Tall Sherbet Shown
Gold Ball Shaped Base
Dorothy Thorpe

Lockheed
Highball Shown
Etched Airplane
Dorothy Thorpe

DTC 6
Double Old Fashioned Shown
Multicolored Floral Decal
Dorothy Thorpe

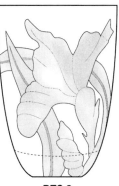

DTC 3
Tumbler Shown
Gray Etched Floral
Dorothy Thorpe

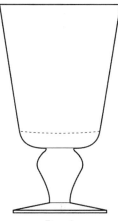

Royal
Clear or Various
Color Bowls
Doyen

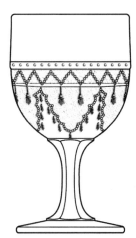

Drapery
Textured Swags,
Pattern Glass
Doyle Glass

DUY 1
Vertical & Crisscross Cuts
Dublin

Avoca Suite
Crisscross & Fan Cuts
Dublin

Europa Suite
Tumbler Shown
Crisscross & Fan Cuts
Dublin

Grapevine Lattice
Tumbler Shown
Amethyst,
Carnival Glass
Dugan Glass

Floral & Grape
Tumbler Shown
Various Colors,
Carnival Glass
Dugan Glass

Aine
Gray Cut Harp & Shamrocks,
Multisided Stem
Duiske Glass

Aine
Wine Shown
Gray Cut Harp & Shamrocks,
Smooth Stem
Duiske Glass

Duncan & Miller Shapes and Lines

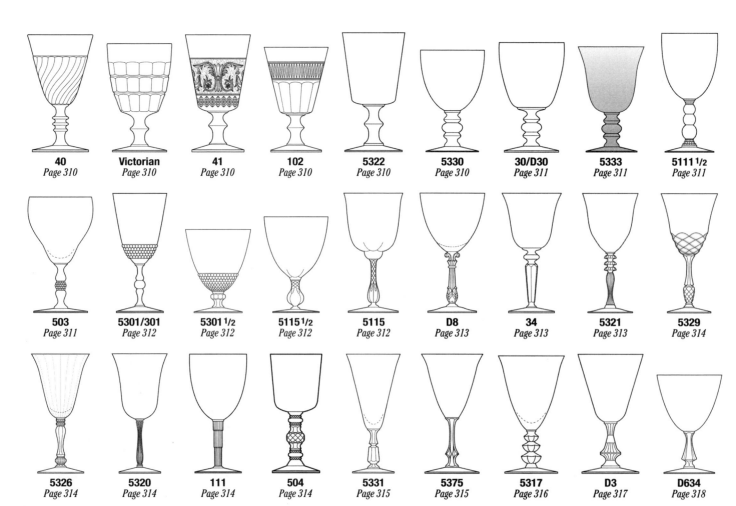

40 Page 310	**Victorian** Page 310	**41** Page 310	**102** Page 310

5322 Page 310 · **5330** Page 310 · **30/D30** Page 311 · **5333** Page 311 · **5111 1/2** Page 311

503 Page 311 · **5301/301** Page 312 · **5301 1/2** Page 312 · **5115 1/2** Page 312 · **5115** Page 312 · **D8** Page 313 · **34** Page 313 · **5321** Page 313 · **5329** Page 314

5326 Page 314 · **5320** Page 314 · **111** Page 314 · **504** Page 314 · **5331** Page 315 · **5375** Page 315 · **5317** Page 316 · **D3** Page 317 · **D634** Page 318

D621
Page 318

D1
Page 318

D7
Page 318

D11
Page 318

D630
Page 319

D613
Page 319

D635
Page 319

D616
Page 319

32
Page 320

D15
Page 320

D13
Page 320

D627
Page 321

D612
Page 321

D4
Page 321

D5
Page 321

D6
Page 321

D2
Page 322

83
Page 322

5323
Page 322

5323
Page 322

UNKNOWN
Page 322

48
Page 323

45
Page 323

42
Page 323

555
Page 323

39
Page 323

22
Page 323

115
Page 323

21
Page 323

112
Page 323

118
Page 323

75
Page 323

103
Page 323

150
Page 323

400
Page 323

500
Page 324

502
Page 324

128
Page 324

UNKNOWN
Page 324

155
Page 324

154
Page 324

Spiral Flutes
Clear or Various Colors,
Swirl Lines
40
Duncan & Miller

Victorian
Clear or Amber,
Thumbprint Panels,
Pressed Glass
Duncan & Miller

Sandwich
Clear or Various Colors,
Textured, Scrolls, Pressed Glass
41
Duncan & Miller

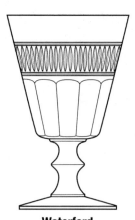

Waterford
Clear, Amber, Green or
Yellow Flash, Pressed Glass
102
Duncan & Miller

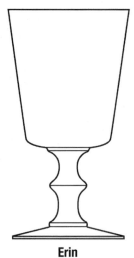

Erin
Plain
5322
Duncan & Miller

Kohinoor
Cut 690, Crisscross
5322
Duncan & Miller

Laurel Diamond
Laurel & Crisscross Cuts
5322
Duncan & Miller

Windermere
Diagonal & Leaf Cuts
5322
Duncan & Miller

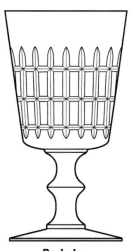

Berkeley
Cut 702,
Vertical & Horizontal
5322
Duncan & Miller

Sun Ray
Cut 691,
Vertical & Crisscross
5322
Duncan & Miller

Dover
Clear or Ruby Bowl
5330
Duncan & Miller

Clematis
Etched Floral
5330
Duncan & Miller

Magnolia
Clear or Pink Tint,
Etched Floral
5330
Duncan & Miller

Wilshire
Cut 767, Leaves & Swags
5330
Duncan & Miller

Sheffield
Cut 768,
Oval & Crisscross
5330
Duncan & Miller

Nobility
Cut 775, Laurel Band
5330
Duncan & Miller

Saratoga
Cut 769,
Crisscross & Circles
5330
Duncan & Miller

Warwick
Cut 632, Crisscross
30
Duncan & Miller

30-1
Crisscross Cuts
D30
Duncan & Miller

Chartreuse
Green, Plain
5333
Duncan & Miller

Terrace
Plain
5111 ½
Duncan & Miller

First Love
Etched Floral
5111 ½
Duncan & Miller

Royal Lace
Etched Floral
5111 ½
Duncan & Miller

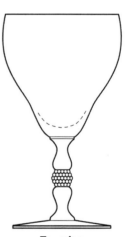

Touraine
Plain
503
Duncan & Miller

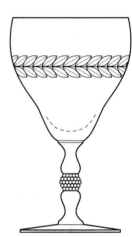

Laurel Wreath
Cut 640, Laurel Band
503
Duncan & Miller

Bridal Bow
Cut 782, Bows & Swags
503
Duncan & Miller

503-1
Vertical & Leaf Cuts
503
Duncan & Miller

503-2
Gray Cut Floral
503
Duncan & Miller

Athene
Cut Floral
503
Duncan & Miller

Dogwood
Etched Floral
503
Duncan & Miller

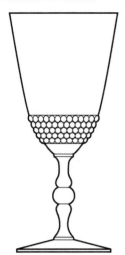

Teardrop
All Clear, Orange or Ruby;
or Smoke Bowl & Foot
5301/301
Duncan & Miller

Royal Lace
Etched Floral
5301
Duncan & Miller

Teardrop
Plain
5301 ½
Duncan & Miller

Canterbury
Plain
5115 ½
Duncan & Miller

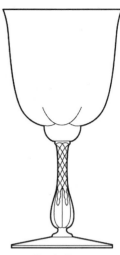

Canterbury
Plain
5115
Duncan & Miller

Azalea
Cut 694, Floral
5115
Duncan & Miller

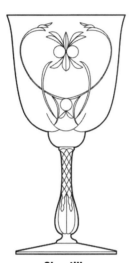

Chantilly
Cut 773, Geometric
5115
Duncan & Miller

Maytime
Cut 698, Floral
5115
Duncan & Miller

Phoebus
Cut 621,
Crisscross & Fans
5115
Duncan & Miller

Tristan
Cut 622, Floral
5115
Duncan & Miller

Tripole
Cut 750, Floral
5115
Duncan & Miller

5115-3
Floral, Crosshatch
& Panel Cuts
5115
Duncan & Miller

Royal Lace
Etched Floral
5115
Duncan & Miller

Remembrance
Etched Floral & Rose
5115
Duncan & Miller

5115-2
Etched Geometric,
Plants, & Dots
5115
Duncan & Miller

Wild Rose
Etched Roses
5115
Duncan & Miller

Patio
Plain
D8
Duncan & Miller

Ethereal
Horizontal Wavy Line Cuts
D8
Duncan & Miller

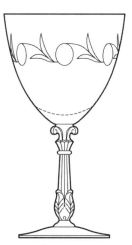

Serenade
Plant Cuts
D8
Duncan & Miller

Astral
Star Cuts
D8
Duncan & Miller

Starlight
Cut Floral & Stars
D8
Duncan & Miller

Country Garden
Cut Floral
D8
Duncan & Miller

Duncan Rose
Cut Rose
D8
Duncan & Miller

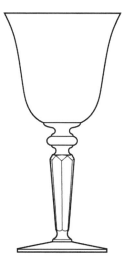

Kent
Plain
34
Duncan & Miller

Marlborough
Cut 628,
Crisscross & Floral
34
Duncan & Miller

Trianon
Plain
5321
Duncan & Miller

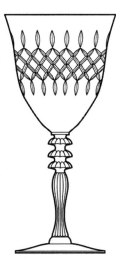

Tiara
Cut 683,
Vertical & Crisscross
5321
Duncan & Miller

Viceroy
Cut 695, Laurel Band,
Panel Cuts
5321
Duncan & Miller

Blossom Time
Cut 705, Floral
& Panel Cuts
5321
Duncan & Miller

Adoration
Etched Floral
5321
Duncan & Miller

Duncan & Miller

5321-1
Gray Cut Stars
5321
Duncan & Miller

Wistar
Crisscross Cuts
5329
Duncan & Miller

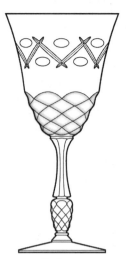

Andover
Cut 760, Crisscross & Dots
5329
Duncan & Miller

Exeter
Cut 758, Crisscross & Dots
5329
Duncan & Miller

Deauville
Optic Bowl
5326
Duncan & Miller

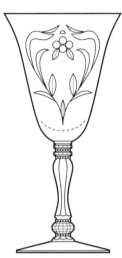

Burgundy
Cut Floral
5326
Duncan & Miller

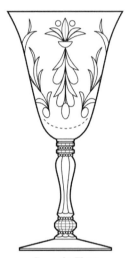

Francis First
Cut 783, Floral
5326
Duncan & Miller

Charmaine Rose
Etched Roses & Butterflies
5326
Duncan & Miller

Indian Tree
Etched Floral
5326
Duncan & Miller

Kimberly
Cut 684, Crisscross
5320
Duncan & Miller

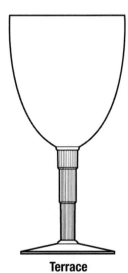

Terrace
Plain
111
Duncan & Miller

Granada
Clear or Various
Color Bowls, Plain
504
Duncan & Miller

Royal Lace
Etched Floral
504
Duncan & Miller

504-3
Crisscross Cuts
504
Duncan & Miller

Stratford
Cut 689, Crisscross
504
Duncan & Miller

Locksley
Cut 635,
Crisscross & Fans
504
Duncan & Miller

504-1
Floral & Crisscross Cuts
504
Duncan & Miller

Alhambra
Floral & Oval Cuts
504
Duncan & Miller

504-2
Cut Floral
504
Duncan & Miller

504-4
Floral & Crisscross Cuts
504
Duncan & Miller

Victory
Plain
5331
Duncan & Miller

Lexington
Cut 764,
Crisscross & Circles
5331
Duncan & Miller

Prelude
Cut 783,
Vertical & Crisscross
5331
Duncan & Miller

Victory
Cut 772,
Leaves & Stars
5331
Duncan & Miller

5331-2
Horizontal & Star Cuts
5331
Duncan & Miller

Eternally Yours
Cut 765, Floral
5331
Duncan & Miller

Language of Flowers
Etched Floral
5331
Duncan & Miller

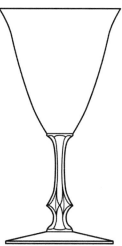

Diamond
Clear or Ruby Bowl, Plain
5375
Duncan & Miller

Garland
Cut Garland Band
5375
Duncan & Miller

Queen's Lace
Cut Floral Band
5375
Duncan & Miller

5375-2
Cut Floral
5375
Duncan & Miller

5375-1
Diamond Cuts
5375
Duncan & Miller

Empress
Cut 696, Crisscross
5375
Duncan & Miller

Monterey
Cut 697, Floral & Crisscross
5375
Duncan & Miller

5375-4
Horizontal, Floral & Dot Cuts
5375
Duncan & Miller

Charmaine Rose
Etched Rose & Butterfly
5375
Duncan & Miller

5375-5
Crisscross & Diamond Cuts
5375
Duncan & Miller

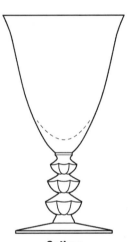

Cathay
Plain
5317
Duncan & Miller

Minuet
Cut 713,
Vertical & Crisscross
5317
Duncan & Miller

Juno
Cut 688,
Vertical & Circles
5317
Duncan & Miller

Coronet
Cut 682, Crisscross
5317
Duncan & Miller

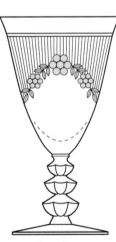

Lovelace
Cut 681, Vertical & Floral
5317
Duncan & Miller

Lucerne
Cut 652, Floral
5317
Duncan & Miller

Rhapsody
Cut 651, Floral
5317
Duncan & Miller

Dogwood
Etched Floral
5317
Duncan & Miller

5317-1
Etched Floral
5317
Duncan & Miller

Wild Rose
Etched Roses
5317
Duncan & Miller

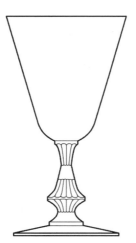

Duncan Phyfe
Plain
D3
Duncan & Miller

Deauville
Vertical Cuts
D3
Duncan & Miller

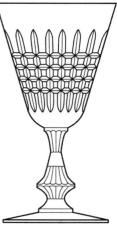

Pickwick
Horizontal & Vertical Cuts
D3
Duncan & Miller

Willow
Curved Leaf Cuts
D3
Duncan & Miller

D3-2
Vertical Cuts
D3
Duncan & Miller

Holiday
Vertical & Circle Cuts
D3
Duncan & Miller

Reverie
Swirl Cuts
D3
Duncan & Miller

Sherwood
Plant Cuts
D3
Duncan & Miller

Silver Wheat
Cut Wheat
D3
Duncan & Miller

D3-1
Grape & Leaf Cuts
D3
Duncan & Miller

Wild Rose
Cut Floral
D3
Duncan & Miller

Thistle
Cut Thistle
D3
Duncan & Miller

D3-3
Gray Cut Rose & Leaves
D3
Duncan & Miller

Thea
Cut Laurel Band
D634
Duncan & Miller

Druid
Cut Leaves
D621
Duncan & Miller

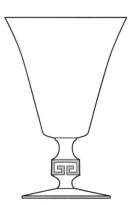

Mandarin
Frosted Greek Key
D1
Duncan & Miller

Athena
Vertical & Horizontal Cuts
D1
Duncan & Miller

Chinese Garden
Cut Floral
D1
Duncan & Miller

Fern
Plant & Panel Cuts
D1
Duncan & Miller

Governor Clinton
Cut Floral
D1
Duncan & Miller

Spring Glory
Cut Floral & Butterfly
D1
Duncan & Miller

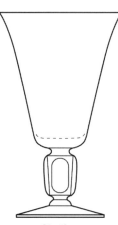

Chalice
Plain
D7
Duncan & Miller

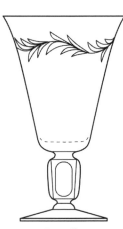

Arcadia
Cut Leaves
D7
Duncan & Miller

Spray
Cut Plant
D7
Duncan & Miller

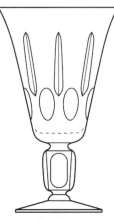

Sundown
Vertical & Oval Cuts
D7
Duncan & Miller

Wheat
Vertical & Wheat Cuts
D7
Duncan & Miller

Simplicity
Plain
D11
Duncan & Miller

Platinum Band
Wide Platinum Band
D11
Duncan & Miller

Petite
Gray Cut Floral
D11
Duncan & Miller

Devon Spray
Cut Floral
D11
Duncan & Miller

Sylvan
Gray Cut Leaves
D11
Duncan & Miller

Radiance
Vertical Cuts
D11
Duncan & Miller

Essex
Cut Plant
D11
Duncan & Miller

Coronet
Gray Cut Plumes & Feathers
D11
Duncan & Miller

Coralbel
Cut Floral
D11
Duncan & Miller

Snowflake
Gold Encrusted Snowflakes,
Gold Bowl & Foot Trim
D11
Duncan & Miller

D11-1
Abstract Cuts
D11
Duncan & Miller

Gold Lahme
Gold Encrusted Leaves,
Gold Trim
D630
Duncan & Miller

Wistaria
Cut Leaves
D613
Duncan & Miller

Marquis
Cut Plant
D613
Duncan & Miller

Tempo
Cut Plant,
Bubble in Stem
D635
Duncan & Miller

Thea
Cut Laurel Band,
Bubble in Stem
D635
Duncan & Miller

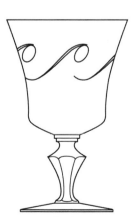

Etude
Swirl Cuts
D616
Duncan & Miller

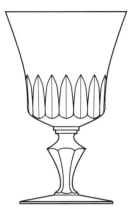

Radcliff
Vertical Cuts
D616
Duncan & Miller

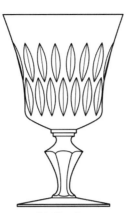

St. Charles
Vertical Cuts
D616
Duncan & Miller

Windsor
Plain
32
Duncan & Miller

Bristol Diamond
Cut 803, Crisscross
32
Duncan & Miller

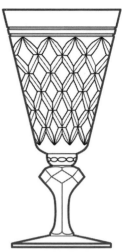

Chesterfield
Cut 717, Crisscross
32
Duncan & Miller

Sherwood
Cut 645,
Crisscross & Vertical
32
Duncan & Miller

32-1
Floral, Crisscross
& Circle Cuts
32
Duncan & Miller

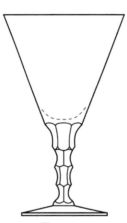

Elegance
Plain
D15
Duncan & Miller

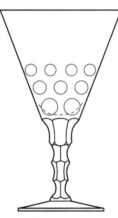

Champagne
Cut Dots
D15
Duncan & Miller

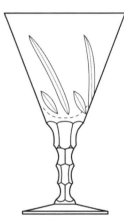

Rhythm
Swirl Cuts
D15
Duncan & Miller

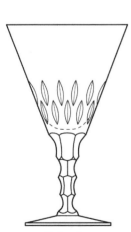

Splendor
Vertical Cuts
D15
Duncan & Miller

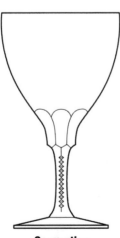

Coronation
Plain
D13
Duncan & Miller

Margaret Rose
Gray Cut Rose
D13
Duncan & Miller

Regency
Swirl & Plant Cuts
D13
Duncan & Miller

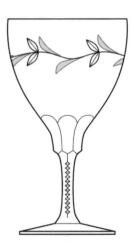

Heritage
Cut Leaves
D13
Duncan & Miller

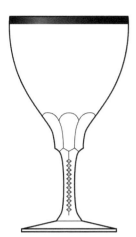

Platinum Band
Platinum Band on Rim
D13
Duncan & Miller

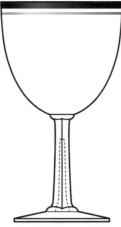

Double Wedding Band
Platinum & Gold Bands,
Bubble in Stem
D627
Duncan & Miller

Lenox Rose
Frosted Cut Rose,
Bubble in Stem
D612
Duncan & Miller

Lily of the Valley
Plain
D4
Duncan & Miller

Lily of the Valley
Gray Cut Floral
D4
Duncan & Miller

Duncan Scroll
Plain
D5
Duncan & Miller

Fleur De Lis
Fan & Circle Cuts
D5
Duncan & Miller

Cretan
Curved & Circle Cuts
D5
Duncan & Miller

Dawn
Circle & Swag Cuts
D5
Duncan & Miller

Spring Beauty
Cut Floral
D5
Duncan & Miller

Hawthorne
Cut Floral
D5
Duncan & Miller

Eternal Life
Plain
D6
Duncan & Miller

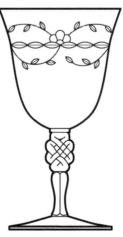

Belvedere
Cut Floral
D6
Duncan & Miller

Concerto
Cut Plants
D6
Duncan & Miller

Wild Flower
Cut Floral
D6
Duncan & Miller

Duncan & Miller

Riviera
Plain
D2
Duncan & Miller

Arcadia
Gray Cut Plants
D2
Duncan & Miller

Candlelight
Vertical Cuts
D2
Duncan & Miller

Mesa
Cut Wheat
D2
Duncan & Miller

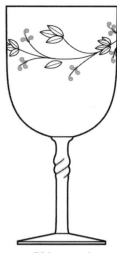

Ridgewood
Cut Floral
D2
Duncan & Miller

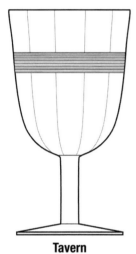

Tavern
Optic Bowl,
Cut Horizontal Bands
83
Duncan & Miller

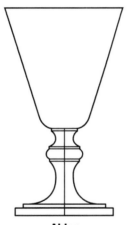

Alden
Clear or Various Color Bowls,
Square Foot
5323
Duncan & Miller

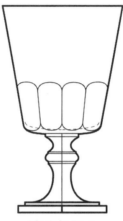

Virginia Dare
Cut 703, Panels
5323
Duncan & Miller

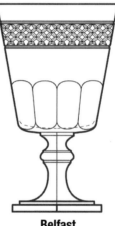

Belfast
Cut 734,
Crisscross & Panels
5323
Duncan & Miller

5323-3
Crisscross Cuts
5323
Duncan & Miller

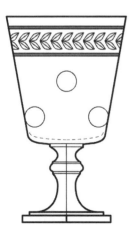

5323-2
Gray Cut Laurel Band,
Rings & Dots
5323
Duncan & Miller

5323-4
Vertical Cuts
5323
Duncan & Miller

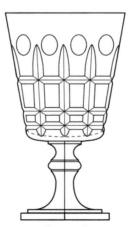

Concord
Cut 701, Dots,
Vertical & Horizontal
5323
Duncan & Miller

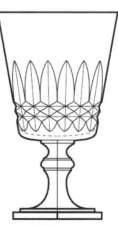

Killarney
Cut 686,
Vertical & Crisscross
5323
Duncan & Miller

DUN 3
Green Bowl, Square Foot
Duncan & Miller

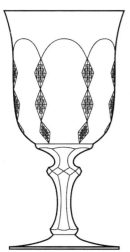

Diamond Ridge
Cordial Shown
Plain or Gold Trim
48
Duncan & Miller

Starred Loop
Plain, Gold Trim
or Ruby Flash
45
Duncan & Miller

Mardi Gras
Plain, Gold Trim
or Ruby Flash
42
Duncan & Miller

Shell & Tassle
Shell & Swags
555
Duncan & Miller

Button Arches
Wine Shown
Plain or Ruby Flash
39
Duncan & Miller

Kimberly
All Ruby or Ruby Flashed,
Crisscross & Crosshatch Cuts
22
Duncan & Miller

Hilton
Clear, Blue Flashed or Solid
Cobalt, Plain or Cut Foot
22
Duncan & Miller

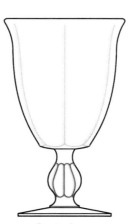

Canterbury
Panels
115
Duncan & Miller

Punties
Pink, Cobalt or Ruby
Ovals & Grooves
21
Duncan & Miller

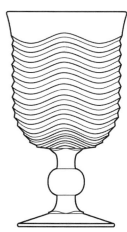

Caribbean
Clear or Various Colors,
Wavy Bands
112
Duncan & Miller

Hobnail
Clear or Various Colors
118
Duncan & Miller

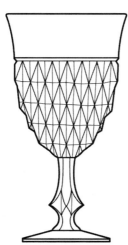

Diamond
Clear or Ruby Flashed
75
Duncan & Miller

Georgian
Clear or Various Colors,
Honeycomb Cuts
103
Duncan & Miller

Flair
Swirls
150
Duncan & Miller

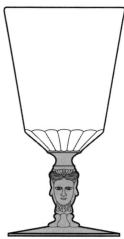

Three Faces
Frosted Stem,
Pressed Glass
400
Duncan & Miller

Three Faces (400-1)
Cut Floral
400
Duncan & Miller

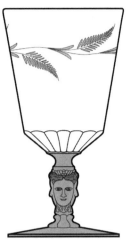

Three Faces
Engraving 53, Cut Plant
400
Duncan & Miller

Fish
Tumbler Shown
Various Color Bases
500
Duncan & Miller

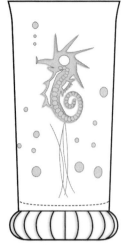

Seahorse
Various Color Bases
502
Duncan & Miller

Chanticleer
Tumbler Shown
Various Colors, Roosters
128
Duncan & Miller

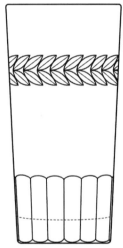

Biltmore
Tumbler Shown
Cut Laurel & Panels,
Barware
Duncan & Miller

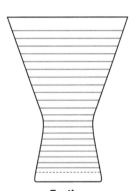

Festive
Clear or Various Colors
155
Duncan & Miller

Laguna
Various Colors
154
Duncan & Miller

Picardie
Multisided Panels
Duralex

Gigogne
Tumbler Shown
Rings
Duralex

Rivage
Dinner Plate Shown
Various Colors, Swirls
Duralex

DRB 1
Plain
Durobor

Vigneron
Plain
Durobor

Napoli
Plain
Durobor

Hostellerie
Plain
Durobor

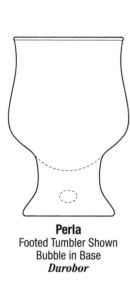

Perla
Footed Tumbler Shown
Bubble in Base
Durobor

Viking
Bubble in Base
Durobor

Galia
Champagne/Tall Sherbet Shown
Plain
Durobor

Brussels
Footed Tumbler Shown
Plain
Durobor

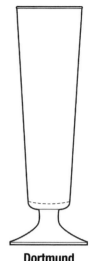

Dortmund
Beer Glass Shown
Plain
Durobor

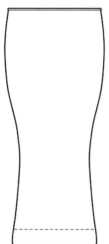

Prague
Beer Glass Shown
Plain
Durobor

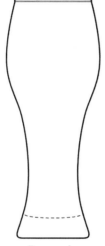

Brasserie
Beer Glass Shown
Plain
Durobor

Windsor
Cooler Shown
Plain
Durobor

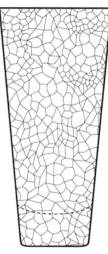

Helsinki
Highball Shown
Textured, Barware
Durobor

Hi-Fi
Highball Shown
Swirl Lines, Square Base
Durobor

Glace
Cooler Shown
Textured, Barware
Durobor

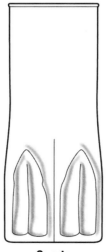

Quartz
Highball Shown
Textured Arches,
Square Base
Durobor

EAG 1
White Shamrocks,
Green Stem Accent
Eamon Glass

EAG 3
White Shamrocks
Eamon Glass

EAG 4
Wine Shown
White Shamrocks, Heart &
Crown, Twisted Stem
Eamon Glass

EAG 2
White Shamrocks
Eamon Glass

Carousel
Vertical & Dot Cuts
Easterling

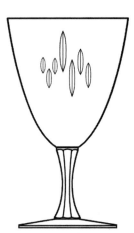

Marquise
Vertical Cuts
Easterling

Venetian Star
Star & Plant Cuts
Easterling

Lady Victoria
Crisscross Cuts
Easterling

Tuscano Love
Red & White Swirls
Eastern Design

Tuscano Palazzo
Red, White & Green Swirls
Eastern Design

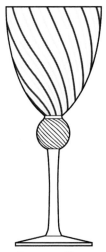

Tuscano Skye
Blue & White Swirls
Eastern Design

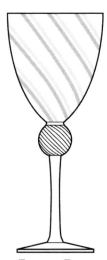

Tuscano Terra
Light Green & White Swirls
Eastern Design

Tuscano Ocean
Blue & Green Swirls
Eastern Design

Tuscano Tropical
Orange & Lime Green Swirls
Eastern Design

Venezia Autumn
Orange, Red, Black, White
& Lime Vertical Stripes
Eastern Design

Venezia Blue Lagoon
Blue, Green, Purple & White
Vertical Stripes
Eastern Design

Venezia Spa
Blue Bowl, White Swirls
Eastern Design

Venezia Deco
Black & White Swirls
Eastern Design

Ruby
Ruby Bowl
Ebeling/Reuss

Mozart
Multisided Bowl
Ebeling/Reuss

Vintage
Wine Hock Shown
Floral, Crisscross & Fan Cuts
Ebeling/Reuss

Sheffield
Crisscross & Fan Cuts
Ebeling/Reuss

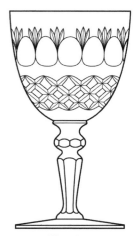

Kingsley
Wine Shown
Crisscross, Oval & Fan Cuts
Ebeling/Reuss

Emperor
Vertical, Horizontal &
Plant Cuts, Gold Trim
Ebeling/Reuss

Emperor
Various Color Bowls,
Vertical, Horizontal
& Plant Cuts, Gold Trim
Ebeling/Reuss

Marquis
Gray Cut Floral &
Crisscross Cuts, Gold Trim
Ebeling/Reuss

Marchioness
Various Color Bowls,
Gray Cut Floral,
Crisscross Cuts, Gold Trim
Ebeling/Reuss

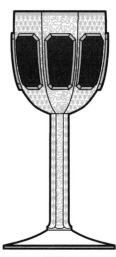

EBC 9
Various Color Panels,
Gold Bowl, Stem & Trim
Ebeling/Reuss

ECN 1
Various Color Bowls,
Textured Swirls
Echo Point

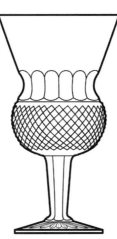

Thistle–Plain
Panel & Crisscross Cuts
Edinburgh

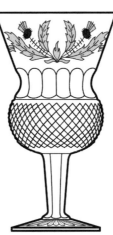

Thistle
Gray Cut Floral,
Panel & Crisscross Cuts
Edinburgh

Thistle–Tall
Gray Cut Floral, Panel &
Crisscross Cuts, Tall Stem
H828
Edinburgh

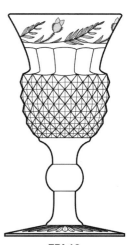

EDI 19
Cordial Shown
Gray Cut Floral,
Panel & Crosshatch Cuts
Edinburgh

Edinburgh

Stirling
Crisscross, Fan
& Swag Cuts
Edinburgh

Balmoral
Crisscross & Fan Cuts
Edinburgh

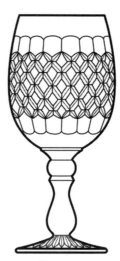

Braemar
Thumbprint &
Crisscross Cuts
84216
Edinburgh

Elegance
Vertical & Crisscross Cuts
Edinburgh

Orkney
Crisscross & Star Cuts
Edinburgh

EDI 16
Vertical, Crisscross
& Fan Cuts
Edinburgh

Argyll
Crisscross & Floral Cuts
Edinburgh

Ness
Crisscross & Fan Cuts
Edinburgh

Royal
Star & Fan Cuts
Edinburgh

Holyrood
Vertical & Crisscross Cuts
Edinburgh

Gleneagles
Vertical Cuts
Edinburgh

EDI 56
Vertical & Crisscross Cuts
Edinburgh

Montrose
Vertical, Crisscross
& Crosshatch Cuts
Edinburgh

Maree
Panel & Crisscross Cuts
Edinburgh

Tiree
Vertical & Crisscross Cuts
Edinburgh

EDI 18
Wine Shown
Crisscross & Fan Cuts
Edinburgh

Tweed
Crisscross & Fan Cuts
Edinburgh

Tay
Crisscross & Fan Cuts
Edinburgh

Kelso
Crisscross, Fan & Star Cuts
Edinburgh

Berkeley
Crisscross & Fan Cuts
Edinburgh

EDI 52
Crisscross, Crosshatch
& Fan Cuts
Edinburgh

EDI 4
Vertical, Crisscross
& Fan Cuts
Edinburgh

King James
Vertical, Crisscross
& Star Cuts
Edinburgh

Tectonic
Frosted Stem
Edinburgh

Synergis
Plain
Edinburgh

Vienna
Crisscross & Fan Cuts
Edinburgh

Finesse
Crisscross, Crosshatch
& Fan Cuts
Edinburgh

EDI 10
Gray Cut Floral
Edinburgh

Serenade
Vertical, Curved Crisscross,
& Fan Cuts
Edinburgh

Duet
Crisscross, Fan & Star Cuts
Edinburgh

Edinburgh

Storm
Slanted Vertical Cuts
Edinburgh

Mirage
Vertical & Crisscross Cuts
Edinburgh

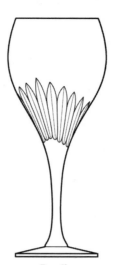

Brodie
Vertical Cuts
Edinburgh

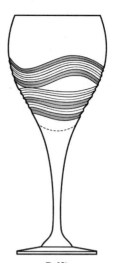

Drift
Gray & Clear
Curved Cut Rings
Edinburgh

Skye
Vertical, Crisscross
& Arch Cuts
Edinburgh

Eclipse
Curved Cut Rings
Edinburgh

Sonata
Vertical Cuts
Edinburgh

Broughton
Vertical & Crisscross Cuts
Edinburgh

Ailsa
White Wine Shown
Vertical Cuts
Edinburgh

EDI 36
Curved Vertical Cuts
Edinburgh

Symphony
Vertical Cuts
Edinburgh

Skibo
Geometric Square Cuts
Edinburgh

Portee
Diamond Cuts
Edinburgh

Spey
Notched Vertical Cuts
Edinburgh

Ayr
Vertical, Crisscross
& Fan Cuts
Edinburgh

Clova
Vertical Cuts
Edinburgh

Orrin
Cut Curved Lines
Edinburgh

Silhouette
Crisscross & Fan Cuts
Edinburgh

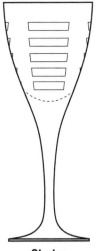

Stratus
Rectangle Cuts
Edinburgh

Tain
Frosted Cut Floral
Edinburgh

Torrent
Crisscross Cuts
Edinburgh

EDI 55
Wine Shown
Crisscross & Fan Cuts
Edinburgh

Cordelia
Curved Vertical Cuts
Edinburgh

Tempest
Wine Shown
Slanted Crisscross Cuts
Edinburgh

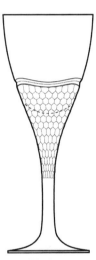

Nimbus
Wine Shown
Curved Horizontal
& Honeycomb Cuts
Edinburgh

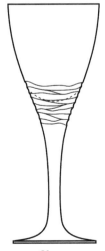

Cirrus
Wine Shown
Uneven Horizontal Cuts
Edinburgh

EDI 47
Crisscross Cuts
Edinburgh

EDI 17
Wine Shown
Crisscross, Fan
& Vertical Cuts
Edinburgh

Romeo
Wine Shown
Crisscross & Fan Cuts
Edinburgh

Rhapsody
Slanted Cuts
Edinburgh

Edinburgh

Isla
Crisscross, Crosshatch
& Fan Cuts
Edinburgh

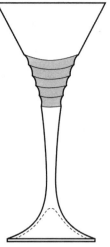

Infinity
Frosted Curved Bands,
Hollow Foot
Edinburgh

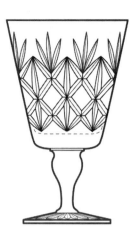

Glenshee
Crisscross & Fan Cuts
Edinburgh

Appin
Vertical & Crisscross Cuts
T601
Edinburgh

EDI 11
Wine Shown
Horizontal &
Crisscross Cuts
Edinburgh

Lomond
Crisscross & Fan Cuts,
Round Bowl
Edinburgh

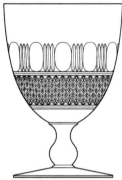

Marlboro
Vertical, Oval
& Crosshatch Cuts
Edinburgh

EDI 46
Wine Shown
Crisscross Cuts
Edinburgh

EDI 5
Crisscross & Fan Cuts
Edinburgh

EDI 13
Wine Shown
Cut Thistle
Edinburgh

Cameron
Crisscross & Fan Cuts
Edinburgh

Lochiel
Crisscross, Fan
& Circle Cuts
Edinburgh

Iona
Vertical, Crisscross
& Fan Cuts
Edinburgh

Sutherland
Crisscross & Fan Cuts
Edinburgh

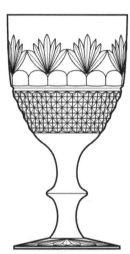

Royal Highland
Panel, Crosshatch
& Fan Cuts
Edinburgh

EDI 21
Wine Shown
Crisscross & Fan Cuts
Edinburgh

EDI 50
Wine Shown
Crisscross & Fan Cuts
Edinburgh

Lomond
Crisscross & Fan Cuts,
Square Bowl
Edinburgh

Star of Edinburgh
Crisscross, Swag & Fan Cuts
Edinburgh

Embassy
Crisscross, Crosshatch
& Fan Cuts
Edinburgh

Lochnagar
Etched Grapevine,
Panel Cuts
L436
Edinburgh

Highland
Vertical & Crosshatch Cuts
79382
Edinburgh

EDI 34
Thumbprint Cuts
Edinburgh

Cameron
Panel & Crosshatch Cuts
Edinburgh

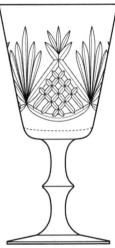

EDI 65
Crisscross & Fan Cuts
Edinburgh

Young Pretender
Gray Cut Floral & Star,
Crisscross & Crosshatch Cuts
Edinburgh

Royal Scot
Panel, Crosshatch
& Star Cuts
71124
Edinburgh

EDI 9
Vertical, Oval &
Crisscross Cuts
Edinburgh

EDI 12
Crisscross Cuts
Edinburgh

EDI 30
Vertical & Crisscross Cuts
Edinburgh

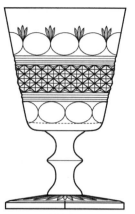

EDI 35
Horizontal, Oval
& Crosshatch Cuts,
Square Foot
Edinburgh

EDI 41
Brandy Glass Shown
Crisscross, Swag
& Fan Cuts
Edinburgh

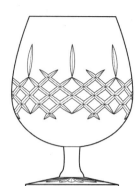

Brodick
Brandy Glass Shown
Vertical & Crisscross Cuts
Edinburgh

Continental
Brandy Glass Shown
Vertical, Crisscross
& Fan Cuts
Edinburgh

EDI 22
Tumbler Shown
Vertical, Fan &
Crisscross Cuts
Edinburgh

Eden
Tumbler Shown
Frosted Wavy Cuts
Edinburgh

EGC 2
Ruby Bowl & Foot,
Scrolls, Deer & Dots
Egermann

EGC 3
Royal Blue or Ruby Panels,
Gold Scrolls & Trim
Egermann

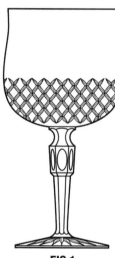

EIS 1
Crisscross Cuts
Eisch

Bolero
Vertical Cuts
173
Eisch

Pirouette
Air Twist Stem
Eisch

Vintec
White Wine Shown
Plain
Eisch

Pyramid
Plain, Square Base
Ekenas

EKE 1
Frosted Cone Shaped Base
Ekenas

ETZ 1
Red Bowl
Elements

Black Toast & Marmalade
Large Wine Shown
English Sayings
in Black Print
Emma Bridgewater

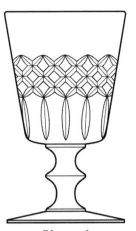

Diamond
Vertical & Crisscross Cuts
English Rock

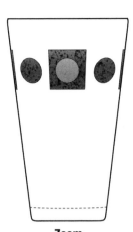

Zoom
Highball Shown
Black Squares, Various Color Dots
E916
Epoch

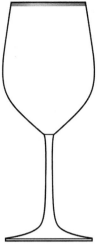

Century Gold
Gold Trim
Epoch

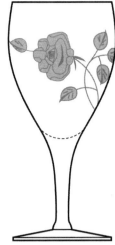

Bridal Rose
Gray Cut Rose & Leaves
Executive House

Pavlova
Wine Shown
Frosted Ballerina in Stem
Fabergé

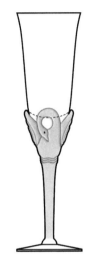

FAC 1
Champagne Flute Shown
Frosted Swan Stem
Fabergé

FAC 2
Champagne Flute Shown
Frosted Floral Stem,
Blue Stone in Center
Fabergé

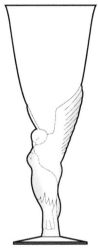

Kissing Doves
Frosted Stem
Fabergé

Viktoria
Fan Cuts
Fabergé

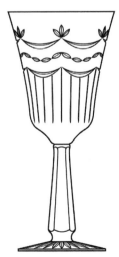

Empire
Vertical, Fan & Swag Cuts
Fabergé

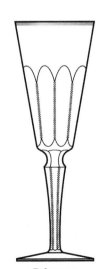

Princess
Champagne Flute Shown
Panel & Dot Cuts, Gold Trim
Fabergé

d'Arcy
Vertical & Crisscross Cuts
Fabergé

Metropolitan
Clear, White or Black,
Vertical & Horizontal Cuts
Fabergé

Palais Royal
Various Color Bowls,
Clear Panels, Fan Cuts
Fabergé

Nobilis
Crisscross, Vertical
& Fan Cuts
Fabergé

Raina
Vertical Cuts
Fabergé

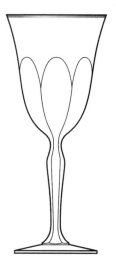

Aurora
Panel Cuts,
Plain or Gold Trim
Fabergé

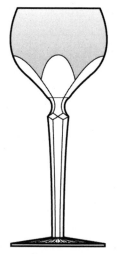

Lausanne
Wine Hock Shown
Various Color Bowls,
Clear Panels
Fabergé

Odessa
Various Color Bowls,
Crisscross & Fan Cuts
Fabergé

Alexandra
Cobalt Bowl, Panel Cuts
Fabergé

Xenia
Liquor Cocktail Shown
Various Color Bowls, Vertical,
Crosshatch & Dot Cuts
Fabergé

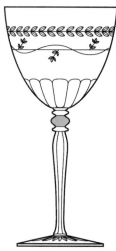

Luxembourg
Laurel Band, Floral Vine
& Panel Cuts
Fabergé

Czar Imperial
Various Color Bowls,
Crosshatch, Fan & Arch Cuts
Fabergé

FAC 4
Gray Cut Floral & Birds,
Various Eggs, Laurel Band,
Crosshatch Cuts, Multi-Motif
Fabergé

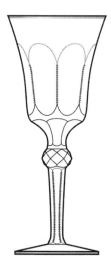

Operetta
Panel Cuts,
Gold Trim on Rim &
Top of Panels
Fabergé

Bubbles
Champagne Flute Shown
Various Color Bowls,
Clear Cut Dots
Fabergé

Galaxie
Martini Shown
Blue Bowl, Cut Stars
Fabergé

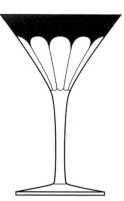

Grand Duke
Martini Shown
Various Color Bands,
Panel Cuts
Fabergé

Blanc de Blanc
White Bowl, Vertical Cuts
Fabergé

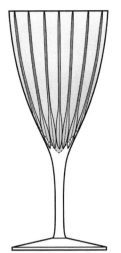

Rouge d'Orient (Ruby)
Bleu de Nuit (Cobalt)
Ruby or Cobalt Bowl,
Vertical Cuts
Fabergé

Crown
Wine Shown
Vertical & Horizontal Cuts
Fabergé

Bristol
Wine Shown
Panel Cuts,
Beaded Vertical Lines
Fabergé

Printemps
Panel & Leaf Cuts
Fabergé

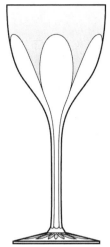

Regency
Various Color Bowls,
Panel Cuts
Fabergé

Foliage
Cut Leaves & Stems
Fabergé

Ville de Lyon
Fan & Garland Cuts
Fabergé

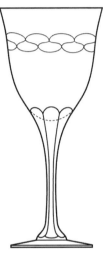

Olivia
Panel & Oval Cuts
Fabergé

Plume
Purple or Red Bowl,
Clear Cut Feather
Fabergé

Na Zdorovye
Cordial Shown
Various Color Bowls,
Multi-Motif
Fabergé

Coronation
Champagne Flute Shown
Crisscross & Starburst Cuts,
Gold Trim
Fabergé

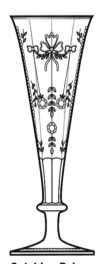

Gatchina Palace
Champagne Flute Shown
Etched Bows & Leaves,
Gold Trim
Fabergé

Paris
Wine Shown
Various Color Bowls,
Panel Cuts, Multisided Foot
Fabergé

Pine Cone
Vodka Shown
Etched Swags & Dots
Fabergé

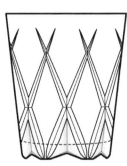

Triomphe
Double Old Fashioned Shown
Crisscross Cuts, Barware
Fabergé

Waffle
Double Old Fashioned Shown
Crisscross & Crosshatch Cuts
Fabergé

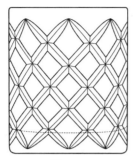

Oberon
Double Old Fashioned Shown
Crisscross Cuts
Fabergé

Farber Holder/Crystal
Chrome Stemware,
Various Color Liners
Farber Brothers

Classic
Plain
Farberware

Optic
Optic Bowl
Farberware

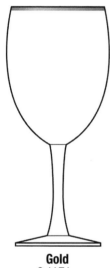

Gold
Gold Trim
Farberware

Pink Coral
Light Pink, Plain
Fashion Royale

Eternal
Optic Bowl, Platinum Trim
Fashion Royale

Blue Mist
Light Blue, Optic Bowl
Fashion Royale

Greenbrier
Light Green, Optic Bowl
Fashion Royale

Mystique
Black, Optic Bowl
Fashion Royale

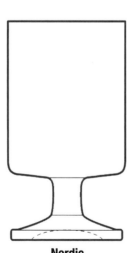

Nordic
Clear, Topaz or Smoke Foot
Federal Glass Company

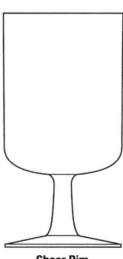

Sheer Rim
Plain
Federal Glass Company

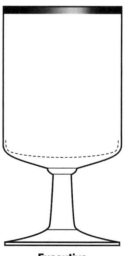

Executive
Platinum Trim
Federal Glass Company

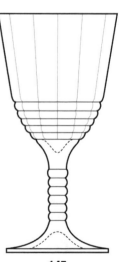

145
Optic Bowl, Plain,
Hollow Foot
Federal Glass Company

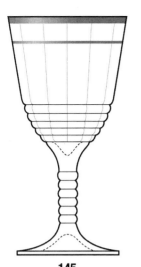

145
Gold or Platinum Trim
Federal Glass Company

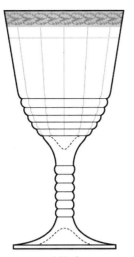

145-2
Gold Laurel Band
145
Federal Glass Company

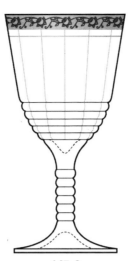

145-3
Gold Floral Band
145
Federal Glass Company

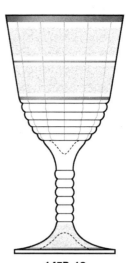

145R-12
Frosted Bands,
Gold Bowl & Foot Trim
145R
Federal Glass Company

145R-14
Gray Cut Floral
145R
Federal Glass Company

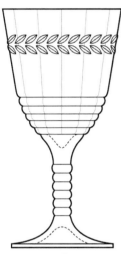

145R-1
Embossed Laurel,
Plain
145R
Federal Glass Company

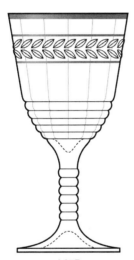

145R
Embossed Laurel,
Optic Bowl, Hollow Foot,
Gold Bands & Trim
Federal Glass Company

145R-3
Embossed Laurel,
Gray Cut Dots & Leaves
145R
Federal Glass Company

Mary Rose
Decoration 472,
White Floral Decal
Federal Glass Company

Parrot
Cone Shaped Footed Sherbet Shown
Clear or Various Colors,
Parrots & Plants
Federal Glass Company

Patrician
Champagne/Tall Sherbet Shown
Clear or Various Colors,
Textured Scrolls
Federal Glass Company

Colonial
Champagne/Tall Sherbet Shown
Clear or Green, Fluted
Federal Glass Company

Georgian
Champagne/Tall Sherbet Shown
Clear or Green,
Birds & Scrolls
Federal Glass Company

Normandie
Champagne/Tall Sherbet Shown
Clear or Various Colors,
Floral & Scrolls
Federal Glass Company

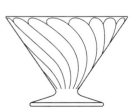

Diana
Champagne/Tall Sherbet Shown
Clear or Various Colors,
Swirls, Plain or Gold Trim
Federal Glass Company

Federal Glass Company

Colonial
Clear or Smoke Iridescent,
Pressed Glass
Federal Glass Company

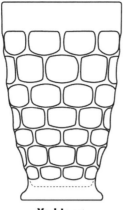

Yorktown
Footed Tumbler Shown
Clear or Various Colors,
Pressed Glass
Federal Glass Company

Home Entertainment Set
Beer Glass Shown
Plain
Federal Glass Company

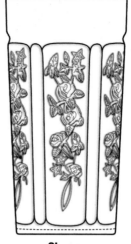

Sharon
Tumbler Shown
Clear or Various Colors,
Embossed Floral
Federal Glass Company

Mayfair
Tumbler Shown
Clear or Various Colors,
Crisscross, Archs & Floral
Federal Glass Company

Rosemary
Tumbler Shown
Various Colors,
Floral & Archs
Federal Glass Company

Madrid
Tumbler Shown
Clear or Various Colors,
Geometric, Floral & Scrolls
Federal Glass Company

Star
Tumbler Shown
Clear or Amber, Fans,
Plain or Gold Trim
Federal Glass Company

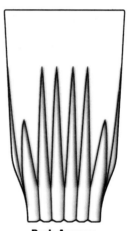

Park Avenue
Tumbler Shown
Ribbed,
1940s–1960s Glassware
Federal Glass Company

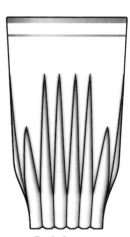

Park Avenue
Tumbler Shown; Ribbed,
Gold Band & Wide Gold Trim
1940s–1960s Glassware
Federal Glass Company

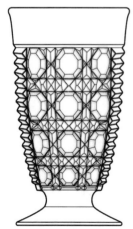

Windsor
Footed Tumbler Shown
Clear or Various Colors,
Button & Cane, Pressed Glass
Federal Glass Company

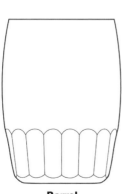

Barrel
Tumbler Shown
Oval Cuts, Barware
Federal Glass Company

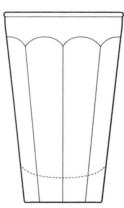

Heritage
Highball Shown
Clear or Various Colors,
Panels
Federal Glass Company

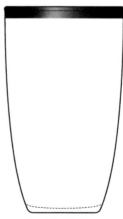

Danish Modern
Tumbler Shown
Platinum Trim, Barware
T-353
Federal Glass Company

Thumbprint
Tumbler Shown
Green
Federal Glass Company

Lido
Tumbler Shown
Amber or Pink, Optic, Ringed
146R
Federal Glass Company

Sportsman
Pilsner Shown
Various Birds, Platinum Trim
Federal Glass Company

Snowflake
Tumbler Shown
Gold & Black Snowflakes
Federal Glass Company

Thumbprint
Clear or Various Colors,
Thumbprint Panels
Fenton Glass

Hobnail
Clear or Various Colors,
Raised Dots
Fenton Glass

Plymouth
Clear or Various Colors,
Horizontal, Vertical & Dots
1620
Fenton Glass

Georgian
Clear or Various Colors,
Honeycomb
1611
Fenton Glass

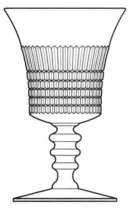

Lincoln Inn
Clear or Various Colors,
Vertical & Crisscross, Pressed
1700
Fenton Glass

Priscilla
Clear or Various Colors,
Panels, Circles & Stars
1890
Fenton Glass

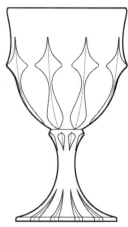

Valencia
Clear or Various Colors,
Vertical Design
Fenton Glass

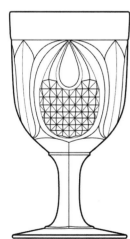

Pineapple
Clear or Various Colors,
Vertical & Crosshatch, Pressed
9045
Fenton Glass

Rose
Various Colors,
Embossed Floral,
Pressed Glass
Fenton Glass

Empress
Various Colors,
Embossed Feather,
Pressed Glass
Fenton Glass

Flower Band
Clear or Various Colors,
Embossed Floral Band,
Pressed Glass
Fenton Glass

Cactus
Various Colors,
Beaded Cactus,
Pressed Glass
Fenton Glass

Stippled Scroll
Various Colors,
Scrolls & Beads,
Pressed Glass
Fenton Glass

Flower Window
Clear or Ruby, Floral,
Twisted Stem,
Pressed Glass
Fenton Glass

Historic America
Various American Scenes,
Pressed Glass
Fenton Glass

Orange Tree
Blue or Marigold, Floral,
Pressed Glass
Fenton Glass

Iris
Marigold Bowl, Floral,
Pressed Glass
Fenton Glass

American Legacy
Clear or Green, Panels
Fenton Glass

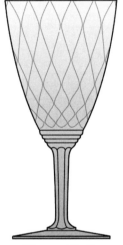

Diamond Optic
Various Colors,
Diamond Optic Bowl
Fenton Glass

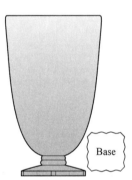

Elizabeth
Footed Tumbler Shown
Various Colors, Scalloped Foot
1639
Fenton Glass

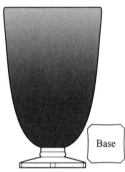

Elizabeth
Footed Tumbler Shown
Various Colors, Square Foot
1639
Fenton Glass

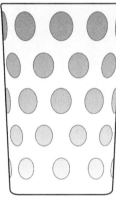

Coin Dot
Tumbler Shown
Various Colors,
Clear or Color Dots
Fenton Glass

Floral & Grape Variant
Tumbler Shown
Various Colors
1012
Fenton Glass

Bouquet
Tumbler Shown
Blue Carnival Glass,
Floral & Dots
Fenton Glass

Butterfly & Berry
Tumbler Shown
Various Colors, Carnival Glass
1124
Fenton Glass

Lattice & Grape
Tumbler Shown
Various Colors,
Carnival Glass
Fenton Glass

Apple Tree
Tumbler Shown
Milk Glass or
Gold Pearl Carnival Glass
Fenton Glass

FIF 3
Wine Hock Shown
Various Color Bowls,
Crisscross & Fan Cuts
Fifth Avenue

FIF 1
Wine Hock Shown
Various Color Bowls, Floral,
Horizontal & Vertical Cuts
Fifth Avenue

Princess
Wine Hock Shown
Various Color Bowls,
Vertical & Swag Cuts
Fifth Avenue

Millenia
Various Color Bowls,
Crisscross & Fan Cuts
Fifth Avenue

Juliet
Plain
Fifth Avenue

Estate
Vertical & Crisscross Cuts
Fifth Avenue

FIF 9
Brown, Optic Bowl
Fifth Avenue

Birthstones
Clear or Various Color
Bowls, Panel Cuts
Fifth Avenue

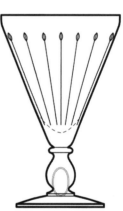

Elegance
Vertical Cuts,
Bubble in Stem
17588
Fine Arts

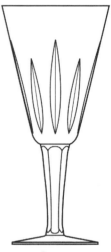

Opera
Wine Shown
Vertical Cuts
Fine Arts

Regency
Gray Cut Arches
Fine Arts

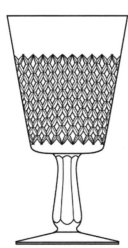

Royal Diamond
Crisscross Cuts
Fine Arts

Romance Rose
Gray Cut Rose
Fine Arts

Romance of the Stars
Gray Cut Stars,
Bubble in Stem
17638
Fine Arts

Tranquility
Swirl Cuts
Fine Arts

Twilight
Smoke Bowl
Fine Arts

Wildflower
Gray Cut Plant
Fine Arts

FLG 1
Cut Stars
Flemington Glass

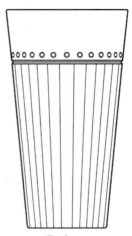

Tapioca
Cooler Shown
Beaded Band,
Vertical Lines
Food Network

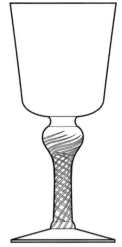

Airtwist
Wine Shown
Air Twist Stem
Foreign Advisory

Baluster
Plain
Foreign Advisory

Belle Isle
Wine Shown
Crisscross & Fan Cuts
Foreign Advisory

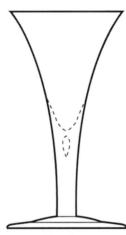

Teardrop
Plain,
Bubble in Stem
Foreign Advisory

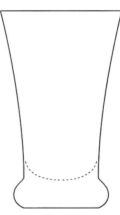

Tavern
Plain
Foreign Advisory

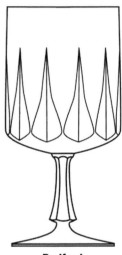

Bedford
Vertical Teardrop Cuts
Forest

Fostoria Shapes and Lines

2056 *Page 352*	**2719** *Page 352*	**1372** *Page 352*	**2496** *Page 352*	**2770** *Page 352*	**2449** *Page 352*	**2412** *Page 352*	**5056** *Page 352*	**5412** *Page 352*
6060 *Page 352*	**2630** *Page 352*	**880** *Page 353*	**661** *Page 353*	**863** *Page 354*	**6106** *Page 355*	**6107** *Page 356*	**UNKNOWN–Romania** *Page 356*	**6102** *Page 356*
UNKNOWN–Romania *Page 357*	**6115** *Page 358*	**UNKNOWN** *Page 358*	**6103** *Page 358*	**802** *Page 359*	**114** *Page 359*	**5025** *Page 359*	**766** *Page 359*	**858** *Page 360*
UNKNOWN–Romania *Page 361*	**867** *Page 361*	**6122** *Page 361*	**867 1/2** *Page 361*	**795, 846, 902, 906, 952, 963** *Page 361*	**879** *Page 362*	**805** *Page 362*	**870** *Page 362*	**892** *Page 362*
890 *Page 363*	**877** *Page 363*	**891** *Page 363*	**869** *Page 364*	**5008** *Page 364*	**660** *Page 364*	**6004** *Page 365*	**6005** *Page 365*	**5082** *Page 365*

5093/5293	5097	UNKNOWN	UNKNOWN	5099/5299	5098/5298	6017	6143	6030
Page 366	*Page 366*	*Page 367*	*Page 367*	*Page 367*	*Page 367*	*Page 368*	*Page 369*	*Page 369*

6031	6110	6007	6008	6013	6026	6016	6024	6108
Page 370	*Page 370*	*Page 370*	*Page 371*	*Page 371*	*Page 371*	*Page 372*	*Page 372*	*Page 373*

6037	6012	6127	6126	6123	6011	6032	6064	6113
Page 373	*Page 373*	*Page 374*	*Page 374*	*Page 374*	*Page 375*	*Page 376*	*Page 376*	*Page 376*

6120	UNKNOWN	6104	6105	6092	6111	6086	6010	6009
Page 377	*Page 377*	*Page 377*	*Page 377*	*Page 378*	*Page 378*	*Page 379*	*Page 379*	*Page 379*

UNKNOWN	6072	6093	6087	6109	6029	6089	6068	6100
Page 380	*Page 380*	*Page 380*	*Page 380*	*Page 381*	*Page 381*	*Page 381*	*Page 381*	*Page 382*

6101	882	6083	6124	6144	MO12	UNKNOWN	5083	6112
Page 382	*Page 382*	*Page 382*	*Page 383*	*Page 383*	*Page 383*	*Page 383*	*Page 383*	*Page 383*

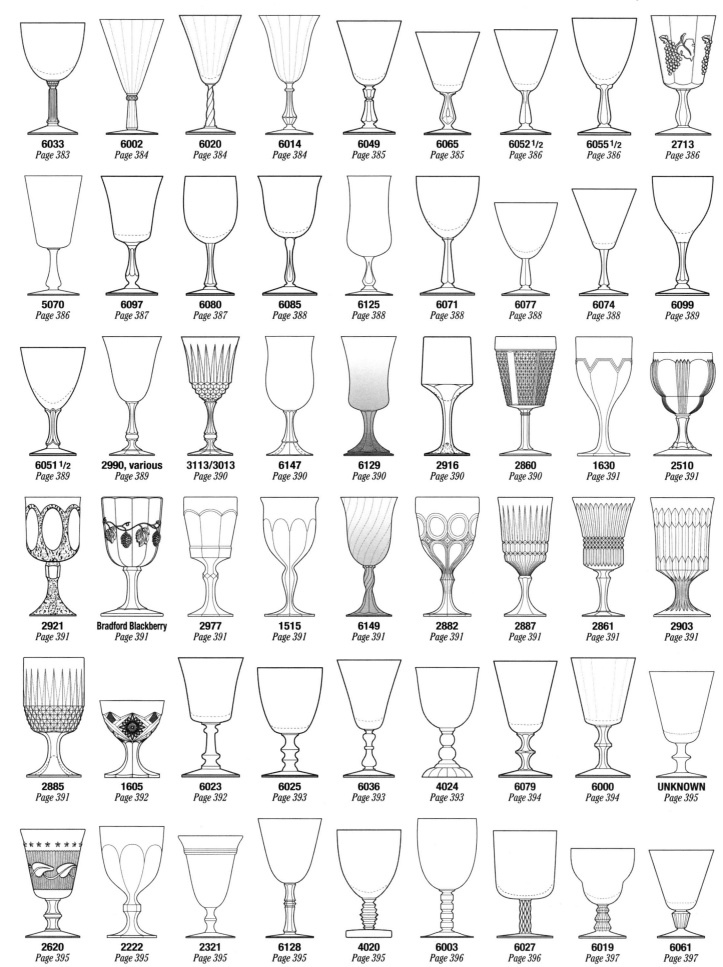

6033
Page 383

6002
Page 384

6020
Page 384

6014
Page 384

6049
Page 385

6065
Page 385

6052 1/2
Page 386

6055 1/2
Page 386

2713
Page 386

5070
Page 386

6097
Page 387

6080
Page 387

6085
Page 388

6125
Page 388

6071
Page 388

6077
Page 388

6074
Page 388

6099
Page 389

6051 1/2
Page 389

2990, various
Page 389

3113/3013
Page 390

6147
Page 390

6129
Page 390

2916
Page 390

2860
Page 390

1630
Page 391

2510
Page 391

2921
Page 391

Bradford Blackberry
Page 391

2977
Page 391

1515
Page 391

6149
Page 391

2882
Page 391

2887
Page 391

2861
Page 391

2903
Page 391

2885
Page 391

1605
Page 392

6023
Page 392

6025
Page 393

6036
Page 393

4024
Page 393

6079
Page 394

6000
Page 394

UNKNOWN
Page 395

2620
Page 395

2222
Page 395

2321
Page 395

6128
Page 395

4020
Page 395

6003
Page 396

6027
Page 396

6019
Page 397

6061
Page 397

347

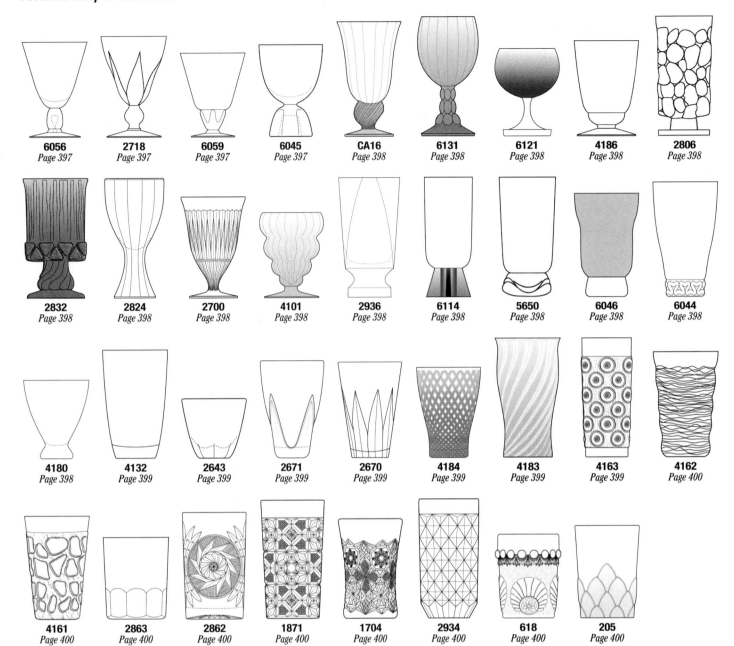

6056 *Page 397*	**2718** *Page 397*	**6059** *Page 397*	**6045** *Page 397*	**CA16** *Page 398*	**6131** *Page 398*	**6121** *Page 398*	**4186** *Page 398*	**2806** *Page 398*
2832 *Page 398*	**2824** *Page 398*	**2700** *Page 398*	**4101** *Page 398*	**2936** *Page 398*	**6114** *Page 398*	**5650** *Page 398*	**6046** *Page 398*	**6044** *Page 398*
4180 *Page 398*	**4132** *Page 399*	**2643** *Page 399*	**2671** *Page 399*	**2670** *Page 399*	**4184** *Page 399*	**4183** *Page 399*	**4163** *Page 399*	**4162** *Page 400*
4161 *Page 400*	**2863** *Page 400*	**2862** *Page 400*	**1871** *Page 400*	**1704** *Page 400*	**2934** *Page 400*	**618** *Page 400*	**205** *Page 400*	

Baroque Line

Round Handled Bowl

Cup & Saucer

Dinner Plate

Candlestick   **Candlestick**   **Iced Tea**

Century Line

Round Handled Bowl

Cup & Saucer

Candlestick

Dinner Plate

Creamer

Sugar

Colony Line

Pickle Dish

Cup & Saucer

Handled Cake Plate

Dinner Plate

Creamer   **Sugar**

Contour Line

Salad Bowl

Cup & Saucer

Serving Plate

Dinner Plate

Creamer

Sugar

Coronet Line

Serving Bowl

Handled Bowl

Cup & Saucer

Fruit/Dessert Bowl

Salad Plate

Sugar

Candlestick

Candlestick

Creamer

Fairfax Line

Flat Cup & Saucer

Footed Cup & Saucer

Bon Bon Plate with Bow Handles

Demitasse Cup & Saucer

Serving Bowl

Oval Platter

Creamer

Sugar

Dinner Plate

Lafayette Line

Serving Bowl

Cup & Saucer

Divided Handled Bowl

Sugar

Oval Platter

Torte Plate   **Creamer**

Mayfair Line

Cup & Saucer

Square Bowl

Dinner Plate

Rectangular Bowl

Raleigh Line

Cup & Saucer

Creamer

Sugar

Sweet Meat Plate

Saucer

Handled Bowl

Candlestick

Fostoria

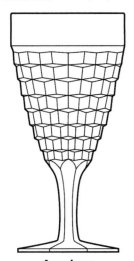

American
Clear or Various Colors,
Raised Blocks
2056
Fostoria

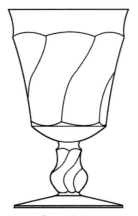

Jamestown
Clear or Various Colors,
Swirled Panels, Pressed Glass
2719
Fostoria

Coin Glass
Clear or Various Colors,
Coin Panels
1372
Fostoria

Baroque
Clear, Blue or Topaz,
Scrolls & Panels
2496
Fostoria

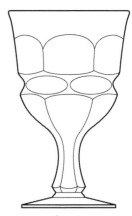

Argus
Clear or Various Colors,
Panels, Pressed Glass
2770
Fostoria

Hermitage
Clear or Various Colors,
Panels, Pressed Glass
2449
Fostoria

Colony
Swirls, Pressed Glass
2412
Fostoria

American Lady
Clear, Blue, Green
or Amethyst Bowls
5056
Fostoria

Colonial Dame
Clear or Green Bowl,
Swirl Stem
5412
Fostoria

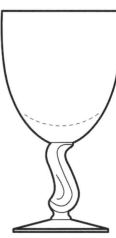

Contour
Clear or Pink Bowl,
Curved Stem
6060
Fostoria

Windfall
Cut 870, Leaves,
Curved Stem
6060
Fostoria

Spring
Cut 844, Plants,
Curved Stem
6060
Fostoria

Sylvan
Etch 1, Falling Leaves,
Curved Stem
6060
Fostoria

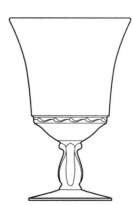

Century
Plain, Pressed Glass
2630
Fostoria

Lacy Leaf
Crystal Print 6,
Etched Leaves
2630
Fostoria

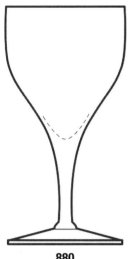

880
Plain
Fostoria

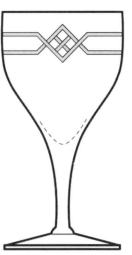

Mission
Geometric Cuts
880
Fostoria

Irish Lace
Etch 36, Crisscross,
Optic Bowl
880
Fostoria

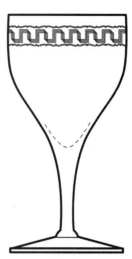

Greek
Etch 45, Geometric,
Plain or Optic Bowl
880
Fostoria

Garland
Etch 237, Floral Swags
880
Fostoria

Rosilyn
Etch 249, Scrolls & Swags,
Optic Bowl
880
Fostoria

Kornflower
Etch 234, Floral
880
Fostoria

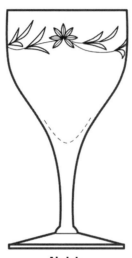

Airdale
Cut 175, Floral
880
Fostoria

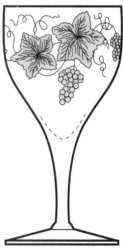

New Vintage
Etch 227, Grapes & Leaves
880
Fostoria

Geneva
Cut 135, Floral
880
Fostoria

Sunburst
Cut 81, Starbursts
880
Fostoria

661
Plain
Fostoria

Ballet
Needle Etch 91, Geometric,
Optic Bowl
661
Fostoria

Miami
Decoration 42, Floral,
Gold Trim
661
Fostoria

Orient
Etch 265, Floral Swags,
Optic Bowl
661
Fostoria

353

Fostoria

Melrose
Etch 268, Floral,
Optic Bowl
661
Fostoria

Virginia
Etch 267, Floral,
Optic Bowl
661
Fostoria

Cynthia
Cut 763, Floral
661
Fostoria

Louisa
Cut 168, Floral,
Optic Bowl
661
Fostoria

Empress
Gold Decoration 29,
Encrusted Floral Band
661
Fostoria

863
Plain
Fostoria

Block
Etch 38 ½, Blocks,
Optic Bowl
863
Fostoria

Chain
Etch 42, Crisscross Band
863
Fostoria

Lunar
Etch 54, Spiral Band
863
Fostoria

Large Cloverleaf
Needle Etch Scrolls
863
Fostoria

Small Cloverleaf
Etch 67, Scrolls
863
Fostoria

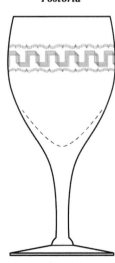

Greek
Etch 45, Geometric
863
Fostoria

Mission
Cut 116, Geometric
863
Fostoria

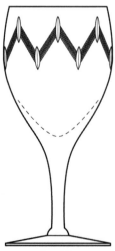

Cut 125
Zigzag Band
863
Fostoria

Etch 210
Scrolls, Plain or Optic Bowl
863
Fostoria

Garland
Etch 237, Floral Swags
863
Fostoria

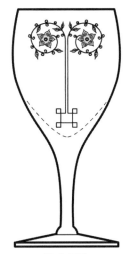

Etch 212
Geometric Floral
863
Fostoria

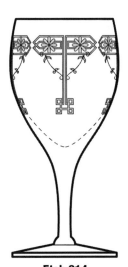

Etch 214
Geometric Floral
863
Fostoria

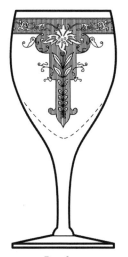

Persian
Etch 253, Floral
863
Fostoria

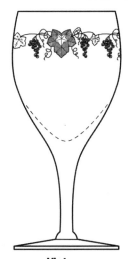

Vintage
Etch 204, Grapes & Leaves
863
Fostoria

New Vintage
Etch 227, Grapes & Leaves,
Plain or Optic Bowl
863
Fostoria

Clover
Cut 132, Gray Floral
863
Fostoria

Cut 104
Plant & Swags
863
Fostoria

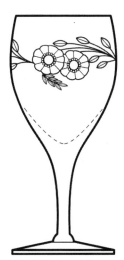

Apple Blossom
Cut 158, Floral
863
Fostoria

Chrysanthemum
Cut 132, Gray Floral
863
Fostoria

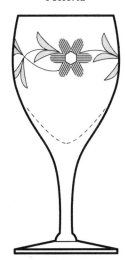

Fairfax
Cut 167, Gray Floral
863
Fostoria

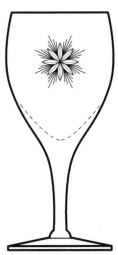

Cut 110
Starburst
863
Fostoria

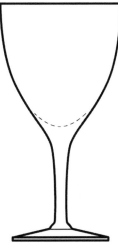

Celebrity
Plain
6106
Fostoria

6106-1
Iridescent Optic Bowl
6106
Fostoria

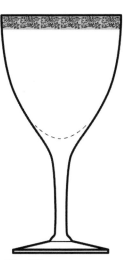

Mantilla (Platinum 675)
Brocade (Gold 674)
Encrusted Floral Band
6106
Fostoria

Fostoria

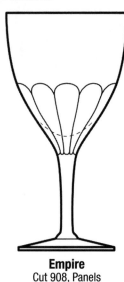

Empire
Cut 908, Panels
6106
Fostoria

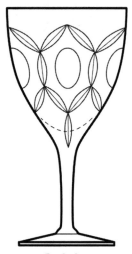

Berkeley
Cut 909, Oval & Leaf
6106
Fostoria

Inspiration
Plain
6107
Fostoria

Inspiration
Narrow Optic Bowl
6107
Fostoria

Lovelight (Platinum Trim)
Remembrance (Gold Trim)
6107
Fostoria

Betrothal (Platinum Trim)
Allegro (Gold Dec. 672)
Optic Bowl
6107
Fostoria

Matrimony
Cut 910, Leaves
6107
Fostoria

Orange Blossom
Cut 911, Floral
6107
Fostoria

Avignon
Plain
Fostoria

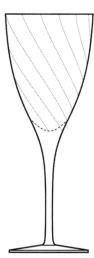

Monticello
Swirl Optic Bowl
Fostoria

Elegance
Gray Cut Swirl
Fostoria

Charleston
Gray Cut Floral
Fostoria

Silhouette
Clear, Blue, Pink or Black
6102
Fostoria

Invitation (Platinum Trim)
Vermeil (Gold Trim)
6102
Fostoria

Bridal Shower
Cut 897, Vertical
6102
Fostoria

Lineal
Cut 899, Gray Lines
6102
Fostoria

Venus
Cut 896, Panels
6102
Fostoria

Fleurette
Etch 26, Floral
6102
Fostoria

Milady
Cut 895, Leaves
6102
Fostoria

Rosalie
Etch 19, Floral
6102
Fostoria

Golden Garland
Etch 664, Floral,
Gold Trim
6102
Fostoria

Platina Rose
Etch 633, Floral,
Platinum Trim
6102
Fostoria

Bianca
Etch 22, Floral
6102
Fostoria

6102-1
Etched Floral
6102
Fostoria

Wedding Flower
Cut 920, Gray Flower Petals
6102
Fostoria

Thunderbird
Etched Thunderbird
6102
Fostoria

Baroness
Vertical Cuts
Fostoria

Monarch
Aida 173, Vertical Cuts
Fostoria

Athens
Cut Laurel Band
Fostoria

Countess
Gray Cut Swirls
Fostoria

Fostoria

Stephanie
Gray Cut Floral,
Swirl Cuts
Fostoria

San Francisco
Plant & Leaf Cuts
80174
Fostoria

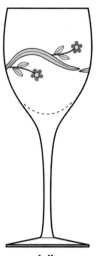

Jolie
Gray Cut Floral
Fostoria

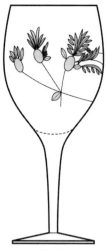

Nadia
Gray Cut Floral
Fostoria

Coronation
Gray Cut Floral
Fostoria

Galleria
Champagne Flute Shown
Blue Outlined
Geometric Shapes
Fostoria

Engagement
Gold Trim
Fostoria

Sommelier Collection
Magnum Wine Shown
Plain
6115
Fostoria

FOS 6
Green Stem, Blue Foot
Fostoria

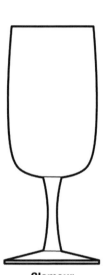

Glamour
Clear, Gray, Green
or Blue Bowl
6103
Fostoria

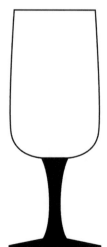

Glamour
Black Stem
6103
Fostoria

Announcement (Plat. Trim)
Rehearsal (Gold Trim)
6103
Fostoria

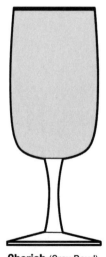

Cherish (Gray Bowl)
Something Blue (Blue Bowl)
Platinum Trim
6103
Fostoria

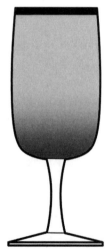

6103-1
Smoke Bowl,
Wide Platinum Trim
6103
Fostoria

Fountain
Cut 901, Curved Lines
6103
Fostoria

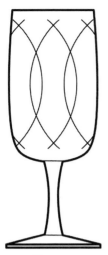

Forever
Cut 904, Geometric
6103
Fostoria

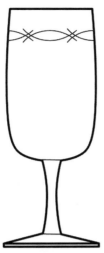

Ballerina
Cut 900, Geometric
6103
Fostoria

Barcelona
Etch 27, Scrolls
6103
Fostoria

Nuptial
Etch 21, Floral
6103
Fostoria

Plume
Cut 141, Laurel
802
Fostoria

Rosedale
Etch 25, Floral & Plants
802
Fostoria

Rosilyn
Etch 249, Wreaths & Plants
802
Fostoria

Etch 47
Needle Etched Scrolls
114
Fostoria

Etch 45
Geometric Bands
5025
Fostoria

Mother of Pearl
Iridescent, Optic Bowl
766
Fostoria

Laurel
Decoration 31,
Gold Encrusted Laurel Band
766
Fostoria

766-2
Gold Encrusted
Geometric Band, Optic Bowl
766
Fostoria

Newport
Gold Decoration 9,
Cut Laurel
766
Fostoria

Cascade
Band 8, Crisscross,
Gold Bands & Trim
766
Fostoria

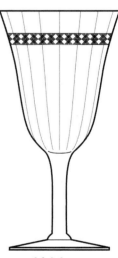

Irish Lace
Etch 36, Geometric,
Optic Bowl
766
Fostoria

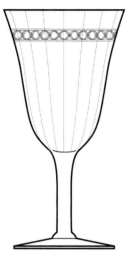

Chain
Etch 42, Crisscross,
Optic Bowl
766
Fostoria

Priscilla
Cut 130, Geometric Band,
Plain or Optic Bowl
766
Fostoria

Victory
Etch 257, Floral Swags,
Optic Bowl
766
Fostoria

766-1
Etched Floral Swags,
Gold Encrusted Band
766
Fostoria

Garland
Etch 237, Floral Swags,
Plain or Optic Bowl
766
Fostoria

Modern Vintage
Etch 255, Grapes & Leaves,
Plain or Optic Bowl
766
Fostoria

Oriental
Etch 250, Birds & Floral
766
Fostoria

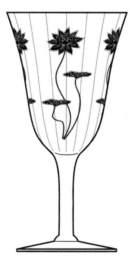

Lotus
Etch 232, Floral,
Optic Bowl
766
Fostoria

Mother of Pearl
Iridescent, Optic Bowl
858
Fostoria

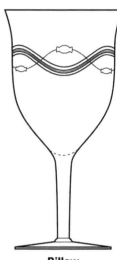

Billow
Cut 118, Curved Lines
858
Fostoria

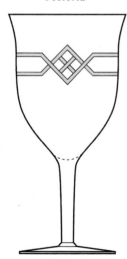

Mission
Cut 116, Geometric
858
Fostoria

Lenore
Needle Etch 73, Geometric,
Clear or Iridescent
858
Fostoria

Greek
Etch 45, Geometric,
Plain or Optic Bowl
858
Fostoria

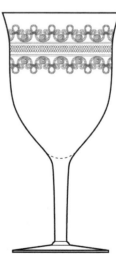

Large Cloverleaf
Etch 47, Scrolls
858
Fostoria

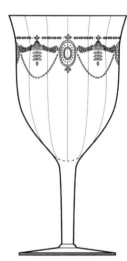

New Adam
Etch 252, Floral Swags,
Optic Bowl
858
Fostoria

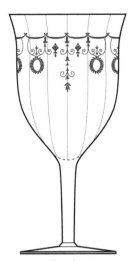

Empire
Etch 238, Scrolls & Swags,
Optic Bowl
858
Fostoria

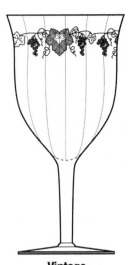

Vintage
Etch 204, Grapes & Leaves,
Plain or Optic Bowl
858
Fostoria

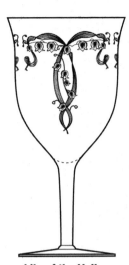

Lily of the Valley
Etch 241, Floral
858
Fostoria

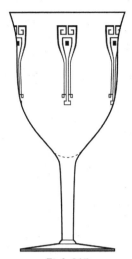

Etch 215
Geometric
858
Fostoria

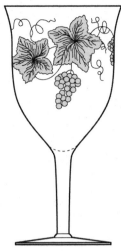

New Vintage
Etch 227, Grapes & Leaves
858
Fostoria

Florid
Etch 256, Floral,
Optic Bowl
858
Fostoria

Dresden
Decoration 12,
Painted Floral, Gold Trim
858
Fostoria

Bluebird
Painted Bluebird,
Blue Trim
858
Fostoria

Atlanta
Crisscross Cuts,
Gold Trim
Fostoria

Parisian
Needle Etch 53,
Optic Bowl
867
Fostoria

Biscayne
White, Blue, Brown,
Black or Yellow
6122
Fostoria

Halo
Black, Platinum Trim
6122
Fostoria

Fresno
Etch 78, Geometric Bands,
Optic Bowl
867 ½
Fostoria

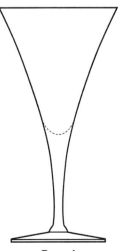

Repeal
Plain, Various Stemware
795, 846, 902, 906, 952, 963
Fostoria

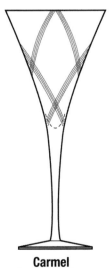

Carmel
Gray Cut Arches
Fostoria

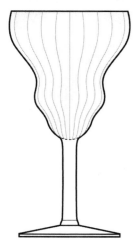

Mother of Pearl
Iridescent, Optic Bowl
879
Fostoria

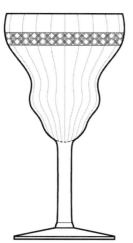

Irish Lace
Crisscross Etch,
Optic Bowl
879
Fostoria

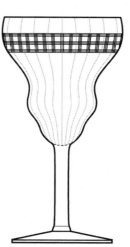

Block
Etch 38 ½, Squares,
Optic Bowl
879
Fostoria

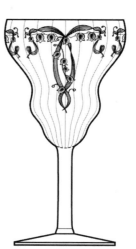

Lily of the Valley
Etch 241, Floral & Swags,
Optic Bowl
879
Fostoria

Apple Blossom
Cut 158, Floral
805
Fostoria

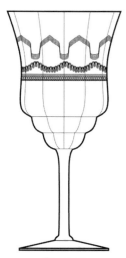

Baronet
Etch 92, Geometric Bands,
Optic Bowl
870
Fostoria

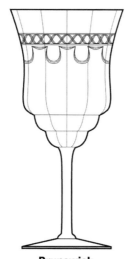

Brunswick
Etch 79, Crisscross & Swags,
Clear or Various Colors
870
Fostoria

Seville
Etch 274, Floral,
Clear or Various Colors
870
Fostoria

Nordic
Plain
892
Fostoria

Ingrid
Cut 794, Dots & Leaves
892
Fostoria

Rosemary
Etch 339, Floral
892
Fostoria

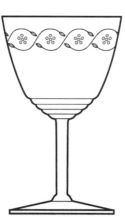

Christine
Cut 798, Floral
892
Fostoria

Ringlet
Tracing 95, Etched Loops
892
Fostoria

Ariel
Etch 93, Scrolls
892
Fostoria

Lyric
Cut 796, Vertical Lines
892
Fostoria

Papyrus
Cut 795, Plants
892
Fostoria

892-1
Frosted Stars
892
Fostoria

Orchid
Carved 48, Gray Floral
892
Fostoria

890
Clear, Green, Rose or
Burgundy, Optic Bowl
Fostoria

Verona
Etch 281, Floral,
Clear, Green or Rose
890
Fostoria

Warwick
Cut 198, Floral
890
Fostoria

877
Clear or Various Colors,
Plain or Optic Bowl
Fostoria

Mother of Pearl
Iridescent Optic Bowl
877
Fostoria

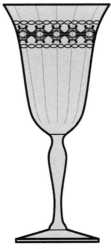

Cordelia
Etch 82, Geometric Band,
Green or Orchid, Optic Bowl
877
Fostoria

Chatteris
Cut 197, Floral,
Optic Bowl
877
Fostoria

Lattice
Cut 196, Plants & Lattice,
Optic Bowl
877
Fostoria

Vernon
Etch 277, Floral,
Clear or Various Colors
877
Fostoria

Oak Leaf
Etch 290, Clear,
Green or Pink
877
Fostoria

Oakwood
Etch 290, Iridescent Clear,
Blue or Orchid, Gold Trim
877
Fostoria

Springtime
Etch 318, Floral,
Clear or Yellow, Optic Bowl
891
Fostoria

Fostoria

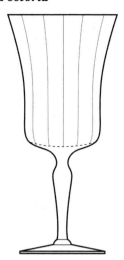

869
Clear or Various Colors,
Optic Bowl
Fostoria

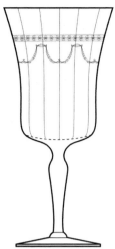

Sherman
Needle Etch 77,
Scrolls & Swags
869
Fostoria

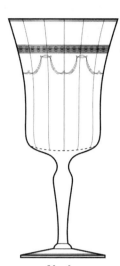

Alaska
Decoration 54, Etched
Scrolls & Swags, Gold Trim
869
Fostoria

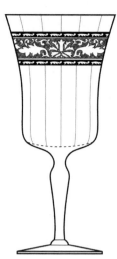

Royal
Etch 273, Scrolls,
Clear or Various Colors
869
Fostoria

Arbor
Cut 184, Lines & Floral,
Amber, Blue or Green
869
Fostoria

Blackberry
Etch 205, Plants
5008
Fostoria

Large Sunburst Star
Cut 81
5008
Fostoria

Mother of Pearl
Iridescent Optic Bowl
660
Fostoria

Pagoda
Needle Etch 90, Scrolls
Optic Bowl
660
Fostoria

Washington
Etch 266, Floral,
Optic Bowl
660
Fostoria

Trellis
Cut 169, Crisscross & Floral,
Optic Bowl
660
Fostoria

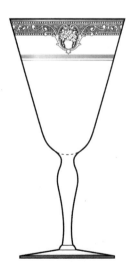

Vase & Scroll
Decoration 25, Blue Etched
Floral, Gold Bands & Trim
660
Fostoria

Black & Gold
Gold Trim with Black Lines
660
Fostoria

Mystic
Etch 270, Floral
660
Fostoria

Woodland
Etch 264, Floral
660
Fostoria

Goldwood
Etch 264, Decoration 50,
Floral, Gold Trim
660
Fostoria

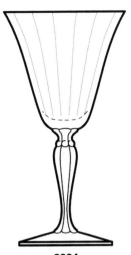

6004
Clear or Blue; or Clear Bowl
with Green or Wisteria Stem,
Various Optic Bowls
Fostoria

Fuchsia
Etch 310, Floral,
Clear or Wisteria Stem
6004
Fostoria

Nairn
Cut 708, Floral
6004
Fostoria

Staunton
Cut 707, Floral
6004
Fostoria

6004-2
India Tree Etch
6004
Fostoria

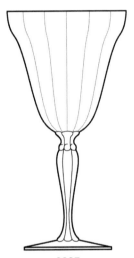

6005
Clear or Iridescent
Optic Bowl; Clear, Green
or Yellow Stem
Fostoria

Florentine
Etch 311, Urn & Floral,
Clear or Topaz Stem
6005
Fostoria

Mayday
Etch 312, Floral,
Green Foot
6005
Fostoria

5082
Various Optic Bowls
& Colors
Fostoria

Mother of Pearl
Iridescent Optic Bowl
5082
Fostoria

Eilene
Etch 83, Scrolls; Clear,
Blue, Green or Pink Bowl
5082
Fostoria

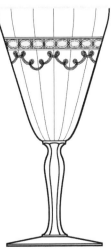

Princess
Needle Etch 74, Scrolls,
Gold Trim & Band
5082
Fostoria

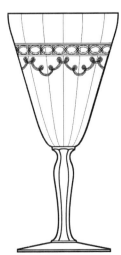

Richmond
Needle Etch 74, Scrolls
5082
Fostoria

Delphian
Etch 272, Floral,
Blue Stem
5082
Fostoria

Duchess
Etch 272, Floral,
Blue Stem, Gold Band & Trim
5082
Fostoria

5082-4
Etched Floral
5082
Fostoria

Rogene
Etch 269, Floral
5082
Fostoria

Mystic
Etch 270 ½, Floral,
Green
5082
Fostoria

5082-1
Etched Floral & People
5082
Fostoria

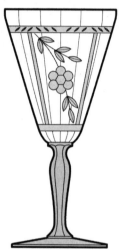

Kenmore
Cut 176, Floral,
Blue Stem
5082
Fostoria

5082-2
Cut Floral, Green Stem
5082
Fostoria

5082-3
Cut Floral, Green Stem
5082
Fostoria

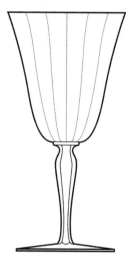

5093/5293
Various Optic Bowls
& Colors
5093
Fostoria

Mother of Pearl
Iridescent Optic Bowl
5093
Fostoria

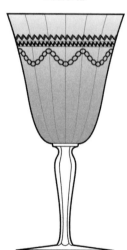

Avalon
Etch 85, Geometric,
Blue or Pink Bowl
5093
Fostoria

Vesper
Etch 275, Floral,
Amber, Blue or Green
5093
Fostoria

5097
Clear, Amber, Green, Orchid, Rose
or Topaz Bowl with Straight or Loop
Optic; Clear, Amber or Green Stem
Fostoria

Spartan
Etch 80; Clear, Amber,
Green or Plum Bowl
5097
Fostoria

Greek
Needle Etch 45; Clear,
Amber, Green or Rose Bowl
5097
Fostoria

Beverly
Etch 276; Clear, Amber
or Green Bowl
5097
Fostoria

5097-1
Etched Hunt Scene, Dogs
5097
Fostoria

5097-8
Gray Cut Floral,
Pink Bowl
5097
Fostoria

5097-5
Gray Cut Floral,
Amethyst Bowl
5097
Fostoria

5097-7
Polished Cut Floral
5097
Fostoria

5097-2
Green Bowl, Gold Trim
5097
Fostoria

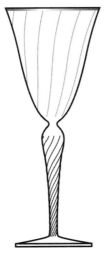

Liana
Swirl Optic Bowl,
Gold or Platinum Trim
Fostoria

Bellwether
Curved Cuts
Fostoria

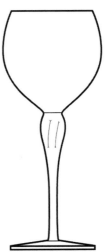

Aura
Plain
Fostoria

5099/5299
Clear, Amber, Blue, Green,
Rose, Topaz or Wisteria
Optic Bowl
Fostoria

Kashmir
Etch 283, Floral,
Topaz or Blue Bowl
5299
Fostoria

Trojan
Etch 280, Topaz or
Rose (Pink) Bowl
5299
Fostoria

Versailles
Etch 278, Topaz Bowl,
Plain or Gold Trim
5299
Fostoria

5098/5298
Clear, Amber, Ameythst, Blue,
Rose, Topaz or Green Optic Bowl
Fostoria

Camden
Etch 84, Geometric,
Amber or Green Bowl
5298
Fostoria

Fostoria

Acanthus
Etch 282, Scrolls
Amber or Green Bowl
5298
Fostoria

Berry
Cut 188, Floral,
Rose or Green Bowl
5298
Fostoria

Fern
Etch 305, Leaves & Scrolls,
Clear or Rose Bowl
5098/5298
Fostoria

June
Etch 279, Floral; Clear,
Blue, Pink or Topaz Bowl
5098/5298
Fostoria

Versailles
Etch 278, Scrolls,
Pink, Blue or Green Bowl
5098/5298
Fostoria

Sceptre
Clear, Blue or Topaz Bowl
6017
Fostoria

Simplicity
Wide Gold Trim 618
6017
Fostoria

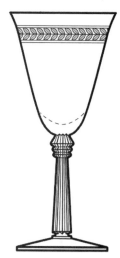

Laurel
Cut 776, Laurel Band
6017
Fostoria

Ripple
Cut 766, Waves
6017
Fostoria

Beacon
Cut 767, Dots &
Vertical Lines
6017
Fostoria

Drape
Cut 784, Swags
6017
Fostoria

Lenox
Etch 330, Laurel
6017
Fostoria

Lucerne
Cut 778, Dots &
Vertical Cuts
6017
Fostoria

Raynel
Cut 777, Dots &
Vertical Cuts
6017
Fostoria

Bridal Shower
Cut 768, Gray Dots &
Vertical Lines
6017
Fostoria

Lido
Etch 329, Floral,
Clear or Blue Bowl
6017
Fostoria

Cynthia
Cut 785, Gray Floral
6017
Fostoria

Romance
Etch 341, Floral
6017
Fostoria

Shirley
Etch 331, Floral
6017
Fostoria

6017-2
Gray Cut Floral & Dots
6017
Fostoria

6017-1
Gray Cut Floral
6017
Fostoria

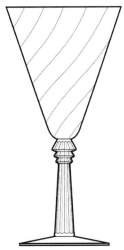

Pavilion
Clear or Smoke
Swirl Optic Bowl
6143
Fostoria

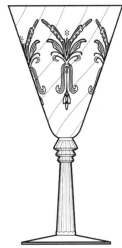

Nouveau
Etch 42, Floral,
Clear or Smoke Bowl
6143
Fostoria

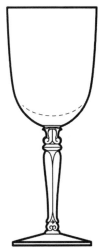

Astrid
Plain
6030
Fostoria

Wavemere
Loop Optic Bowl
6030/3
Fostoria

Holly
Cut 815, Laurel Band
6030
Fostoria

Gadroon
Cut 816, Leaves & Swirls
6030
Fostoria

Buttercup
Etch 340, Floral,
Plain or Gold Encrusted
6030
Fostoria

Christiana
Cut 814, Floral
6030
Fostoria

Trellis
Cut 822, Gray Leaves,
Crisscross & Curved Lines
6030
Fostoria

Fostoria

6030-1
Dot & Scroll Cuts
6030
Fostoria

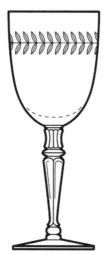

Mt. Vernon
Cut 817, Laurel Band
6031
Fostoria

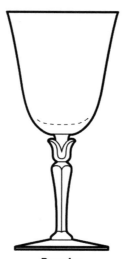

Promise
Plain
6110
Fostoria

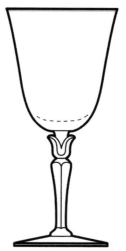

Reception (Platinum Trim)
Golden Belle (Gold Trim)
6110
Fostoria

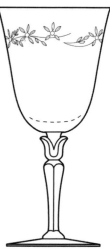

Glendale
Cut 919, Floral
6110
Fostoria

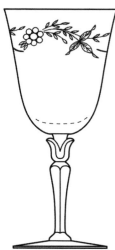

Greenfield
Cut 916, Floral
6110
Fostoria

6007
Clear, Green, Topaz or Wisteria
Straight or Loop Optic Bowl;
or with Amber Stem
Fostoria

Bristol
Cut 710, Floral
6007
Fostoria

Castle
Needle Etch 87
6007
Fostoria

Eton
Cut 713, Floral
6007
Fostoria

Inverness
Cut 711, Floral
6007
Fostoria

Oxford
Cut 714, Floral
6007
Fostoria

York
Cut 709, Floral
6007
Fostoria

Manor
Etch 286, Floral
6007
Fostoria

Morning Glory
Etch 313, Floral,
Clear or Amber Stem
6007
Fostoria

6007-1
Cut Floral
6007
Fostoria

6008
Clear, Topaz or Wisteria
Straight or Dimple
Optic Bowl
Fostoria

Carlisle
Cut 715, Floral & Dots
6008
Fostoria

Canterbury
Cut 716, Floral & Dots
6008
Fostoria

Chateau
Etch 315, Floral & Scrolls
6008
Fostoria

Marlboro
Cut 717, Floral
6008
Fostoria

6013
Clear, Burgundy,
Regal Blue or Ruby Bowl
Fostoria

Allegro
Cut 748, Floral
6013
Fostoria

Bouquet
Cut 756, Floral
6013
Fostoria

Daisy
Etch 324, Floral,
Clear or Green
6013
Fostoria

Fantasy
Cut 747, Plants
6013
Fostoria

Society
Cut 757, Leaves & Swags
6013
Fostoria

Greenbriar
Straight Optic Bowl
6026
Fostoria

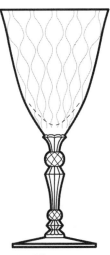

Niagara
Niagara (Wavy) Optic Bowl
6026/2
Fostoria

Chintz
Etch 338, Floral
6026
Fostoria

Fostoria

Mulberry
Cut 799, Plants
6026
Fostoria

Rheims
Cut 803, Crisscross
6026
Fostoria

Selma
Cut 800, Plants
6026
Fostoria

6026-1
Gray Cut Floral
6026
Fostoria

Wilma
Clear, Blue, Pink or
Iridescent Optic Bowl
6016
Fostoria

Regis (Gold Trim 697)
Victoria (Platinum Trim 796)
6016
Fostoria

Meadow Rose
Etch 328, Floral,
Clear or Blue Bowl
6016
Fostoria

Navarre
Etch 327, Floral,
Clear, Pink or Blue Bowl
6016
Fostoria

Melba
Cut 761, Floral
6016
Fostoria

Cumberland
Cut 762, Crisscross &
Vertical Cuts
6016
Fostoria

6016-1
Floral & Wheat Cuts
6016
Fostoria

Cellini
Straight or Loop Optic Bowl
6024
Fostoria

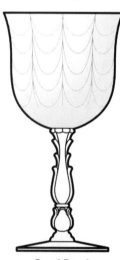

Coral Pearl
Iridescent Loop Optic Bowl
6024
Fostoria

Regal
Cut 782, Swags
6024
Fostoria

Willowmere
Etch 333, Floral
6024
Fostoria

372

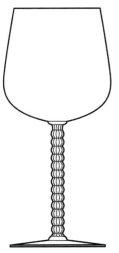

Precedence
Clear, Gray or
Onyx (Black) Bowl
6108
Fostoria

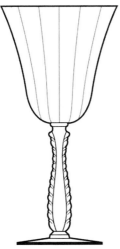

Silver Flutes
Narrow Optic Bowl
6037
Fostoria

Heather
Etch 343, Floral
6037
Fostoria

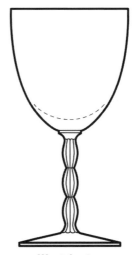

Westchester
Clear, Amethyst, Cobalt,
Green or Ruby Bowl
6012
Fostoria

Mother of Pearl
Iridescent Bowl
6012
Fostoria

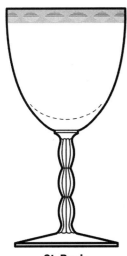

St. Regis
Gold Cut Decoration 616
6012
Fostoria

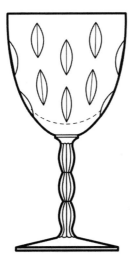

Pierette
Cut 764, Vertical Cuts
6012
Fostoria

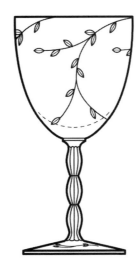

Ivy
Cut 745, Leaves
6012
Fostoria

Gossamer
Cut 746, Floral
6012
Fostoria

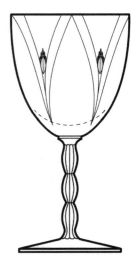

Heraldry
Cut 743, Gray Cut Floral
6012
Fostoria

Cyrene
Cut 763, Leaves & Swirls
6012
Fostoria

Festoon
Cut 738, Vertical & Swags
6012
Fostoria

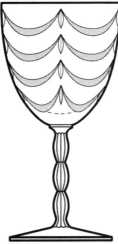

Regency
Cut 744, Gray Swags
6012
Fostoria

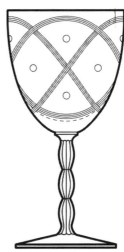

Orbit
Cut 742, Dots & Arches
6012
Fostoria

Watercress
Cut 741, Floral & Dots
6012
Fostoria

Fostoria

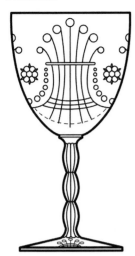

Rondeau
Cut 640, Geometric & Floral
6012
Fostoria

Rambler
Etch 323, Floral,
Plain or Gold Trim
6012
Fostoria

Springtime
Etch 318, Floral
6012
Fostoria

Rock Garden
Cut 739, Floral
6012
Fostoria

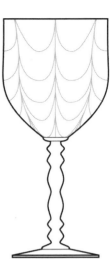

Festive
Clear, Blue or Yellow
Loop Optic Bowl
6127
Fostoria

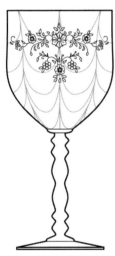

Serenity
Etch 35, Floral,
Clear, Blue or Yellow Bowl
6127
Fostoria

Wimbledon
Optic Bowl
6126
Fostoria

Gazebo
Rust or Black Stem
6126
Fostoria

Corsage
Plum Stem
6126
Fostoria

Tara
Etch 34, Floral
6126
Fostoria

Princess
Clear, Blue or Green Bowl
6123
Fostoria

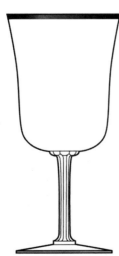

Princess
Platinum Trim
6123
Fostoria

Princess
Gray Bowl, Black Stem
6123
Fostoria

Tenderness
Green Bowl, Platinum Trim
6123
Fostoria

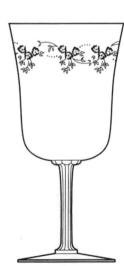

Poetry
Etch 32, Floral
6123
Fostoria

Cameo
Etch 28, Floral,
Green Bowl
6123
Fostoria

Intimate
Etch 31, Floral,
Blue Bowl
6123
Fostoria

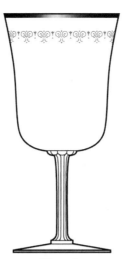

Marquis
Etch 692, Scrolls,
Platinum Trim
6123
Fostoria

Petit Fleur
Cut 922, Floral
6123
Fostoria

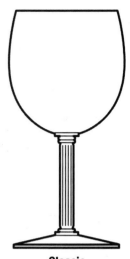

Classic
Clear, Amethyst, Cobalt, Green or
Ruby Bowl; or with Amber Stem
6011
Fostoria

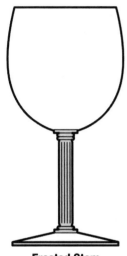

Frosted Stem
Plain
6011
Fostoria

Mother of Pearl
Iridescent Bowl
6011
Fostoria

Athenian
Cut 770, Laurel
6011
Fostoria

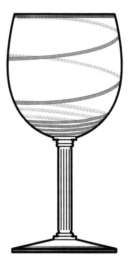

Golden Swirl
Cut 730, Gold Swirl & Trim
6011
Fostoria

Whirlpool
Cut 730, Gray Swirl
6011
Fostoria

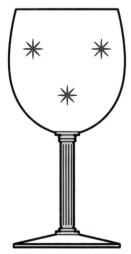

6011-1
Star Cuts, Frosted Stem
6011
Fostoria

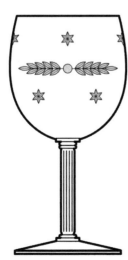

Directoire
Cut 736, Stars & Laurel
6011
Fostoria

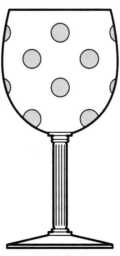

Mardi Gras
Cut 765, Gray Dots
6011
Fostoria

Quinfoil
Cut 737, Plants
6011
Fostoria

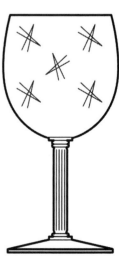

Rocket
Cut 729
6011
Fostoria

Fostoria

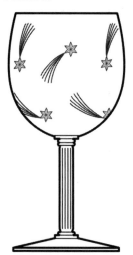

Shooting Stars
Cut 735
6011
Fostoria

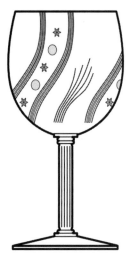

Celestial
Cut 731, Swirls & Dots
6011
Fostoria

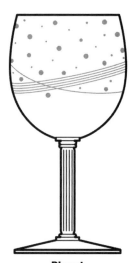

Planet
Etch 734, Rings & Circles
6011
Fostoria

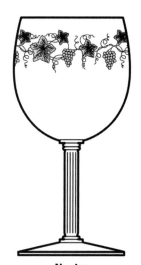

Nectar
Etch 322, Grapes & Leaves
6011
Fostoria

Tempo
Plain
6032
Fostoria

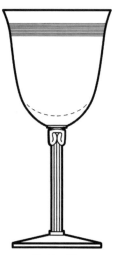

Formality
Cut 818,
Gray Horizontal Lines
6032
Fostoria

Greek Key
Geometric Cuts
6032
Fostoria

Patrician
Plain
6064
Fostoria

Elegance
Rib Optic Bowl
6064 ½
Fostoria

Cascade
Iridescent Optic Bowl
6064 ½
Fostoria

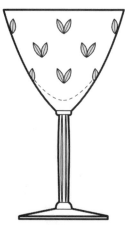

Skylark
Cut 846, Gray Leaves
6064
Fostoria

Maytime
Cut 845, Leaves
6064
Fostoria

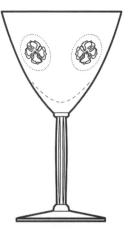

Rosette
Etch 3, Dots & Floral
6064
Fostoria

Moon Mist
Frosted Stem Accent
6113
Fostoria

Versailles
Gold Stem Accent
6113
Fostoria

Eloquence
Plain, Gold or Platinum Trim
6120
Fostoria

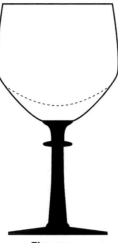

Eloquence
Black Stem
6120
Fostoria

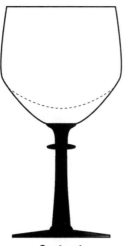

Contrast
White Bowl, Black Stem
6120
Fostoria

Venise
Etch 688, Floral,
Platinum Trim
6120
Fostoria

Kristina
Frosted Ball,
Gold Band Accents
Fostoria

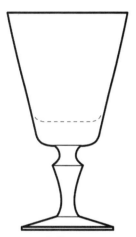

Jefferson
Plain
6104
Fostoria

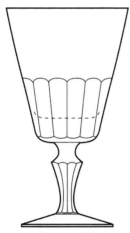

Beacon Hill
Cut 917, Panels
6104 ½
Fostoria

Carillon
Cut 915, Slanted Leaves
6104
Fostoria

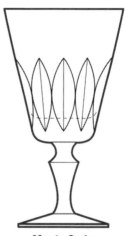

Monte Carlo
Cut 912, Leaf Panels
6104
Fostoria

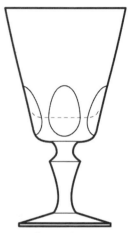

Queen Anne
Cut 905, Ovals
6104
Fostoria

Savannah
Cut 902, Floral
6104
Fostoria

Tiara
Cut 903, Vertical Cuts
6104
Fostoria

Berkshire
Plain
6105
Fostoria

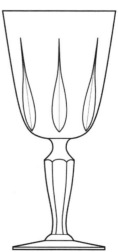

Cantata
Cut 907, Teardrop
6105
Fostoria

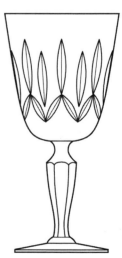

Georgetown
Cut 906, Vertical & Slanted
6105
Fostoria

Fostoria

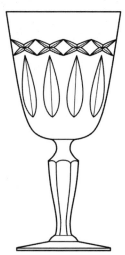

Stratford
Cut 915, Vertical &
Crisscross
6105
Fostoria

Priscilla
Plain
6092
Fostoria

Engagement (Platinum Trim)
Aurora (Gold Trim)
6092
Fostoria

Regal
Stainless Steel Overlay
6092
Fostoria

Burgundy
Cut 878, Gray Floral
6092
Fostoria

Spring Song
Cut 884, Plants
6092
Fostoria

Sweetbriar
Cut Plants
6092
Fostoria

Sweetheart Rose
Cut 877, Floral
6092
Fostoria

Twilight
Cut 883, Stars
6092
Fostoria

6092-2
Polished Swirl Cuts
6092
Fostoria

6092-3
Vertical & Arch Cuts
6092
Fostoria

Illusion
Plain
6111
Fostoria

Olympic
Cut 679, Laurel Band,
Gold or Platinum Trim
6111
Fostoria

Renaissance
Etch 678, Floral,
Gold or Platinum Trim
6111
Fostoria

First Love
Cut 918, Crisscross
& Leaves
6111
Fostoria

6111-1
Diagonal Thumbprint Cuts
6111
Fostoria

Vesper
Plain
6086
Fostoria

Fantasy
Etch 17, Floral
6086
Fostoria

Overture
Cut 867, Laurel Band
6086
Fostoria

Serenade
Cut 864, Leaves
6086
Fostoria

Star Song
Cut 871, Floral
6086
Fostoria

6010
Optic Bowl
Fostoria

Leicester
Cut 722 ½, Floral
6010
Fostoria

Sheraton
Etch 317, Urn & Floral
6010
Fostoria

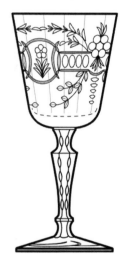

Wellington
Cut 722, Floral
6010
Fostoria

Westminster
Cut 723, Floral
6010
Fostoria

Camelot
Clear or Blue Optic Bowl
6009
Fostoria

Cameo
Etch 88, Geometric Bands
6009
Fostoria

Midnight Rose
Etch 316, Rose Floral
6009
Fostoria

Grand Majesty
Etch GRO3/GRO4, Floral,
Clear or Blue Bowl
6009
Fostoria

Fostoria

Buckingham
Cut 721, Floral
6009
Fostoria

Doncaster
Cut 718, Floral
6009
Fostoria

Lancaster
Cut 719, Floral
6009
Fostoria

Nottingham
Cut 720, Floral
6009
Fostoria

6009-1
Clear or All Pink,
Cut Plants
6009
Fostoria

Ambassador
Vertical Cuts
Fostoria

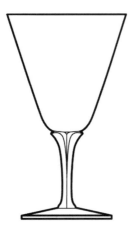

Celeste
Plain
6072
Fostoria

Bridal Belle
Cut 639, Plants,
Platinum Trim
6072
Fostoria

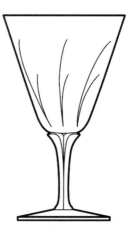

Melody
Cut 881, Gray Lines
6072
Fostoria

Moonbeam
Cut 856, Panels
6072
Fostoria

Serenity
Cut 868, Leaf Band
6072
Fostoria

Stockholm
Cut 879, Panels
6093
Fostoria

Bristol
Cut 880,
Crisscross & Vertical
6093
Fostoria

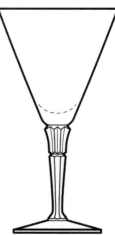

Chateau
Plain
6087
Fostoria

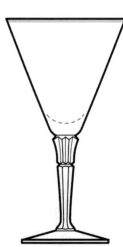

Golden Flair
Gold Trim
6087
Fostoria

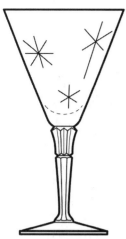

Evening Star
Cut 869, Stars
6087
Fostoria

Exeter
Clear or Amethyst
6109
Fostoria

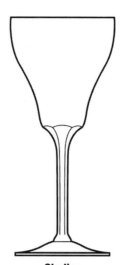

Chalice
Cut 812
6029
Fostoria

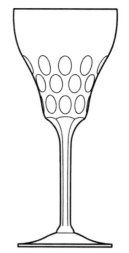

Saybrooke
Cut 813, Ovals
6029
Fostoria

Orleans
Plain
6089
Fostoria

Beloved
Platinum Trim
6089
Fostoria

Bridal Crown
Cut 882, Vertical Cuts
6089
Fostoria

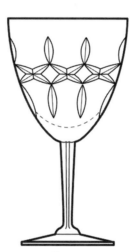

Devon
Cut 876, Crisscross
& Vertical
6089
Fostoria

Whisper
Cut 875, Leaves
6089
Fostoria

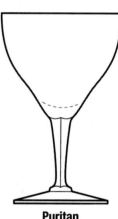

Puritan
Plain
6068
Fostoria

Victoria
Narrow Optic Bowl
6068 ½
Fostoria

Rainbow
Narrow Optic
Iridescent Bowl
6068 ½
Fostoria

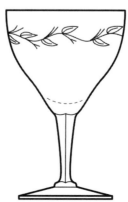

April Love
Cut 866, Leaves
6068
Fostoria

Autumn
Cut 850, Leaves
6068
Fostoria

Duchess
Cut 853, Vertical Cuts
6068
Fostoria

Gossamer
Cut 852, Swirls
6068
Fostoria

Stardust
Cut 851, Stars
6068
Fostoria

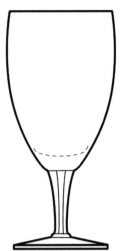

Debutante
Clear or Gray Bowl
6100
Fostoria

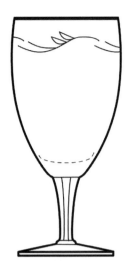

Bridesmaid
Cut 658, Leaves,
Platinum Trim
6100
Fostoria

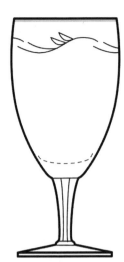

Flower Girl
Cut 659, Leaves,
Gold Trim
6100
Fostoria

Cotillion
Cut 892, Swirls
6100
Fostoria

Evening Breeze
Cut 891, Plants
6100
Fostoria

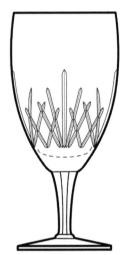

Princess Ann
Cut 893, Vertical
& Crisscross
6100
Fostoria

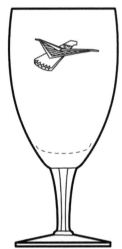

Thunderbird
Etched Emblem
6100
Fostoria

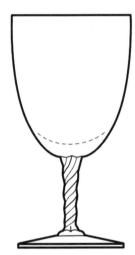

Crystal Twist
Plain
6101
Fostoria

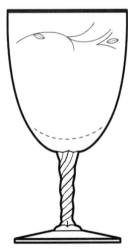

Coronet
Cut 656, Platinum Trim
6101
Fostoria

Flower Song
Cut 894, Plants
6101
Fostoria

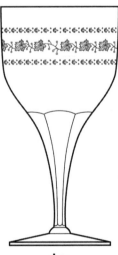

Ivy
Etch 235, Ivy Leaves
882
Fostoria

Grille
Etch 236, Floral Swags
882
Fostoria

Embassy
Plain
6083
Fostoria

Golden Grail
Gold Encrusted 644
6083
Fostoria

6083-1P
Platinum Encrusted Band
6083
Fostoria

St. Regis
Cut 873, Vertical & Ovals
6083
Fostoria

Westminster
Cut 872, Crisscross
& Vertical
6083
Fostoria

Splendor
Plain
6124
Fostoria

Brocade
Etch 30, Floral
6124
Fostoria

Granada
Cut 923, Geometric
6124
Fostoria

Lotus
Clear, Black, Frosted
or Pink Frosted Stem
6144
Fostoria

Monet
Clear, Blue, Gray, Peach,
Pink or Purple Optic Bowl
MO12
Fostoria

FOS 10
Wine Shown
Cobalt/Clear Petal Stem
See Duo by *Colony*
Fostoria

5083
All Green or Clear Bowl with
Blue, Green or Amber Stem;
Straight, Loop or Spiral Optic Bowl
Fostoria

Triumph
Gold or Platinum Metal Base
6112
Fostoria

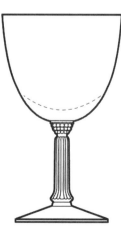

Mademoiselle
Plain
6033
Fostoria

Reflection
Platinum Band 625
6033
Fostoria

Bouquet
Etch 342, Floral
6033
Fostoria

Sprite
Cut 823, Leaves
6033
Fostoria

Spinet
Cut 821, Leaves & Dots
6033
Fostoria

6002
All Clear, Topaz, Pink or
Green; or Clear Bowl with
Ebony Stem & Foot
Fostoria

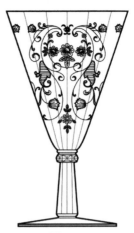

Minuet
Etch 285, Floral,
Yellow Bowl
6002
Fostoria

New Garland
Etch 284, Floral,
All Pink
6002
Fostoria

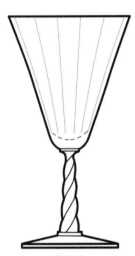

Melody
Optic Bowl
6020
Fostoria

Gothic
Cut 774, Plants
& Crisscross
6020
Fostoria

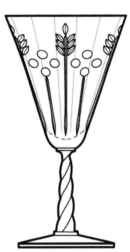

Kimberley
Cut 775, Plants
6020
Fostoria

Mayflower
Etch 332, Floral
6020
Fostoria

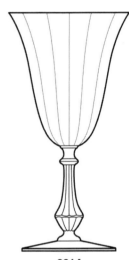

6014
Optic Bowl
Fostoria

Wavecrest
Clear, Blue or Amber
Loop Optic Bowl
6014
Fostoria

Arcady
Etch 326, Floral
6014
Fostoria

Corsage
Etch 325, Floral
6014
Fostoria

Bordeaux
Cut 758, Dots & Lines
6014
Fostoria

Cavendish
Cut 754
6014
Fostoria

Palmetto
Cut 755, Plants
6014
Fostoria

Weylin
Cut 759, Crisscross
& Dots
6014
Fostoria

6014-1
Floral & Swag Cuts
6014
Fostoria

6014-2
Clear & Gray Cut Floral
6014
Fostoria

Windsor
Plain
6049
Fostoria

Avalon
Cut 832, Floral
6049
Fostoria

Bridal Wreath
Cut 833, Vines
6049
Fostoria

Starflower
Etch 345, Floral
6049
Fostoria

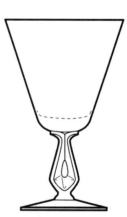

Symphony
Plain
6065
Fostoria

Legacy (Platinum Trim)
Ambassador (Gold Trim)
6065
Fostoria

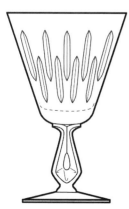

Baronet
Cut 847, Vertical Cuts
6065
Fostoria

Swirl
Cut 848
6065
Fostoria

Lynwood
Etch 4, Plants
6065
Fostoria

Heritage
Cut 849, Crisscross
6065
Fostoria

Living Rose
Etch 5
6065
Fostoria

Continental
Plain
6052 ½
Fostoria

Moon Ring
Optic Bowl
6052
Fostoria

Ingrid
Cut 836, Dots & Leaves
6052 ½
Fostoria

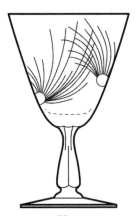

Pine
Cut 835, Dots & Swirls
6052 ½
Fostoria

Thistle
Etch 346
6052 ½
Fostoria

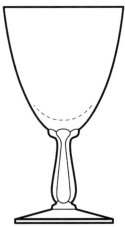

Rhapsody
Clear or Turquoise Bowl
6055 ½
Fostoria

Marilyn
Loop Optic Bowl
6055
Fostoria

Shell Pearl
Iridescent Loop Optic Bowl
6055
Fostoria

Anniversary
Wide Gold Band
6055 ½
Fostoria

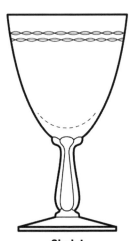

Circlet
Cut 840, Horizontal Bands
6055 ½
Fostoria

Spray
Cut 841, Gray Floral
6055 ½
Fostoria

Vintage
Embossed Grapes,
Milk Glass
2713
Fostoria

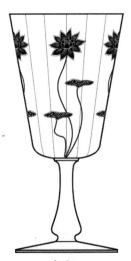

Lotus
Etch 232, Floral,
Optic Bowl
5070
Fostoria

Poppy/Poupee
Etch 231, Floral,
Optic Bowl
5070
Fostoria

5070-1
Geometric Etch, Optic Bowl
5070
Fostoria

Sheraton
Plain
6097
Fostoria

Harvest
Brown Optic Bowl
6097
Fostoria

Sheffield (Platinum Trim)
Richmond (Gold Trim)
6097
Fostoria

Andover
Gold Encrusted Band
6097
Fostoria

Sentimental
Etch 25, Floral
6097
Fostoria

Georgian
Cut 885, Panels
6097
Fostoria

Gloucester
Cut 898, Crisscross & Fan
6097
Fostoria

Monticello
Cut 88, Crisscross
6097
Fostoria

6097-1
Gray Cut Rose
6097
Fostoria

Northampton
Panel Cuts, Romania
Fostoria

Fascination
Clear, Lilac or Ruby Bowl
6080
Fostoria

Firelight
Iridescent Loop Optic Bowl
6080 ½
Fostoria

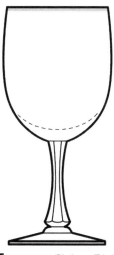

Trousseau (Platinum Trim)
Classic Gold (Gold Trim)
6080
Fostoria

Carousel
Cut 863, Plants
6080
Fostoria

True Love
Cut 862, Plant
6080
Fostoria

Fostoria

Petite
Plain
6085
Fostoria

Golden Lace
Etch 645, Floral,
Gold Trim
6085
Fostoria

Juliet
Cut 865, Floral
6085
Fostoria

Moonglow (Platinum Trim)
Sunglow (Gold Trim)
Cut 649 (Plat.), Cut 650 (Gold)
6085
Fostoria

Distinction
Clear, Cobalt, Light Blue,
Plum or Ruby Bowl
6125
Fostoria

Prelude
Plain
6071
Fostoria

Kimberly
Cut 855,
Honeycomb & Fans
6071
Fostoria

Wildwood
Cut 854, Floral
6071
Fostoria

Nordic
Plain
6077
Fostoria

American Beauty
Cut 858, Floral
6077
Fostoria

Encore
Cut 860, Vertical Cuts
6077
Fostoria

Garland
Cut 859, Leaves
6077
Fostoria

Enchantment
Plain
6074
Fostoria

Golden Love
Cut 640, Floral,
Gold Trim
6074
Fostoria

Sweetbriar
Cut 857, Plants
6074
Fostoria

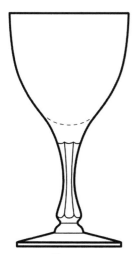

Vogue
Clear or Gold Tint Bowl
6099
Fostoria

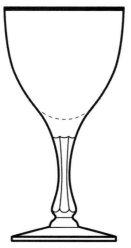

Candlelight
Platinum Trim
6099
Fostoria

Love Song (Platinum Trim)
Golden Song (Gold Trim)
Cut 655, Leaves
6099
Fostoria

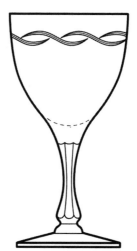

Embrace
Cut 887, Woven Lines
6099
Fostoria

Chapel Bells
Cut 888, Swirls
6099
Fostoria

Courtship
Plain
6051 ½
Fostoria

Ringlet
Optic Bowl
6051
Fostoria

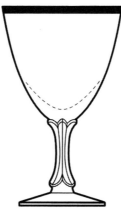

Wedding Ring
¼" Wide Platinum Trim
6051 ½
Fostoria

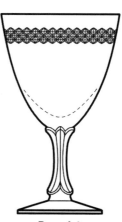

Bracelet
Cut 838, Crisscross Band
6051 ½
Fostoria

Nosegay
Cut 834, Floral
6051 ½
Fostoria

6051 ½-2
Cut 833
6051 ½
Fostoria

6051 ½-1
Cut Floral
6051 ½
Fostoria

Plume
Cut 839, Gray Feather
6051 ½
Fostoria

Wheat
Cut 837
6051 ½
Fostoria

Chippendale
Etched Floral
CH05
Fostoria

Fostoria

Satin Ribbon
Etched Ribbons
SA05
Fostoria

Juniper
Arch & Fan Cuts
JU05
Fostoria

Bennington
Vertical & Crisscross Cuts
BE04
Fostoria

Kimberly
Plain, Gold or Platinum Trim
Vertical Cuts
2990
Fostoria

Radiance
Vertical Cuts
3113/3013
Fostoria

Gala
Plain
6147
Fostoria

Celebration (Platinum Trim)
Jubilee (Gold Trim)
6147
Fostoria

Festival
Etch 45, Floral & Ribbons
6147
Fostoria

Icicle
Clear, Blue or Yellow,
Frosted Stem
6147
Fostoria

Misty
Blue, Brown or Yellow
6129
Fostoria

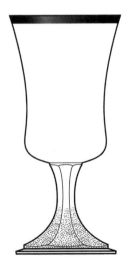

Misty
Clear, Decoration 695,
Platinum Trim
6129
Fostoria

Fairlane
Plain, Barware
2916
Fostoria

Bracelet
Platinum Trim
2916
Fostoria

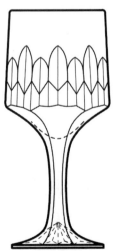

Greenfield
Vertical Cuts
2916
Fostoria

Diamond Point
Pressed Glass
2860
Fostoria

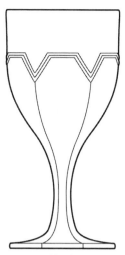

Alexis
Geometric Panels
1630
Fostoria

Sunray
Clear, Amber, Blue, Green,
Ruby or Topaz
2510
Fostoria

Glacier
Frosted Ribs
2510
Fostoria

Golden Glow
Decoration 513,
Yellow Ribs
2510
Fostoria

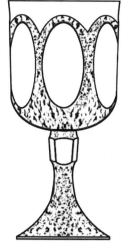

Woodland
Clear, Blue, Brown, Green,
Pink or Yellow
2921
Fostoria

Bradford Blackberry
Blackberry Vine, Panels
Fostoria

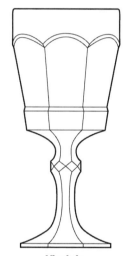

Virginia
Clear or Various Colors,
Panels, Pressed Glass
2977
Fostoria

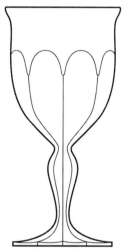

Lucere
Arched Panels,
Pressed Glass
1515
Fostoria

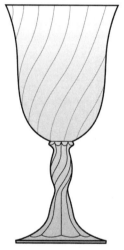

Maypole
Yellow, Blue, Peach or Ruby,
Swirl Optic Bowl
6149
Fostoria

Moonstone
Clear, Dark Blue, Light Blue, Green,
Peach, Plum, Pink, Taupe or Yellow
2882
Fostoria

FOS 3
Cobalt or Light Blue,
Cameos
Fostoria

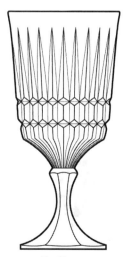

Heritage
Clear, Pink or Blue,
Vertical Cuts
2887
Fostoria

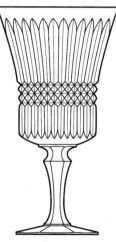

Aspen
Plain or Gold Trim,
Vertical Cuts, Barware
2861
Fostoria

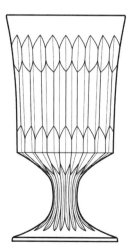

Monarch
Vertical Cuts, Barware
2903
Fostoria

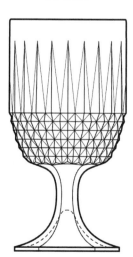

Stratton
Vertical Cuts
2885
Fostoria

Fostoria

Sherwood
Champagne/Tall Sherbet Shown
Geometric, Pressed Glass
1605
Fostoria

Colfax
Plain
6023
Fostoria

Dolly Madison
Cut 786, Panels
6023
Fostoria

Spencerian
Needle Etch 94, Scrolls
6023
Fostoria

Colonial Mirror
Etch 334
6023
Fostoria

Willow
Etch 335
6023
Fostoria

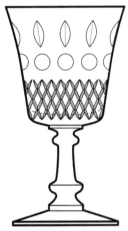

Brighton
Cut 801, Geometric
6023
Fostoria

Wentworth
Cut 802, Geometric
6023
Fostoria

Chippendale
Cut 788, Geometric
6023
Fostoria

Revere
Cut 825, Geometric
6023
Fostoria

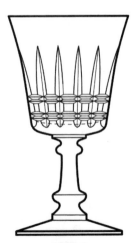

6023-1
Horizontal & Vertical Cuts
6023
Fostoria

Wakefield
Cut 820, Crisscross & Fans
6023
Fostoria

Spire
Cut 793,
Dots & Vertical Cuts
6023
Fostoria

Cathedral
Cut 792, Arches
6023
Fostoria

Pilgrim
Cut 787, Crisscross & Dots
6023
Fostoria

Cabot
Plain or Dimple Optic Bowl
6025
Fostoria

Georgian
Cut 791, Panels
6025
Fostoria

Hawthorn
Cut 790, Leaves
6025
Fostoria

Minuet
Cut 826, Plants & Panels
6025
Fostoria

Plymouth
Etch 336
6025
Fostoria

Sampler
Etch 337
6025
Fostoria

Suffolk
Cut 789, Leaves & Dots
6025
Fostoria

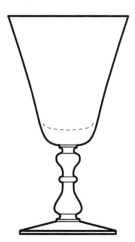

Rutledge
Plain
6036
Fostoria

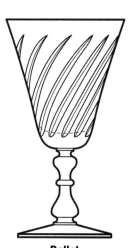

Ballet
Cut 828, Vertical Curves
6036
Fostoria

Camellia
Etch 344, Floral
6036
Fostoria

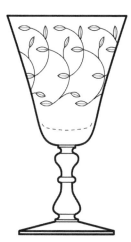

Chatham
Cut 829, Leaves
6036
Fostoria

Rose
Cut 827, Floral
6036
Fostoria

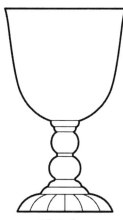

Victorian
Clear, Amethyst, Cobalt, Green or Ruby
Bowl; or Clear Bowl with Ruby Stem
4024
Fostoria

Silver Mist
Frosted
4024
Fostoria

Elsinore
Etch 89,
Geometric Bands
4024
Fostoria

Embassy
Cut 728, Vertical
& Floral Cuts
4024
Fostoria

Manhattan
Cut 725, Crisscross
& Vertical Cuts
4024
Fostoria

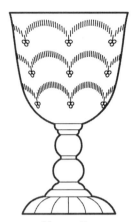

Marquette
Cut 733, Waves & Floral
4024
Fostoria

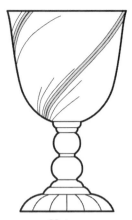

Meteor
Cut 726, Gray Curved Lines
4024
Fostoria

National
Cut 727, Frosted Stars
4024
Fostoria

Seaweed
Cut 732, Frosted Dots,
Swirled Lines
4024
Fostoria

Kent
Plain
6079
Fostoria

Empress
Cut 861, Vertical Cuts
6079
Fostoria

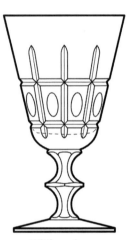

Williamsburg
Cut 874, Vertical & Ovals
6079
Fostoria

6000
Clear or Various Colors,
Optic Bowl
Fostoria

Monroe
Etch 86, Geometric Bands
6000
Fostoria

Waterbury
Cut 712, Crisscross & Fans
6000
Fostoria

Legion
Etch 309, Floral
6000
Fostoria

Celebrity
Cut 749, Geometric
6000
Fostoria

Memories
Cut 750, Crisscross & Fans
6000
Fostoria

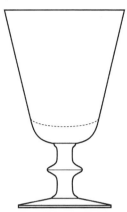

FOS 8
Plain
Fostoria

Wistar
Clear or Milk Glass,
Pressed Glass
2620
Fostoria

Colonial
Clear or Amber, Panels,
Pressed Glass
2222
Fostoria

Priscilla
Clear, Blue, Green,
Black, Pink or Amber
2321
Fostoria

Regency
Plain
6128
Fostoria

Heirloom
Etch 36, Floral
6128
Fostoria

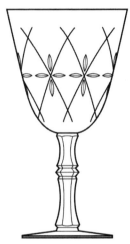

Nova
Cut 934, Geometric
6128
Fostoria

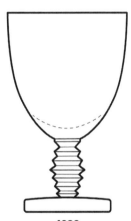

4020
All Clear; Amber, Cobalt, Pink or
Lavender Bowl; or Clear Bowl
with Amber, Black or Green Stem
Fostoria

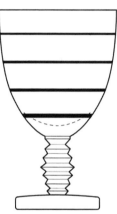

Saturn
Decoration 605, Black Lines
4020
Fostoria

Polka Dot
Cut 607, Dots,
Black Stem & Foot
4020
Fostoria

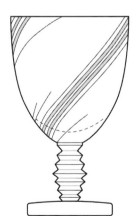

Comet
Cut 702, Gray Curved Lines,
Clear, Black or Green Stem
4020
Fostoria

Millefleur
Cut 195, Floral,
Clear or Black Stem
4020
Fostoria

New Garland
Etch 284, Floral; All Pink,
Topaz Bowl or Amber Stem
4020
Fostoria

Tapestry
Cut 701, Gray Wheat
4020
Fostoria

Formal Garden
Cut 700, Floral
4020
Fostoria

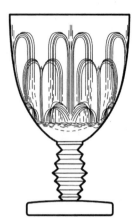

Fountain
Etch 307, All Clear
or with Green Stem
4020
Fostoria

Kashmir
Etch 283, Green Stem
4020
Fostoria

Minuet
Etch 285, Floral,
Green or Amber Stem
4020
Fostoria

Queen Anne
Etch 306, Floral,
All Clear or with Amber Stem
4020
Fostoria

Fern
Etch 305, Plants,
All Clear or with Black Stem
4020
Fostoria

New Yorker
Cut 703, Crisscross & Vertical,
Clear, Black or Green Stem
6020
Fostoria

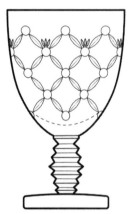

Chelsea
Cut 783, Geometric
4020
Fostoria

Rhythm
Cut 773, Geometric
4020
Fostoria

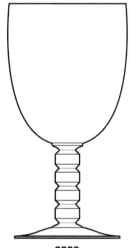

6003
All Clear; Green or Topaz
Bowl; or Clear Bowl with
Wisteria Stem & Foot
Fostoria

Manor
Etch 286, Floral,
Clear, Green or Topaz Bowl
6003
Fostoria

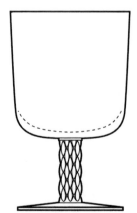

Envoy
Plain
6027
Fostoria

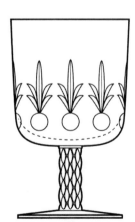

Aloha
Cut 805, Dots & Fans
6027
Fostoria

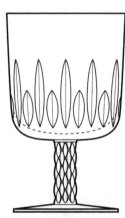

Cadence
Cut 806, Vertical Cuts
6027
Fostoria

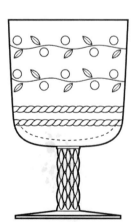

Princess
Cut 824,
Rope & Laurel Bands
6027
Fostoria

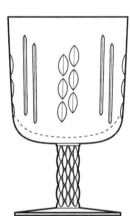

Salon
Cut 804,
Vertical Cuts
6027
Fostoria

Rondel
Clear, Blue or
Topaz Bowl
6019
Fostoria

Federal
Cut 771, Stars
6019
Fostoria

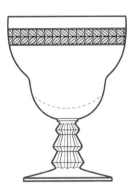

Laurel
Cut 776, Laurel Band
6019
Fostoria

Tulip
Cut 772, Dots & Fans
6019
Fostoria

Lyric
Clear or Pink Stem
6061
Fostoria

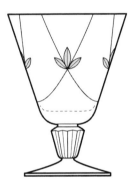

Crest
Cut 843, Fans
& Swirl Lines
6061
Fostoria

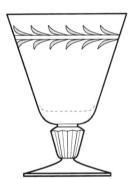

Regal
Cut 842, Gray
Laurel Band
6061
Fostoria

Skyflower
Etch 2, Floral
6061
Fostoria

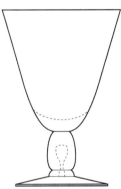

Diadem
Bubble in Stem
6056
Fostoria

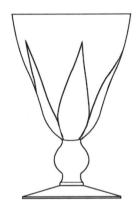

Fairmont
Clear, Amber,
Blue or Green
2718
Fostoria

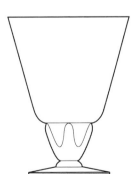

Chalice
Plain
6059
Fostoria

Chalice
Black Stem
6059
Fostoria

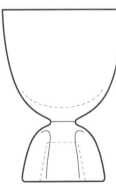

Capri
Clear, Green or
Cinnamon Base
6045
Fostoria

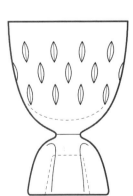

Marquise
Cut 831, Vertical Cuts
6045
Fostoria

Rondo
Cut 830, Straight
& Curved Lines
6045
Fostoria

Fostoria

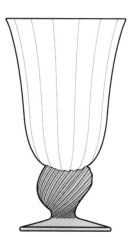

Captiva
Clear, Blue, Peach,
Pink & Smoke
CA16
Fostoria

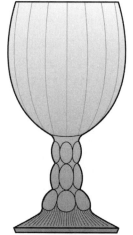

Splendor
Blue or Rust,
Optic Bowl
6131
Fostoria

Sphere
Brown, Gray or
Green Bowl
6121
Fostoria

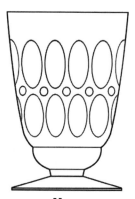

Mesa
Clear, Amber, Blue, Brown,
Olive Green or Red
4186
Fostoria

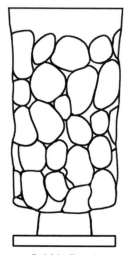

Pebble Beach
Clear, Brown, Orange, Pink,
Smoke or Yellow
2806
Fostoria

Sorrento
Blue, Brown, Green,
Pink or Plum
2832
Fostoria

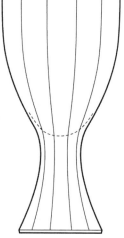

Module
Clear, Dusk (Smoke),
or Sunrise (Topaz)
2824
Fostoria

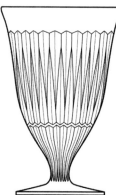

Radiance
Iced Tea Shown
Vertical Ribs
2700
Fostoria

4101
Amber, Blue, Green,
Pink or Topaz
Block Optic Bowl
Fostoria

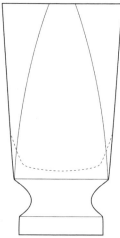

Transition
Highball Shown
Plain, Square Base
2936
Fostoria

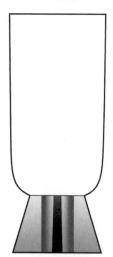

Venture
Gray 4-Toed Base
6114
Fostoria

Horizon
Iced Tea Shown
Clear, Brown or Green Bowl
5650
Fostoria

Catalina
Iced Tea Shown; Brown,
Chartreuse, or Spruce Green Bowl
6046
Fostoria

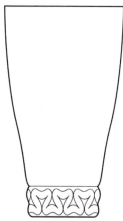

Tiara
Flat Iced Tea Shown
Clear, Brown or Green Bowl
6044
Fostoria

Casual Flair
Tumbler Shown
Clear, Fawn or Sky Blue
4180
Fostoria

398

Blue Meadow
Tumbler Shown
Sky Blue, Etch 8, Floral
4180
Fostoria

Country Garden
Tumbler Shown
Sky Blue, Etch 13, Floral
4180
Fostoria

Golden Twilight
Tumbler Shown
Fawn, Etch 12, Stars
4180
Fostoria

Greenbriar
Tumbler Shown
Etch 14, Leaves
4180
Fostoria

Kismet
Tumbler Shown
Sky Blue, Etch 10, Leaves
4180
Fostoria

Plain 'n Fancy
Tumbler Shown
Amber, Etch 11, Floral
4180
Fostoria

Ring O' Roses
Tumbler Shown
Fawn, Etch 9, Floral
4180
Fostoria

Sun Valley
Tumbler Shown
Etch 15, Stars
4180
Fostoria

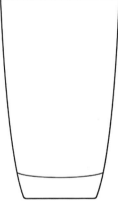

Standish
Highball Shown
Plain
4132
Fostoria

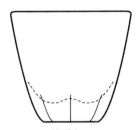

Holiday
Liquor Cocktail Shown
Plain
2643
Fostoria

Dusk
Flat Iced Tea Shown; Clear, Honey
(Amber), Lime Green or Tokay (Taupe)
2671
Fostoria

Dawn
Tumbler Shown; Clear, Honey (Amber),
Lime Green or Tokay (Taupe)
2670
Fostoria

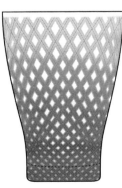

Needlepoint
Highball Shown
Gold, Green or Teal Blue
4184
Fostoria

Homespun
Highball Shown
Gold, Moss Green or Teal Blue
4183
Fostoria

Inca
Cooler Shown
Clear, Amber, Blue, Pink or Smoke
4163
Fostoria

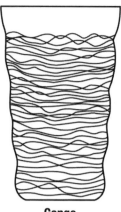

Congo
Tumbler Shown; Clear, Amber,
Marine (Green), Pink, or Smoke
4162
Fostoria

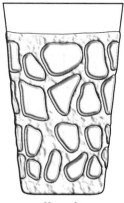

Karnak
Highball Shown; Clear, Amber,
Marine Blue, Pink, or Smoke Brown
4161
Fostoria

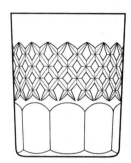

Alta
Old Fashioned Shown
Cut 924, Crisscross & Panels
2863
Fostoria

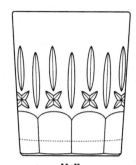

Vail
Old Fashioned Shown
Cut 925, Vertical & Star Cuts
2863
Fostoria

Stowe
Highball Shown
Pressed Glass, Barware
2862
Fostoria

Heritage
Highball Shown
Pressed Glass, Barware
1871
Fostoria

Rosby
Tumbler Shown
Clear or Green
1704
Fostoria

Winburn
Tumbler Shown; White, Aqua
(Turquoise) or Peach (Pink) Milk Glass
1704
Fostoria

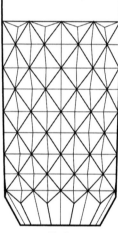

York
Highball Shown
Pressed Glass, Barware
2934
Fostoria

Shell & Jewel
Tumbler Shown
Pressed Glass
618
Fostoria

Frosted Artichoke
Tumbler Shown
Pressed Glass
205
Fostoria

Bacchus
Frosted Clear or Blue
Male Nude Stem
France Crystal

FNC 1
Champagne Flute Shown
Frosted Cherub Stem
France Crystal

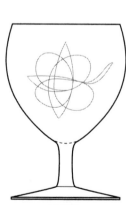

Mobile
Abstract Cuts
Francis Ruhe

Biarritz
Fan & Oval Cuts
17715
Franciscan

Zinfandel
Crisscross & Vertical Cuts
17711
Franciscan

Belvedere
Crisscross & Vertical Cuts
17700
Franciscan

Mademoiselle
Vertical Cuts
17683
Franciscan

Genesis
Plain
17708
Franciscan

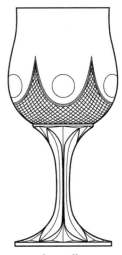

Acapella
Dots & Crisscross Cuts
17708
Franciscan

Angelique
Crisscross & Panel Cuts
17708
Franciscan

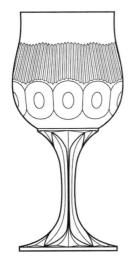

Madrigal
Vertical & Circle Cuts
17708
Franciscan

Nouvelle
Arch & Floral Cuts
17708
Franciscan

Ondine
Vertical & Oval Cuts
17708
Franciscan

Sonnet
Vertical Teardrop Cuts
17708
Franciscan

17708-1
Gold Inlay Etched Floral
17708
Franciscan

17708-2
Gold Inlay Etched Floral
17708
Franciscan

17708-3
Etched Floral
17708
Franciscan

17708-4
Etched Floral
17708
Franciscan

17708-5
Etched Floral
17708
Franciscan

17708-6
Etched Floral & Wreath
17708
Franciscan

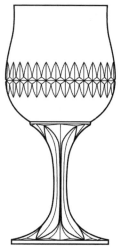

17708-7
Vertical Cuts
17708
Franciscan

Jubilation
Clear or Various Colors,
Optic Bowl
17707
Franciscan

Revelation
Aqua
See *"Tiffin"* for other colors
17702
Franciscan

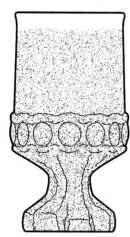

Madeira
Clear or Various Colors,
Pressed Glass
120
Franciscan

Cabaret
Various Colors,
Pressed Glass
121
Franciscan

Flambeau
Clear or Various Colors,
Optic Bowl
Franciscan

Alfresco
Various Colors
Franciscan

Arietta
Gray Cut Plants & Stars
Franconia

Vignette
Gray Cut Leaves
Franconia

Summer Bloom
Gray Cut Floral
Franconia

Delphine
Gray Cut Floral
Franconia

Delphine Rosalie
Cut Floral
Franconia

Silver Thistle
Etched Thistle
Franconia

Dorette
Thick Gold Band
Franconia

Silver Crown
Platinum Trim
Franconia

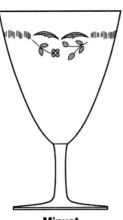

Minuet
Gray Cut Floral & Lines
Franconia

Athena
Gray Cut Vertical Lines,
Gold Trim
Franconia

Carillon
Blue or Smoke Bowl
Franconia

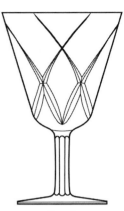

Karat
Crisscross Cuts
Franconia

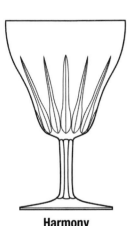

Harmony
Vertical Cuts
Franconia

Aura
Vertical Cuts
Franconia

Prism
Vertical Cuts
Franconia

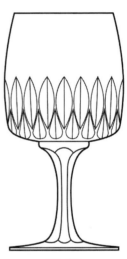

Manila
Vertical Cuts
Franconia

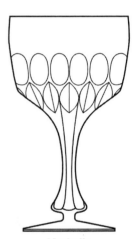

Marbella
Oval Cuts
Franconia

Salamanca
Vertical Cuts
Franconia

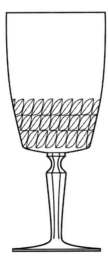

Embassy
Slanted Cuts
Franconia

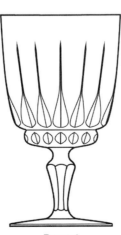

Regent
Vertical Cuts
Franconia

Continental
Vertical Cuts
Franconia

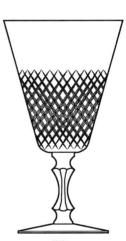

Elite
Crisscross Cuts
Franconia

Millefleurs
Gray Cut Floral
Franconia

Hawthorn
Gray Cut Floral
Franconia

Laurel-Oak
Gray Cut Floral
Franconia

Stella
Gray Cut Stars
Franconia

Fascination
Gray Cut Floral
Franconia

Irina
Plain
Franconia

Lyric
Plain
Franconia

Regal
Vertical Cuts
Franconia

Lima
Plain
Franconia

Classic
Plain
Franconia

Argenta (Platinum Trim)
Jewel (Gold Trim)
Franconia

Bridal Gold (Gold Band)
Sterling (Platinum Band)
Wide Band on Bowl &
Trim on Foot
Franconia

Senate
Frosted Stem
Franconia

Polaris
Plain
Franconia

FSC 1
Wine Shown
Gray Vertical Cuts
William Fraser

FSC 3
Wine Hock Shown
Various Color Bowls,
Fan & Dot Cuts
William Fraser

Thistle
Etched Floral, Optic Bowl
Fry

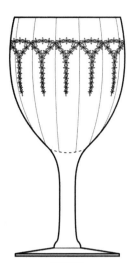

DE103
Etched Floral, Optic Bowl
7761
Fry

King
Etched Floral, Optic Bowl
Fry

Rose
Etch 18, Floral; Optic Bowl
DE18
Fry

Sheraton
Etched Floral; Plain or
Gold Trim on Bowl & Foot
7715
Fry

Morning Glory
Etched Floral, Optic Bowl
7715
Fry

FRY 3
Etched Floral, Optic Bowl
Fry

DE107
Etched Swags, Optic Bowl,
Plain or Gold Trim
Fry

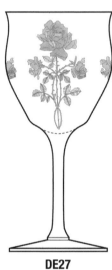

DE27
Etched Floral
7816
Fry

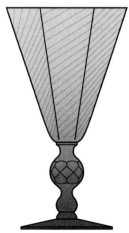

FRY 64
Sapphire Blue, Multisided
Slant Optic Bowl
7816
Fry

FRY 13
Blue, Multisided Slant
Optic Bowl
Fry

FRY 17
Various Colors & Optics
• ***Fry***

FRY 27
Blue or Pink, Etched
Geometric, Optic Bowl
Fry

FRY 48
Blue, Gray Cut Floral,
Optic Bowl
Fry

FRY 49
Amber, Gray Cut Floral,
Optic Bowl
Fry

FRY 21
Pink, Gray Cut Floral,
Optic Bowl
Fry

FRY 23
Blue, Gray Cut Floral,
Optic Bowl
Fry

FRY 24
Pink Optic Bowl,
Light Blue Stem
Fry

FRY 56
Aqua, Gray Cut Floral
& Geometric, Optic Bowl
Fry

7553
Clear or Blue,
Optic Bowl
Fry

7553-1
Cut Floral & Ribbon,
Optic Bowl
7553
Fry

7553-2
Cut Floral & Ribbon,
Optic Bowl
7553
Fry

7553-3
Gray Cut Lattice & Floral,
Optic Bowl
7553
Fry

DE63
Clear, Pink, Blue or Green,
Etch 63, Floral
7553
Fry

FRY 10
Various Color Optic Bowls,
Twisted Stem
Fry

FRY 41
Optic Bowl,
Black Twisted Stem
Fry

FRY 16
Etched Floral, Optic Bowl,
Black Twisted Stem
Fry

FRY 38
Green Optic Bowl,
Black Twisted Stem
Fry

FRY 11
Cobalt Optic Bowl,
Needle Etched Geometric,
Twisted Stem
Fry

FRY 28
Amethyst Optic Bowl,
Twisted Stem
Fry

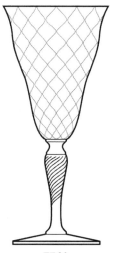

7541
All Clear or Various Color
Bowls & Stems; Diamond or
Straight Optic Bowls
Fry

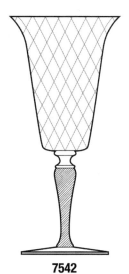

7542
All Clear or Various Color
Bowls & Stems; Diamond or
Straight Optic Bowls
Fry

FRY 26
Light Blue,
Diamond Optic Bowl
Fry

FRY 61
All Blue, Optic Bowl
Fry

FRY 1
Various Colors, Diamond or
Straight Optic Bowls
Fry

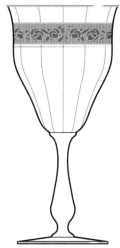

FRY 9
Clear or Pink,
Gold Encrusted Rose Band,
Gold Bowl & Foot Trim
Fry

FRY 30
Clear or Pink,
Etched Cameos,
Optic Bowl
Fry

DE107
Pink, Etched Floral & Scrolls,
Optic Bowl
Fry

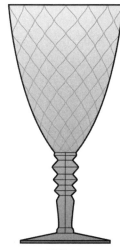

FRY 42
Green or Blue,
Diamond Optic Bowl
Fry

FRY 7
Various Color Bowls
Fry

FUG 5
Wine Shown
Gold Scroll Band
Fumo Brothers

FUG 2
Wine Shown
Wide Gold Greek
Key Band
Fumo Brothers

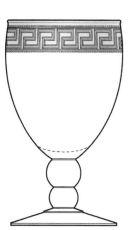

FUG 3
Wide Gold Greek
Key Band
Fumo Brothers

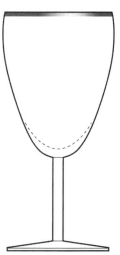

Sovereign
Platinum Trim
Furstenberg

Signed Products and Makers Marks

Listed below are many of the manufacturers pictured in the Crystal Stemware ID Guide series that most commonly sign their names or otherwise mark their glassware. Some of the makers will almost always mark their glassware, while others only mark certain patterns or lines. Companies listed with a " • " will typically sign most of their product, though some unmarked product in those companies could signify a second quality piece. In cases where the manufacturer marked their product other than by using their own name, marks they often used are represented.

Anchor Hocking		Dorothy Thorpe	
Arcoroc		Dugan	
Arnolfo Di Cambio		Duralex	
Atlantis		Eamon Glass	
Baccarat •		Edinburgh •	
Bartlett & Collins		Fabergé •	
Blenko		Federal Glass	
Calvin Klein		Fenton	
Cambridge	NEAR-CUT NEARCUT	Fostoria	
Cartier •		Galway	
Cavan		Gorham	
Cera		Hawkes	
Ceska •		Hazel-Atlas	
Christian Dior •		Heisey	
Christinenhutte		Higbee	
Cofrac Art Verrier		Imperial	NUCUT
Colle •		Jeannette Glass	J
Cristal d'Arques/Durand		Josair	
Cristal De Sevres	SEVRES	Kemple Glass	K K Kw
Da Vinci Crystal		Kosta/Boda	
Dartington		Kusak	
Daum •		Lalique •	
Degenhart Glass Co		Ralph Lauren •	

Lenox • (Second)	Spode
Libbey	St. Louis •
L.S. Collection	Steuben •
Lorraine	Stevens & Williams
McKee Glass	Stuart
Moser	Summit Art Glass
Mosser Glass	Sussmuth
Nachtmann	Theresienthal
New Martinsville	Tiffany & Co •
Noritake	Tiffin
Northwood	Tipperary
Oneida	Tudor •
Orrefors •	Tyrone
Peill •	U.S. Glass
Pilgrim Glass	Val St. Lambert
Riedel	Villeroy & Boch •
Riekes Crisa	Waterford •
Rogaska	Waterford Marquis 2nd
Rosenthal •	Webb Corbett •
Royal Brierly	Thomas Webb •
Royal Doulton	Wedgwood
Royal Leerdam	Westmoreland •
Sasaki	Wheaton Glass
Seneca	L.G. Wright
Sinclair	William Yeoward •
L.E. Smith Glass	Schott Zwiesel/Cristallerie Zwiesel
Spiegelau •	Schott Zwiesel

The History of Replacements, Ltd.

The World's Largest Retailer of Old and New China, Crystal, Silver & Collectibles

In 1981, Bob Page, an accountant-turned-flea-marketer, founded Replacements, Ltd. Since then, the company's growth and success can only be described as phenomenal. Today, Replacements, Ltd. locates hard-to-find pieces in over 383,000 patterns — some of which have not been pro-

Some of the 60,000 shelves which hold over 13 million pieces of inventory.

duced for more than 100 years. Now serving more than 10 million customers, with an inventory of nearly 13 million pieces, Replacements emails and mails more than 2 million inventory listings weekly to customers seeking additional pieces in their patterns.

The concept for Replacements, Ltd. originated in the late 1970s when Page, then an auditor for the state of North Carolina, started spending his weekends combing flea markets for china and crystal. Before long, he was filling requests from customers to find pieces they could not locate. "I was buying and selling pieces primarily as a diversion," Page explains. "Back when I was an auditor, no one was ever happy to see me. And, quite frankly, I wasn't thrilled about being there either."

Page began placing small ads in shelter publications and started building a file of potential customers. Soon, his inventory outgrew his attic, where he had been storing the pieces, and it was time to make a change. "I reached the point where I was spending more time with dishes than auditing," Page says. "I'd be up until one or two o'clock in the morning. Finally, I took the big step — I quit my auditing job and hired one part-time assistant. Today I'm having so much fun, I often have to remind myself what day of the week it is!"

Replacements, Ltd. continued to grow quickly. In 1986, *Inc.* magazine ranked Replacements, Ltd. 81st on its list of fastest-growing independently-owned companies in the US. "Our growth has been incredible," says Page, who was named 1991 North Carolina Entrepreneur of the Year. "I had no idea of the potential when I started out." Providing high-quality merchandise and the highest possible levels of customer service are the cornerstones of the business, resulting in a shopping experience unparalleled in today's marketplace. Page also attributes much of the success of Replacements, Ltd. to a network of about 450 dedicated suppliers from all around the U.S. The company currently employs more than 400 people in its facilities covering half a million square feet.

A major contributor to the company's success is Replacements, Ltd's internally developed suite of computer applications

A View of Replacements' 12,000 square foot Retail Store

and services. The benefits from continuous investment in state-of-the-art software development tools, the latest in computer server and data storage technologies and, most of all, from the efforts of a competent and enthusiastic Information Services team help support top-level customer service. In addition to conventional business components, the system includes tools that enable quick and accurate responses to customers whether they are buying, selling or requesting research.

For those who are unsure of the name and/or manufacturer of their patterns, Replacements, Ltd. also offers a free pattern identification service. In addition, numerous books and publications focusing on pattern identification have been published by Replacements, Ltd. for both suppliers and the general public.

Replacements, Ltd. receives countless emails, phone calls and letters from its many satisfied customers. Some need to replace broken or lost items while others want to add to the sets they have had for years. A constant in the varied subjects customers write about is their long and fruitless search — a search that ended when they learned what Replacements, Ltd. could offer. "Since many patterns are family heirlooms

Aerial view of the expanded Replacements, Ltd.

that have been handed down from generation to generation, most customers are sentimental about replacing broken or missing pieces," Page says. "You know, some of the stories that we get from our customers telling us how much finding those pieces means to them are really very emotional. I have read some of the letters and emails that literally bring tears to my eyes. And it's just great to be able to satisfy that need and be able to make so many people happy to be able to find those patterns."

Replacements' museum and retail store are one of the top destination attractions for the Piedmont Triad area of North Carolina, drawing people from around the world. Visitors can browse through unique pieces in the museum or watch artisans restore damaged treasures. Offering free tours every thirty minutes, Replacements is pet friendly, thus a great pit stop for those traveling with furry friends. Rand McNally even named Replacements as one of the Top 25 Free Attractions in the United States.

The Replacements, Ltd. Retail Store and Museum in Greensboro, NC is a 12,000 square-foot retail facility locat-

ed in front of the massive warehouse. It is decorated with late 19th century hand-carved showcases, 20-foot ceilings and classic chandeliers. Inside, one can view an incredibly varied selection of merchandise — from figurines, mugs and ornaments to the china, crystal and silver that made the company famous.

For More Information

- **Call** 1-800-REPLACE (1-800-737-5223) from 9 am to 10 pm, ET, 7 days a week.

- **Write to:** Replacements, Ltd.
  PO Box 26029
  Greensboro, NC 27420

- **Fax:** 336-697-3100

- **Internet:** www.replacements.com

- **Visit** the Replacements, Ltd. Retail Store and Museum, at exit 132 off I-85/40 in Greensboro, NC.

  The Retail Store and Museum are open 7 days a week, from 9 am to 7 pm.

About the Authors

Bob Page was born April 19, 1945 and grew up working the fields of his family's small farm in Ruffin, North Carolina. He attended the University of North Carolina at Chapel Hill and graduated with a degree in business and a major in accounting. After two years in the U.S. Army, he obtained his CPA certificate and worked in public accounting for eight years. In 1978, he took a position as an auditor for the State of North Carolina.

In March of 1981, Bob left his accounting career forever to found Replacements, Ltd. He and his company have received extensive publicity and public recognition. Awards include: 1986 North Carolina Small Businessman of the Year; 1990 Retail Entrepreneur of the Year for the State of North Carolina; ranked among *Business North Carolina's* NC Top 100 Private Companies from 2009-2011; Society of Financial Services Professionals 2004, Triad Business Ethics Award; and Better Business Bureau Torch Award for Marketplace Ethics in 2005 and 2012.

Ryan, Dale, Owen, Bob (Front)

Bob is involved in numerous charitable endeavors in North Carolina as well as the nation and is a tireless advocate for the rights of gay and lesbian individuals, supporting the campaigns of local, state and national political candidates, regardless of party, who will best support and promote the rights of lesbian, gay, bisexual and transgender (LGBT) citizens. Bob was named one of America's Top 25 "Out" Executives in 1999 and 2001. He also won the Human Rights Campaign's Torch Award in 1996, and was named the LGBT Business Owner of the Year in 2005 by the National Gay & Lesbian Chamber of Commerce. Replacements is the only North Carolina company, and one of nine nationally, to receive a perfect score of 100% in the Human Rights Campaign Foundation's Corporate Equality Index (a measure of workplace equality for LGBT employees, vendors, and investors) from 2002 through 2013. Bob has been invited to the White House on several occasions.

Dale Frederiksen was born June 15, 1962 in Pontiac, Michigan and attended Waterford Township High School. In 1980, Dale moved to Chattanooga, Tennessee to attend Tennessee Temple University, graduating in 1984 with a BS degree in secondary education. He taught junior and senior high mathematics for three years in Kansas City, Kansas, before returning to Chattanooga in 1987 to teach mathematics and to coach volleyball at Ooltewah Middle School.

In 1989, he joined the staff of Replacements, Ltd. as an inventory purchasing agent and later trained in the field of computer graphics, where he specialized in drawing crystal images, some of which appear in this book. He remains involved in the creation and production of various china, crystal and silver identification guides, and he takes an active role in purchasing product for Replacements. Dale enjoys researching and discovering patterns that have previously been undocumented, along with spending time with Bob, his partner of 23 years, and their twin boys, Owen and Ryan.

Tableware Reference Guides

Noritake Jewel of the Orient

Over 3000 pattern images in full color, beautifully organized for identification. Includes price guide, company history, and special sections featuring Azalea, Tree in the Meadow, and 175. Hardcover, 315 pages. ISBN: 1-88997777-11-X

Suggested Retail $29.95
Our Price $19.99

Tiffin is Forever

This helpful guide includes comprehensive, detailed illustrations of over 2,700 stems and patterns of Tiffin Glass. A must for the glass enthusiast or collector. Hardbound, 175 pages.

Suggested Retail $29.95
Our Price $19.99

A Collection of American Crystal

Descriptions of crystal by Glastonbury/ Lotus, Libbey/ Rock Sharpe and the TG Hawkes glass companies. Over 1,000 patterns and 200 stems Hardbound, 140 pages. ISBN: 1-88997777-11-X

Suggested Retail $24.95
Our Price $9.99

Franciscan–An American Dinnerware Tradition

The foremost comprehensive book on Franciscan dinnerware. Full color, beautifully designed for identification. Includes company history and price guide! Hardcover, 272 pages. ISBN: 1-889977-70-1

Suggested Retail $24.95
Our Price $19.99

Stainless Flatware Guide

More than 5,000 stainless patterns from over 100 manufacturers. Over 700 pages of detailed, digital images organized by shape and style. Softbound, 798 pages. ISBN: 1-57432-067-X

Suggested Retail $39.95
Our Price $19.99

Homer Laughlin Decades of Dinnerware

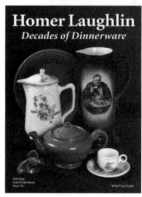

The definitive book on Homer Laughlin dinnerware. More than 3,000 patterns in full color. Pre-1900 to current Fiesta® patterns. Plus a separate price guide! Hardcover, 559 pages. ISBN: 1-889977-13-6

Suggested Retail $39.95
Our Price $23.99

Seneca Glass Company: 1891-1983

Includes information on over 1,200 different stems and patterns, along with a history of the Seneca Glass Company by West Virginia glass authority Dean Six. Hardbound, 132 pages.

Suggested Retail $24.95
Our Price $11.99

Johnson Brothers English Classic Dinnerware

Arranged by shape, this is the most inclusive guide to Johnson Brothers dinnerware patterns. Colorful, easy to use and well indexed. ISBN: 1-889977-15-2

Suggested Retail $29.95
Our Price $19.99

Haviland A Pattern Identification Guide

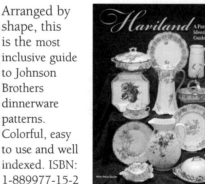

The most comprehensive book on Haviland with over 5,000 patterns in full color. Includes company, blanks and shapes, histories, plus price guide. Hardcover, 577 pages. ISBN: 978-1-889977-16-4

Suggested Retail $29.99
Our Price $19.99

China Identification Guides

Each guide features full color and black & white digital images of dinner plates from various companies. Each manufacturer is organized by shape and style. Quickly identify patterns with no markings or other patterns which are difficult to identify due to multiple shapes, etc. We've also included brief histories of each manufacturer.

Guide #1
Heinrich, Hutschenreuther, and Rosenthal. Softbound, 119 pages.
ISBN: 1-57432-131-5

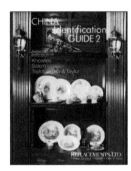

Guide #2
Edwin M. Knowles, Salem, and Taylor, Smith & Taylor. Softbound, 144 pages.
ISBN: 1-889977-06-3

Guide #3
Canonsburg, Cronin, Crooksville, Cunningham & Pickett, French Saxon, Leigh Potters, Mt. Clemens Pottery, Paden City Pottery, Pope Gosser, Sebring Pottery, Stetson, Universal China, and W.S. George. Softbound 213 pages.
ISBN: 1-889977-08-X

Guide #4
Altrohlau, Epiag, Jean Pouyat, Paul Müller, Schumann, and Wm. Guerin. Softbound 163 pages.
ISBN: 1-889977-09-8ISBN: 1-889977-08-X

Guide #5
Bawo & Dotter, Charles Ahrenfeldt, Tirschenreuth, and Tressemann & Vogt. Softbound 187 pages.
ISBN: 1-889977-10-1

Guide #6
Arcadian, Harker, Limoges (American), Princess, Royal, Shenango, Steubenville, and Warwick. Softbound 197 pages.
ISBN: 1-889977-12-8

Guide #7
Meito, Celebrate, Craftsman, Diamond, Empress, Hira, Imperial, Jyoto, National, Princess and Regal. Softbound 219 pages.
ISBN: 1-889977-14-4

China Identification Guide Set Volumes 1-7

Special Set Price *(Suggested Retail $419.65)* **$69⁹⁵**

Item Code
RB3REPBOOK CHIDGS

To Order Call 1-800-REPLACE (1-800-737-5223)   OUTSIDE USA: 1-336-697-3000

Manufacturer Index

Pattern Index

421

427

~ F ~

433

Rock Crystal Cuttings
d Blown Stemware

441

Duncan's Rock Crystal Cuttings
Lead Blown Stemware

No. 34 Kent Pattern
Cutting No. 628 R. C.
Marlbor...

No. 32 Windsor Pattern
Cutting No. 645 R. C.
Sherwood Design

74

Central Glass Works,
Wheeling, W. Va.,

MANUFACTURERS OF

Lead Blown Stemware.

TUMBLERS,
Plain, Cut and Etched.

ALSO FULL LINE OF PRESSED GOODS.

Our new 700 line is made
Plain, Optic and Optic and
Etched   There is nothing
made to-day to equal our 700
for the money.

66 West Broadway New York.
George R. Reinhart.
619 Arch St., Philadelphia.
Green & Seeman,
Baltimore, Md.
H. E. Wardell,
419 Alton Block, Chicago.

John H. Dubbs,

700

No. 537...
Cuttin...
Flora...

Caprice
by Cambridge

you'll love its rippling brilliance...
grace... practical and inexpensive...

Select your Caprice from 65 open stock pieces...
Crystal or Moonlight Blue. Because this fine Americ...
hand-made crystal highlights your table with such match...
less sparkle and charm, you will want to use it every day.

THE CAMBRIDGE GLASS COMPANY, Cambridge, Ohio

No. 5322 Erin Pa...
Cutting No. 702 ...
Berkeley Design

No. 5322 Erin Pattern
Cutting No. 690 R. C.
Kohinoor Design

No. 5322 Erin...
Cutting No. 691 R. C.
Sun Ray Design

30 York Pattern
...ting No. 632 R. C.
Warwick Design

Most Complete Lines of Deep Etched Ware
"MADE IN AMERICA"

Our lines of blown glassware embrace not only the staple stemware and tableware
items, but a large variety of odd pieces for special uses, making them the most complete
lines shown by any American glass factory.

We believe, too, that we make the largest variety of shapes, and show the widest
choice of patterns—deep plate and needle etchings and light cuttings.

For 1915 several new lines have been prepared.   These will be on show at all our
branch offices after January 1.

FOSTORIA GLASS COMPANY
MOUNDSVILLE, W. VA.

NEW YORK CITY, 66 West Broadway
CHICAGO, ILL., 807 Masonic Temple
BOSTON, MASS., 105 Federal St.
PHILADELPHIA, 213 Commercial Bldg.

PERMANENT SAMPLE ROOMS:

John Nixon
H. A. Marshall
Geo. K. Marshall
Jos. Tomkinson

BALTIMORE, MD., 304 W. Baltimore St.   W. T. Owen
BUFFALO, N. Y., 311 Main St.   A. H. Sharpe
SAN FRANCISCO, 718 Mission St.,room 302 B.F.Heastand
DENVER, COLO., 1523 Glenarm St.   Chas. E. Hilliker
DALLAS, TEXAS, Cor. Elm and Poydras St. H. J. Blakeney

Note: A complete line of stemware is available in all patterns and cuttings shown on this page.

442